Information Technology and Global Governance

Series Editor
Derrick L. Cogburn
American University
Bethesda, Maryland, USA

Information Technology and Global Governance focuses on the complex interrelationships between the social, political, and economic processes of global governance that occur at national, regional, and international levels. These processes are influenced by the rapid and ongoing developments in information and communication technologies. At the same time, they affect numerous areas, create new opportunities and mechanisms for participation in global governance processes, and influence how governance is studied. Books in this series examine these relationships and influences.

More information about this series at
http://www.springer.com/series/14855

Trisha Meyer

The Politics of Online Copyright Enforcement in the EU

Access and Control

Trisha Meyer
Institute for European Studies and Vesalius College
Vrije Universiteit Brussel
Brussels, Belgium

Information Technology and Global Governance
ISBN 978-3-319-50973-0   ISBN 978-3-319-50974-7   (eBook)
DOI 10.1007/978-3-319-50974-7

Library of Congress Control Number: 2017932405

Cover design by Samantha Johnson

Printed on acid-free paper

This Palgrave Macmillan imprint is published by Springer Nature
The registered company is Springer International Publishing AG
The registered company address is: Gewerbestrasse 11, 6330 Cham, Switzerland

For Evan, Elisabeth and Peter

Acknowledgments

This book results from research conducted for my PhD. Choosing the academic path can at times make for a solitary journey, but it is infinitely more enjoyable when others travel alongside. I am deeply grateful for the confidence bestowed in my ability and the concern for my wellbeing. To my PhD supervisor, Leo Van Audenhove, thank you for taking me on board. You provided me with pointed guidance each step of the way. You know when to speak, and when to be silent, in order to help push boundaries. To my doctoral committee, Tuomas Mylly, Caroline Pauwels and Peggy Valcke, thank you for your input. Your enthusiasm for online copyright enforcement kept me going. To my doctoral jury, Karen Donders, Luciano Morganti and Milton Mueller, thank you for taking on the weighty task of evaluating the merit of my work. Thank you for pointing out the strengths *and* weaknesses of my research. To my many interview respondents, thank you for the invaluable insight you provided. Speaking with you was crucial for my understanding of the policy dynamics at play and the final argumentation of this study. Over the past years I have been welcomed into several academic homes: the Institute for European Studies, the center for Studies on Media, Information and Telecommunication, Vesalius College and the University of Turku. Thank you for the amazing support and stimulating work environment. A researcher could not ask for more. I am particularly grateful for the funding provided by the Academy of Finland, through the eCoherence project, which proved crucial for adapting the PhD into this present monograph. To my colleagues and mentors, Harri Kalimo and Jamal Shahin, thank you for your consistent and selfless action on my behalf. It is a great honor to work with you. To Marjon, Claire,

Ernesto, Lynn, Klaas, Marie, Katja, Steffi, Caterina, Ilse and Julia, thank you for your friendship. I cherish the fun and serious moments we shared. On a personal level, Evan, you are stoically patient. Thank you for your unwavering love; thank you for dreaming with me. I dedicate this book to you and our children. To Dad and Mom Meyer, Dad and Mom Lamos, Grandma, Kevin and Lori, Jan and Melinda, Todd and Nathanja, Jonathan and Grace, Sjoerd and Kimberly, Matt, Evan and Erin, thank you for your faith and support. I am blessed to call you family. Last but not least, to Zack and Joëlle, Andrew and Julie, Catherine, Katharina, Vera, Pieter and Annelise, Melissa, Jen, Koos and Elise, thank you for being examples of the Christian faith to me. You remind me, "to do justice, and to love kindness, and to walk humbly with your God" (Micah 6:8). "*Soli Deo Gloria*".

CONTENTS

Key (handwritten annotation pointing to 5.2.2 Shared Responsibility)

Important (handwritten annotation pointing to 5.3.2 Social and Economic Reality)

Abbreviations[1]

3Is	Ideas, Interests and Institutions
ACTA	Anti-Counterfeiting Trade Agreement
ADA	Argumentative Discourse Analysis
ADSL	Asymmetric Digital Subscriber Line
AGCOM	Autorità per la Garanzie nelle Communicazioni (Italian Communications Authority)
ALDE	Alliance of Liberals and Democrats for Europe (European Parliament)
ARCEP	Autorité de Régulation des Communications Électroniques et des Postes (French Regulatory Authority for Electronic Communications and Post)
ARMT	Autorité de Régulation des Mesures Techniques (French Authority for the Regulation of Technical Measures)
ARPA	Advanced Research Projects Agency (United States Defense Department)
AVMS	Directive on the Coordination of Certain Provisions Laid Down by Law, Regulation or Administrative Action in Member States concerning the Provision of Audiovisual Media Services (Audiovisual Media Services Directive, EU)
BSA	Business Software Alliance
CCO	Creative Content Online
CD	Compact Disc
CJEU	Court of Justice of the European Union
CNIL	Commission Nationale de l'Informatique et des Libertés (French Data Protection Authority)

Copyright in the Information Society Directive	Directive on the Harmonization of Certain Aspects of Copyright and Related Rights in the Information Society (EU)
CSA	Conseil Supérieur de l'Audiovisuel (French Audiovisual Regulator)
DADVSI	Loi du 1 août 2006 sur le Droit d'Auteur et les Droits Voisins dans la Société de l'Information (French Law on Author's Right and Related Rights in the Information Society)
DG CONNECT	Directorate General for Communications Networks, Content and Technology (European Commission)
DG INFSO	Directorate General for the Information Society and Media (European Commission)
DG MARKT	Directorate General for Internal Market and Services (European Commission)
DG Trade	Directorate General for Trade (European Commission)
DMCA	Digital Millennium Copyright Act (Unites States)
DNS	Domain Name System
DPI	Deep Packet Inspection
DRM	Digital Rights Management
DVD	Digital Versatile Disc
E-Commerce	Electronic Commerce
E-Commerce Directive	Directive on Certain Legal Aspects of Information Society Services, in particular Electronic Commerce, in the Internal Market (EU)
EC	European Commission
EDPS	European Data Protection Supervisor
EP	European Parliament
EPP	European People's Party (European Parliament)
EU	European Union
EUIPO	European Union Intellectual Property Office
GAO	Government Accountability Office (United States)
GATT	General Agreement on Tariffs and Trade
GDP	Gross Domestic Product
Green/EFA	Greens/European Free Alliance (European Parliament)
GUE/NGL	European United Left/Nordic Green Left (European Parliament)
HADOPI	Haute Autorité pour la Diffusions des Œuvres et la Protection des Droits sur Internet (French High Authority on the Distribution of Works and the Protection of Rights on the Internet)

HADOPI 1	Loi du 12 juin 2009 favorisant la Diffusion et la Protection de la Création sur Internet (French Law favoring the Dissemination and Protection of Creation on the Internet)
HADOPI 2	Loi du 28 octobre 2009 relative à la Protection Pénale de la Propriété Littéraire et Artistique sur Internet (French Law relating to the Criminal Protection of Literary and Artistic Property on the Internet)
HTML	HyperText Markup Language
HTTP	HyperText Transfer Protocol
IANA	Internet Assigned Number Authority
IAP	Internet Access Provider
ICANN	Internet Corporation for Assigned Names and Numbers
ICCC	International Conference on Computer Communications
ICT	Information and Communications Technology
IETF	Internet Engineering Task Force
IFPI	International Federation of the Phonographic Industry
IG	Internet Governance
IGAC	Ispecção Geral Das Actividades Culturais (Portuguese Ministry's Inspector General of Cultural Activities)
IGF	Internet Governance Forum
IMP	Interface Message Processor
IP	Internet Protocol
IPR	Intellectual Property Rights
IPR Enforcement Directive	Directive on the Enforcement of Intellectual Property Rights (EU)
ISP	Internet Service Provider
ITU	International Telecommunications Union
JRC	Joint Regulatory Committee
MEP	Member of European Parliament
MPAA	Motion Picture Association of America
MR	Mouvement Réformateur (Belgian French-Speaking Liberal Political Party)
NCP	Network Control Protocol
NSA	United States National Security Agency
NYC	New York City
OECD	Organization for Economic Cooperation and Development
OSI	Open Systems Interconnection
P2P	Peer-to-Peer
PDF	Portable Document File
PEC	Political Economy of Communications
PIPA	Preventing Real Online Threats to Economic Creativity and Theft of Intellectual Property Act (United States)

RIR	Regional Internet Registry
S&D	Progressive Alliance of Socialists and Democrats (European Parliament)
SME	Small- to Medium-Sized Enterprise
SOPA	Stop Online Piracy Act (United States)
TCP/IP	Transmission Control Protocol & Internet Protocol
TFEU	Treaty on the Functioning of the European Union
TPM	Technical Protection Measure
TRIPS	Agreement on Trade Related Aspects of Intellectual Property Rights
UCLA	University of California, Los Angeles
UK	United Kingdom
UN	United Nations
UNCTAD	United Nations Conference on Trade and Development
UNESCO	United Nations Educational, Scientific and Cultural Organization
URL	Uniform Resource Locator
US	United States of America
VCR	Video Cassette Recorder
W3C	World Wide Web Consortium
WIPO	World Intellectual Property Organization
WSIS	World Summit on the Information Society
WTO	World Trade Organization

NOTE

1. This list does not include the abbreviations of stakeholders active within the selected online copyright enforcement policies. For these abbreviations, I kindly refer to the endnotes in the relevant Chaps. 3, 4, 5, and 6.

LIST OF FIGURES

LIST OF TABLES

LIST OF BOXES

CHAPTER 1

Introduction

The Internet developed in the 1960s, but took until the introduction of the World Wide Web in the 1990s to truly become popular. Indeed *the Internet has evolved from a scientific to a mass medium.* This fast and fairly recent adoption of the Internet by industry and citizens has given rise to issues which previously had been contained and regulated by a much smaller group of computer experts (Zittrain 2008). Cybersecurity, copyright enforcement, the privacy of Internet users and the responsibility of Internet intermediaries are examples of topics which have caught the attention of those regulating (see for instance, Mueller 2010; G8 2011; European Commission 2010a). However *there is no agreement among public authorities, industry or civil society on how the Internet should be regulated.* This book analyzes recent controversies in one Internet governance (IG) field in particular—online copyright enforcement policies.

If we consider IG from the popularization of the Internet in the 1990s onwards, then *IG is currently entering its third phase* (Brown and Marsden 2013). The first regulatory phase corresponds with the liberalization of the telecommunications sector. It was a *laissez-faire,* libertarian approach to the Internet, with declarations that cyberspace was radically different from the offline world and beyond the reach of governments (Barlow 1996; Shapiro 1999). The second regulatory phase started after the dot.com bubble burst and 09/11. There was a recognition of the need for government intervention and specific rules for the online environment were set up. Think of

© The Author(s) 2017
T. Meyer, *The Politics of Online Copyright Enforcement in the EU,* Information Technology and Global Governance,
DOI 10.1007/978-3-319-50974-7_1

the European Union Directive on Copyright in the Information Society (European Parliament & Council 2001). Despite legislation, however, governments cannot get a grip on the online environment and technology continues to develop quickly. In the current third phase of regulation, *IG is still very much in flux and the conflict of interests and opinions between stakeholders is high.* As the importance of the Internet has increased for businesses in different sectors, but equally for citizens, each stakeholder group is vocal on the need for a regulatory approach meeting their needs. Rights holders vocally question the open character of the Internet, seeking to step beyond the careful feeling-around of regulators in the first decade of the twenty-first century. They advocate proactive involvement of Internet intermediaries for enforcement purposes. Filtering, blocking and blacklisting of Internet content—using the technology of the Internet to regulate—alternatively seem on and off the table again. France chose to protect its copyright holders by monitoring, sending warning messages and (potentially) sanctioning Internet users (French Parliament 2009a, b). This public policy is called graduated response. The United Kingdom initially followed suit (UK Parliament 2010), but then shifted its focus to discouraging and blocking illicit content (providers) through court and voluntary action of Internet intermediaries. Spain and Italy passed legislation to fast track the blocking of infringing websites (Spanish Parliament 2011; AGCOM 2013). The European Commission and Council sought to pass a multilateral Anti-Counterfeiting Trade Agreement (ACTA, 2011 Accession Ongoing)—however without success. Citizens protested both the substance and negotiation procedure of the Treaty. We observe *a tendency toward more governance of the Internet, but also a divergence in opinions on how this should take shape.*

In this study, I start from a *concern about the increased proactive use of technology and surveillance in dealing with regulatory problems on the Internet.* Mandating Internet intermediaries to intervene, block and filter out content changes is currently the most efficient means of gaining control over content on the Internet. *It makes the Internet more regulable, but also much more centralized and complex at the center*—reversing two key characteristics of the Internet's design that have made it so valuable to democracy and society (McIntyre and Scott 2008; Lessig 2006). Furthermore surveillance of Internet uses prioritizes the interests and rights of those regulating over the interests and right to privacy of Internet users (Meyer and Van Audenhove 2010). In this book, I argue that surveillance is not only a policy measure, but more generally a societal phenomenon. It serves to encourage particular values, behavior and definitions of problems in policy. This is not a problem as such, but *careful consideration is needed of whose viewpoints are being legitimized for which purpose.* Surveillance is about more than just privacy, it is an approach to regulating society (Lyon 2007). Therefore careful consideration is necessary in how and why we regulate through technology.

The purpose of this introductory chapter is to provide an overview of the guiding elements in the book. It expands on the research topic, selected case studies, theoretical and analytical approach, methodology and chapter outlines.

1.1   Research Topic: Online Copyright Enforcement[1]

As indicated, this study chooses to focus on one area within IG—*online copyright enforcement policies.*[2] I believe online copyright enforcement is exemplary of the conflict of interests and opinions on the regulatory role of online intermediaries in IG. Indeed some of its policies lean toward more regulation of the Internet through the involvement of Internet intermediaries, filtering, blocking and blacklisting. It is obvious that *the Internet and technological innovation significantly challenge copyright.* The ease of copying and distributing creative content on the Internet strain the old business models of the media industries. The difficulty to enforce copyright has also contributed to a questioning of the current definition and scope of copyright. Movements such as open source, access to knowledge and the Pirate Party resist the proprietarian model of knowledge creation that copyright offers artists and society. They argue that copyright (and intellectual property rights (IPR) more generally) have been captured by business interests and are not aimed at fostering knowledge and creativity in society anymore (Krikorian and Kapczynksi 2010). The scope and length of copyright have steadily increased in the 300 years of its existence. The media industries have also had the tendency to declare the demise of their profession each time a new technology is developed. Jack Valenti infamously compared the danger of Video Cassette Recorder (VCR) for the film industry to the Boston strangler for a woman alone at home. The level of uncertainty in business and resistance to copyright should not be underestimated. At the same time it is not necessarily the disaster that is often portrayed. *The impact of the Internet on the media industries is not straightforward.* Moreover, the effects of this new technology are not the same for each sector (for instance, music, film, publishing and gaming, Winseck 2011). An important claim of this study is that *neither technology nor policy is neutral.* The Internet's design enables widespread distribution of creative content, yet equally online copyright enforcement policies can contribute to a change in the Internet's design by requesting centralized and complex control. As this book will show, *online copyright enforcement policies are battlegrounds for debating the role of Internet intermediaries in regulating the Internet and the nature of knowledge and cultural creation.* The rest of this section provides a brief introduction to online copyright enforcement to date.

Rights holders and public authorities use a wide range of techniques to enforce copyright online. These measures aim at addressing both the demand for and the supply of infringing content: they target Internet users on the one hand, and Internet intermediaries and content providers on the other. Box 1.1 outlines online copyright enforcement techniques according to target audience. The techniques are implemented through litigation, public policy and self/co-regulation.

Box 1.1 Online copyright enforcement techniques (according to target audience)

Internet users: demand-side

- Awareness raising and educational campaigns
- Legal offers and subsidies
- Graduated response toward recurring infringing behavior
- Litigation on infringement

Sanctions: throttling of Internet speed, termination of access, fines, imprisonment.

Internet intermediaries and content providers: supply-side

- Notice-and-takedown of Internet content, links and sites
- Follow-the-money approach involving online advertising networks and payment processors
- Litigation on injunctions and intermediary (secondary) liability

Sanctions: blocking and takedown, damages and compensation, imprisonment.

Based on: BOP Consulting with DotEcon 2015. International Comparison of Approaches to Online Copyright Infringement. London: UK Intellectual Property Office. DeBeer, Jeremy, and Christopher Clemmer 2009. "Global Trends in Online Copyright Enforcement: A Non-Neutral Role for Network Intermediaries?" *Jurimetrics* 49 (4):375. Yu, Peter. 2004. "The Escalating Copyright Wars." *Hofstra Law Review* 32:907–951.

Drawing on existing legislation, rights holders seek to enforce copyright through *litigation*. In the late 1990s and early 2000s, lawsuits were brought against peer-to-peer (P2P) file sharers, such as the protracted case against Jammie Thomas-Rasset in the United States (September 11, 2012). The strategy underlying the legal pursuit of Internet users is one of settlements and fines to set examples and deter further file sharing. In graduated response proceedings, technical measures, such as throttling and disconnection of Internet access, are also considered. Litigating against individuals is considered highly unpopular and of limited success, however. Now rights holders primarily focus on those providing (access to) infringing content, such as the renown P2P network, the Pirate Bay, and on Internet access and service providers, who act as intermediaries between Internet users and the illicit content providers. The main reasons for litigating against Internet intermediaries and content providers are to seek access to the personal data of Internet users and to block and take down copyright infringing content, links and sites. To the frustration of rights holders in the EU, there is currently much divergence in the national requirements and procedures for online copyright enforcement litigation, as well as in the actual outcome of cases (European Commission 2010b; IFPI 2015). As a result, litigation is only one of multiple strategies pursued.

Adapting *public policy* on copyright enforcement to fit the online environment is deemed necessary and desirable as well. In the United States, the Digital Millennium Copyright Act (DMCA) forms the foundation for online copyright enforcement (US Copyright Office 1998). In Europe, copyright is a shared competence between the EU and its member states. The E-Commerce, Copyright in the Information Society, Intellectual Property Rights (IPR) Enforcement Directives (European Parliament & Council 2000, 2001, 2004) jointly provide guidance for rights holders and Internet intermediaries. The EC has considered adapting (or at the very least clarifying) all three legislative acts, as technology has rapidly changed since their adoption in the early 2000s. However, despite organizing multiple public consultations and working groups, there is currently no consensus among stakeholders on the extent of reform necessary in the fields of copyright and Internet regulation. For instance, the E-Commerce Directive provides the possibility to develop notice-and-takedown mechanisms for hosting service providers. National procedural practices differ, however, and stakeholders disagree on important issues, such as which intermediaries fit the category of a hosting service provider, how promptly a hosting service provider should take action, whether a judge needs to be involved and more. Meanwhile, during this stalemate at a European level, member state governments have added to the present fragmentation by taking independent legislative action. Most notably, France and the United Kingdom have passed laws encouraging a graduated response scheme that targets recurring infringing behavior of Internet users (although the British system has not been implemented); and Spain and Italy have set mechanisms in place that allow for rapid blocking and takedown of infringing content and sites (BOP Consulting with DotEcon 2015).

Finally, perhaps not surprisingly, many public authorities, including the EU institutions (Council of the European Union 2014, European Commission 2014, European Parliament Committee on Legal Affairs 2014), encourage *self/co-regulatory measures* in the field of online copyright enforcement. Through awareness raising rights holders and public authorities emphasize the importance of copyright and the harm caused by its infringement. Some graduated response and notice-and-takedown schemes are voluntary. For instance, in the United States and the United Kingdom, rights holders and Internet intermediaries collaborate to send educational messages to users (BOP Consulting with DotEcon 2015; Center for Copyright Information 2016; UK Department for Business Innovation & Skills et al. 2014); and many social networks and Internet service providers (ISPs) have developed policies and tools for reporting and taking down content (YouTube Content ID is one example, YouTube 2016). Lastly, so-called follow-the-money and stoplight approaches are encouraged (see BAE Systems Detica 2012; Council of the European Union 2014; European Commission 2014; European Parliament Committee on Legal Affairs 2014; IFPI 2015; Weatherley 2014a, b for a sample of supporting actors). Follow-the-money seeks to stop the flow of money to illicit websites through the involvement of online advertising networks and payment processors; while search engines using a stoplight system would provide ratings, highlighting legal offers and discouraging consumption of infringing content (BOP Consulting with DotEcon 2015).

Copyright protection online is multifaceted, yet piecemeal. Underlying these enforcement techniques is surveillance technology to identify and monitor infringement. Moreover Internet intermediaries are requested to alter the availability of content. Online copyright enforcement thus clearly intersects with the issues of data protection and net neutrality, raising the important question how we balance rights and interests in this domain. Scholars show particular concern for the rise in private regulation using technology (Bridy 2010; Coudert and Werkers 2010; DeBeer and Clemmer 2009). Self/co-regulatory measures by nature focus on flexible solutions, but to which extent is parliamentary, judicial and civil society oversight necessary in regulating content online?

1.2   RESEARCH SCOPE: POLICY PROPOSALS IN THE EUROPEAN UNION

The case studies analyzed in this book focus on online copyright enforcement policy proposals in the EU after the implementation of the 2004 IPR Enforcement Directive (European Parliament & Council). As mentioned, in the EU, the E-Commerce, Copyright in the Information Society and IPR Enforcement Directives (European Parliament & Council 2000, 2001, 2004) are the three key legislative texts for copyright and its enforcement in an online environment. The IPR Enforcement Directive was adopted last and harmonizes the civil enforcement of IPR within the EU. The EU has not passed additional legislation on online copyright enforcement since these three texts. It is a starting point that all case studies have in common. The selected case studies cover EU, member state and international policy proposals. They deal with enhanced cooperation, increased involvement of Internet intermediaries and monitoring of Internet users.

- *2008 European Commission public consultation on Creative Content Online* (European Commission 2008): policy actors provide a wide range of views on stakeholder cooperation, graduated response in France and filtering measures. The public consultation and its related initiative were non-legislative and had a limited outcome.
- *2009 proposal to adopt graduated response in France* (French Parliament 2009a, b). In graduated response, the monitoring of Internet users is considered an educational measure to change P2P file-sharing behavior. France was the first EU member state to pass legislation supplementing the IPR Enforcement Directive. The adoption of graduated response has been controversial.

- *2010 European Commission public consultation on the E-Commerce Directive* (European Commission 2010c): the E-Commerce Directive stipulates the conditions for limiting the liability of intermediary service providers when illegal activity or content is present on their networks (European Parliament & Council 2000). Stakeholders express opinions on the interpretation of the liability provisions, notice and takedown procedures, filtering measures and investment in law enforcement. This public consultation also had a limited outcome. The EC has since held two additional public consultations on aspects of the E-Commerce Directive.
- *2010–2012 European Parliament debates on the Anti-Counterfeiting Trade Agreement* (ACTA, 2011 Accession Ongoing): this Treaty deals with international cooperation on IPR enforcement. In 2012 the EP refused to give its consent to ACTA, in effect prohibiting its ratification by the EU.

The case studies described in this book date from 2008 to 2012, but their results remain remarkably pertinent. The struggle to enforce copyright in an online environment continues and policy developments move at a snail's pace. *The case studies clearly show the complex and diverging views on copyright enforcement and IG within the EU. The policies all take stands on the regulatory use of technology and surveillance, have clear links with both copyright enforcement and IG, and are limited to the EU and its member states.* The case studies explain the intense conflict and resulting stalemate on online copyright enforcement in the EU and reflect on the Internet as an enabler but also target of regulation. Careful consideration is necessary on how and why we govern technology. In order to find a way forward in online copyright enforcement policies and IG, we need to come to the point where nuance and details provide the most interesting story to tell.

There are plenty of private arrangements and practices to deal with online copyright infringement. I focus on public policy proposals, because they set the scope for possible private action. If adopted, they embed particular ideas and interests into an institutional and enforceable framework. They are also well documented and therefore are easier to capture. Moreover, the Internet does not stop at national borders, but its international governance is fairly fragmented. The same applies to copyright. Within the EU, Internet and copyright are both policy areas where the European public authorities and member states share responsibilities (Mathijsen 2010). Copyright is a particularly sensitive domain of shared competence, as it relates to the cultural policies of the countries. The EU seeks to develop common visions on IG and copyright, as these will strengthen the digital single market and thus the economic competitiveness of the Union. Agreements found between twenty-eight countries at a regional level, could also go a long way in influencing debates at an international level. It is impossible to study the policies of an EU member state without taking into account the regional institutional influences. Nor is it possible understand the EU's international positioning without a proper study of internal policy developments. As the subject area of online copyright enforcement is vast, this demarcation is advisable as it allows me to investigate the policy approach of one influential actor in the regulatory debate more deeply.

Figure 1.1 is a timeline of the selected case studies; Table 1.1 provides a quick scan of main policy developments in EU online copyright enforcement. This table cannot cover all policy proposals and changes that have taken place at EU and national levels since 2004—in particular it does not do justice to the multitude of court cases that have taken place. Its aim is to serve as a point of reference for further discussion in the book by highlighting the parallel, yet fragmented policy endeavors to tackle copyright infringement across the EU. Section 2.4 goes into further detail on the legacy and developments of policy in this field.[3]

Further, the following two sections outline the theoretical and analytical framework, as well as the questions and methodology guiding the research conducted for this work, as it will enable the reader to better understand the focus, structure and outcome of the analysis presented in the following chapters. Analytically, I have found value in distinguishing between ideas, interests and institutions (the 3Is) present in the policymaking processes. Moreover, as I hope will become clear in the pages to come, focusing on discourses provides unique insight into how policy problems and solutions are framed in the debate. Language gives utterance to viewpoints and can create either bonds or barriers between stakeholders.

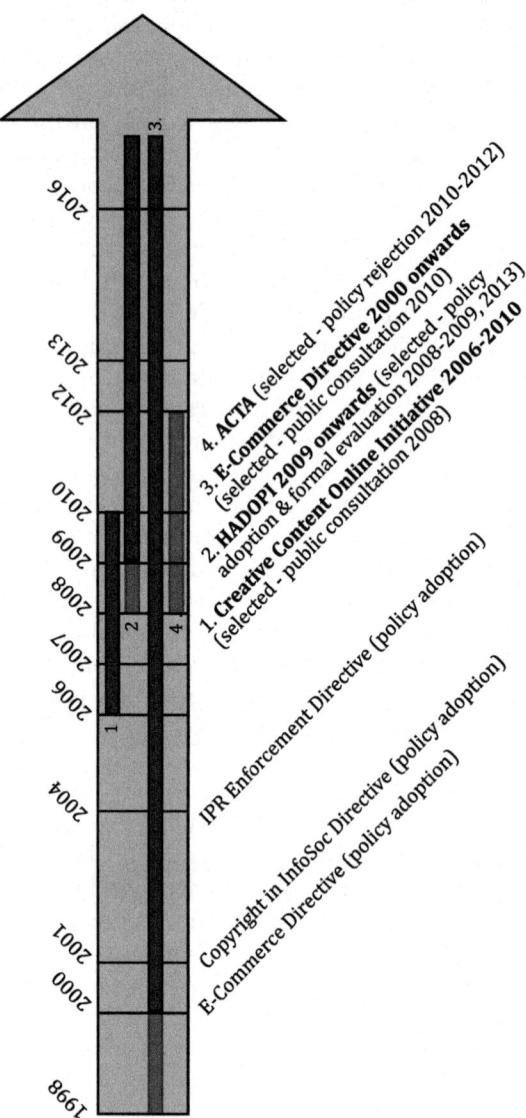

Fig. 1.1 Case study timeline (2008–2012)

Table 1.1 EU policy developments in online copyright enforcement (2004–2016)

Member state	Policy development	Details
EU	International negotiations Legislative reviews Legislative and non-legislative proposals to modernize online copyright and IPR enforcement frameworks Litigation and competition inquiries Stakeholder dialogues on online licensing, and follow-the-money	Anti-Counterfeiting Trade Agreement (ACTA): signed, not ratified Directives on multiterritorial licensing of musical works online, and permitted uses of orphan works E-Commerce Directive: evaluation and non-legislative guidelines IPR Enforcement & copyright in InfoSoc Directives: evaluation to determine review Audiovisual Media Services Directive (AVMS): review and legislative proposal to include certain online content providers Legislative proposal for regulation on cross-border content portability CJEU IPR Enforcement, copyright in InfoSoc and E-Commerce Directives cases, such as *Promusicae, Scarlet, Netlog, Padawan, Google France, eBay, Telekabel*: on balance of fundamental rights, restrictions on filtering, private copying levies, keyword advertising and injunctions Stakeholder dialogues on online licensing and follow-the-money approach: information sharing
Austria	Litigation	Pirate Bay case: blocked CJEU *UPC Telekabel vs. Constantin Film and Wega Filmproduktionsgesellschaft*: web blocking injunctions by intermediaries are permitted
Belgium	Legislative proposals to reform and enforce copyright Litigation	MR legislative proposal (initially graduated response, then levy on Internet connection) and Ecolo-Groen! legislative proposal (levy on Internet connection): retracted CJEU *SABAM vs. Scarlet, Netlog*: all encompassing, preventive intermediary filtering prohibited
Denmark	Litigation	Pirate Bay case: blocked

(continued)

Table 1.1 (continued)

Member state	Policy development	Details
France	Legislation on graduated response Non-legislative proposals to modernize online copyright and IPR enforcement frameworks Litigation Stakeholder cooperation on follow-the-money	HADOPI legislation: passed, implemented, evaluation Dailymotion, YouTube cases: not liable Allostreaming, Pirate Bay cases: blocked CJEU *Google vs. Louis Vuitton Mattelier & Others*: AdWords & trademarks, whether reasonably well-informed and reasonably observant Internet user can ascertain origin Charter of good practices in advertising for copyright protection (follow-the-money)
Finland	Legislative proposals to amend copyright Litigation	Copyright reform campaign: sufficient signatures obtained for government consideration, however limited outcome Legislative review of Copyright Act (607/2015): includes possibility to order a preventive injunction Open WiFi case: not liable Right to Internet access
Germany	Legislation on ancillary copyright Litigation	Google Tax law: passed, prevents search engines from displaying news content without fee Rapid share: no filtering YouTube case: not liable Hamburg case: low damages Individual liability Pirate Party elected
Ireland	Litigation Private agreement on graduated response	EMI Records case: Irish transposition of IPR Enforcement Directive does not allow judges to order non-infringing ISPs to take action against copyright infringing customers Eircom case settlement: graduated response mandated and implemented UPC case: graduated response mandated
Italy	Legislation on web blocking Litigation	AGCOM regulation on web blocking (Resolution no. 680/13/CONS): passed and implemented, allows Italian communications authority (AGCOM) to order injunction Yahoo! case: not liable after successful appeal Google case: not liable Break Media case: liable despite non-detailed notice

Table 1.1 (continued)

Member state	Policy development	Details
Netherlands	Litigation	Pirate Bay, Mininova cases: blocked FTD case: liable Downloading legal
Portugal	Stakeholder cooperation on online copyright protection	Memorandum of Understanding includes procedure for web blocking, involves Portuguese Ministry's Inspector General of Cultural Activities (IGAC)
Spain	Legislation on web blocking Legislation on ancillary copyright, contributory and vicarious liability for online copyright infringement, blocking of advertising on illicit sites, reform of private copying levies and more Litigation	Ley Sinde (2/2011, part of Sustainable Economy Act): passed and implemented Ley 21/2014 (law amending the Intellectual Property Act): passed and implemented Cinetube, Scaremule, YouTube cases: not liable CJEU *Promusicae vs. Telefónica:* ISPs not obliged to disclose subscriber information for civil proceeding, but member states can oblige if balance between various fundamental rights CJEU *Padawan SL vs. SGAE:* private copying levies prohibited when devices not made available to private users and clearly reserved for uses other than private copying
Sweden	Litigation	Pirate Bay employees case: guilty B2 case: injunction denied Pirate Party elected
United Kingdom	Legislation on graduated response Legislative and non-legislative proposals to make copyright fit for purpose (included licensing and exceptions) Litigation Stakeholder cooperation on licensing, graduated response and follow-the-money	Digital Economy Act: passed, not implemented Legislation on additional copyright exceptions: passed, exception on private copying levies repealed Litigation: extensive use of s.97A of Copyright, Designs and Patents Acts to obtain blocking injunctions CJEU *L'Oréal vs. eBay:* keyword advertising & trademarks, echoes Google France; intermediary liability, whether intermediary has active role and knowledge; need to ensure injunction possible Copyright Hub (licensing), Voluntary Copyright Alert Programme (graduated response) and Operation Creative and Infringing Website List (follow-the-money)

1.3   Theoretical/Analytical Approach
and Questions

This study builds on the *theory of political economy of communications (PEC)*. In essence, the central question in the PEC regarding the Internet is how to make money from content online. *The theory perceives online copyright enforcement primarily as a struggle between market actors to gain the upper hand.* The media industries seek to stay afloat by enforcing exclusive rights to reproduce, distribute and make their creative content available online. However in the digital and online environment, copyright as a means of creating scarcity is undermined. The Internet and technology industries have an interest to protect their own IPR, but equally gain from widespread distribution of content online. They are hesitant to enforce the rights of the media industries. For both industries, the value of content is primarily economic rather than social. The PEC argues that content on the Internet is increasingly commodified—it is perceived as a product to buy and sell. This book contends that while market interests are important, there is more at play in the online copyright enforcement debate. The theory of *PEC grapples with the "open character" of the Internet.* In its original design the Internet encourages decentralization, flexibility, interoperability and cooperation. The Internet was built with open, unfettered communication in mind, and has renewed hopes for alternative ways of creating knowledge and culture based on community sharing rather than market exchange. I argue that *the online copyright enforcement debate is about resistance to the copyright model of the media industries not only in terms of stakeholders' interests, but also their rationales for copyright and the Internet.* Along these same lines, I find in PEC that there is a lack of attention for the possibilities that the Internet's design permits for strong online copyright enforcement. Rights holders call to fight fire with fire—to use technology to regulate the availability of content it encourages. This perspective on technology is fairly narrow and focuses on threats. There is no regard for the Internet's added value to democracy through the facilitation of free speech, deliberation between citizens and community building. *Investigating the online copyright enforcement debate is important because it contributes to the framing and definition of the Internet's functions and values.* IG as a field is only just being determined.

In order to operationalize these theoretical insights, I developed a framework based on the analysis of ideas, interests, institutions and discourses present in policy. The framework provides a holistic explanation of selected online copyright enforcement policies in the EU. It is important to note that the outcome is not clear. Online copyright enforcement is a contested area and *there is a need for a thick description* to understand how stakeholders interact under which circumstances and how policy developments play themselves out. The main research question guiding this study has been *how and why selected policies in the EU dealing with the online enforcement of copyright have developed.* I seek to understand developments in this third phase of IG policymaking. Through the analysis I reveal explanatory factors for the events taking place, but I do not wish to infer causality. I contribute to the theory of PEC by researching how and why ideas, interests, institutions and discourses play a role in online copyright enforcement policies. *Answers to the five sub-research questions of this study, set out in Box 1.2, provide rich and valuable insight into the divergence in policy opinions and results.* The emphasis is on the perceptions of actors, on recovering "the individual and shared meanings that motivated actors to do what they did" (Wendt 1998, 102). I can only give a partial answer to the last two sub-research questions based on this study's empirical evidence. The questions are included because they refer to the study's theory on why it is important to investigate online copyright enforcement in the first place. The problems, solutions and goals presented and adopted, the views on knowledge creation and technological governance advocated, the stakeholder coalitions formed and the institutional rules and settings chosen in policy all shape the future governance of the Internet. The purpose of this study is to elucidate the contention in the debate, thereby hoping to clarify opportunities and pitfalls and contribute to a way forward.

Box 1.2   Research questions

How and why have selected policies in the EU dealing with the online enforcement of copyright developed?
- Which actors are involved with which ideas and interests?
- Which discourses are used in these policies to argue different ideas and interests?
- Which institutional rules and settings are chosen to develop these policies?
- Do these policies affect the control of creative content on the Internet?
- Do these policies form a possible threat to the "open character" of the Internet?

1.3.1   Political Economy of Communications

The study of political economy is about how societies are organized and controlled, and thus involves the analysis of power. The study of political economy of the media is about the production, distribution, and consumption of media. Importantly, this approach is interested in how the media are organized and controlled within the larger political economy. In other words, it is concerned with who has power to make decisions about the media, and who benefits from these decisions. It is about understanding how power relations actually work within and around the media. (Sirois and Wasko 2011, 332)

The study of *political economy* provides a macro-level perspective on why it is interesting to consider policy. Political economy studies the interactions of economics, law and politics, investigating how institutions develop in different economic systems. It deems that *our economic and political systems are intertwined*. Political economy argues that the economy does not operate independently of political decision making. The two influence each other. I have a keen desire to understand the factors and processes at play in policymaking. Online copyright enforcement is about who controls information on the Internet. I start from the premise that the high and often opposing economic stakes surrounding copyright in the online environment matter greatly for the development of its policies. Political economy as a theoretical approach places market transactions central in its investigations. Further, the study of political economy provides a normative perspective on how our economic and political systems should evolve. It is important to understand that the study of political economy comes in many shades and colors. Marxist political economy, institutional economics, Keynesian economics and neoclassical economics are a few examples of political economic perspectives on our current capitalist system. In this study I define capitalism as an economic and political system in which trade and industry are controlled by private actors (rather than the state) whose ultimate goal is to maximize profit. I appreciate the *normativity* of political economic approaches. Our worldviews and ideals determine how we define problems and what we consider as possible solutions—in economics, politics and research alike. In the rest of this section I expand further on these thoughts. However as this study pertains to media, I limit myself to the PEC. I explain PEC's economic and normative focus, the added value of investigating media, the definition of power and two PEC schools of thought.

The PEC studies *power relations* in media. Central to its investigations are mechanisms and strategies used to control the production, distribution and consumption of media (Winseck 2011). Media here are conceived of as the press, radio and television, but more broadly also include industries such as film, music, gaming, publishing and performance. The Internet can be considered both telecommunications (its hardware and software) and media (its content). The PEC seeks to counter negative consequences of our capitalist market system (Wasko et al. 2011).[4] It emphasizes that our economic structures are intrinsically bound up in the organization of society, and view power as "a resource that is structured or rooted in [...] a feature built into a system that rewards market position with privileged status within social hierarchies" (Mosco 2009, 220). The PEC contends that our capitalist system's reliance on the production of exchange value and the exploitation of labor results in injustice and inequality. Inherent to its approach is a *commitment to social praxis*. This means PEC scholars strive for social justice and democratic practice through their work (Wasko et al. 2011; Mosco 2009).

The PEC deems *media* important to investigate, because media serve a *double role in society*, as "industries in their own right and as the major site of the representations and arenas of debate through which the overall system is imagined and argued over" (Wasko et al. 2011, 2). Media are subject to market dynamics, but can also serve as agents of economic, social and cultural change (Hesmondhalgh 2007; McChesney 2008; Watson 2003). The PEC argues that media require extra scrutiny as they are *socially and democratically important* in their contribution to our daily lives through the provision of information, culture and entertainment. One arena where struggles over media play out is in policymaking. PEC starts from the premise that policy developments are never neutral and often (but not invariably) result in the support of dominant economic interests. At the same time, leading scholar in the PEC, Vincent Mosco (2009), critiques the PEC for its lack of analysis of policy processes. Detailed studies of power relations in policy are missing.

In line with Manuel Castells (2009, 10), I define *power* as "the relational capacity that enables a social actor to influence asymmetrically the decisions [and actions] of other social actor(s) in ways that favor the empowered actor's will, interests, and values". David Betz and Tim Stevens (2011,

42–53) usefully translate four basic forms of power (Barnett and Duvall 2005) into cyberpower:

- *Compulsory cyberpower* involves direct coercion through control of computers or their networks. It is a technical and material form of power. As I elaborate in Chap. 2, technological governance is compulsory cyberpower. Threats of sanctions by a state through legal, military or economic action are also compulsory cyberpower.
- *Institutional cyberpower* is about influencing the behavior of actors through the formal and informal institutions that govern the Internet. It not only relates to the global and local institutional context, but also to the characteristics, values and standards of the Internet.
- *Structural cyberpower* concerns the strategic positioning of actors in the Internet environment to directly influence the actions of other actors. It is about the organization of the Internet economically and socially, and the possibilities which these arrangements allow and preclude.
- *Productive cyberpower* uses discourse and symbolism. It is the shaping of actions and behavior through the language, defining the Internet, policy issues and actors in a particular way. Old discourses are reproduced in the digital environment, but the Internet is equally a medium for the emergence of new discourses. Productive cyberpower is the softest form of power in this typology and is closely linked with institutional power in the sense that it relates to the culture of the Internet.

The PEC focuses primarily on structural (economic and social) power. It considers other forms of power (regulation, formal and informal institutions, discourses and ideas) mainly in function of structural power. As the discussion of Betz and Stevens' four forms of cyberpower indicates, I lean toward *complexity and resistance* in power relations. This fits closely with the European strand of PEC. Although economic position and ownership give much power, oppositional forces are continually at work in our capitalist system. Technology, regulation, institutions and discourses are different ways in which this dialectic between domination and resistance is played out.

For this study the most relevant *schools of thought* in the PEC are North American and European. On the one hand, *North American PEC* has strong Marxist ties, stressing class relations, monopoly and imperialism in the media (Mosco 2009; Winseck 2011). It is deeply concerned with the *dangers of capitalism for the democratic potential and diversity of the media*. The most prominent North American PEC scholars are Dallas Smythe (1977, 1981), Herbert Schiller (1969, 1973), Dan Schiller (2000, 2008) and Robert McChesney (2008). Dwayne Winseck (2011) identifies the lack of the complexity in its analysis of the media system and the lack of attention for audience agency as the main weaknesses of North American PEC. Nicholas Garnham (2011) adds that some of the sweeping claims about collusion between state and economy to maintain hegemony in society are untenable. There is a need to investigate the conflict of interests among actors. The cultural studies approach has extensively addressed the latter criticism. In cultural studies, the users play an active role in the reproduction, but also reinterpretation and resistance of discourses and ideologies in media and culture. On the other hand, *European PEC* deals with the expansion of commercial media and related defense of public service media, class struggles and labor within media industries (Mosco 2009; Hesmondhalgh 2007). It is closely linked with the work of Nicholas Garnham (1990, 2000) and Golding and Murdock (2005), as well as the cultural industries approach advanced by Bernard Miège (1989). David Hesmondhalgh (2007) argues that European PEC is better in dealing with contradiction, historical variation and the specific conditions of media industries. This is because it focuses on the *media's role in the reproduction of but also the resistance to social class divisions*, and studies the labor processes and internal organization of media industries. European PEC acknowledges "the partial and incomplete process of commodifying culture" (Hesmondhalgh 2007, 35). "It allows for contradiction *within* industrial, commercial cultural production, rather than assuming a simplistic polarity *between* corporations and non-profit 'alternative' producers" (Hesmondhalgh 2007, 36, italics in original). This resistance is crucial to consider when analyzing policymaking. Thus although important, it is not merely economic interests determining public policy. Moreover we cannot assume that all actors within the media industries share the same policy goals. Finally in the online environment, it is important to note that both media and Internet & technology industries pursue commercially motivated goals. This study identifies more closely with European PEC.

In summary the PEC adds value by pointing my analysis of online copyright enforcement policies to the interaction between economics and politics. PEC scholars emphasize the double role of media in society, with the explicit aim of encouraging social justice and democratic practice. They view economic power as particularly influential, but leave room for resistance and social change. Chapter 2 shows how the PEC applies to the two main components of this research: Internet and copyright. I try to expound both on its contributions *and* shortcomings. In particular additional perspectives are necessary and included to deal with surveillance and technological governance.

1.3.2   Ideas, Interests and Institutions (3Is)

The neoclassical economist *Jagdish Bhagwati* published a book entitled *Protectionism* in which he used a typology of *3Is—ideas, interests and institutions*—to analyze and contest developments in international trade policy. Bhagwati (1989, 17) states that, "[p]rofound commitments to policies are generally due to a mix of ideological factors (in the forms of ideas and example), interests (as defined by politics and economics), and institutions (as they shape constraints and opportunities)." He argues that it was the conjunction of these 3Is that favored postwar liberalization of trade. For Bhagwati, ideas are theories that underlie policy thinking and examples are historical perceptions and experiences that can be used to argue for or against policy change. Although he recognizes that, "it would be vulgar to claim that interests dominate exclusively, the appropriate ideology being chosen simply to legitimate the triumphant interests", he believes that, "a good cause seldom triumphs unless someone's interest is bound up in it" (Bhagwati 1989, 17–18). Institutions then create the mechanism and momentum for ideas and interests, shaping them while at the same time being shaped by them. I believe Bhagwati's holistic typology is useful as the basis for analyzing online copyright enforcement policies, even though the political economic approach adopted in this study grew out of a reaction to neoclassical economics. I adopt the terms not the underlying economic views.

Much needs to be done to further unveil the black boxes of these 3Is. This requires a look into political science literature where Bhagwati's typology has become a popular means of analyzing change. My interest lies in literature that has consciously moved beyond rationalist and positivist perspectives where self-interest is in the driving seat and ideas play an exogenous and minority role (see for instance Goldstein and Keohane 1993; Laffey and Weldes 1997; Schmidt 2010; McGillivray et al. 2001). Policymaking is more complex than that. These scholars (who identify closely with *the cultural/linguistic turn* in research) emphasize that ideas matter, but are divided among themselves whether ideas cause or constitute change. Said differently, *they disagree whether ideas influence alongside interests and institutions, or whether they define and create meaning for interests and institutions.* So for instance Judith Goldstein and Robert Keohane (1993, 3) state that, "ideas influence policy when the principles or causal beliefs they embody provide road maps that increase actors' clarity about goals or ends-means relationships, when they affect outcomes of strategic situations in which there is no unique equilibrium, and when they become embedded in political institutions." Mark Laffey and Jutta Weldes (1997) object. They argue that in Goldstein and Keohane's interpretation, "ideas—although explicitly defined as shared beliefs—are thus implicitly conceptualized as commodities that are 'supplied' by 'political entrepreneurs' on a 'market-place' in response to 'demands', and then 'circulate' through that market-place to be 'peddled' and 'consumed'" (Laffey and Weldes 1997, 207). They counter that ideas cannot be understood as separate variables, as objects that can exist apart from people. Laffey and Weldes offer an alternative metaphor "ideas as capital" in response, to emphasize that ideas are socially constructed and dynamic.

I elaborate on this tension in the literature, because it illustrates that we do not need to resign either to developing a model of causal relations between the 3Is, or to an approach where ideas and language determine all. In essence this is about identifying our position on the ontological and epistemological spectrum. *The question is how far we need to move away from positivism,* from capturing an objective reality through causal inference. How much is our perception of the world and knowledge colored by human subjectivity (della Porta and Keating 2008)? In line with the PEC, this study is critical realist and postpositivist. As Donatella della Porta and Michael Keating (2008, 24, italics in original) explain, "*[c]ritical realist* epistemology holds that there is a real material world but that our knowledge of it is often socially conditioned and subject to challenge and reinterpretation." *The dynamic and dialectical nature of the 3Is is continually emphasized.*

Moving beyond disagreement then, what can we learn from literature to help define the 3Is for policy analysis? First, *ideas* need to be further unpacked. Goldstein and Keohane (1993) distinguish between worldviews, principled beliefs and causal beliefs. Worldviews concern ideas about reality and define the universe of possibilities for action; principled beliefs are normative ideas that help distinguish between right and wrong, just from unjust; and *causal beliefs are beliefs about cause and effect rela-*

tionships which provide guides for attaining particular goals (Goldstein and Keohane 1993, 8–11). These ideas move on a scale from abstract to concrete, and from stable to changeable—worldviews are the most abstract and stable, causal beliefs are the most concrete and changeable. Ideology, ideals and ideas run parallel to this categorization. As we saw above, the New Oxford American Dictionary defines ideology (worldviews) as a system of ideals and ideas, especially one that forms the basis of economic or political action. Examples of ideology within this study are "neoliberalism" and "representative democracy", and the critiques thereof. Further ideals (principled beliefs) are values and norms, in this context, on economics and policymaking. Examples could be "free market" versus "fairness", "efficiency" versus "representability". With the clear understanding that ideology and ideals shape ideas (and interests and institutions!) I limit myself to the study of ideas (causal beliefs).

> Ideas are defined as the proposed definitions of a policy problem, the subsequent proposed policy solutions, and the theories upon which these problem definitions and solutions are built.

These ideas can be gathered more easily from stakeholders' contributions to policy debates than their underlying ideology and ideals. This means I can analyze the dialectic between domination and resistance in more detail. Second, *interests* are easier to pin down. On the one hand Frank Fischer (2003) and Maarten Hajer (1995) point out that interests are not a given, they can change throughout the policy process. They are referring to actors' reasons for involvement in the policy. On the other hand statements (such as can be found in certain political economic circles) that politics are driven by material interests, view interests as powerful market positioning. This study covers both interpretations.

> Interests are defined as the policy goals of involved actors, and the social and economic reality in which the policy develops.

Involved actors in this definition are individuals, organizations and businesses who seek to influence the development of the policy at hand (including policymakers themselves). Third, *institutions* broadly defined are "any formalized (or semi-formalized) regular pattern of behaviour" (McGillivray et al. 2001, 21). They are the formal and informal rules of the game, which determine the opportunities and constraints for policy action (Kern 2011). In this study, I approach institutions as *settings rather than actors*.

Institutions are defined as the policy legacy, and the political and legal reality in which the policy develops.

Scholars point out that changes in the socioeconomic and politico-legal realities (whether perceived or real) can create junctures in policies, opening windows of opportunity for policy development (Goldstein and Keohane 1993; Bradford 1999; Schmidt 2010). Finally, I believe it is necessary to not just discuss 3Is but a *D—discourse* as well. I perceive discourse as stakeholders' argumentation of their ideas and interests. Discourse is about the stories and metaphors used in policy debates. It is different from a simple presentation of problem definitions, policy solutions and goals. Treating discourse separately allows me to take the *language of policy* into account. Moreover I have found that the specific discourse analysis adopted in this study adds value through its identification of discourse coalitions, structuration and institutionalization in policy. As I explain below, it points to interactions between the 3Is. The following section defines discourse and brings all four elements together into an analytical framework for online copyright enforcement policies.

1.3.3 Argumentative Discourse Analysis

Argumentative discourse analysis (ADA) is an example of the linguistic turn in policy analysis. It stresses language and its environment, and considers *discourses central to the creation and representation of meaning*. Argumentative discourse analysis (Hajer 1995, 2002, 2006), argumentative policy analysis (Gottweis 2006), frame-critical policy analysis (Fischer 2003, Rein and Schön 1996), critical semiotic analysis (Jessop 2004, 2009) and discursive institutionalism (Schmidt 2010) are very similar in approach. Among these discourse analyses, two overarching features are particularly relevant from the perspective of the PEC. First as mentioned, *discourse in context* is emphasized. Hajer (2002, 63) argues that, "ADA is not simply about analysing arguments—it is much more about analysing politics as a play of 'positioning' at particular 'sites' of discursive production." Further Fischer (2003, 45) states that, "political action is constituted by discourses, from hegemonic discourses embedded in the existing institutions (for example, the theories and practices of liberal capitalism) to the oppositional efforts of other groups attempting to create new discourses (for example, environmentalism). Public policies are not only influenced by the discourses of particular groups, they are shaped and supported by the institutional processes in which specific discursive practices are embedded, processes which can have a life of their own." The focus is primarily on the *shaping role of ideas and discourse on our perception of reality*. This is positive but needs to be balanced with a thorough analysis of interests and institutions. Second, these linguistic approaches stress *strong empirical research and engagement in the field*. For example in "Frame-Critical Policy Analysis and Frame-Reflective Policy Practice", Martin Rein and Donald Schön (1996) indicate that they study controversial policy issues specifically to work toward solutions. Moreover the approach keeps close ties with networked governance and deliberative democratic thinking (Hajer and Wagenaar 2003; Fischer 2003), an active search to improve decision making. In other words, similar to the PEC, social praxis is encouraged. I opt for ADA in this study, because I have found Maarten Hajer's (1993, 1995, 2002, 2006) work concrete and easy to apply in policy analysis. He marks his discourse analysis as realist, materialist and radical (Hajer 2002), which is closer to my study in terms of ontology and epistemology than other linguistic research (of those mentioned here, Gottweis 2006, in particular). In the following paragraph, I define and explain how certain ADA terms are used in this book.

Hajer (2006, 67) defines discourse as, "an ensemble of ideas, concepts, and categories through which meaning is given to social and physical phenomena, and which is produced and reproduced through an identifiable set of practices". Discourse is a means to study ideas and interests in policy. In line with the operationalization of the 3Is,

> Discourses are defined here as involved actors' argumentation of their policy problem definitions, solutions, theories and goals.

In ADA, discourses are identified in policy by searching texts for emblematic issues and story lines. *Emblematic issues are metaphors or sensitizing concepts; story lines are "condensed statements summarizing complex narratives, used by people as 'short hands' in discussions"* (Hajer 2006, 69). Two examples in this study are "piracy is theft" (metaphor) and "losses in the media industries are due to online piracy requiring strong government intervention" (story line). The power of emblematic issues and story lines lies in their ambivalence and reinterpretability. Story lines serve to simplify and suggest unity in policy reasoning. Hajer (1995, 64–65) states that story lines "not only help construct a problem, they also play an important role in the creation of a social and moral order in a given domain. Story-lines are devices through which actors are positioned, and through which specific ideas of 'blame' and 'responsibility', and of 'urgency' and 'responsible behaviour' are attributed". Discourses are not necessarily coherent sets of arguments and can change throughout the policy process.

ADA also allows us to study the *(re)production of discourses* by analyzing policy practices. I focus on the formation of coalitions and the gradual structuration and institutionalization of discourses. *A discourse coalition is "a group of actors, that in the context of an identifiable set of practices, shares the usage of a particular set of story lines over a particular period of time" (within this definition the practices are embedded routines and shared ideals); discourse structuration refers to the adoption of a discourse by the majority of actors in the policy process; discourse institutionalization is the final step when a particular discourse is embedded into legal and political arrangements* (Hajer 2006, 70).[5] Discourse coalitions, structuration and institutionalization form a scale. Once a discourse has been institutionalized, change in the dominant discourse (and consequently policy approach) will be hardest to achieve. These three analytical concepts convey the struggle for productive and institutional power in policy and thus add to the analysis of the 3Is. They provide insight into how stakeholders advocate their problem definitions, policy solutions and goals, and who is successful in this endeavor. Hajer focuses on the constitutive role of arguments, while taking the dynamic interactions of actors and structural constraints of institutions on board.

Finally to complete the analysis of interests and institutions according to the definitions provided in the previous section, I also map the social, economic, political and legal realities in the setting-the-scene chapter and in each policy case study through literature review and expert interviewing. Combining the analysis of the 3Is with argumentative discourse provides nuance yet flexibility. In my view this analytical framework addresses the need to operationalize policy analysis for the PEC at a micro level. It is attentive to the formative role that ideas and discourses play, yet recognizes that the material reality contains resourceful market players and institutions with long legacy. It is a tool to elucidate the dialectic between domination and resistance that defines whether and how we control creative content online (CCO). In the penultimate section of this chapter I expand on which methods and cases I use to put this analytical framework into practice.

1.4   Research Methodology

This book presents the analysis of four case studies in-depth to better understand the uniqueness of each case and explain the EU's approach to enforce copyright on the Internet. Within the case studies, I seek to get a grip on the *ideas, interests, institutions and discourses influencing the policy, with a particular focus on actors' perceptions in and on the policymaking process.* The aim is to reconstruct the process and meaning of the policy development in each case study. The research for each case is conducted in six steps. To avoid repetition at the beginning of each case I summarize the different steps here.

1.4.1   Setting the Scene

First, Chap. 2 provides an in-depth political economic analysis of online copyright enforcement. This sets the scene for the case studies. For each individual case I also perform a review of existing literature.

1.4.2   Document Gathering

Second, most documents are gathered online. The selected documents firstly consist of legislative proposals, supporting policy documents, consultations and press releases from involved government and Parliament officials and departments. I also consult relevant related legislation and litigation to understand the institutional dynamics of each case. The second important source of documents are policy advocates' contributions through consultation responses and press releases. Media texts have been taken into account where they contribute directly to the policy debate. The policy advocates are identified through government websites and media texts. The selection of documents and actors has been verified during the interviews with specific questions aimed at identifying actors' main texts, partners and opponents.

Selected documents are given equal weight, as they all contribute to the policymaking process. When identifying discourse structuration and institutionalization, I restrict the analysis to government and Parliament officials and departments' documents. Operationalizing the definitions above, discourse structuration occurs when discourse is (re)produced by government or Parliament officials and departments during the policy-making process. Discourse institutionalization means discourse has been embedded into legal and supporting policy documents at the end of the policymaking process.

1.4.3 Selection of Key Incidents in the Policymaking Process

Third, determining key incidents in the policy development helps limit the overall number of documents. For the case studies on CCO and the E-Commerce Directive, the relevant consultation is the key incident. For ACTA, the analysis centers around the events leading up to the policy rejection in the EP. The French case study covers the time period from the introduction of legislative proposals to its adoption in Parliament.

1.4.4 3Is and ADA

Fourth, I conduct the analysis of the 3Is and argumentative discourse. I code the emblematic issues, story lines, problem definitions, policy solutions, theories on copyright and the Internet, and policy goals in each document. It should be noted that this coding is complemented with literature review and expert interviews, which aid my understanding of the socioeconomic and politico-legal realities.

1.4.5 Expert Interviewing

Fifth, interviews have been conducted with a wide range of policy advocates from civil society, media industries and Internet & technology industries. Where possible, I have also interviewed government and Parliament officials. Moreover academics have been contacted to provide alternative views on policy developments. For the media industries I cast the net particularly wide, expecting views to differ between sectors and within the value chain. I have contacted policy actors across the value chain from the music, audiovisual, gaming and publishing sectors, major as well as independent. In total fifty-four interviews have been conducted related to these case studies: thirty-nine on EU online copyright enforcement policies, and fifteen on the French HADOPI laws.

In my research, interviewing is a complementary tool to verify preliminary results and gather data not available in the documents. The knowledge sought in the interviews relate to policy details (technical), policy interactions and development (process related) and/or actors' beliefs (interpretive) (Bogner et al. 2009). Importantly not only the documents, but also the interviews are subject to the analysis of 3Is and argumentative discourse.

1.4.6   Interpretation and Conclusion

Lastly, these steps are brought together in a structured reporting of the cases. This can be found in Chaps. 3 through 6. Each case follows the same format (Box 1.3).

Box 1.3   Structure of case studies

Ideas

Problem Definitions and Policy Solutions
Copyright and Internet Rationales

Discourses

Discourses
Discourse Coalitions, Structuration and Institutionalization

Interests

Policy Goals
Social and Economic Reality

Institutions

Policy Legacy
Political and Legal Reality

Conclusion: PEC Considerations

1.5   CHAPTER OUTLINES

This study consists of three main parts. Chapter 2 provides theoretical reflections on online copyright enforcement. Chapters 3 through 6 set out the four analyzed case studies. Chapter 7 brings the various threads woven through the study together.

Chapter 2 sets the scene for the empirical research. It studies the history, rationales and discourses of the Internet and copyright (ideas and discourses). The history of the Internet and copyright teaches us that choices are continually made in the development of a technology or policy. The current debate on online copyright enforcement is not unique. It is not the first time that a balance needs to be found between contradicting ideas and interests in copyright. What is remarkable is that the majority of Internet and copyright rationales clash. While the Internet promotes widespread distribution of information, copyright limits and protects. Stakeholders' views on knowledge creation greatly influence whether they assess online copyright infringement as a positive or a negative development. Throughout the study, I highlight power struggles in online copyright enforcement. Socially, the Internet is portrayed as a means of obtaining political participation and freedom of expression. Economically, we notice strong consolidation in the media, telecommunications, ICT and Internet industries. These sections of Chap. 2 illustrate the tensions within and between the Internet and copyright. Further, I analyze the costs and benefits of copyright infringement (interests). Copyright infringement causes loss in the media industries, but benefits other parts of the economy, and according to some studies, even society as a whole. It also expands on the characteristics and challenges of the media industries. Here again a historical and holistic perspective is necessary. The media industries have continually had to adapt to technological advancements. At the same time the turmoil of the media industries should not be underestimated. Digitization and the Internet exasperate one very important media strategy: the creation of artificial scarcity. Finally, Chap. 2 explains the regulatory history and framework of IG and online copyright enforcement policies (institutions). IG is increasing, but opinions diverge on which of the 3Is it should advance. Online copyright enforcement policies are likely to be framed as extensions of existing offline approaches. I contend that policymakers should not ignore the opportunities that the Internet offers for creativity, collaboration and freedom of expression. Much comes down to balancing market and non-market concerns.

Chapters 3 through 6 report on the four selected case studies—CCO, HADOPI, the E-Commerce Directive and ACTA. Each case study is analyzed according to the framework set out in Chap. 1. I investigate involved actors' proposed problem definitions and policy solutions on online copyright enforcement, the theories used on copyright and the

Internet (ideas); the presence of discourses and stakeholder coalitions, the adoption of discourses during and at the end of the policymaking process (discourses); involved actors' policy goals, the social and economic reality in which the policy develops (interests); the policy legacy, and the political and legal reality (institutions). The case studies teach us that stakeholders compete for control over cultural production and distribution, the Internet infrastructure and the policymaking process. There is no agreement on problem definitions nor policy solutions for copyright in the online environment. The EU case studies result in stalemates. Importantly, the role of Internet intermediaries in intervening in the network is at the crux of the EU online copyright enforcement debate. Filtering measures are off the table, but a compromise might be found on notice and takedown procedures. Further, the EU case studies show that the institutional setting of the EU affects the framing of problems and possibilities for action. At the same time, ACTA took a surprising turn. Stakeholders are not afraid to pitch policy objectives, legal provisions and case law against each other in the hope of gaining legal and political clout. The EU "*acquis communautaire*" provides high protection of IPR, yet there is much pressure to complete the digital single market. EU level policymaking has turned out to be a difficult setting for advocating strong online copyright enforcement. France provides an example where online copyright enforcement policy did find support. Graduated response is a monitoring, warning and sanction mechanism aimed at changing Internet users' P2P file-sharing behavior. Graduated response in France is government driven, creates a new administrative authority and advocates the suspension of Internet access as a sanction. In France, public authorities deem a strong legal framework necessary for the further development of legal offers. In the analysis I found that stakeholders' objections were reduced to the procedure rather than the principle of graduated response. They manage to bring in judicial and procedural safeguards, but fail to convince public authorities that graduated response is a disproportionate policy solution. I criticize graduated response on grounds of its threatening discourse on the Internet and bias toward regulating through technology.

Finally, Chap. 7 provides structured answers to the study's research questions. The case studies confirm that ideas, interests, institutions and discourses are deeply intertwined in public policy. In terms of ideas and discourses, there is no agreement among stakeholders on the problem definitions, policy solutions or goals for online copyright enforcement in the EU. It is clear however that policy actors' approach to knowledge creation and stance on the role of copyright and the Internet in society determine their positions on online copyright enforcement. They compete for the adoption of their views and framing in policy, but need to bear in mind that proposed and adopted online copyright enforcement laws are economic rather than social in outlook. In terms of interests, the empirical evidence shows that the views of the media and Internet & technology industries are opposed on online copyright enforcement. At the same time ACTA reveals that civil society can be successful in demanding change. In terms of institutions, stakeholders select institutional rules and settings that support their views best. Proponents of strong online copyright enforcement call for the use of technology to regulate. Opponents point to the importance of the Internet in everyday life. Chapter 7 also expands on the policy implications, theoretical and analytical lessons learned in this study. In order to find a way forward in online copyright enforcement policies and IG, we need to come to the point where nuance and detail provide the most interesting story to tell. If we are willing to move beyond fragmentation and polarization, this book has taught us that the approach needs to be comprehensive. Viewing problem definitions holistically, taking into account the various causes of copyright discontentment and media change, will lead to policy solutions that are multifaceted. Further from this study's perspective it is important that the Internet can be an enabler but also a target of regulation. I argue that careful consideration is necessary on how and why we govern technology. We should not accept that technology plays the role of adjudicator. Finally, I include improvements for future research. These pertain to the tradeoff between the number of case studies and the level of detail in analysis, and the emphasis on ideas and discourses while using PEC as the theoretical basis.

NOTES

1. As we start this chapter, it is important to remark that the terms, theories and demarcations presented in this chapter are explained and defined in due detail in subsequent chapters.
2. Two clarifications are due. First, the term governance in this study refers to a manner of controlling, influencing or regulating a person,

action or course of events. This implies that governance is not restricted to legislation or the government as an actor. Second, the importance of IPR and the increase in infringement have led to the development of policies to enforce existing legislation. The term copyright enforcement in this study refers to policies to enforce copyright rather than the enforcement of copyright policies.

3. In case the reader is interested in receiving regular updates and analysis on online copyright enforcement, I can strongly recommend consulting the European Audiovisual Observatory's IRIS Newsletter (http://merlin.obs.coe.int/newsletter.php), the 1709 Blog (http://the1709blog.blogspot.be), the London School of Economics Media Policy Project Blog (http://blogs.lse.ac.uk/mediapolicyproject/) and/or the Internet & Jurisdiction Project Retrospect (http://www.internetjurisdiction.net).

4. Political economy as approached here is a reaction to neoclassical economics. Consequently some authors prefer the term critical political economy. It must be recognized that in comparison to other political economic studies, PEC adopts a more explicit normative standpoint (for a discussion see Mosco 2009; Winseck 2011).

5. For the purpose of clarity, it is necessary to remark on the difference between institutions and institutionalization in this study. Institutions refer to policy structures and settings; institutionalization is the process of embedding discourses into those policy structures and settings.

BIBLIOGRAPHY

September 11, 2012. N. 11-2858 Capitol Records, Inc vs. Thomas-Rasset. United States Court of Appeals for the Eight Circuit.

AGCOM. 2013. Delibera n. 680/13/CONS, Regolamento in materia di tutela del diritto d'autore sulle reti di comunicazione elettronica e procedure attuative ai sensi del decreto legislativo 9 aprile 2003, n. 70. Naples: Italian Communications Regulatory Authority.

Australia, Canada, the European Union and its member states, Japan, the Kingdom of Morocco, New Zealand, the Republic of Korea, the Republic of Singapore, the Swiss Confederation, the United Mexican States, and the United States of America. 2011 Accession Ongoing. Anti-Counterfeiting Trade Agreement.

BAE Systems Detica. 2012. *The Six Business Models for Copyright Infringement. A Data-Driven Study of Websites Considered to Be Infringing Copyright.* Guildford: Google and PRS for Music.

Barlow, John Perry. 1996. *A Declaration of the Independence of Cyberspace*. Davos: Electronic Frontier Foundation.

Barnett, Michael, and Raymond Duvall. 2005. Power in International Politics. *International Organization* 59(1): 39–75.

Betz, David, and Tim Stevens. 2011. In *Cyberspace and the State. Toward a Strategy for Cyber-Power*, ed. International Institute for Strategic Studies, *Adelphi*. Oxon: Routledge.

Bhagwati, Jagdish. 1989. *Protectionism*. Cambridge: MIT Press.

Bogner, Alexander, Beate Littig, and Wolfgang Menz. 2009. Expert Interviews – An Introduction to a New Methodological Debate. In *Interviewing Experts*, ed. Alexander Bogner, Beate Littig, and Wolfgang Menz, 1–13. Houndmills: Palgrave Macmillan.

BOP Consulting with DotEcon. 2015. *International Comparison of Approaches to Online Copyright Infringement*. London: UK Intellectual Property Office.

Bradford, Neil. 1999. The Policy Influence of Economic Ideas: Interests, Institutions and Innovation in Canada. *Studies in Political Economy* 59(Summer): 17–60.

Bridy, Annemarie. 2010. Graduated Response and the Turn to Private Ordering in Online Copyright Enforcement. *Oregon Law Review* 89: 81–132.

Brown, Ian, and Christopher Marsden. 2013. *Regulating Code: Good Governance and Better Regulation in the Information Age*. Cambridge/London: MIT Press.

Castells, Manuel. 2009. *Communication Power*. Oxford/New York: Oxford University Press.

Center for Copyright Information. 2016. The Copyright Alert System. http://www.copyrightinformation.org/the-copyright-alert-system/. Accessed 6 Oct 2016.

Coudert, Fanny, and Evi Werkers. 2010. In the Aftermath of the Promusicae Case: How to Strike the Balance? *International Journal of Law and Information Technology* 18(1): 50–71.

Council of the European Union. 2014. *Draft Council Conclusions on IPR Enforcement*. Brussels: Council of the European Union.

DeBeer, Jeremy, and Christopher Clemmer. 2009. Global Trends in Online Copyright Enforcement: A Non-Neutral Role for Network Intermediaries? *Jurimetrics* 49(4): 375.

della Porta, Donatella, and Michael Keating. 2008. How Many Approaches in the Social Sciences? An Epistemological Introduction. In *Approaches and Methodologies in the Social Sciences. A Pluralist Perspective*, ed. Donatella della Porta and Michael Keating, 19–39. Cambridge: Cambridge University Press.

European Commission. 2008. *COM(2007) 836 final. Communication from the Commission to the European Parliament, the Council, the European Economic and Social Committee and the Committee of the Regions on Creative Content Online in the Single Market*. Brussels: European Commission.

————. 2010a. *COM(2010a) 245 Final/2. Communication from the Commission to the European Parliament, the Council, the European Economic and Social Committee and the Committee of the Regions. A Digital Agenda for Europe.* Brussels: European Commission.

————. 2010b. *COM(2010b) 779 final. Communication of the Commission to the European Parliament, the Council, the European Economic and Social Committee and the Committee of the Regions on the Application of Directive 2004/48/EC of the European Parliament and the Council of 29 April 2004 on the Enforcement of Intellectual Property Rights.* Brussels: European Commission.

————. 2010c. *Public Consultation on the Future of Electronic Commerce in the Internal Market and the Implementation of the Directive on Electronic Commerce (2000/31/EC).* Brussels: European Commission.

————. 2014. *Communication from the Commission to the European Parliament, the Council and the European Economic and Social Committee. Towards a Renewed Consensus on the Enforcement of Intellectual Property Rights: An EU Action Plan.* Brussels: European Commission.

European Parliament & Council. 2000. *Directive 2000/31/EC of the European Parliament and of the Council of 8 June 2000 on Certain Legal Aspects of Information Society Services, in particular Electronic Commerce, in the Internal Market.* Luxembourg: Official Journal of the European Communities.

————. 2001. *Directive 2001/29/EC of the European Parliament and of the Council of 22 May 2001 on the Harmonisation of Certain Aspects of Copyright and Related Rights in the Information Society.* Luxembourg: Official Journal of the European Communities.

————. 2004. *Directive 2004/48/EC of the European Parliament and of the Council of 29 April 2004 on the Enforcement of Intellectual Property Rights.* Luxembourg: Official Journal of the European Union.

European Parliament Committee on Legal Affairs. 2014. *Draft Report on 'Towards a Renewed Consensus on the Enforcement of Intellectual Property Rights: An EU Action Plan'.* Brussels: European Parliament.

Fischer, Frank. 2003. *Reframing Public Policy.* Oxford: Oxford University Press.

French Parliament. 2009a. *Loi n. 2009a-669 du 12 Juin 2009a favorisant la Diffusion et la Protection de la Création sur Internet.* Paris: Journal officiel de la République française.

————. 2009b. *Loi n. 2009b-1311 du 28 Octobre 2009b relative à la Protection Pénale de la Propriété Littéraire et Artistique sur Internet.* Paris: Journal officiel de la République française.

G8. 2011. G8 Declaration. Renewed Commitment for Freedom and Democracy. G8 Summit of Deauville – May 26–27, 2011. Deauville: French Government.

Garnham, Nicholas. 1990. *Capitalism and Communication: Global Culture and the Economics of Information.* Thousand Oaks: Sage.

————. 2000. *Emancipation, the Media and Modernity: Arguments About the Media and Social Theory.* Oxford: Oxford University Press.

————. 2011. The Political Economy of Communication Revisited. In *The Handbook of Political Economy of Communications*, ed. Janet Wasko, Graham Murdock, and Helena Sousa, 41–61. Chichester: Wiley-Blackwell.

Goldstein, Judith, and Robert Keohane. 1993. Ideas and Foreign Policy: An Analytical Framework. In *Ideas and Foreign Policy: Beliefs, Institutions and Political Change*, ed. Judith Goldstein and Keohane Robert, 3–30. Ithaca/London: Cornell University Press.

Gottweis, Herbert. 2006. Argumentative Policy Analysis. In *Handbook of Public Policy*, ed. Guy Peters and Jon Pierre, 461–479. London: Sage.

Hajer, Maarten. 1993. Discourse Coalitions and the Institutionalization of Practice: The Case of Acid Rain in Great Britain. In *The Argumentative Turn in Policy Analysis and Planning*, ed. Frank Fischer and John Forester, 43–76. Durham: Duke University Press.

————. 1995. *The Politics of Environmental Discourse: Ecological Modernization and the Policy Process*. Oxford: Oxford University Press.

————. 2002. Discourse Analysis and the Study of Policy Making. *European Political Science* 2(1): 61–65.

————. 2006. Doing Discourse Analysis: Coalitions, Practices, Meaning. In *Words Matter in Policy and Planning. Discourse Theory and Method in the Social Sciences*, ed. Margo van den Brink and Tamara Metze, 65–74. Utrecht: Koninklijk Nederlands Aardrijkskundig Genootschap & Netherlands Graduate School of Urban and Regional Research.

Hajer, Maarten, and Hendrik Wagenaar, ed. 2003. *Deliberative Policy Analysis: Understanding Governance in the Network Society*. Cambridge: Cambridge University Press.

Hesmondhalgh, David. 2007. *Cultural Industries*. 2nd ed. London: Sage.

IFPI. 2015. *Digital Music Report 2015. Charting the Path to Sustainable Growth*. London: International Federation of the Phonographic Industry.

Jessop, Bob. 2004. Critical Semiotic Analysis and Cultural Political Economy. *Critical Discourse Studies* 1(1): 1–16.

————. 2009. Cultural Political Economy and Critical Policy Studies. *Critical Policy Studies* 3(3–4): 336–356.

Kern, Florian. 2011. Ideas, Institutions, and Interests: Explaining Policy Divergence in Fostering 'System Innovations' Towards Sustainability. *Environment and Planning C: Government and Policy* 29: 1116–1134.

Krikorian, Gaelle, and Amy Kapczynksi, eds. 2010. *Access to Knowledge in the Age of Intellectual Property*. New York: Zone Books.

Laffey, Mark, and Jutta Weldes. 1997. Beyond Belief: Ideas and Symbolic Technologies in the Study of International Relations. *European Journal of International Relations* 3(1): 193–237.

Lessig, Lawrence. 2006. *Code: And Other Laws of Cyberspace, Version 2.0*. New York: Basic Books.

Lyon, David. 2007. *Surveillance Studies: An Overview*. Cambridge/Malden: Polity.

Mathijsen, P.S.R.F. 2010. *A Guide to European Union Law as Amended by the Treaty of Lisbon*. 10th ed. London: Sweet & Maxwell.

McChesney, Robert Waterman. 2008. *The Political Economy of Media: Enduring Issues, Emerging Dilemmas*. New York: Monthly Review Press.

McGillivray, Fiona, Iain McLean, Robert Pahre, and Cheryl Schonhardt-Bailey. 2001. *International Trade and Political Institutions: Instituting Trade in the Long Nineteenth Century*. Cheltenham: Edward Elgar.

McIntyre, T.J., and Colin Scott. 2008. Internet Filtering: Rhetoric, Legitimacy, Accountability and Responsibility. In *Regulating Technologies: Legal Futures, Regulatory Frames and Technological Fixes*, ed. R. Brownsword and K. Yeung, 109–124. Oxford: Hart Publishing.

Meyer, Trisha, and Leo Van Audenhove. 2010. Graduated Response and the Emergence of a European Surveillance Society. *Info* 12(6): 69–79.

Miège, Bernard. 1989. *The Capitalization of Cultural Production*. New York: International General.

Mosco, Vincent. 2009. *The Political Economy of Communication*. 2nd ed. London/Thousand Oaks: Sage.

Mueller, Milton. 2010. *Networks and States. The Global Politics of Internet Governance*. Cambridge/London: MIT Press.

Murdock, Graham, and Peter Golding. 2005. Culture, Communication and Political Economy. In *Mass Media and Society*, ed. J. Curran and M. Gurevitch, 70–92. London: Arnold.

Rein, Martin, and Donald Schön. 1996. Frame-Critical Policy Analysis and Frame-Reflective Policy Analysis. *Knowledge and Policy: The International Journal of Knowledge Transfer and Utilization* 9(1): 85–104.

Schiller, Herbert. 1969. *Mass Communications and American Empire*. New York: Augustus M. Keeley Publishers.

———. 1973. *The Mind Managers*. Boston: Beacon Press.

Schiller, Dan. 2000. *Digital Capitalism: Networking the Global Market System*. Cambridge, MA: MIT Press.

———. 2008. *How to Think About Information*. Urbana: University of Illinois Press.

Schmidt, Vivien. 2010. Taking Ideas and Discourse Seriously: Explaining Change Through Discursive Institutionalism as the Fourth 'New Institutionalism'. *European Political Science Review* 2(1): 1–25.

Shapiro, Andrew L. 1999. *The Control Revolution: How the Internet Is Putting Individuals in Charge and Changing the World We Know*. 1st ed. New York: PublicAffairs.

Sirois, André, and Janet Wasko. 2011. The Political Economy of the Recorded Music Industry: Redefinitions and New Trajectories in the Digital Age. In *The

Handbook of Political Economy of Communications, ed. Janet Wasko, Graham Murdock, and Helena Sousa, 331–357. Chichester: Wiley-Blackwell.

Smythe, Dallas. 1977. Communications: Blindspot of Western Marxism. *Canadian Journal of Political and Social Theory* 1(3): 1–27.

———. 1981. *Dependency Road: Communications, Capitalism, Consciousness and Canada*. Norwood: Ablex Publishing.

Spanish Parliament. 2011. *Ley 2/2011, de 4 de marzo, de Economía Sostenible*. Madrid: Boletín Oficial del Estado.

UK Department for Business Innovation & Skills, Intellectual Property Office, Department for Culture Media & Sport, Vince The Rt Hon Dr Cable, and Sajid The Rt Hon Javid. 2014. New Education Programme Launched to Combat Online Piracy. https://www.gov.uk/government/news/new-education-programme-launched-to-combat-online-piracy. Accessed 6 Oct 2016.

UK Parliament. 2010. *Digital Economy Act 2010*. London: Her Majesty's Stationery Office.

US Copyright Office. 1998. *The Digital Millennium Copyright Act of 1998. U.S. Copyright Office Summary*. Washington, DC: US Copyright Office.

Wasko, Janet, Graham Murdock, and Helena Sousa. 2011. Introduction: The Political Economy of Communications: Core Concerns and Issues. In *The Handbook of Political Economy of Communications*, ed. Janet Wasko, Graham Murdock, and Helena Sousa, 1–10. Chichester: Wiley-Blackwell.

Watson, James. 2003. *Media Communication: An Introduction to Theory and Process*. 2nd ed. Basingstoke/New York: Palgrave Macmillan.

Weatherley, Mike. 2014a. 'Follow the Money': Financial Options to Assist in the Battle Against Online IP Piracy. A Discussion Paper by Mike Weatherley MP Intellectual Property Adviser to the Prime Minister. http://www.olswang.com/media/48204227/follow_the_money_financial_options_to_assist_in_the_battle_against_online_ip_piracy.pdf. Accessed 6 Oct 2016.

———. 2014b. Search Engines and Piracy. A Discussion Paper by Mike Weatherley MP Intellectual Property Adviser to the Prime Minister. http://www.olswang.com/media/48165108/search_engines_and_piracy_mike_weatherley_mp.pdf. Accessed 6 Oct 2016.

Wendt, Alexander. 1998. On Constitution and Causation in International Relations. *Review of International Studies* 24: 101–118.

Winseck, Dwayne. 2011. The Political Economies of Media and the Transformation of the Global Media Industries. In *The Political Economies of Media. The Transformation of the Global Media Industries*, ed. Dwayne Winseck and Dal Yong Jin, 3–48. London/New York: Bloomsbury Academic.

YouTube. 2016. Copyright on YouTube. https://www.youtube.com/yt/copyright/. Accessed 6 Oct 2016.

Zittrain, Jonathan. 2008. *Future of the Internet – And How to Stop It*. London: Yale University Press.

CHAPTER 2

The Internet Versus Copyright?

This chapter sets the scene for the case studies on online copyright enforcement policies. It expands on the preliminary political economic views expressed in Chap. 1. The aim of the chapter is to expose differences *and* connections between the Internet and copyright in their development, functioning and governance, providing an initial, yet comprehensive power analysis of online copyright enforcement in the EU. It explores online copyright enforcement from a theoretical perspective, yet adopts the same analytical structure as the case studies. In terms of ideas, Sect. 2.1 explains the history and rationales underlying the Internet and copyright today. In light of the contention over copyright, it also draws on literature that discusses the costs and benefits of copyright as a means of fostering knowledge and creativity. Perceptions on how we can and should create knowledge are a key part of the PEC puzzle. Building on this discussion, Sect. 2.2. briefly highlights existing online copyright enforcement discourses as identified in literature. Regarding interests, Sect. 2.3 expands on the social and economic reality in which online copyright enforcement policies develop. Reasons for copyright infringement, as well as costs and benefits are discussed. The section seeks to understand how copyright infringement fits within the wider changes at hand in the media industries. Lastly in terms of institutions, Sect. 2.4 explains the political and legal reality of online copyright enforcement policies. It is worth repeating that this study

© The Author(s) 2017
T. Meyer, *The Politics of Online Copyright Enforcement in the EU*, Information Technology and Global Governance,
DOI 10.1007/978-3-319-50974-7_2

interprets institutions as settings rather than actors. How we regulate the Internet shapes what we can do with it. For this reason I expand on the history and proposed models of governing this young medium. Moreover Sect. 2.4 discusses specific technologies of governance. These offer direct and compulsory power. Finally, the legacies and developments of online copyright enforcement policies at an international, EU and national level are addressed.

2.1   IDEAS

2.1.1   The Internet

2.1.1.1   History [1]

The Internet developed after the Second World War within computer science research groups as an alternative data transmission system to the circuit-switched telephone networks and as a means of connecting computers across distances. In the United States, the context was the Cold War, and there was a willingness within the US government to fund research that would advance their world position in science and technology. With an escalating threat of nuclear attacks, the Department of Defense was also concerned about the survivability of the communication networks (Abbate 1999). Paul Baran (the United States) and Donald Davies (the United Kingdom) developed *packet-switching,* which was a radically new way of transmitting data. In simple terms, messages are broken up into packages, sent across the network along the fastest and most efficient routes and then reassembled as one message at the other end. The data transmission is more resilient and the network is decentralized. Building on Baran and Davies' work, Joseph Licklider, Robert Taylor, Lawrence Roberts and others at ARPA (the US Defense Department's Advanced Research Projects Agency) developed what would be the main precursor to the Internet: ARPANET, an American and later international packet-switched network of computers and their respective research groups (Abbate 1999; Bing 2009).[2]

Throughout the decades, the nature of collaboration within the *ARPANET research community* was built on consensus, decentralization of authority and open exchange of information. In "Inventing the Internet," Jane Abbate (1999, 5) emphasizes how the values of this group of users shaped the technology:

"[i]n the early days of the ARPANET, the distinction between producers and users did not even exist, since ARPA's computer experts were building the system for their own use. Their dual role as users and producers led the ARPANET's builders to adopt a new paradigm for managing the evolution of the system: rather than centralize design authority in a small group of network managers, they deliberately created a system that allowed any user with the requisite skill and interest to propose a new feature."

Even when the ARPANET extended to include other users, these values remained. Abbate (1999) and other scholars (Castells 2001; Bing 2009; Zittrain 2008) believe *this commitment to flexibility and diversity endorsed by its users and built into the network, is key to the survival and success of the network, because it allowed for unforeseen developments.*[3]

One example of an unforeseen development was email. The ARPANET was designed as a way of sharing resources and teleworking on other computers, useful for computer scientists but much less for other user groups. With email, the ARPANET became a communications means as well. It was a "smash hit" which increased the value of the network for current and future users (Abbate 1999). The switch-over from the Network Control Protocol (NCP) to the *Transmission Control Protocol & Internet Protocol (TCP/IP)* was another unplanned step. The main instigators in this change were Robert Kahn and Vincent Cerf, although—as with the other innovations—more researchers were involved (Abbate 1999). TCP/IP enable interconnection between different networks, and with them, the Internet (the "network of networks") was born. Similar to packet-switching, TCP/IP assume that networks are unreliable and depend on the endpoints of the network (Bing 2009). Complexity is pushed to the edges of the network, and flexibility is favored. TCP/IP are the overarching, common protocols bringing diverse networks together.

Looking ahead to the governance of the Internet, it is important to point out that TCP/IP were not accepted as standard protocols immediately. The 1980s were marked with a standards war between research groups and organizations favoring the largely US-developed TCP/IP and those promoting the protocol of the International Organization for Standardization called Open Systems Interconnection (OSI). Jamal Shahin (2006) describes how the European Community (later the EU) before the 1990s perceived foreign research and development in computing and telecommunications as a threat. The reasoning went that Europe was running behind technologically and needed to foster national/European champions that could compete at an international level. This—as well as a desire to be part of a global "institutional" effort to develop a global network—made them favor OSI rather than TCP/IP. OSI was more closed and in line with the interests of the incumbent European telecommunications companies, whose support the European Community needed to develop a pan-European communications network. From the perspective of inter-connectivity (and openness) however, TCP/IP have more to offer and eventually the European Community's reluctance gave way.

A final big step which brought the Internet into the form we are familiar with today was its *commercialization and the introduction of the world wide web*. From the 1990s onward businesses were permitted online, and Tim Berners-Lee at CERN[4] developed HTML (HyperText Markup Language) and HTTP (HyperText Transfer Protocol) to link and search for information on the Internet (to form the world wide web, Abbate 1999; Bing 2009). These two developments, along with the increased use of personal computers, led to a boom in Internet adoption. Jane Abbate (1999, 217–218) states that,

> "[t]he Web completed the Internet's transformation from a research to a popular medium by providing an application attractive enough to draw the masses of potential Internet users into active participation. It solidified the Internet's traditions of decentralization, open architecture, and active user participation, putting in place a radically decentralized system of information sharing. On the Web, the links between sites were made laterally instead of hierarchically, and each individual could be a producer as well as a consumer of information."

At the same time, the growth of the Internet has made the consensus-based regulation of the early ARPANET unsustainable. All users cannot be involved in decision making. The question of how the Internet should then be governed is answered in very diverse manners. An important message to carry with us throughout the book is that the outcome of the development of the Internet was not inevitable. *Choices were made and clear values were embedded in the technology of the Internet. Characteristics of early Internet architecture such as flexibility and decentralization, but also interoperability, peer review and consensus point to an openness in the Internet's original design* (Castells 2001; Lessig 2006). The Internet was built with open, unfettered communication in mind. In this study, references to the open (character) of the Internet imply these characteristics. Figure 2.1 highlights in a different manner the points made in this section about the history of the Internet.

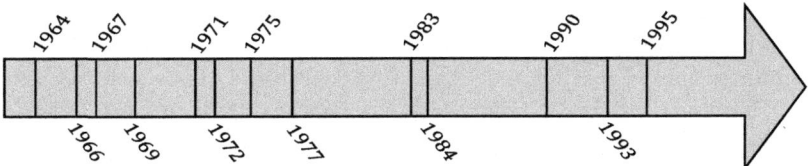

1964   Distributed communications: Paul Baran publishes work
1966   Packet-switching: Donald Davies presents ideas in the UK
1967   MARK I: first packet-switching network launched in the UK
1969   ARPANET: first IMP (interface message processor) installed at UCLA
1971   Email: Ray Tomlinson creates first network mail program
1972   ICCC: ARPANET welcomed with enthusiasm at computer conference
1975   Personal computer: Altair 8800 arrives on the market
1975   TCP/IP: Stanford University implements Internet working protocols
1977   Internet: TCP/IP demonstrated, networks start to interconnect
1980s International standards war: TCP/IP wins
1983   End of NCP: ARPANET switches over to TCP/IP
1983   MILNET: ARPANET splits into military and research/civilian networks
1984   DNS: system to structure domain names introduced
1990   End of ARPANET: NSFNET takes over backbone, ARPANET retires
1990   World Wide Web: Tim Berners-Lee develops HTML/HTTP
1990   Privatization: first commercial provider offering Internet access arrives
1993   Mosaic: first web browser launched
1995   Commercialization: the Internet opens up to all activities & services

Based on: Abbate, J. (1999). *Inventing the Internet.* London & Cambridge, MA: MIT Press.

Fig. 2.1   Internet history timeline

2.1.1.2 Rationales[5]

In "Internet Galaxy: Reflections on the Internet, Business, and Society," Manuel Castells (2001) explains how the Internet is used for different reasons by four distinct user groups who together build up a unique Internet culture. I interpret these as four rationales for the existence of the Internet. A rationale is a set of reasons for a course of action (in this case for Internet use).

Pursuit of Science

First, as highlighted in the previous section, the early Internet was the product of *shared pursuit of technological advancement among computer scientists.* Academics sought to build a decentralized communication network through building on each other's research and allowing peer review of one's own research. This first layer of the culture of the Internet is techno-meritocratic: merit is based on the contribution to technological discovery and on recognition and respect by other scientists.

Technological Sharing

The second group of users—hackers—gives this *shared pursuit of technological advancement* a countercultural twist. Hackers also work on technical aspects of the Internet, but are part of loosely organized networks grounded in society. They are *autonomous of corporate or institutional assignments*. They have a distinct (at times anti-capitalist) worldview of open access and freedom to create and share knowledge. Similar to the academic setting, cooperation and free communication are again important values.

Social Interaction and Symbolic Belonging

Third, the Internet is also *a tool to bring likeminded users together to work, discuss and play on common topics*. Hackers form a community focused on computer programming, but non-technical groups have also adopted the Internet as their means of communication and networking. In this context, the Internet is widely appreciated as a potential tool for democratization. Users can easily gather and share information with others. The Internet facilitates bottom-up and horizontal communication and can also be a medium of self-expression.

Entrepreneurship

Fourth, the Internet would not have boomed without its take-up by entrepreneurs for purposes of commerce. The Internet is essential as *a collaboration and distribution medium in our information economy,* but it is also *a commercial space of its own*. In this fourth layer of Internet culture, the capitalist values of domination and profit maximization are supreme. This entrepreneurship transformed the Internet into a mass medium. The nature of a network is that the more users and uses there are, the more valuable a network becomes—not just economically but also socially (Castells 2001, 36–63).

These four uses of the Internet build upon each other. The fourth rationale of entrepreneurship and capitalism can sit ill at ease with the other three purposes of the Internet, which are technically or socially oriented. The Internet can contribute to democracy through the facilitation of free speech, deliberation between citizens and community building. At the same time, the Internet is an important tool for innovation in managing businesses as well as an increasing business sector of its own (Castells 2009; Foster and McChesney 2011). Tensions arise between technical, social and economic uses of the Internet, in particular when it may not be economically efficient or profitable to maintain a flexible, decentralized, interoperable and cooperative space (Lessig 2003; McChesney 2008; Shapiro 1999).

Economically information is a strange commodity, because it is a public good.[6] One person's use of information does not preclude another's (Winseck 2011). The Internet allows for the development of a *digital commons*, an alternative market system based on gifting or sharing rather than commodity exchange (Castells 2009; Winseck 2011; Murdock 2011). This has sparked hopes for the development of a more equal society (Benkler 2006; Mansell 2012; Shapiro 1999). However it also significantly challenges copyright (the exclusive right to reproduce and distribute information).

From a PEC perspective, the Internet has *intensified contradictions* between alternative market systems and capitalism. PEC scholars hope for a digital commons, but equally are aware that market exchange logic has expanded aggressively online. They tend to observe continuity rather than change on the Internet. For instance, the Marxist communications scholar Christian Fuchs (2009) argues that narratives on the potential of the Internet for democracy are often techno-deterministic and serve as ideological legitimization of existing modes of domination, because everyone can voice opinions but nobody cares about them. He deems that real decisions are still taken by elite groups (see also McChesney 2013).

While I agree that *capitalist values increasingly dominate the Internet environment,* I have found that the theory of PEC grapples with understanding the (dis)continuities of the Internet. Counterpower is fairly quickly dismissed, making phenomena, such as DRM (digital rights management) hacking, WikiLeaks and ACTA hard to explain. Indeed, *the PEC does not sufficiently consider the impact of architectural features of the Internet on power relations.* On the one hand, the Internet in its setup facilitates global networks, giving stakeholders new platforms to collaborate and share. This is an alternative form of structural power. Resistance is made easier. On the other hand, through use of its architecture the Internet has opened up new avenues for monitoring and censoring information. This governance through technology offers compulsory power to those in charge. Domination is made easier. These thoughts will be further explored in Sect. 2.4 on institutions.

Figure 2.2 visualizes the environment in which IG develops. In this figure I have grouped Castells' first two rationales together. In my case studies I investigate how rationales for the Internet interact with one another in online copyright enforcement policies—with the clear belief that the open character of the Internet should be preserved. Let us look at the history and rationales of copyright next.

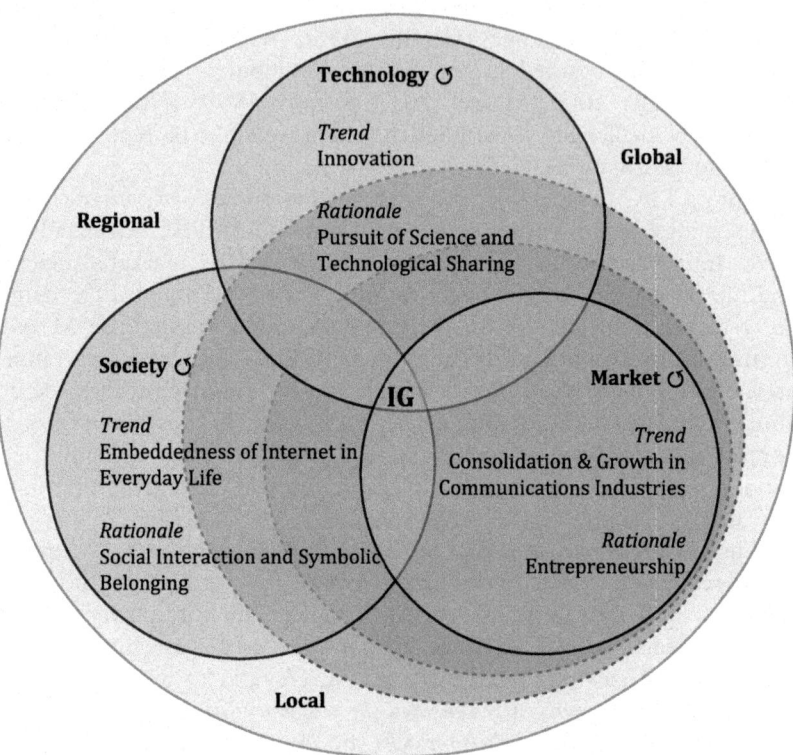

Fig. 2.2 Convergence and conflict in Internet Governance

2.1.2   Copyright

2.1.2.1   History

On the one hand, copyright is acknowledged to be a motor for stimulating creative activity, thereby promoting learning and progress for the benefit of the public; on the other, limitations and exceptions to copyright answer to the public interest in the widest possible availability of copyright material. A successful copyright law must find a balance between these two goals of public policy. (Davies 2002, x)

The oldest recognized copyright law is the 1709 Statute of Anne in the United Kingdom. As literacy increased, printing presses improved and industrialization boomed, the book market started to flourish. There was a concern among printers that books were published and distributed in an unauthorized manner. The Statute of Anne granted authors or purchasers of their works (printers) a monopoly to protect the works for a limited period (two consecutive sets of fourteen years) (Davies 2002; Burkitt 2001). In the course of the eighteenth and nineteenth centuries, other countries followed suit. For instance, the United States included a clause in the Constitution in 1790 conferring power on Congress "to promote the Progress of Science and useful Arts, by securing for limited times to Authors and Inventors the exclusive Right to their respective Writings and Discoveries" (United States of America 1790, Article 1, Section 8, Burkitt 2001).[7] After the French Revolution, France passed copyright decrees in 1791 and 1793. It took Germany until the unification of its *Länder* to enact a copyright law in 1870. Copyright abolished a system of privileges that had been active in Europe since the late fifteenth century. This had been an effective means of censorship, as rulers could control the (re)production and distribution of books by restricting privileges to a select group of printers. The system of privileges came to a gradual end as absolute monarchies were overturned (Davies 2002; Burkitt 2001). Indeed, with the exception of the United Kingdom, this is the case in each of the countries mentioned. As we can tell then, *the spread of copyright was uneven.* What is more, *its origins in each country differ* as well. A brief look into the history of copyright in the United Kingdom, France, Germany and the United States reveals a range of arguments used to defend copyright.[8]

In the United Kingdom, John Locke's philosophy of individual possessivism weighed through heavily. Copyright is justified, because property is considered a natural right and the intellectual efforts of an author are his property. This approach emphasizes the individual and an author's entitlement to the fruits of his labor (Menell 2000; Burkitt 2001). Further, France and Germany used Kantian and Hegelian idealist theory to defend copyright. A creative work bears the personality of its author and thus copyright is a natural right. In addition to copyright, an author is granted moral rights of personality (Menell 2000; Burkitt 2001). There is a marked difference between European and American justifications for copyright. The United States acted on utilitarian considerations that copyright is an efficient stimulus to foster creative production and distribution. Public interest concerns about education in the early United States lay at the base of the law, and mass production through industrialization and competition was encouraged. Due to this stress on economics, the United States did not offer authors moral rights to their works until its accession to one of the main copyright treaties, the Berne Convention, in 1989 (Handke 2010; Davies 2002; Burkitt 2001). Of course however, developing (rationales for) a policy is not a one-off process. Peter Burkitt (2001, 151) states that "[t]he droit moral, now a distinctive feature of French and international law, was not driven inevitable author-ward by some underlying process of cultural development, but emerged piecemeal through an unplanned accumulation of court decisions." Interestingly, another example is that prior to the signing of the US Constitution natural law justifications were floated in the United States as well (Davies 2002; Burkitt 2001).

Copyright has grown significantly over the past 300 years. It has increased in coverage, scope and length. Copyright is granted when a creative work is original and has a concrete form. While copyright originally only protected printed works, today it *covers* many forms of media: paintings, sculptures, photography, film and sound recordings, architectural plans, software, (in some countries) databases and much more (Gotzen and Janssens 2009). In this process of technological innovation, copyright was extended to a new range of stakeholders. For instance, performers, musicians, producers and broadcasters are entitled to rights related to copyright (related rights, Fisher 2004). Furthermore, the *scope* of protection has grown. Copyright gives its holders temporary exclusive rights to reproduce, adapt and make a work of their mind available to the public (economic rights). Holders are also granted certain moral and personality rights, such as the right of attribution and to integrity of a work (Gotzen and Janssens 2009; Bently et al. 2010). As new forms of media emerged, so did new types of rights. Broadcasting rights, rental rights and rights to employ technical protection measures (TPMs) to protect digital works are examples of how technology has extended the scope of protection in copyright (Halbert 1999; Westkamp 2007; Vaidhyanathan 2001). Finally, the *length* of protection is not universal, but it has made quite the jump from the Statute of Anne's initial arrangement of two sets of fourteen years. In the EU, it is currently seventy years after the death of the author (for copyright) and seventy years after the first performance of a work (for related rights, European Parliament & Council 2011; Gotzen and Janssens 2009).

All policymaking involves the weighing of conflicting arguments and interests. At each step of the policymaking process, involved stakeholders seek to shape the law in their favor. *Copyright today is the result of choices made to balance the rights and interests between rights holders and with other stakeholders throughout its history.* It is a complex set of rights. Recognizing that authors are often the weaker party among rights holders in contracting, copyright seeks to protect their interests especially, for instance by making it impossible to transfer moral rights or to stand down from unknown future exploitations of a creative work (Gotzen and Janssens 2009; Torremans 2004). Furthermore as the quote at the beginning of this section indicates, balancing between private and public interests in creative production and distribution is inherent to copyright. *Copyright includes a social responsibility* (Davies 2002). For this reason, copyright expires after a length of time. A creative work then falls into the public domain where it can be freely used. In addition, copyright legislation includes limitations and exceptions to exclusive rights, such as the right to a private copy and use for commentary or research (Bently et al. 2010; Gotzen and Janssens 2009; Torremans 2004). Limitations and exceptions often represent the balance in copyright law. In copyright, there is an emphasis on protection, but equally a tension between protection of and access to works. Neil Netanel (2008) speaks of "copyright's paradox" in which copyright is granted to spur on free speech, yet imposes unacceptable burdens on speech when private and public interests are not well balanced. Holders and users of copyright have quite different definitions of where this balance between interests lies.

What I wish to underline in this section is copyright's diverse and dialectic policymaking history. *National historical particularities combined with the complexity of rights and exceptions included in copyright have resulted in a fragmentation that is difficult to overcome.* Despite international harmonization, there are still differences between countries in the legal definitions of what is covered, how and for what time. This burdens cross-border trade and enforcement of copyright. Moreover, it is important to realize that the current copyright debate is not unique. *Finding the balance between private and public interests is a recurring exercise and discussion.* The early rationales for copyright continue to be relevant in today's policy. They have marked out a strong defense for copyright on property, personality, economic and social grounds, and are used cumulatively and sometimes interchangeably in discourses. The following section offers a short summary of these traditional rationales for copyright and delves into alternative interpretations. Opposing views on copyright are even more emphasized in Sect. 2.1.2.3 on costs and benefits of our current copyright system.

2.1.2.2   Rationales[9]

The following three rationales for copyright demonstrate common ways of thinking about the protection for creative works:

Natural Law

First, a cultural work is the fruit of a creator's mind. According to this first reasoning, the fruit of a person's mind should be considered *property*, because a person has a similar natural right of property to the fruit of his labors. A cultural work is also viewed as being *the expression of a creator's personality* and thus intrinsically linked to that person. This reasoning provides the basis for moral rights (Davies 2002; Menell 2000; Yu 2007a). Copyright is included as a human right in the Universal Declaration of Human Rights (Article 27) and the Covenant on Economic, Social and Cultural Rights (Article 15, Torremans 2004).

Economic Incentive

Second, information acts as a public good. Here the thought process is that cultural works will be underproduced due to the free riding of users and a stimulus is required to encourage the creation of works. Copyright is an exception to competition, offering means of obtaining remuneration and ensuring that there are continuous contributions to science and culture. This rationale gives copyright a firm utilitarian foundation (Yu 2007a; Menell 2000; Gordon and Bone 2000). It reasons that a creator needs *a just reward for his labor.* Similarly, media industries need to be able to expect a reasonable profit and *return on investment* to endeavor in the risky business of cultural production and distribution (Davies 2002; Yu 2007a). This rationale strongly underpins industrial property rights (patents, trademarks, geographical indications and industrial designs) as well.

Social Requirements
Third, a creator should be rewarded not only for his own private interest, but also for *the public interest of society*. Through his creation, he enriches the national cultural patrimony. The third rationale encourages creators and the media industries to spread their works widely. Copyright is granted in the wider interest of society. For this reason, limitations and exceptions to copyright's time and use are set in place (Davies 2002; Yu 2007a).

These three rationales are interdependent. They provide moral, economic and social reasons for copyright. They show how a balance needs to be found between protection of and access to copyrighted works in order to encourage knowledge creation. Currently copyright is in trouble. "Copyright is important in an economy based on the market exchange of information, yet it is also easily infringed in the digital and online environment." The Internet aims at reproducing and distributing works widely. Information scarcity and abundance are set up against each other. Robin Mansell (2012) considers this a paradox. Two statements are correct and contradictory at the same time: "information is initially costly to produce and intellectual property rights create the optimal incentives for creativity, diversity, and growth" *and* "information is virtually costless to reproduce and the optimal incentives for creativity, diversity, and growth occur when it is freely distributed" (Mansell 2012; 179).

Bridging this gap can signify two things: either protection and enforcement of copyright need to increase dramatically or copyright needs to be reformed for the digital age. The study of PEC deems the regulatory responses formulated to the lack of control over copyrighted works significant, because *copyright sets the rules for the creation of knowledge and culture in our society*. A growing group of scholars, political economists and also legal scholars and academics from the South (for instance May and Sell 2005; Bettig 1996; Vaidhyanathan 2001; Lessig 2004; Tian 2009; Yu 2007b; Burkitt 2001) argue against what they call, the commodification of information and enclosure of the intellectual commons.[10] The gradual lengthening, extending and strengthening of copyright are seen as part of a global movement toward more proprietarian control in information and knowledge. These scholars point to repeated instances of inequality in the long history of IPR. Indeed *copyright is the result of power struggles* to maintain the capitalist market system. Only, our global and digital surroundings have now made it easier to detect and vocalize domination and resistance to the ways in which we create knowledge and culture. It should be noted that resistance to copyright comes in different strands. For instance, Fuchs (2009) points out that the open source movement is not necessarily anti-capitalist (see also Dyer-Witheford 2002; Mueller 2010). Although copyright's strongest critics (which include Marxist political economists) view it as a repressive means of mind control (Fuchs 2009; Strangelove 2005), many advocate use of *the Internet as an alternative market system.* Commons and control can operate side by side (Lessig 2003; Mansell 2012; Boyle 2003).

This study is not a justification for or against copyright. In line with mainstream PEC, I am critical of copyright law that ignores users' needs, but emphasize studying the complexity and detail of the law. My case studies deal with developments in copyright enforcement policies that encourage technological governance. At stake is the fact that copyright enforcement policies can shape the future Internet through use of the Internet's architecture for surveillance and regulation. I value the open character of the Internet and believe we need to study how this is potentially changed by government, right holders and Internet intermediaries alike. This does not mean that I think copyright has become redundant or the Internet should be unregulated. I can heartily sign up to Mansell's political economic analysis in "Imagining the Internet: Communication, Innovation and Governance." Mansell (2012) argues that the Internet tussle is an aggravation of age-old social imaginaries on the role of technology and information to achieve a good society. Is technological change exogenous or endogenous? Do we need strong or weak copyright, a closed or open Internet? *Mansell calls for rereading these paradoxical relationships and suggests a new social imaginary of the Internet that recognizes both economic growth and social justice, information scarcity and abundance as crucial in good society.* She argues that we should resist the choice between top-down and bottom-up governance. Importantly in this new social imaginary we need to counter monopolies wherever we see them (value information diversity in and outside the market space), facilitate online creativity (foster new business models and open sharing of information, and limit but not abandon IPR enforcement and surveillance) and make governance accountable (whether top down or bottom up, especially through technology).

2.1.2.3 Costs and Benefits

What are the costs and benefits of our current copyright model? To a large extent the benefits have already been addressed while discussing its rationales: copyright was set into place to protect the moral rights of creators, and to deal with the underproduction of creative works, by overcoming the non-excludability of creative works and minimizing transaction costs (Gordon and Bone 2000; Handke 2010). Christian Handke (2010) and Wendy Gordon and Robert Bone (2000) argue that it is very unclear to which extent copyright infringement decreases the production of creative works. To be certain the premise that more protection leads to more supply should be questioned. Handke (2010, 10) states that, "studies have found no evidence that copyright term extensions or the diffusion of digital copying technology (that diminish the de facto strength of copyright protection) have affected supply significantly." Gordon and Bone (2000, 203) add that, "[g]iven the increasing economic importance of today's copyright industries, the assumption of low-cost copyright monopoly must be re-examined. The easily-granted, long-lived copyright monopoly may prove more costly than usually expected." These authors do not question the benefits of copyright, but rather the response given in light of technological change.

Let us consider two sets of arguments on copyright costs dealing with diversity and economics. First, YiJun Tian (2009) argues that our copyright model (despite the divergences between countries) mainly offers *a one-size-fits-all solution to very different types of creators, creative works, industries, economies and cultures.* Creators do not always need an economic incentive to contribute to culture and knowledge. Artistic passion or peer recognition may be far more important. For instance, most academics are already remunerated for their work and publish to demonstrate their expertise in a field. In this regard, Creative Commons is a welcome alternative. Creative Commons is an initiative that allows creators to decide how much control they wish to have over their works. It requires forward thinking by creators and is difficult to manage for (corporate) works with multiple creators. However it is a positive development, as it introduces flexibility into the copyright system. Moreover, copyright no longer is an "arcane technical matter" (Harhoff 2009, 1) relevant to the media industries only. It was already a challenge to fit the differences between media products and structures under one copyright umbrella. However with the shift to an information economy, copyright covers many more industries, requiring integration of these new interests into the copyright balance as well (see Sect. 2.3.2). This explains the high level of interest in copyright enforcement. Finally, Daniel Burkitt (2001) argues that our copyright model does not integrate non-Western ways of thinking about creativity well. The Chinese Confucianist tradition and Australian aboriginal art conceptualize creation as a process of past transmission and emphasize collective ownership. It seems clear that more flexibility is needed. At the same time, this could further fragment the copyright system.

The second set of arguments on copyright costs concerns *the economics of our model*. Handke (2010), Gordon and Bone (2000) point to three drawbacks. To start, copyright involves *administrative costs*. These pertain to the reform and enforcement of regulation. Public authorities and rights holders bear the majority of administration costs (Gordon and Bone 2000; Handke 2010). One contestation of the French graduated response system relates to its high administrative price tag. It is argued that the costs of enforcing copyright are far higher than the income generated by increased sale of creative works. Second, *transaction costs* are the costs of identifying copyright holders and licensing creative works. These costs can be partially reduced through consolidating ownership and collective rights societies (Handke 2010; Gordon and Bone 2000). However, the complexity of digital licensing and opaque functioning of collective rights management societies are two important points of criticism in the copyright debate. Lack of efficient licensing hinders the development of new business models and thus the legal consumption of creative works. Third, *access and innovation costs for users* (short and long term) deal with societal losses. Short term, creators have monopoly rights over their works and often charge more than the reproduction cost. This excludes users unable or unwilling to purchase the content at this higher price (Gordon and Bone 2000). Long term, copyright can chill future creativity as it "increases the cost of borrowing from previous works and thus weakens the incentive to create" (Gordon and Bone 2000, 195). Incumbent rights holders might also seek to hold back technological change if it endangers their business models and favors newcomers—such as in the case of online sampling. Through sampling, more information is available on creative works, decreasing the need for branding and making the market more contestable (Handke 2010).

Looking at the benefits and costs of copyright helps understand the complexity of the system. This analysis acknowledges weaknesses in the system and can help identify points of improvement. For instance, Handke (2010) advocates *an open-ended approach to technological change and using ICT to decrease copyright's costs.* This includes accepting the contestability that new technology creates between newcomers and incumbents. The final section on ideas summarizes alternative ways of thinking about copyright.

2.1.2.4 Knowledge Creation

Throughout my narration, I have introduced several *strands of resistance to copyright.* I believe that these arguments target two aspects of copyright. A first mild critique contests the current *(im)balance between the protection of and access to creative works.* This critique emphasizes the social requirement rationale of copyright. A second harsher criticism questions the *economics underlying copyright,* seeking openness in knowledge production. PEC analyses of copyright will fit either criticism, depending on the views of the scholar. Importantly, PEC scholars view copyright as a mechanism to control the production and distribution of creative works. In addition to resistance on copyright rationales, I think there are *two sources of discontentment: international IPR policy and copyright on the Internet.* Madhavi Sunder (2006, 266–267, italics in original) states that, "calls for reforming intellectual property law can be heard from the *New York Times* to the *Times of India,* the World Trade Organization (WTO) to World Intellectual Property Organization (WIPO), and the west coast to the east coast." At the base of these criticisms are differing views on how to foster

Table 2.1 Copyright resistance—views on knowledge creation

Rationale and source	International trade	Technological change
Social		
Adapt copyright balance	Copyright for development	ICT to reduce copyright costs
Economic		
Reduce/abolish copyright system	Cultural specificity of creativity	Open and free creativity based on gift exchange

knowledge creation. Let me explain this further. Table 2.1 summarizes the strands of resistance in copyright.

Internationally, critique of copyright is linked to trade and development. The inclusion of Trade Related Aspects of Intellectual Property Right (TRIPS) in the formation of the WTO caused much contestation, as it seemed that other fora known for being more lenient to the interests of developing countries such as United Nations Educational, Scientific and Cultural Organization, United Nations Conference on Trade and Development or even WIPO were avoided (Tian 2009; Sunder 2006). Reaching an agreement through WTO meant that economic value of copyrighted works was underlined. This trend has continued through the inclusion of IPR provisions in regional and bilateral free trade agreements (Yu 2016). As stated above, this international IPR critique stresses the value of having access to knowledge (Tian 2009) and contests the Western view of individualist knowledge creation (Gibson 2007; Burkitt 2001).

Technologically, resistance to copyright originates in its perception as being challenging or even oppositional to "the promises by new Internet technologies: active participation and sharing" (Reyman 2009, 6). Quite controversially, copyright now protects software and technological protection measures have been used to aid enforcement (Netanel 2008; Shemtov 2007). Lawrence Lessig (2003, 2004) and Yochai Benkler (2006) contend against the spread of intellectual property to include Internet content and architecture. They argue that the Internet is used to tip the copyright balance in favor of the media industries, leading to an enclosure of the digital commons (see also Dyer-Witheford 2002; Fuchs 2009; Murdock 2011). In PEC terms, the Internet is a source of compulsory and institutional power to control voices and culture (Mylly 2009; Bettig 1996; Gillespie 2007):

> Technologies do not deterministically impose the development of the society; they mirror it and may allow for different and competing interpretations. However, different technologies also imply different political possibilities that depend also on the social environment. Which way societies develop does not thus primarily depend on the code itself, but on the ability and willingness of societies and their institutions to impose, resist and modify the code. The control of code has thus emerged as a fundamental source of power in the information society. Intellectual property rights, in turn, are the primary instruments enabling their control. (Mylly 2009, 94)

Underlying these international and technological copyright arguments is a contrarian view on how knowledge should be produced. In her book

"Controlling Voices: Intellectual Property, Humanistic Studies, and the Internet," TyAnna Herrington (2001) presents *three views of knowledge creation: objective, subjective and transactional.* Contenders of objective knowledge creation are positivist, preferring evidence obtained in a scientific manner. Supporters of subjective knowledge creation are expressivist and Romantic, viewing truth as being produced by "the lone author." Finally, advocates of transactional knowledge creation stress the interaction between subject, object and community. Herrington (2001, 121) studies the views of academia in the copyright debate and points out that, "[w]here the Internet and academic humanist communities view authorship and control of intellectual products as community-based, the legal community follows a foundational, Romantic ideology and treats intellectual products as property, thus placing control of information in the hands of few but powerful individual and corporate entities." Indeed, *the New Enlightenment* (Sunder 2006), *Access to Knowledge, Cultural Environmentalism* (Boyle 2003) *or Creative Commons movements all point to this transactional view of knowledge creation.* This thinking is currently particularly strong. Parallels are drawn with the enclosure of the English commons (the privatization of public grounds) in the sixteenth and seventeenth centuries (Linebaugh and Rediker 2000; Oudenampsen and Haegens 2009; Boyle 2003). James Boyle (2003) also links this resistance to the green movement, viewing environment and intellectual property as part of a global commons and emphasizing intellectual property as recyclable and reusable resources (Herrington 2001).

In broader terms, the discussion here is not only about how open or closed we wish the production of and access to knowledge to be, but also politics, society and the Internet. Clearly there is a significant dissimilarity between the rationales and functions of copyright and the Internet. *There are tensions within copyright and the Internet about the balance between various uses; but more profoundly, their approach to information is different.* Two out of the three copyright rationales favor protection (natural law and economic incentive), while the Internet rationales opt for widespread distribution of information (pursuit of science, technological sharing, social interaction & symbolic belonging and entrepreneurship). Neither copyright nor the Internet should be used to impose a one-sided view on the production, distribution and consumption of information. Property and the commons can coexist. As the following section shows, however, the debate is heated, often lacking the necessary nuance.

2.2   DISCOURSES

Language frames how problems, solutions and goals are defined, offering productive power to those whose discourse is dominant. Equally however, discourse is never stagnant and windows of opportunities to introduce alternative discourses exist. I believe *we need to look in more detail at the processes of domination and resistance through use of language*. I emphasize discourses as constitutive elements in online copyright enforcement policy developments. Maarten Hajer (2006, 67) states that, "language has the capacity to make politics, to create signs and symbols that can shift power-balances and that can impact on institutions and policymaking. It can render events harmless, but it can also create political conflicts. It can suggest that we should discuss the problem in terms of operational solutions, but it might also suggest that this is meaningless, as solutions would require substantial institutional or cultural change." Discourses are not more important than the market structure, alliances between actors or the institutional context in policymaking, but *words construct the problem, scope and available solutions and thus set the tone for the whole policy process*. The dominant discourse on strong copyright enforcement is fiercely resisted on the Internet. Depending on the issue at hand (copyright and privacy are the most striking), new players such as Google or Facebook will speak quite differently about openness on the Internet. Looking at discursive relations is another way of underlining the dynamic nature of power in the PEC.

Scholars have summarized the main discourses in the online copyright enforcement debate as proprietarian and communitarian (Breindl and Briatte 2010; Reyman 2009). These discourses are very much tied to views on knowledge creation.

2.2.1   Property

Arguments in favor of online copyright enforcement commonly use terms such as "piracy," "theft" and "stealing." Indeed copyright is emphasized as a property right and a distinction is made between producers and users of creative works (Reyman 2009; Gillespie 2007). Further internationally, copyright infringement is construed as part of organized crime threatening national security (Farrand 2011). "Piracy" and "counterfeiting" are also used interchangeably. In relation to US foreign policy, Debora Halbert (1999, 93) puts it in the following way: "[p]irates serve a function in the narrative the United States is constructing on intellectual property and the way it should be protected internationally. Conceptual fences are being built around intangible property and pirates serve as justification for tough laws and harsh penalties." By defining unauthorized distribution and copying of creative works as a crime, copyright infringement is branded as deviant and socially undesirable behavior, hiding contentions between the rationales and exceptions of the law. Yana Breindl and François Briatte (2010) and Jessica Reyman (2009) contend that the complexity of copyright law helps maintain this dominant proprietarian discourse. Moreover, while technology is presented as a threat, it is used as a means to enforce copyright. Here technology joins arms with discourse. Compulsory power is harnessed not only to make infringement more difficult, but also to naturalize the discourse. As Reyman (2009, 138) states: "[i]nstitutionalized support for regulating technology through copyright law legitimizes the property steward narrative, in which creative works retain exclusivity, ownership is individualized, and access is granted only by buying discrete, commodified packages of copyrighted goods."

2.2.2   Commons

Arguments against online copyright enforcement often point to the slowness of the media industries in adapting their business models to the online environment. There is also the perception that big, bad corporations pocket the majority of the income rather than the just reward for labor returning to the artists themselves (Lessig 2004; Yu 2011). Technology and piracy are welcomed as challenging the logic of capital which results in "the concentration of ownership and control of the communications system in the hands of the richest members of the capitalist class" (Bettig 1996, 1). Proposals for change include a Creative Commons (Lessig 2003; Benkler 2006), focusing on active participation and sharing of creative works (Reyman 2009; Aigrain 2012). In the online environment this movement strongly favors free/open source software. Non-market modes of production and distribution are viewed as preferable for our economy and society. Breindl and Briatte (2010) and Reyman (2009) argue that the property lobby is weakened by this alternative discourse of knowledge creation. However, overall it has only met with mixed success, as it fails to fit in the (dominant discursive) legal landscape. Quite importantly Reyman (2009, 24) points out that this communitarian discourse does not make "a clear distinction between a free pass to consume entertainment products and the freedom to access, build on, and contribute to an information commons." Indeed it can be misused (or misinterpreted) as a justification for mass copying and at times lacks the nuances necessary to appreciate the complexity of copyright.

The debate on online copyright enforcement is certainly perceived and portrayed as polarized. At the same time, I think this split representation hides the nuances of how problems and solutions are framed within particular policy debates and have evolved over time. Importantly it begs the question where market-based Internet intermediaries stand and interests come in. These actors may be critical of the property discourse, but they do not necessarily fit the commons bill either. As I have argued, their underlying rationale of entrepreneurship does not always sit well with technical or social views of the Internet. My case studies cover a variety of online copyright enforcement measures and institutional settings over a period of five years. They serve to test the presence of these proprietarian and communitarian discourses (and undoubtedly variations thereof) in policy. *Nuance is needed in the debate, but equally in our analysis of the debate.* Investigating online copyright enforcement policies is important, because they serve as arenas of debate in setting the rules for the creation of knowledge and culture. They are part of the dialectic between domination and resistance in media.

In this context, Bob Jessop (2009, 339), one of the leading scholars in cultural political economy, makes the following statement. It links our discussions on discourse, technology and social practices beautifully:

> Technologies have a key role in the selection and retention of specific imaginaries insofar as they provide reference points not only in meaning-making but also in the coordination of actions within and across specific personal interactions, organizations and networks, and institutional orders. In this sense they are important meaning-making instruments deployed by agents to translate specific social construals into social construction and hence to structure social life.

His interpretation of technologies[11] is broader than the use of the term in this book, nonetheless it is helpful because it emphasizes the role of technology in selecting and retaining discourses. Importantly I study the flip side as well: through meaning-making, technology and the Internet are being (re)defined. The Internet is a new medium open to change.

2.3   INTERESTS

The following sections expound on the social and economic reality of online copyright enforcement. They analyze the reasons, costs and benefits of copyright infringement, the characteristics, changes and challenges of the media industries and consolidation in the online environment. Our capitalist market system is subject to both conflict and convergence, continuity and change.

2.3.1   Copyright Infringement

2.3.1.1   Additional Reasons

> At the most basic level, there are two reasons why P2P file sharers won't behave: (1) they don't have to, and (2) they don't want to. (Bridy 2009, 600)

We have looked into alternative thinking and discourses about copyright, but motivations to copy and distribute creative works are at times mixed. Not all people opt for non-compliance due to crystallized views on the Internet or copyright. I identify four additional and interrelated reasons for non-compliance in literature. Ideas are still at play, although perhaps not on the foreground. These reasons tend to focus on everyday experiences.

Ease of Infringement and Circumvention

First, law enforcers cannot stop the majority of unauthorized distribution due to the *widespread and ephemeral nature of copyright infringement*. The chances of being caught are low. Digital distribution and copying is quick, cheap and of high quality (OECD 2009). With P2P sharing technologies downloading creative works often involves uploading as well. Thus the architecture of these platforms encourages sharing. Further, TPMs have not succeeded in decreasing copyright infringement much. As Annemarie Bridy (2009, 601) states, "[f]rom a technical standpoint, illegal file sharers have always managed to stay a step ahead of rights owners: When content is locked, they pick the locks; the better the locks get, the better they get at lock-picking. When they're being watched, they hide; the better the surveillance gets, the better they get at hiding."

Reciprocity and Individual Nature of Infringement

Second, many have turned a blind eye to copyright infringement, justifying it as we saw above in all manners. The figures of copyright infringement are astounding. Because so many distribute and copy, it seems socially permissible. In some cases, reciprocity plays a role: if you have received, you are *expected to share* (OECD 2009). Additionally, the act of copying itself is often done *without a motive of profit and in private* (Jones 2005).

This allows individuals to diminish the impact of actions and creates a false feeling of anonymity. In this regard, the Organization for Economic Cooperation and Development (OECD) (2009) identifies lack of parental supervision as one cause of piracy among the youth.

Lack of Legitimacy

Importantly and in line with alternative thinking on copyright, there is a widespread *feeling that copyright is out of sync with the digital environment* (Bridy 2009). Constraining encounters with copyright, such as the unavailability of legal content due to licensing issues, the overreach of DRM into legitimate uses or the takedown of YouTube clips, frustrate people. The complexity of copyright and the (ab)use of harsh enforcement measures delegitimize the law. In combination with the imposition of unadapted copyright policies in developing countries (Mattelart 2009), it fosters the image that big rights holder interests have captured copyright.

Illegal Profitability and Supply-Demand Mismatch

Finally, the media industries have had difficulty competing against the quick and cheap supply of creative works available through illicit sources. The *lucrativeness of distribution* without the initial production costs has attracted copyright infringements on a commercial scale (OECD 2009). However, *adapting business models* to the digital environment has also been a slow process, in particular if this involves ceding control over content. Consumers expect creative works to be widely available at low prices, anytime and anywhere. In some smaller and developing markets, there is little legal content available (Mattelart 2009).

Annemarie Bridy (2009) is right. People simply don't have to and don't want to abide by copyright. *What is particularly striking about copyright infringement is the disconnect between what the law says and what people think and feel.* Even if everyone had to behave, they would not. Although necessary (indeed indispensable for commercial infringement) coercion alone does not solve the problem of copyright infringement (Bridy 2009). Education and awareness campaigns help, but are not the panacea either. There is a need to address the deep roots of the lack of legitimacy of copyright and societal permissibility of copyright infringement. Much returns then to the social requirements of copyright, adapting the copyright balance not to legitimize infringement or to favor one economic interest over another, but to accommodate the coexistence of market and non-market modes of knowledge creation.

Table 2.2 Copyright infringement data

Scale of Copyright Infringement

Media	Percentage	Reference year	Source
Film	80	Unknown	NPD/IFPI *in* EC (2009a, b, c, d)
Music	28	2011	IFPI (2012)
Software	39	2015	BSA (2016)
Online audiovisual	30	2008	EC (2009a, b, c, d)
P2P	98	Unknown	Netnames (2015)

Cost of Copyright Infringement per Year

Place	Media	Cost	Reference year	Source
World	All IPR, excl. digital	Up to US$ 461 billion	2013	OECD and EUIPO (2016)
World	All IPR	Up to US$ 650 billion	2008	Frontier Economics (2011)
World	All IPR	Up to US$ 1.7 trillion	Projection for 2015	Frontier Economics (2011)
World	Software	US$ 52 billion	2015	BSA (2016)
World	US Film	US$ 6.1 billion	2005	MPAA *in* US GAO (2010)
EU	Music, film, TV, software	€10 billion (US$ 14.7 billion)	2008	TERA (2010)
EU	Recorded music	€336 million (US$ 446 million)	2014	EUIPO (2016)

Based on: BSA. (2016). *Seizing Opportunity through License Compliance. BSA Global Software Survey. May 2016.* Washington DC: Business Software Alliance; EUIPO. (2016). *The Economic Cost of IPR Infringement in the Recorded Music Industry.* Alicante: European Union Intellectual Property Office; European Commission. (2009d). *SEC(2009) 1103 Final. Commission Staff Working Document. Accompanying Document to the Communication from the Commission to the European Parliament, the Council, the European Economic and Social Committee and the Committee of the Regions. Europe's Digital Competitiveness Report. Volume 1: i2010 – Annual Information Society Report 2009 Benchmarking i2010: Trends and Main Achievements.* Brussels: European Commission; Frontier Economics. (2011). *Estimating the Global Economic and Social Impacts of Counterfeiting and Piracy.* London: Frontier Economics; IFPI. (2012). *Digital Music Report 2012. Expanding Choice. Going Global.* London: International Federation of the Phonographic Industry; NetNames. (2015). *Counting the Cost of Counterfeiting. A NetNames Report.* London: NetNames; OECD & EUIPO. (2016). *Trade in Counterfeit and Pirated Goods. Measuring the Economic Impact.* Paris: Organization for Economic Co-Operation and Development; TERA Consultants. (2010). *Building a Digital Economy: The Importance of Saving Jobs in the EU's Creative Industries.* Paris: International Chamber of Commerce/BASCAP; US Government Accountability Office. (2010). *GAO-10-423. Intellectual Property. Observations on Efforts to Quantify the Economic Effects of Counterfeit and Pirated Goods.* Washington DC: US Government Accountability Office.

The comparative cost of copyright infringement in the EU has been calculated, using the annual average US$ per 1€ for 2008 and US$ per 1€ for 2014. This data was retrieved from X-Rates.com 2016a, b.

2.3.1.2   Costs and Benefits

To continue, similar to copyright, we can analyze the costs and benefits of infringement. The conflicting data on the extent and cost of the problem must be tackled first. *Accuracy is difficult to obtain* (Handke 2010; OECD Secretary General 2007; US Government Accountability Office 2010; Rogers 2013). Table 2.2 give an indication of the wide spread of figures used among industry and government actors. According to the studies, the scale of copyright infringement ranges from 28 to 98% of media trans-actions. Perhaps even more striking, the cost of copyright infringement per year is estimated globally at US\$ 6.1 billion for the film industry, but US\$ 52 billion for the software industry (BSA 2016; US Government Accountability Office 2010).

There are at least two reasons for inaccuracy in the infringement data. First, the extent of the problem is not clear, because it is *difficult to obtain data on illegal activities*. Governments often rely on industry statistics, of which the origin is not always known. Infringement of tangible copyrighted goods can be determined by looking at border seizures. However, these do not take into account domestic production and consumption and are dependent on the efficiency of border agencies (US Government Accountability Office 2010). Visible transactions of intangible goods are perhaps easier to track, but the gray areas of copyright need to be considered. Not all P2P activities are illegal for instance. Second, the scale of the problem is *highly dependent on the assumptions underlying the calculations*. Not all infringements can be considered an economic loss, because they would not have led to a purchase if copyright enforcement had prevented the infringement. The assumption that infringement is a one-to-one substitution of legal consumption is false (US Government Accountability Office 2010; Huygen et al. 2009; Aguiar and Martens 2013). This also relates to the estimated value attributed to the infringed goods. Infringement studies use different economic multipliers to calculate loss (US Government Accountability Office 2010). In 2010 the US Government Accountability Office (GAO) published a report damning the infringement data used by the US Government. One example from the report concerned the shortcomings of "RIMS II" economic multipliers to estimate losses to the media industries, jobs and the economy. Although these figures accurately indicate that the effects of infringement reach beyond the media, they do not take into account economic gains that other sectors, consumers or the economy may experience from copyright infringement (such as increased uptake of broadband and higher levels of cultural consumption, US Government Accountability Office 2010).

A further point on infringement data concerns *comparability*. They are often specific to a particular medium, location or simply ask different questions. For instance, in their 2016 study on "Trade in Counterfeit and Pirated Goods. Measuring the Economic Impact," the OECD and the European Union Intellectual Property Office (EUIPO) calculated the value of tangible IPR infringements in world trade. However, this does not take domestic or online infringement into account. Finally, the drop in copyright sales is not only caused by infringement. The media industries have been highly concentrated and undergoing major structural changes

Table 2.3 Costs and benefits of IP infringements by stakeholder (in the United States)

Stakeholders	Potential effects
Consumers	Negative effects Damage to health and safety Costs incurred when product fails due to lower quality of counterfeit good Positive effects Perceived benefits from lower prices of counterfeit and pirated goods
Industry	Negative effects Lost sales Lost brand value or damage to public image Cost of IP protection Decreased incentive to invest in research and development Positive effects Increased sales of legitimate goods based on consumer "sampling" of pirated goods
Government	Negative effects Lost tax revenue due to illegal sales of counterfeit and pirated goods Cost of IP enforcement Risks of counterfeits entering supply chains with national security or civilian safety implications
Economy as a whole	Negative effects Lower economic growth as a result of reduced incentives to innovate Lost revenue from declining US trade in countries with weak IP rights regimes

Source: US Government Accountability Office. (2010). *GAO-10-423. Intellectual Property. Observations on Efforts to Quantify the Economic Effects of Counterfeit and Pirated Goods.* Washington DC: US Government Accountability Office. 9–10.

in the past twenty years (Oberholzer-Gee and Strumpf 2010). I elaborate on these thoughts in Sect. 2.3.2.

Beyond the numbers, what does literature have to say about the *costs* of copyright infringement for various stakeholders? Here again the US GAO (2010) offers helpful insight (Table 2.3). For *consumers*, copyright infringing goods can be a security risk (for instance, to their computer). The good might also be of a lesser quality (US Government Accountability Office 2010; OECD Secretary General 2007). Further for *rights holders*, the costs are large. Short term they suffer lost sales and are pressured to lower prices and revise business models. Long-term copyright infringement can lead to a loss of brand value and reputation, an increase in enforcement costs (administration costs), a reduction in their operations, and importantly, a decreased incentive to create and invest (US Government Accountability Office 2010; OECD Secretary General 2007; Handke 2010). A third stakeholder who is not always remembered when thinking of copyright infringement costs is the *government*. Indeed they incur less tax revenue due to copyright infringement and invest more in copyright enforcement (administration costs, for instance border seizures). Government agencies also point out that copyright enforcement has been linked to cybercrime (US Government Accountability Office 2010; OECD Secretary General 2007). Finally, for the *economy as a whole*, copyright infringement can negatively affect growth through reduced innovation, less product variety and lower trade levels (Handke 2010; US Government Accountability Office 2010; OECD Secretary General 2007). This has close ties with copyright's functioning as an economic incentive.

To complete the story however, the *benefits* of copyright infringement need to be discussed as well. Short-term benefits for *consumers* are higher consumption of creative works, as well as better awareness through sampling infringed goods (Handke 2010; Huygen et al. 2009; Aguiar and Martens 2013). Further for *rights holders,* the producer side of sampling are new consumers, free promotion, increased complementarity of goods (for instance merchandise and concerts) and more brand recognition (Huygen et al. 2009; Handke 2010; US Government Accountability Office 2010). Additionally, the short-term pressure imposed by copyright infringement on rights holders to revise business models can be interpreted positively. According to Joel Waldfogel (2012), the quality of new recorded music has not decreased since Napster, and technological change has helped independent labels in particular. Moreover in 2009 three research centers TNO, SEO and IvIR conducted a study for the Dutch Ministries for Education, Culture and Science, Economic Affairs, and Justice on the economic and social consequences of file sharing for music, film and games (Huygen et al. 2009). Two conclusions of this study are that downloaders purchase as much music and film and more games than non-downloaders, and that file sharing benefits *societal welfare* in the short and long term. They estimate that the welfare of consumers increases by €200 million compared to a €100 million loss for music producers and record labels on a yearly basis (Huygen et al. 2009).

These studies provide a broader perspective on the problem. *Very often what is at play is not a denial of the costs associated with copyright infringement, but rather a questioning of the necessary level of copyright protection to foster creativity.* Copyright infringement can lead to more access to knowledge and a democratization of knowledge creation. Moreover for the *economy* as a whole, there is possibly not a loss, but rather a redistribution in the economy for other purposes (US Government Accountability Office 2010). Copyright infringement certainly benefits the ICT sector and Internet intermediaries. It can also lead to innovation in circumvention technologies (US Government Accountability Office 2010; Handke 2010). As available data are inaccurate and difficult to compare, studies on costs and benefits of copyright infringement very much become a war of numbers and words, used to advocate particular problem definitions and policy interests in the online copyright enforcement debate. *I seek to point to the ambiguity, not to judge which studies are right or wrong.*

2.3.2   Media Industries[12]

In the next section I explore how media industries are changing in recent years. The context is the rise, boom and commodification of information in the twentieth century. Large societal developments have been taking place, explained by many as a transition to an information society. The challenges for the media industries today are certainly not limited to the Internet and copyright infringement. This is important to keep in mind when discussing online copyright enforcement policies. Copyright and its enforcement are only one mechanism in the continual struggle to become a market leader and obtain the upper hand in the production and distribution of information.

Before we start two remarks are due. First, *online copyright infringement affects more than the media industries.* Entertainment is perhaps an important but certainly not the only type of information available on the Internet. Many different content actors could be interested in developing copyright enforcement policies. This being said, second, I have decided to shed extra light on the media industries. These industries have known significant *convergence with the Internet, ICT and telecoms sectors,* resulting in an (at times strained) intertwining of interests and policies (see Sect. 2.3.2.3). Moreover, in online copyright enforcement policy debates, the media industries are among the most vocal actors.

2.3.2.1 Characteristics

The PEC recognizes that the media are distinctive industries. There are important differences between media types and thus sectors (for instance file size, adaptive ability, consumption of content and delivery methods, Searle 2011). However, there is also a collective set of characteristics which set them apart from other industries. David Hesmondhalgh (2007, 17–25) provides a good summary in the second edition of his book "Cultural Industries." He describes four enduring problems and five responses of the media industries:

A first problem for the media industries is that they are *risky businesses.* It is difficult for users to evaluate a product before experiencing it, which makes success quite unpredictable. Thus media producers are heavily dependent on the positive publicity by others. Further, the media are distinctive, because of the dialectic between *creativity and commerce.* Cultural and social aims play a role alongside economic goals. Remember that copyright pertains economic rights, but also personality rights, and societal exceptions and limitations. For some artists, the creative aspect or the desire to be a celebrity may well be more important than the paycheck at the end of the month. Additionally, media products tend to have *high production costs, but low reproduction costs.* On the one hand, the high initial costs can be an entry barrier for smaller businesses and even lead to monopolistic behavior in the market. On the other hand when there is a hit, large profits can be made due to the low reproduction costs. However, as information is a *public good,* others can also copy the media product at a fairly low cost without competing with or excluding others of its use, resulting in lost revenue on the side of media producers (Rooke 2009; Hesmondhalgh 2007).

Box 2.1   Distinctive features of the media industries

Problems

• Risky business
• Creativity versus commerce
• High production costs and low reproduction costs
• Semi-public goods; the need to create scarcity

Responses

• Misses are offset against hits by building a repertoire
• Concentration, integration and co-opting publicity
• Artificial scarcity
• Formatting: stars, genres and serials
• Loose control of symbol creators; tight control of distribution and marketing

Source: Hesmondhalgh, D. (2007). Cultural Industries. 2nd Edition. London: Sage. 18.

A standard response of the media industries to relieve the risky nature of the business is overproduction. The more media content is produced, the more likely one will be a success. *Misses are offset against hits*. Moreover, media industries use strategies of networking, *integration* (horizontal and vertical), internationalization and *co-opting* with those creating publicity. These allow for better management of the information flows by decreasing competition between products, increasing the distribution market, cross-promoting and more. Further, another important means of information control is the creation of *artificial scarcity*. IPR, installing a release schedule, technically limiting access to products all serve to cope with the public good characteristic of information. *Formatting* is a fourth response of the media industries. It targets the unpredictability of media use, seeking to limit the amount of misses by developing stars, genres and serials. Finally, *"symbol creators"* or media producers are only *loosely controlled* given the artistic and creative nature of media products. This is compensated with a *tighter control of the distribution and marketing*. These problems and responses remain constant in the media industries (Rooke 2009; Hesmondhalgh 2007; Rogers 2013).

2.3.2.2   Changes and Challenges

Having defined the distinctive and constant features of the media, Hesmondhalgh (2007) continues his study by evaluating change in these industries over the past thirty years. His analysis starts in the 1980s, but the origins of change can be found in the period 1945–1990 (see also Michalis 2007). I first link his insights to the wider political economic discussion. Within this context, I look at changes and challenges in the media industries attributed specifically to technological advances of digitization and the Internet. Finally, I provide some concrete examples within five media sectors: music, film, gaming, broadcasting (private & public television and radio) and publishing (including the press).

Hesmondhalgh (2007, 83–84) tracks down the context of change in the media industries to what he terms the "*long downturn.*" Following a two-decade period of economic growth and prosperity after the Second World War, the global economy was hit with multiple recessions from the late 1960s onward. The manufacturing industries in particular suffered great losses. Political shifts led to the *endorsement of free market regulation* and importantly *investments in the tertiary sector.* There was a push for innovation in the computing and telecommunications industries and a growing importance for the media industries in an economy focusing on information and knowledge. The media industries fit right in: internationalizing, collaborating and networking (see next section). In addition to political and economic factors, the West developed socioculturally. On the one hand, there was a strong *questioning of values* (for instance the dismantling of social authority and shifts in family life, sexuality and identity). The media industries have both reflected and contributed to these developments; they are an arena for contesting dominant forces. On the other hand, the *increase in leisure and disposable income* has been important (Hesmondhalgh 2007, 80–102; Michalis 2007).

Moreover, the media industries have been continually adapting to *technological advancements.* The digitization of information and the Internet have incited *efficient changes for the media industries in terms of costs, quality, reach and interactivity* (Henten and Tadayoni 2008; Waldfogel 2012; Rogers 2013). First, advances in ICT and digitization have lowered the cost and barrier of making media products. There are masses of user-generated content. Second, they also enable identical reproduction of content, compression of files and easy storage on personal computers (Fisher 2004). Third, the Internet allows for inexpensive and widespread distribution of media products. This decreases the need for physical storage while it dramatically increases the target audience, making it possible to develop niche markets and offer more diverse media products (Fisher 2004). Finally, the Internet is a two-way medium and consequently enhances user interaction. Media experiences can be individualized through hyper-linking and own research. New funding possibilities through crowd-sourcing also arise (Henten and Tadayoni 2008; Fisher 2004). Media production, distribution and consumption have been democratized.

Of course, these changes have not only created new opportunities, but also *challenges*. Here there are parallels to our discussion on the costs of copyright infringement. A first challenge of the digitization of information and the Internet is obvious then: *copyright infringement is facilitated*. This means rights are infringed and revenue is lost for the media industries. Second, the transnational nature of digital media use has accentuated the *cost of copyright and differences between copyright laws*. For instance, licensing is notoriously complex and has hindered the development of new business models. There are also many new gray areas in use, as litigation on intermediary liability and fair use shows. Third, the rise of user-generated content can be evaluated positively in terms of interactivity and creative output. From the media industries' perspective, however, this use (similar to copyright infringement) may be unwanted and cause the *blurring of the media brand and characters* (Fisher 2004). Fourth and finally, for most media industries the transition to digital and online business models has not been a smooth one. In the 1990s, there was a *high turnover of CEOs* in large media companies, such as Bertelsmann, Time Warner and Vivendi (Küng et al. 2008). Today there is still a *rapid pace of change in business models* (Searle 2011). Mergers and acquisitions, networking and alliances have resulted in non-linear value chains and complex management (Küng et al. 2008). New markets have developed, but equally *new competitors* have arrived and existing actors' roles are challenged and changing. Box 2.2 provides brief outlines of sectoral developments in the media industries. Change has not been uniform among the media sectors.

2.3.2.3 Consolidation and Growth

Finally, it is necessary to situate the media industries within the broader communications industries.[13] As stipulated above, the media and telecommunications industries have gone through processes of not only

Box 2.2   Sectoral developments in the media industries

Music

The music industry has been at the forefront of change. The small file size has made music particularly susceptible to pirating, but diverse new business models are also developing. Some artists have taken advantage of the distribution means of the Internet to circumvent record companies, effectively leapfrogging the traditional music value chain. Overall while sales on recorded music has been declining, total music sales are increasing (Winseck 2011; Rogers 2013). There has been an increase in live performances to compensate for losses in recorded music (Winseck 2011). Hearing an artist perform live at a concert venue or festival is an experience that cannot be digitized. Further, the way of selling music has changed. While CDs tended to bundle music into albums, online the sale of singles is more popular. There has also been a greater focus on developing music for ringtones and gaming (Ala-Fossi et al. 2008; Rogers 2013). Finally, as copyright licensing difficulties are gradually solved, streaming through digital music services such as Spotify and Deezer has picked up (Henten and Tadayoni 2008). These services tend to operate on the basis of advertising and subscriptions.

Film

Films are traditionally released on an exclusive basis through consecutive distribution channels. This is called the window release system, including theatrical release, sale of DVDs, movie rental, and paid and broadcast television licensing. Media users' attitudes have changed to expect that entertainment is available anytime, anywhere (Fisher 2004). Films are also easily accessible online. These factors strain the window release system, forcing a fundamental rethinking of how revenue can be maximized in distribution (Rooke 2009). The Internet offers new opportunities for film promotion and distribution. Similar to music, (online) film services that operate on advertising and subscriptions such as Hulu and Netflix are popular. However, the conflation of the windows release system remains worrying for actors who do not benefit from the new distribution models. Movie theaters in particular are not only pressured to equip their screens for digital films, but also compete with the early availability of films elsewhere and high-end home entertainment sets.

Broadcasting

The relations between public and private broadcasting sector (radio and television) have always been strenuous. The possibilities of online interactivity

(continued)

Box 2.2 (continued)

with media users and decline in advertising have resulted in a redefining of the public service broadcasting remit (Papathanassopoulos and Negrine 2010). Private broadcasters eagerly advocate limiting the role of public broadcasters asserting that the latter's alternative sources of income (license fee; public funding) grant them an unfair advantage in the online environment. Thus, regulatory issues play an important role in the broadcasting sector today (Papathanassopoulos and Negrine 2010). In television, alternative access technologies (digital TV, IPTV, mobile TV) have fragmented the audience and encouraged non-linear viewing (Rooke 2009; Henten and Tadayoni 2008).* Despite these changes, television remains the most popular medium (Henten and Tadayoni 2008). In radio, Internet-streamed and time-shifted models are complementary to broadcast stations: online radio allows for more niche content, while terrestrial radio is relatively unique because of its ubiquity, cheapness and portability (Ala-Fossi et al. 2008).

Gaming

The interactive and digitally native nature of computer games has been an asset for the gaming industry. Gaming was an early use of the Internet, which can easily accommodate for multiplayer contexts. Mobile and social networking games are performing well. The gaming industry has suffered from copyright infringements, but technical restrictions on gaming hardware are still widely used (and accepted) to limit the reproduction of games (Searle 2011).

Publishing

Finally, print is the oldest media technology. The publishing industry mainly includes newspapers, books, magazines and journals, and advertising (Rooke 2009). Online advantages for the publishing industry are the possibilities of customization, updating and user interaction (Henten and Tadayoni 2008). Further, after an arduous start, ereaders and tablet computers such as the Kindle and iPad have taken off. Their assets are digitization and portability. At a sectoral level, newspapers use their web pages as an extension of offline activities, often with optional premium services such as archival access. A real danger for the newspaper industry is the loss of readers to the abundance of information available online. Advertising is in decline and a sustainable Internet business model has yet to be found. Magazines similarly need new revenue streams. The Internet does support the community aspect of magazines, however, which in turn gives magazine publishers more insight into users' interests (Ala-Fossi et al. 2008). Finally, as books are low-risk

(continued)

Box 2.2   (continued)

and low-cost products that can easily be described, their sale has gone well online (Ala-Fossi et al. 2008). New big distributors such as Amazon have emerged; new products are audiobooks and ebooks.

*Audience fragmentation and non-linear viewing are two reasons for decline in television advertising. An obvious third are the many opportunities for advertising online.

privatization, globalization and growth but also consolidation. In the current communications landscape, *vertical integration is common*. The News Corporation is a prime example. Through its ties with British Sky Broadcasting, Fox News and Twentieth Century Fox, it has stakes in the telecommunications, broadcasting, news and cinema production sectors. Further, most ISPs offer triple or even quadruple plays, combining telephone, television, broadband and mobile services. Apple sells computers and other electronic devices, but also has an important content and application store. Google is a search engine, owns YouTube and has developed a social network. The strong growth of the Internet industry does not imply that it has been a smooth process. New (structurally very powerful) players have entered the market and value chain, but many have disappeared as well. The 1990s saw great amounts of venture capital poured into the Internet industry. The bubble burst in the late 1990s. *Companies compete across the value chain to get a slice of the Internet pie*. Media deals help attract consumers to websites and platforms. At the same time, those involved in the distribution of content do not necessarily want to contribute to its production. Rivalry among media and Internet companies is strong. As I discuss below, the current policy debate centers on increasing the responsibility of Internet intermediaries. Having said that, it is obvious but important to restate that we are not dealing with inherent oppositions between the Internet and media industries. Production and distribution of content can go hand in hand. Similarly, companies do not operate on exclusively open or closed systems. They use a *mix of mechanisms and strategies to control and create economic value*. In "The Death and Life of the Music Industry in the Digital Age," Jim Rogers (2013) analyzes the struggles and strategies of the music industry to adapt to the online environment. He argues that the music industry has not seen the decline that many predicted in the 1990s. Change has certainly occurred, but it has not been nearly as earthshaking as projected. Instead through continued and increased integration, profits have remained "under the roofs of a small handful of superpowers" (Rogers 2013, 181). Political economic analyses like this remind us that structural power should not be underestimated.

My study of online copyright enforcement fits in this changing, converging and complex environment. The technology is quickly evolving, actors and interests are intertwined, and offline rules (such as competition and copyright legislation) apply but might need adaptation. In regulatory terms, it is often difficult to determine whether the Internet can be integrated in existing telecoms and media policies or if it is something completely new. *Striking the right balance between competing economic interests, creating a level playing field and seeking the best way forward to encourage innovation and economic growth is undoubtedly difficult.* Tensions run high among actors. An approach only focusing on those elements however forgets the Internet's open approach to information distribution. This offers great *opportunities for creativity, collaboration and freedom of expression.* More than economics are at stake. Public acceptance is an important additional dimension in developing media-related policies. There is strong resistance to the proprietary basis of some media business models.

2.4   INSTITUTIONS

These last sections explore the third I—institutions. Institutions pertain to the formal and informal rules that determine the opportunities and constraints of policymaking. On the one hand, I analyze the history and contentions over the governance of the Internet. *Policy is never neutral and developments in online copyright enforcement contribute to the young and moldable governance of this medium.* On the other hand, the policy legacy and developments in online copyright enforcement are sketched. They form the political and legal reality of the case studies.

2.4.1   *Internet Governance*

2.4.1.1 *History*
According to the New Oxford American Dictionary, governance is a manner of controlling, influencing or regulating a person, action or course

of events. I opt for this broad definition, firstly because it emphasizes that there are actors other than the government who can control, influence and regulate. Secondly the use of the term governance is preferable over regulation, as this latter term has a narrow legal significance in the EU. "Regulations are the most direct form of EU law – as soon as they are passed, they have binding legal force throughout every Member State, on a par with national laws" (European Union 2016). Thirdly governance is widely used in the IG community to refer to politics and policies dealing with the Internet. The United Nations (UN) Working Group on Internet Governance (2005) defined IG as "the development and application by Governments, the private sector and civil society, in their respective roles, of shared principles, norms, rules, decision-making procedures, and programmes that shape the evolution and use of the Internet" (UN Working Group on Internet Governance 2005, 5). Governance draws attention to the fact that control over the Internet needs to be regarded more broadly than laws and rules passed by national governments. Other forms of regulation (norms, market, technology/architecture) and other actors (international organizations, private industry, civil society) also play a role. At the same time, it is important to note that national governments impact IG significantly. While issues related to the Internet cross borders, the implementation and enforcement of IG remain largely in national hands. Indeed *IG is today fragmented—territorialized*. This makes it all the more important that I analyze the international, EU *and* national levels of online copyright enforcement in my case studies. In addition IG relates to more than the architecture of the Internet. The WGIG definition includes both content-related and technical aspects of IG. In "Networks and States. The Global Politics of Internet Governance," Milton Mueller (2010) contends that intellectual property, security threats, content regulation and management of critical Internet resources are key drivers of change in IG today. This inclusiveness points to the fact that the Internet is more than a network of computers. Indeed it is important for civil liberties,[14] commerce and innovation,[15] and foreign policy.[16]

Most early IG, however, was limited to the underlying infrastructure and its users. Indeed *governance of the Internet has grown synchronous with the network itself*. As we explored in the early history of the Internet, there was a unique culture of decision making through consensus and requests for comments. Self-regulation was the norm, as the group of computer scientists developing ARPANET and later other similar packet-switched networks was relatively small. In the 1980s with the switch-over to the Internet, the scale of the network and its users grew. One problem that arose in the new Internet environment was the numbering and naming of Internet protocols (IPs). This led to the establishment of the Internet Assigned Number Authority (IANA) and Regional Internet Registries (RIRs) (Bing 2009). Gradually other aspects of the Internet infrastructure became more formally regulated, as the groups behind the following acronyms reveal: IEEE (Institute of Electrical and Electronics Engineers), Internet Engineering Task Force (IETF), ISOC (Internet Society), World Wide Web Consortium (W3C). These actors and more deal with the governance of the Internet infrastructure. Although the network has grown, *these groups still share that early techno-meritocratic culture and IG is their core concern*. They were the first generation of Internet governors (Bygrave and Michaelsen 2009).[17]

The *boom in the1990s* took IG to a different level: not only did it expand from a technical to a policy discussion, it also brought in a whole new set of actors including national governments, intergovernmental organizations, businesses and civil society. The core concern of these actors was not necessarily IG and they certainly did not share a common framework of openness in the Internet architecture and decision making (Bygrave and Michaelsen 2009). An example of this can be seen in the previously discussed US-European Community debacle over TCP/IP and OSI. The European Community favored the OSI protocol, the more closed standard, and has historically sought to influence the development of a communications network to a larger extent than the United States. However, in the late 1990s a shift also occurred in the birthplace of the Internet. For many years, the US government had funded Internet research, but not exerted a regulatory role. This hands-off approach changed in 1998 with the creation of the *Internet Corporation for Assigned Names and Numbers (ICANN)*. ICANN is a non-profit, private entity registered in California and overseen by the Department of Commerce. ICANN (2016) coordinates and manages the domain name system (DNS), IP addresses, space allocation, root server system and more. IANA's tasks were incorporated into ICANN. The oversight of the US government on ICANN has been heavily disputed in academic and international circles. As a result, in

2014, the US government announced that they would transition stewardship of ICANN's IANA functions to the international IG community.The transition to a multi-stakeholder governance model started to take place in October 2016.

The most recent actor in IG is the *Internet Governance Forum (IGF)*. Desiring a global discussion on the societal, political and economic changes caused by the Internet and ICT, the intergovernmental UN International Telecommunications Union (ITU) organized a World Summit on the Information Society (WSIS) in 2003 and 2005. The IGF was recommended during the second phase of the World Summit (ITU 2006). This forum is a prime example of the fragmentation that we need to deal with when governing the Internet. First, the IGF covers a broad set of issues, such as cloud computing and Internet infrastructure, but also access and diversity, openness, security and privacy. *The Internet is currently governed through many different policies and practices trying to adapt to the Internet environment* (Mueller 2010; Dutton et al. 2011). William Dutton and Malcolm Peltu (2007) offer a useful categorization of IG issues. They divide these issues into Internet centric; Internet-user centric; and non-Internet centric. Internet centric covers the core technical areas of IG, such as IPs, standards and addresses. Internet-user centric deals with uses and abuses of the online space. Problems concerning privacy, (child) pornography, spam, cybercrime and security are considered Internet-user centric. Non-Internet centric are broader issues that have extensive legacy in policy and practice. Dutton and Peltu (2007) include IPR, as well as human rights and telecommunications transmissions in this last category. The significant difference with the Internet and Internet-user centric categories is the approach taken to the issues at hand. *In non-Internet centric areas existing non-digital regulatory processes are dominant. This means new online copyright enforcement rules are likely to be framed as extensions of existing offline issues, marginalizing discussions on the values and functioning of the Internet.* Actions taken to regulate this area have a significant impact, however, especially when the infrastructure of the Internet itself is used to regulate. In these early stages IG can still quite easily be shifted to one direction or another. Second, the IGF illustrates contentious fragmentation in its governance structure. It favors bottom-up regulation, bringing together a wide range of stakeholders on an annual basis to discuss Internet issues. However, it does not have a mandate to produce binding agreements and it is not necessarily accepted as a global forum for IG affairs. Certain national governments, such as China, have been open advocates to dissolving the IGF and giving the ITU a more significant mandate. Online copyright enforcement policy is an additional arena in which the battle over the preferred and future model of IG is played out. The following section discusses various proposed models.

2.4.1.2 Models

Lawrence Solum (2009) identifies five governance models advocated for the Internet. These approaches are not only reflected in IETF/ICANN/IGF IG, but also the broader policies and practices related to the Internet (Solum 2009; Mueller 2010). *There is significant divergence between the models in terms of the level of governance, the stakeholders involved and the means of governing the Internet.* Particularly important for this study is whether the early open Internet norms of flexibility, decentralization, interoperability, peer review and consensus are considered essential to governance of the medium today.

Cyberspace and Spontaneous Ordering

The first model postulates that *the Internet is beyond the reach of national governments and other regulators.* John Perry Barlow's (1996) "A Declaration of the Independence of Cyberspace" is indicative of this approach: "[g]overnments of the Industrial World, you weary giants of flesh and steel, I come from Cyberspace, the new home of Mind. On behalf of the future, I ask you of the past to leave us alone. You are not welcome among us. You have no sovereignty where we gather." The Internet is perceived as separate from physical space; new rules and norms apply. There is hope for more liberty and fairness. This *libertarian* view was popular in the mid-1990s as the Internet boomed (Solum 2009; Mueller 2010; Paré 2003).

Transnational Institutions and International Organizations

The second model focuses on the global impact of the Internet. Solum (2009) captures two views of IG with this second model. On the one hand, the early Internet approach based on user collaboration and consensus fits this mold. The IETF, IGF and to a lesser extent ICANN promote *a multistakeholder, open and inclusive governance of the Internet.* The transnational institutions model calls for the preservation of the unique nature of early Internet culture on a global level (Solum 2009; Mueller 2010). On the other hand, the Internet creates international issues, which could benefit from *cooperation within the framework of an international organization.* This latter view gives a larger role to national governments and advocates formal agreements within (for instance) the ITU (Paré 2003).

Code and Internet Architecture
The third model is based on the work of Lawrence Lessig (2006). *Regulation of the Internet can also occur through technical changes in the network.* The design of the Internet encourages decentralization, flexibility and diversity, which make control over data flows in the network difficult (Abbate 1999; Shapiro 1999). Different from the first libertarian view of the Internet, however, this model contends that these technical features are neither neutral nor inevitable (Solum 2009). The Internet can be captured. For example, blocking and filtering of content on the Internet are interventions in the way that data are transmitted over the network. Code and architecture of the Internet are the most direct means of governing the Internet, as the changes are immediately implemented (Zittrain 2008; Lessig 2006; Reidenberg 1998).

National Governments and Law
The fourth model does not make a distinction between online and offline activities. *The principles underlying the legislation are transposed onto the Internet and importantly the nation state is considered the main regulatory actor* (Solum 2009; Paré 2003). Most adaptation of legislation so far has been premised on this model. The reasoning in this model assumes that copyright infringements on the Internet are the same as in the physical world—theft—leading to civil and/or criminal sanctions. The consequences of the design of the Internet on governance are not acknowledged. Furthermore, by focusing on the role of the national governments, this model also partitions the Internet. State are responsible for control over the Internet, and thus have the sovereignty to erect borders as they deem appropriate (Deibert 2008).

Market and Economics

The fifth model advocates a *laissez-faire* approach toward the Internet. The functioning of the Internet and related problems are analyzed through *an economic lens,* viewing the Internet primarily as a market place. In this fifth model, political or social motivations for governance are downplayed. State regulatory intervention is only considered necessary to remedy negative externalities of an economic approach (Solum 2009). The debate on the neutrality of the Internet illustrates how the premise of the analysis of a regulatory problem can lead to very different solutions. Does net neutrality pertain to the market functioning of a network or much more broadly to the role of the Internet in promoting civil liberties? Depending on the definition given to the problem and to the Internet, the answers proposed for net neutrality emphasize different Internet rationales, levels of regulatory intervention and importantly degrees of Internet openness (Marsden 2010; Solum 2009).

These models are seldom used or advocated in pure form. They are ideal types, and most are to a certain extent combinable (Solum 2009). Depending on the issue at hand, stakeholder coalitions are formed around a specific IG model. Thus international organizations and national legislation clearly favor nation state intervention. However, these models will not only be supported by governments. Copyright holders and civil liberty advocates might seek hard law guarantees for their rights on the Internet as well.

IG is squarely linked to actors' ideas and interests. *Our views and goals (ideas and interests) for the Internet and copyright determine the model we propose for controlling the Internet.* For instance, do we emphasize use of the Internet for the pursuit of science, technological sharing, social interaction and symbolic belonging or entrepreneurship? Further, do we prefer market or non-market-based knowledge creation? *At the same time the existing rules and structures (institutions) on the Internet and copyright reinforce particular ways of thinking and organizing society.* It is hard to step away from a non-Internet centric approach to online copyright enforcement. We maneuver within the legacy of past policies. In line with IG scholars, I emphasize that IG is neither fixed nor neutral. It is continually shaped and constructed by policy and practice.

Finally, the IG models bring a wider debate on governance to the fore. Do we solve problems relying on norms and technology, transnational and international organizations, governments or the market?

I pick up on regulation through surveillance, code and the architecture of the Internet. In particular, this study seeks to contribute to the development of a political economic perspective on the Internet by engaging with literature on surveillance and governance through technology. *Surveillance and technological governance allow close and direct control over Internet content and use, by political and economic actors alike.* Online surveillance is consistently the first step in implementing blocking or filtering measures. Technology provides a coercive form of power, embedding the ideas and interests of those who govern. Technological governance influences our use and perception of the Internet. Furthermore it changes key features of the Internet such as flexibility and decentralization. It is the flip side of the story, how governance through the Internet shapes and constructs in a very direct way. The design of the Internet is moldable. Such influence cannot be ignored in the PEC. The case studies delve into policymaking on online copyright enforcement. Rights holders consistently advocate surveillance and use of technology to tackle piracy online. I seek to better understand how and why domination *and* resistance work in this arena. The following sections take a closer look at this trend. With their common objective to counter abuses of power, the theories of PEC and surveillance complement each other well.

2.4.1.3 Surveillance[18]

David Lyon (2001, 2), a leading contemporary scholar in surveillance studies, defines surveillance as "the collection and processing of personal data, whether identifiable or not, for the purposes of influencing or managing those whose data have been garnered." He argues that surveillance has two faces, care and control, and can be used in an enabling or a constraining way. Surveillance scholars underline that whether for care or control, surveillance has the *aim to influence or manage the surveilled.* Surveillance is more than monitoring, it is a means of social control. On the basis of selected criteria, those monitored are put in categories and a profile of them is built up (Campbell and Carlson 2002). Michel Foucault argues that surveillance and visibility are central to modern power. The knowledge of constant surveillance disciplines citizens into behaving according to certain norms and surveillance is part of the "apparatus," in French *"dispositif"*—how power is maintained in society through a complexity of institutional, discursive and physical mechanisms (van Peperstraten 1999; Foucault 1980).

Surveillance is *inherent to our societies and economies* (Giddens 1984). We monitor and classify information constantly to understand and make sense of the world around us. Both in our personal lives and in our economy, we seek to gather information to manage risks and reduce uncertainty (Los 2006; Lyon 2001). Pertaining to capitalism in particular, John Campbell and Matt Carlson (2002, 587) state that, "[t]he capitalist state depends on the gathering and processing of information to ensure both the greatest possible extraction of surplus value from production and consumption (in essence, efficiency), and the social and political stability necessary to expand its enterprise." Surveillance's role in maintaining the capitalist system (Andrejevic 2007; Campbell and Carlson 2002) is abundantly clear in its use to regain control over information on the Internet. On the grounds of discourses on national security, child safety or intellectual property, online activities are monitored to detect and discourage undesired behavior. Didier Bigo (2006) explains that there has been a *normalization of emergency*, a feeling of insecurity that allows governments to take extreme measures to monitor and control since 9/11. The current risk management discourse in security emphasizes threats and calls for stabilization and increased control (Lievrouw 2012). My focus on surveillance is mostly for the purposes of disciplining or enforcement.

Surveillance for economic purposes is slightly different. It also seeks to influence but is more subtle in nature. Here surveillance is communicated as benign and beneficial for consumers, and consumers allow surveillance for fear of missing out or being excluded (Campbell and Carlson 2002). Privacy is traded for perceived benefits, such as participation in social network sites, ease of search online and awareness of the latest great deals on the market (Mattelart 2010). Political economists contend that privacy is commodified and the value of humans reduced to economics. Here too Internet technology is used to discriminate, because "the purpose of online data collection is to forecast and influence consumer behavior and target those groups of individuals that are predicted to be of greatest value" (Lyon 2003; Campbell and Carlson 2002, 598). Surveillance *legitimizes the values, opinions and rhetoric of those monitoring* which are "frozen into codes" (Lyon 2003). It is important to point out that surveillance is not inherently good or bad, but it does serve as a means of endorsing particular interests and power relations in society.

In an article entitled "Power through the algorithm? Participatory web cultures and the technological unconscious," David Beer (2009) takes these thoughts a step further and points to the everyday shaping of our lives through online surveillance and use of technology. He argues that Internet software is taken for granted, sunk into the "technological unconscious," yet in its treatment of information it classifies and prioritizes our options and actions. For instance, Google uses a series of parameters to determine our search results. Beer contends that this affects us, firstly because these parameters filter what we see and secondly because a profile is built up on who we are. Surveillance and technology don't just help us in our daily activities, they also actively construct them. Building on the work of Scott Lash (2007), he signals that the power provided by technology is subtle, it works from the inside and thus is difficult to detect (see also Campbell and Carlson 2002). Surveillance is present in the very mundane aspects of our lives. Indeed its *ease and pervasiveness on the Internet* make it almost impossible to escape. In 2013 whistleblower Edward Snowden disclosed top secret documents on mass surveillance practices of the United States National Security Agency (NSA) and its security partners. The documents reveal the extensive use of commercial surveillance for security purposes. Often we are not even aware that our personal data is collected and processed. Surveillance gives power and legitimacy to those monitoring.

In policy debates on online copyright enforcement surveillance is suggested as a soft deterrent to change Internet users' behavior, disregarding the societal consequences of widespread monitoring. At the very least transparency is necessary. Similar to political economy, a sense of *social injustice* underlies many surveillance studies. Privacy and data protection laws are set in place, yet cannot adequately address the societal aspects of surveillance (Stalder 2002). Surveillance scholars emphasize that these laws shift the attention away from any discussion on power, because they focus on the individual rather than the system. According to Lyon (2001), the weak resistance to surveillance in politics is due to its limitation to complaints about violation of rights and a general consent that surveillance is necessary in society. However, *resistance* does occur (Lyon 2001). Anthony Giddens (1985, 314) contends that, "surveillance promotes the possibility of the consolidation of power in the hands of dominant classes or elites. At the very same time, however, this process is accompanied by counter-influences brought to bear in the dialectic of control." Whether it is in the opposition against a copyright or privacy policy development through campaigning, in the exposure of government officials' actions through *"sousveillance"* (bottom-up surveillance), or in the circumvention of filtering and blocking measures through anonymization of IP addresses, surveillance is not always accepted. Power is relational and not fixed.

2.4.1.4 Technological Governance

Surveillance studies add to the PEC by arguing that surveillance legitimizes and reproduces the values, opinions and rhetoric of those monitoring. Literature on technological governance complement surveillance studies and PEC through its emphasis on the politics and policies of technology.[19] On the one hand, the technological governance literature details how the architecture of the Internet is called upon to halt the widespread distribution of information that its design permits. On the other hand, it analyzes developments in the regulatory and institutional arrangements to govern the Internet. Underlying (technological governance literature and this study) is the strong belief that technology is never neutral (Feenberg 1999; Green 2002; Harbers 2005). Technology reflects the choices of its developers, users and regulators. Technological governance scholars argue that the Internet contains unique characteristics (flexibility, decentralization, interoperability and cooperation) worth preserving.

The Internet can be defined in many ways. On one level, it is hardware: electronics, wires, waves and so on. On another level, it is protocols telling computers how to interact. On yet another level, it is a social network site, a search engine or a blog. The Internet is many things. At all these different levels, *choices are made about the functionality and nature of the technology*, and importantly that these choices not only have technical but also social and regulatory consequences. Laura DeNardis (2010, 1) argues that the architecture of the Internet "is not external to politics and culture but, rather, deeply embeds the values and policy decisions that ultimately structure how we access information, how innovation will proceed, and how we exercise individual freedom online." Internet specifications result from decisions taken about what the technology should achieve, allow, facilitate *and* prohibit (Abbate 1999; DeNardis 2009; Wu 2010; Lessig 2006). This implies that the Internet can change—an important point to reflect on when considering use of Internet architecture in online copyright enforcement policies.

As government and private actors feel the heat of lack of control over information on the Internet, they have resorted to various means of regulation. One of these is *controlling the architecture which facilitates the spread of information*. The use of technology to regulate copyright infringement for instance, can be seen in allowing surveillance of Internet content and seeking to involve the Internet intermediaries to throttle the Internet speed, block or even filter out information (Brown and Marsden 2013; Mueller 2010).[20] Robin Mansell is one of the few political economists of communications who analyzes foundational and regulatory aspects of the Internet. She calls this the paradox of complexity: the Internet leads to decreased control through traditional means of governance *and* at the same time to enhanced control through programming within a decentralized system (Mansell 2012).

Technology creates a *direct, coercive form of power* for those who create and implement. Roger Brownsword (2008) and Lawrence Lessig (2006) argue that technological governance is potentially even a stronger form of coercive power than the law. While laws need enforcement, here none is needed. The architecture or specification in the technology can preemptively stop actions. It just happens. This has at least three very significant consequences (McIntyre and Scott 2008; Brownsword 2008; Zittrain 2008). Firstly, there is no role for human arbiters after the technology has been set in place; no margin for interpretation; the technology "rules." Secondly, there is no choice to be made by Internet users; no moral dilemma; the technology "decides." Thirdly, technological governance can be less visible than other regulatory means, it is not always clear that a restraint has been put in place. Thus technological governance is powerful. *Fundamental rights concerns* have been flagged as technological governance has not necessarily been implemented with robust regulatory oversight. In particular scholars fear a chilling effect on free speech, a breach of privacy and lack of due process. Moreover there are strong *reserves about relocating power back to the center* of network because this erodes the end-to-end functionality of the Internet (Fuchs 2013; Mueller et al. 2012). Lessig explores these latter arguments in two of his works:

> [In 'Code'] I argued that the original Net protected fundamental aspects of liberty – free speech, privacy, access to content, freedom from excessive regulation; I argued that those freedoms flowed from the architecture of the Net; but, I argued, that architecture was not fixed; nothing guaranteed it would survive unchanged; and, in fact, this architecture was being changed

in ways that took away some of these fundamental liberties. [In 'The Future of Ideas'] I've now told the same story about innovation and the Net. The original Net protected fundamental aspects of innovation. End-to-end meant new ideas were protected; open code meant innovation would not be attached; free distribution meant new ways of connecting would be assured. These protections were largely architectural. This architecture is now changing. And as it changes, as with the threats to liberty, there is a threat here to innovation. (Lessig 2003, 238–239)

IG scholars emphasize that the Internet in its development and design contains *unique characteristics (flexibility, decentralization, interoperability and cooperation)* which challenge our traditional economic and political values, interests and structures. One example is the guiding principle of the IETF to run code based on rough consensus among members. Essentially the IETF gradually improves code as it rolls out (propagating cooperation and flexibility). This Internet principle runs counter to the close control desired by those traditional interests advocating technological governance. IG scholars study the development of policies and institutions to govern the Internet, guided by the conviction that these unique Internet characteristics are crucial to the success of the Internet and should be maintained. Much ink has flowed among IG scholars on whether and how government should be involved in regulating the Internet. Laura DeNardis (2012) and Daniel Paré (2003) sign up the IG's conviction of an open Internet but contend that the strong focus on characteristics has led to an underestimation of the *significance of the sociopolitical dynamics of governance processes*. Paré (2003, 4) states that, "[t]here is also a need to recognize that the interplay between social actors influences, in a multitude of ways, the manner and extent to which the values embedded in the architecture manifest themselves." In essence this is an argument for combining IG with the PEC. IG literature has eye for Internet characteristics and processes; the PEC points to stakeholders and their interests. Both perspectives gain in exercises linking technology, policy and power. The policy debates on online copyright enforcement include advocacy for technological governance. This is significant for both the future of copyright and of the Internet, because *regulation through technology means regulation of technology*. Often the value of the Internet's design is not acknowledged. It is worth restating that use of technology to regulate is not necessarily wrong. However it does merit a cautious approach. The compulsory power granted to stakeholders is significant.

2.4.1.5 Content Control

> Battles over the control of information online are increasingly fought at the level of Internet infrastructure. Forces of globalization and technological change have diminished the capacity of sovereign nation states and media content producers to directly control information flows. This loss of control over content and the failure of laws and markets to regain this control have redirected political and economic battles into the realm of infrastructure and, in particular, technologies of IG. (DeNardis 2012, 721)

Research projects such as the OpenNet Initiative[21] reveal that Internet surveillance, blocking and filtering practices are increasing across the globe.[22] Access to Internet content is restricted at different levels of the Internet (Internet backbones, ISPs, organizations and individual computers) for a multitude of reasons (copyright infringement, but also child pornography, national culture and security to name a few). The OpenNet Initiative studies (2016a) show that these practices on the Internet are certainly not limited to authoritarian states only. As a fairly open and transparent medium, *the Internet has provided many opportunities for innovation and creativity, but equally has its drawbacks for control and security. Technological governance offers compulsory power to those whose actions it protects.*

The media industries were early advocates of governance through technology. One way in which the media industries have protected their works is through use of technological protection measures, such as requiring acceptance of their terms & conditions to access content (clickwrap licenses), inserting limitations in the ability to copy, transfer or play content (DRM)[23] and embedding watermarks in content to facilitate tracking (Fisher 2004). Circumvention of these measures is prohibited by law.[24] Further, the media industries have sought voluntary cooperation with Internet intermediaries, however, in most cases without result.[25] To be clear, Internet intermediaries not only include ISPs, but also search engines, advertisers, payment providers and more. The latest technological governance efforts have concerned how to "follow the money"—how to involve advertising and payment providers to effectively starve illegal file sharing services of their revenues. Lastly, the media industries have also sought to obtain indirect liability of Internet intermediaries through lobbying and litigation. Within the EU, France, the United Kingdom, Spain and Italy have stepped up with extra legislative action. Graduated response permits copyright holders to monitor Internet activities, obliges ISPs to reveal the identity of their subscribers and implements sanctions against recurrent copyright infringers. These legal developments are discussed in detail in the next section.

Internet intermediaries can control content in numerous ways. Some available (although always controversial) means are the blocking of Uniform Resource Locators (URLs), protocols, ports or even Internet access, the seizure of domain names, the filtering and takedown of content and the removal of search results (DeNardis 2012). Box 2.3 explains more about the technologies behind the identification and action against Internet content. *Deploying the Internet infrastructure for online copyright enforcement entails a privatization of governance.* At the core is the shaping of technology and society. As Lessig (2006, 78) states, "code codifies values." Moreover we know that, "[t]he power to shape traffic flows redistributes agency and control among actors" (Mueller and Asghari 2012, 473). The question to be asked then is, which values are codified and whose interests do they serve. This study argues that serious deliberation of the consequences of technological governance is imperative.

Box 2.3   Content identification technologies

Digital Rights Management (DRM)

Digital rights management (DRM) refers to a system that manages rights on digital content. Many different DRM standards have been developed (such as FairPlay by Apple). DRM had the potential of protecting content from widespread illegal distribution, while encouraging new business models and ways of content consumption (Cooper and Sohn 2006). In the music sector, however, DRM has been virtually abandoned. Having found an agreement with the four major music labels, Apple (2009) started to offer all music in the iTunes store DRM-free in early 2009. Such developments had also already taken place on other sites, such as Amazon. Why discard DRM when it had been propagated as an essential part of new business models for copyrighted works online? Essentially for two reasons: ease of circumvention and non-interoperability. The first frustrates content

(continued)

Box 2.3   (continued)

providers, the second dissatisfies consumers. Aaron Weiss (2008) argues that, "the only people restrained by digital rights management are its paying customers." While DRM has been set aside by most of the music industry, its use is still widespread in the film, gaming and publishing sectors. In the fight against copyright infringement, a one-size-fits-all solution cannot be sought.

Watermarking

Further, watermarking helps in the identification of content. It involves embedding an inaudible/invisible mark containing copyright information into an audio/video signal (Gomes et al. 2003). Watermarks can be compared to tattoos on a human being and should not degrade the quality of a work. The most common uses of watermarking are content identification, serial or transactional identification and usage control. Content identification can range from proof of ownership to usage monitoring for remuneration. Serial or transactional identification seeks to trace the distribution of media files. Finally, similar to DRM, usage control implements the rights and obligations put forward by the owners of a work (Metois 1999). It is important to note that watermarks can also be used in a non-restrictive way to convey extra information to consumers. Basic requirements for watermarking are inaudibility, robustness, capacity, reliability and low complexity (Gomes et al. 2003). Because watermarking requires prior processing, unlabeled content is out of its reach. Watermarking also faces the "trade-off between watermark power (and audibility) and detection performance" (Gomes et al. 2003, 78).

Fingerprinting

Fingerprinting is a second technical tool to identify content. It looks at unique features in a media file and then compares them with a database. Fingerprints can be compared to human fingerprints and are inherent to the work. They do not require prior intervention and thus can be used for unlabeled content (Cano et al. 2005). The main uses of fingerprinting are identification, integrity verification, watermarking support, and content-based audio retrieval and processing. First, a fingerprint needs to be extracted, identified and a database created. The identification of media files aids monitoring and tracking (e.g. by rights holders and advertisers). Second, the purpose of integrity verification is to check whether a media file has been altered. This application requires a fragile fingerprint that can detect changes

(continued)

Box 2.3   (continued)

made to a work. A third use of fingerprinting is the support of watermarks by embedding perceptual hashes into a media file. A fingerprint is also an additional protection for a work, because even if the watermark is cracked, a fingerprint can still be extracted and compared. Finally, content-based fingerprinting can be used to detect similarities between works. Consequently, it can add value to services by allowing content-based navigation, search by similarity, content-based processing and so on (Cano et al. 2005). Basic requirements for fingerprinting are accuracy, security, versatility, scalability and robustness (Gomes et al. 2003). Fingerprinting does not rely on embedded data and thus is essentially more robust. However, the necessity to build, update and connect to a database entails higher computational requirements.

Deep Packet Inspection (DPI)

Finally, deep packet inspection (DPI) is a technology to scan *and* act on Internet traffic in real time (Mueller and Asghari 2012). DPI looks into TCP/IP packets for patterns. Importantly, the patterns that the technology searches for need to be predefined and continually updated (Mueller 2011). The two previously described technical tools, digital watermarks and fingerprints, can help define these search criteria. Even in its scanning, DPI is neither neutral nor static. After identification, DPI can also be used to intervene in the network either by manipulating or notifying actors about the analyzed Internet traffic. The main use cases for DPI are network visibility and bandwidth management, user profiling and monetization, lawful interception, network security, copyright policing, and censorship or content regulation (Mueller 2011). Clearly then DPI serves many interests and is highly attractive to right holders. Christian Fuchs (2013, 25) harshly criticizes DPI, arguing that it is part of a "political-economic complex that combines profit interests, a culture of fear and security concerns, and surveillance technologies." Further he states that DPI serves to reinforce a moral panic that "distracts the attention from the political-economic and social causes of societal problems, constructs certain groups as scapegoats, and promises easy solutions (policing, surveillance technologies, law and order politics that include harsh sentences) to complex problems" (Fuchs 2013, 26). It should be noted that Internet intermediaries are not keen to use DPI (or other means of technological governance) for copyright enforcement purposes, as it does not serve their commercial interests. However here too power struggles are present. Technology, surveillance and discourse embed ideas and interests.

2.4.2   Online Copyright Enforcement Policies

2.4.2.1   Legacy and Developments: International

Finally then, let us have a closer look at past and current policies on online copyright enforcement at an international, EU and member state level. As I discussed previously, legislation on copyright goes back a long way—in the case of the United Kingdom 300 years. Until the 1990s, IPR were an arcane topic (Harhoff 2009). Their importance grew in parallel with the economic value of information. The most important international treaties in copyright for this study are the 1994 WTO TRIPS Agreement and the 1996 WIPO Internet Treaties. They form the basis of the 2001 EU Copyright in the Information Society Directive (European Parliament & Council). First, *the WTO Trade-Related Aspects of Intellectual Property Rights (TRIPS) Agreement* is part of the Marrakech Agreement establishing the World Trade Organization (Annex 1C, WTO 1994). It lays down minimum protection and enforcement requirements on its member countries by bringing together the provisions in the preceding international IPR treaties (European Union 2011). Developing countries heavily opposed the inclusion of TRIPS in the Marrakech Agreement, fearing that an IPR trade agreement would deny them affordable access to new technologies (Gotzen and Janssens 2009). Parallels can be drawn with the access to knowledge movement. Second, *the WIPO Internet Treaties* were an act of modernization of copyright and related rights on an international level (WIPO 1996a, b). They provide authors, artists, performers and producers of phonograms with the rights of reproduction, communication to the public, distribution and commercial rental on the Internet. They also include provisions on the protection of computer programs and databases, and importantly prohibit the circumvention of technological protection measures (Gotzen and Janssens 2009; European Union 2006). Finally, governments have been engaged in cross-border collaboration to enforce copyright and have included *IPR provisions in trade and investment agreements*. A recent example has been ACTA. Negotiations on ACTA started in 2008, shrouded with secrecy. In 2011 an agreement was found. The EP whose consent was needed to join ACTA, voted against it on July 4, 2012 (European Parliament 2012). As a consequence, the multilateral treaty has not come into force in the EU (or anywhere else for that matter). One case study in this book analyzes the EU debate on ACTA in detail. ACTA is a sublime example of the opposing views on online copyright enforcement in today's society. ACTA has been criticized for its avoidance of the WTO and WIPO, where developing countries have more voice.

2.4.2.2 Legacy and Developments: The European Union

In the last twenty-five years the EU has passed ten directives on copyright and related rights, and one directive on their enforcement. The adoption of legislative acts slowed down significantly in the early 2000s. Box 2.4 provides an overview. Most relevant for this study are the Copyright in the Information Society and the IPR Enforcement Directives. In 2001 the Directive on Harmonization of Certain Aspects of Copyright and Related Rights in the Information Society (European

Box 2.4   EU directives on copyright and related rights

- Legal Protection of Topographies of Semiconductor Products (Council of the European Communities 1986)
- Legal Protection of Computer Programs (Council of the European Communities 1991; European Parliament & Council 2009a, b, c, d)
- Rental and Lending Rights (Council of the European Communities 1992; European Parliament & Council 2006)
- Copyright and Related Rights in Satellite Broadcasting and Cable Retransmission (Council of the European Communities 1993a)
- Harmonization of the Term of Protection of Copyright and Related Rights (Council of the European Communities 1993b; European Parliament & Council 2011)
- Legal Protection of Databases (European Parliament & Council 1996)
- Resale Right for the Benefit of the Author of an Original Work of Art (European Parliament & Council 2001b)
- Harmonization of Certain Aspects of Copyright and Related Rights in the Information Society (Copyright in the Information Society, European Parliament & Council 2001a)
- Enforcement of Intellectual Property Rights (IPR Enforcement, European Parliament & Council 2004)
- Orphan Works (European Parliament & Council 2012)
- Collective Rights Management and Multi-Territorial Rights Licensing of Music Online (European Parliament & Council 2014)

Parliament & Council) came about, based on the international WTO and WIPO Treaties. The directive translates existing economic rights to the Internet and introduces anti-circumvention rules for technological protection measures. It also includes an exhaustive, yet non-compulsory list of exceptions and limitations. Further, in 2004 the EU addressed the issue of infringement with the IPR Enforcement Directive (European Parliament & Council). This directive deals with the civil enforcement of IPR. Follow-up proposals for legislation on criminal measures (European Commission 2005) proved too controversial and were finally withdrawn in 2010.

Overall, it has been difficult to reach agreements on the adaptation and protection of copyright in the digital context. Figure 2.3 compiles the EC's efforts on online copyright enforcement since 2000. Immediately striking are the number of non-legislative activities in recent years. For instance, as can be observed, review of the Copyright in the Information Society and IPR Enforcement Directives has been considered for quite some time. Currently the EU is focusing both on the *adaptation of copyright legislation to the Internet environment and the protection of intellectual property.* As regards adaptation, a Directive on Certain Permitted Uses of Orphan Works has been passed (European Parliament & Council 2012). Slow and arduous progress also resulted in a Directive on the Collective Management of Copyright and Related Rights and Multi-Territorial Rights Licensing of Musical Works Online (European Parliament & Council 2014). On the one hand, this directive targets non-transparent practices of collective rights management societies. On the other hand, it seeks to facilitate cross-border licensing of musical works for online uses. As regards protection, major efforts went into the multilateral negotiations of the failed ACTA. Further, in 2009 the EC (2009a) set up a European Observatory on Counterfeiting and Piracy.[26] Finally, the term of copyright protection for performers and record producers was increased from fifty to seventy years after the fixation on a record or performance (European Parliament & Council 2011).

Most recently, the EC has taken bold steps to start a more comprehensive process to modernize EU copyright. In December 2015 and September 2016, the EC published two communications entitled *Towards a modern, more European copyright framework* (European Commission 2015a) and *Promoting a fair, efficient and competitive European copyright-based economy in the Digital Single Market* (European Commission 2016a). The documents outline a process for "making EU copyright rules fit for

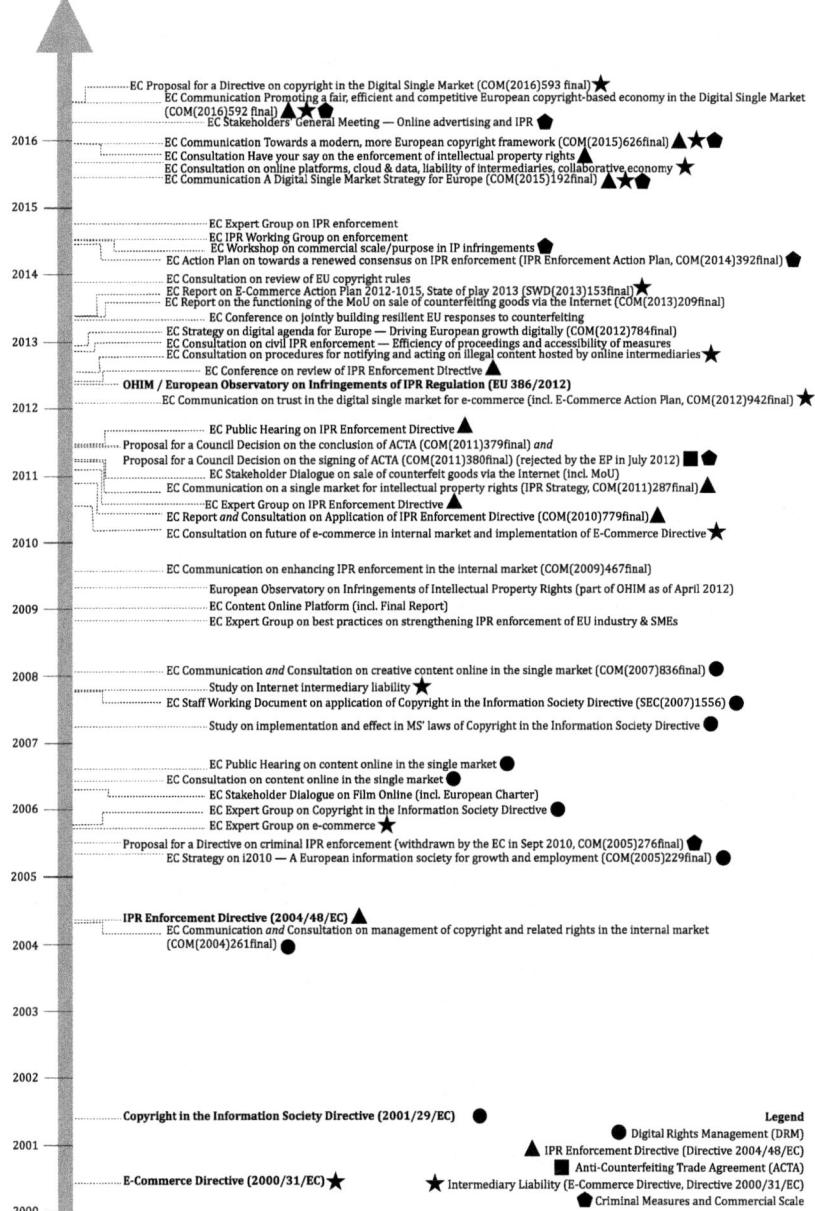

Fig. 2.3 EC policy measures on online copyright enforcement (2000–2016)

the digital age" (European Commission 2015b) by addressing access to content across EU borders, adapting exceptions and limitations, sharing value among market players through new licensing schemes and additional rights (including ancillary copyright) and modernizing online enforcement. Proposals include several regulations and directives. Importantly an additional Directive on Copyright in the Digital Single Market (European Commission 2016b) is foreseen. Language in the proposed directive calls for hosting providers to "take appropriate and proportionate measures to ensure protection of works or other subject-matter, such as implementing effective technologies" (recital 38, see also article 13). It is unclear whether and how this obligation would be compatible with the limited liability provisions in the E-Commerce Directive (see more below). Further announcements regarding enforcement are expected in Fall 2016. Here, the non-legislative follow-the-money approach is expected to feature prominently, along with possible legislative changes to civil enforcement and notice-and-action procedures. Considering the lack of consensus over the way forward on the adaptation and the protection of copyright online among stakeholders so far, heavy battles can be expected before these measures are adopted.

Interestingly, Article 118 of the Treaty on the Functioning of the European Union (TFEU, European Parliament & Council 2010) allows for the adoption of a single EU IPR title. Academically there are some calls to harmonize copyright at a European level. The most prominent example is the Wittem Group's European Copyright Code (2010), the result of eight years of international academic collaboration. Politically however, an EU IPR title does not seem to be on the agenda.

Finally, online copyright enforcement is not dealt with exclusively within copyright law. At an EU level we need to discuss *two pieces of telecommunications legislation: the Telecoms Package and the E-Commerce Directive.* First, *the regulatory framework for electronic communications and services* was first passed in 2002 and then revised in 2009. It is a package of five directives: a Framework Directive, Authorization Directive, Access Directive, Universal Service Directive and Data Protection Directive (European Parliament & Council 2009b, c, d). In 2002 the regulatory framework was also accompanied by a Decision on Radio Spectrum (European Parliament & Council 2002). The framework aims to foster competition by regulating the market entry conditions and behavior of players in the shifting telecommunications market. It also deals with public interest aspects of telecommunications and puts down rules for universal service and data protection (Harcourt 2008; European Union 2015). In 2009 the adoption of the revised telecoms package was held up for several months over a *provision dealing with the suspension of Internet access*. This provision stipulates that restrictions on Internet users' access or use of services and applications through electronic communications networks "may only be imposed if they are appropriate, proportionate and necessary within a democratic society" and "their implementation shall be subject to adequate procedural safeguards in conformity with the European Convention for the Protection of Human Rights and Fundamental Freedoms and with general principles of Community law, including effective judicial protection and due process" (European Parliament & Council 2009c, Article 1.3a). In a spillover of domestic politics, the Telecoms Package (which initially did not relate to copyright infringement) was used to decide on the permissibility of the French graduated response laws. It is a compromise between right holders and citizens, as restrictions on Internet access or use are allowed but only with judicial review.

A second important piece of EU legislation to discuss in telecommunications (but that clearly also reaches beyond) is the *Directive on Certain Legal Aspects of Information Society Services, in particular Electronic Commerce, in the Internal Market* (E-Commerce Directive, European Parliament & Council 2000). For this study, the *limited liability provisions* in the directive are most relevant (Articles 12–15). The E-Commerce Directive stipulates that intermediary service providers (mere conduit, caching and hosting) are not liable for illegal activity or content on their networks as long as they are not aware of its presence. They do not have the obligation to monitor, but need to take action when they are notified of illegal activity or content on their networks (notice-and-action procedure). Articles 12 through 15 of the E-Commerce Directive provide a scale of responsibility: liability increases proportionally with the editorial role of service providers. In other words, the more service providers intervene on their networks, the more responsibility they bear to ensure that activities and content are legal. A provider who offers a service only consisting of the transmission of information (Article 12, mere conduit) has the smallest editorial role and the least responsibility. Next follows a provider who offers a service consisting of the transmission with an automatic, intermediate and temporary storage of information (Article 13, caching). Lastly, a provider offering a service consisting of the storage of information (Article 14, hosting) has the largest editorial role and the most responsibility. I include the text of the limited liability provisions in Box 2.5, as they are central to heated debate in online copyright enforcement. The liability provisions have also

Box 2.5   Limited liability provisions in the e-commerce directive

"Article 12
'Mere conduit'

1. Where an information society service is provided that consists of the transmission in a communication network of information provided by a recipient of the service, or the provision of access to a communication network, Member States shall ensure that the service provider is not liable for the information transmitted, on condition that the provider:

    (a)   does not initiate the transmission;
    (b)   does not select the receiver of the transmission; and
    (c)   does not select or modify the information contained in the transmission.

2. The acts of transmission and of provision of access referred to in paragraph 1 include the automatic, intermediate and transient storage of the information transmitted in so far as this takes place for the sole purpose of carrying out the transmission in the communication network, and provided that the information is not stored for any period longer than is reasonably necessary for the transmission.

3. This Article shall not affect the possibility for a court or administrative authority, in accordance with Member States' legal systems, of requiring the service provider to terminate or prevent an infringement.

Article 13

'Caching'

1. Where an information society service is provided that consists of the transmission in a communication network of information provided by a recipient of the service, Member States shall ensure that the service provider is not liable for the automatic, intermediate and temporary storage of that information, performed for the sole purpose of making more efficient the information's onward transmission to other recipients of the service upon their request, on condition that:

    (a)   the provider does not modify the information;
    (b)   the provider complies with conditions on access to the information;

(continued)

Box 2.5 (continued)

(c) the provider complies with rules regarding the updating of the information, specified in a manner widely recognised and used by industry;

(d) the provider does not interfere with the lawful use of technology, widely recognised and used by industry, to obtain data on the use of the information; and

(e) the provider acts expeditiously to remove or to disable access to the information it has stored upon obtaining actual knowledge of the fact that the information at the initial source of the transmission has been removed from the network, or access to it has been disabled, or that a court or an administrative authority has ordered such removal or disablement.

2. This Article shall not affect the possibility for a court or administrative authority, in accordance with Member States' legal systems, of requiring the service provider to terminate or prevent an infringement.

Article 14

Hosting

1. Where an information society service is provided that consists of the storage of information provided by a recipient of the service, Member States shall ensure that the service provider is not liable for the information stored at the request of a recipient of the service, on condition that:

(a) the provider does not have actual knowledge of illegal activity or information and, as regards claims for damages, is not aware of facts or circumstances from which the illegal activity or information is apparent; or

(b) the provider, upon obtaining such knowledge or awareness, acts expeditiously to remove or to disable access to the information.

2. Paragraph 1 shall not apply when the recipient of the service is acting under the authority or the control of the provider.

3. This Article shall not affect the possibility for a court or administrative authority, in accordance with Member States' legal systems, of requiring the service provider to terminate or prevent an infringement, nor does it affect the possibility for Member States of establishing procedures governing the removal or disabling of access to information.

(continued)

Box 2.5   (continued)

> **Article 15**
>
> No general obligation to monitor
>
> 1. Member States shall not impose a general obligation on providers, when providing the services covered by Articles 12, 13 and 14, to monitor the information which they transmit or store, nor a general obligation actively to seek facts or circumstances indicating illegal activity.
> 2. Member States may establish obligations for information society service providers promptly to inform the competent public authorities of alleged illegal activities undertaken or information provided by recipients of their service or obligations to communicate to the competent authorities, at their request, information enabling the identification of recipients of their service with whom they have storage agreements."
>
> Source: European Parliament & Council. (2000). *Directive 2000/31/EC of the European Parliament and of the Council of 8 June 2000 on Certain Legal Aspects of Information Society Services, in particular Electronic Commerce, in the Internal Market.* Articles 12–15.

been heavily tested in court. This study analyzes stakeholder responses to a public consultation that the EC held in 2010 on the functioning of the E-Commerce Directive. Since then, two further consultations have taken place on intermediary liability and notice-and-action procedures (in 2012 and 2015). Striking the balance between the policy aim to provide high protection for intellectual property in the Copyright in the Information Society and IPR Enforcement Directives and the limited liability provisions in the E-Commerce Directive has been a challenging endeavor to say the least.

2.4.2.3   *Legacy and Developments: EU Member States*

In the EU, four member states have passed additional laws to combat online copyright infringement. Legislation in France (French Parliament 2009a, b), the United Kingdom (UK Parliament 2010), Spain (Spanish Parliament 2011, 2014) and Italy (AGCOM 2013) envisage a more active role of Internet intermediaries in the enforcement of rights. *France and the United Kingdom* promote graduated response. Graduated response is a means of enforcing copyright by monitoring the Internet, followed by warnings and sanctions (such as the suspension of Internet access, imprisonment and fines) related to copyright infringement. While France initially emphasized the suspension of Internet access as a sanction, the United Kingdom seemed to prefer technical measures, such as Internet filtering. In 2013 France amended its policy, limiting the sanction mechanism to fines. The United Kingdom did not implement graduated response. Instead its focus has shifted to discouraging and blocking illicit content (providers) through court and voluntary action of online intermediaries. Further, the 2011 *Spanish* "Sinde Law" is part of a broader legislative act aimed at improving the functioning of the Spanish economy. It created an expedited procedure for the blocking of websites with copyright infringing material, reported by rights holders to a government commission and judge. This law was subject to protests, not least because WikiLeaks revealed that the United States had issued heavy pressure on Spain to change its approach to copyright infringement (El País 2010a, b). Fairly soon afterward, however, in 2014, Spain passed a second set of legislation dealing with copyright more broadly. The new legislation includes provisions that target contributory and vicarious online copyright infringement of intermediaries, creating a new type of liability and facilitating the blocking of advertising on website with copyright infringing material. Finally, *Italy* passed additional legislation on online copyright enforcement in 2013. The Italian communications authority AGCOM had been keen to remedy the country's narrow transposition of the E-Commerce Directive. The authority issued an administrative regulation implementing a notice-and-takedown and blocking procedure. Concerns were raised on its compatibility with EU law (IPKat 2014), but the regulation has since been implemented. It allows the Italian communications authority (rather than a judge) to order injunctions. Table 1.1 in Chap. 1 summarizes these legislative but also non-legislative policy developments in EU member states. Similar to the EU level, informal initiatives among a limited set of stakeholders are noticeable, due to the difficulty to find broad consensus between various ideas and interests in a fast-changing technological environment. In the United Kingdom, stakeholder cooperation on licensing, graduated response and follow-the-money is ongoing; France has also opted for the more informal route in the hope to set up a follow-the-money procedure; in Ireland, a private and lawsuit-based version of graduated response has been implemented; and Portuguese stakeholders signed a

Memorandum of Understanding setting out a procedure for blocking copyright infringing websites.

2.4.2.4 *Litigation*

As a last measure, when policy and stakeholder cooperation fail, litigation serves to restore order and cover harm done by infringement. Right holders have taken three types of actors to court: users, copyright infringement facilitators (for instance P2P networks) and Internet intermediaries in general (Fisher 2004; Yu 2004). First, lawsuits against *users* often end in settlements. These court cases have, however, been controversial and are consequently kept on a low profile, targeting the most egregious uploaders of copyrighted content. Second, *lawsuits against copyright infringement facilitators* challenge the limited liability provisions of Internet intermediaries. The outcome has not been uniform across countries. In many places some form of contributory infringement has been recognized. Here, examples are cases against Napster, Limewire, Mininova and Pirate Bay. Third, right holders have sought more active involvement from *other Internet intermediaries,* such as Google, eBay and ISPs (Werkers 2011). Often the lawsuits deal with the limited liability provisions and the notice-and-action procedure. Here too, the results have been mixed, but tend to emphasize the need to balance rights.

Several cases in the Court of Justice of the European Union (CJEU) have dealt specifically with intermediary involvement in the fight against online copyright infringement. The Belgian collective rights management society SABAM had demanded an ISP Scarlet and a social network Netlog to monitor and filter illegal content on their networks. In both cases (*SABAM vs. Scarlet*, November 24, 2011, *SABAM vs. Netlog*, February 16, 2012), the Court considered that these actions would require general monitoring by the Internet intermediaries and thus breach Article 15.1 of the E-Commerce Directive. The Court also pointed to the necessity to strike a fair balance between IPR and (other) fundamental rights, such as the freedom to conduct business and the rights to data protection and to receive or impart information (Van Asbroeck and Cock 2012). In an earlier copyright infringement case (*Promusicae vs. Telefónica*, January 29, 2008), the Court of Justice had ruled that member states are not obliged to put in place a rule for the disclosure of personal data of Internet users in the context of a civil procedure (Coudert and Werkers 2010). Some court decisions have been more favorable for rights holders, however. For instance, in the CJEU case concerning online trademark infringements on the online auction platform eBay (*L'Oréal vs. eBay*, July 12, 2011), the Court found that eBay could not rely on the limited liability provisions for hosting providers, as it plays an active role in promoting sales on its site. Moreover, in the *CJEU UPC Telekabel vs. Constantin Film* case (March 27, 2014), the Court clarified that web blocking injunctions by intermediaries are permissible. At a member state level, the organizers behind the peer-to-peer (P2P) file-sharing network Pirate Bay in Sweden were found guilty of inciting copyright infringement (Hetland 2009). Rights holders have also won cases in Belgium, Denmark, Finland, the Netherlands and the United Kingdom (among others), obliging intermediaries to block access to copyright infringement facilitators. In Italy, despite AGCOM's regulation, attempts to block websites in Italy have been mixed. The last word on the involvement of Internet intermediaries in the enforcement of rights on the Internet has certainly not yet been spoken. Whether it concerns voluntary or mandatory takedown of links and blocking of sites, rights holders point to the need for more efficient procedures. Often takedown only occurs on an intermediary-to-intermediary basis and injunctions are granted per jurisdiction. All this, while copyright infringing links and sites pop up elsewhere only a short period after the takedown or blocking has occurred. At the same time, automatizing procedures must be carefully considered. Many copyright cases might seem clear, but it is not always evident when a copyright exception or limitation is at play (see, for instance, *Deckmyn vs. Vandersteen*, September 3, 2014, on the use of parody). At the very least, a transparent and clear rebuttal process is necessary.

2.5 CONCLUSION

Online copyright enforcement is about *ideas and discourses*. It is about *debating and deciding how we shape the production and distribution of information and which characteristics of the Internet we deem important*. The Internet's openness provides critics of the dominant market system with a counterpower. It has revived hopes for a non-capitalist market system. At the same time, however, current discourses and regulatory practices lean toward closer involvement of Internet intermediaries and technological governance. We must bear in mind that the Internet is not fixed and its future is in part determined by developments in online copyright enforcement policy.

Online copyright enforcement is about *interests*. It is about controlling information to create economic value. The issue at hand is how we can make money in an online environment. A political economic lens on the matter means that *the policy field is perceived as a struggle for power between actors* who attempt to shape online copyright enforcement policies to best serve their own interests. Media, Internet & technology industries and civil society all pursue their own policy goals. Policy influences and is influenced by market relations. It is never neutral. This study aims to lay bare actors' market or alternative strategies in a capitalist media system.

Online copyright enforcement is about *institutions. Existing structures and rules don't change that quickly.* I have argued that capitalism continues in the online environment. Moreover copyright is 300 years old in Europe. The history and legacy of previous policies and the institutional setting restrain possibilities for action. Equally, however, *it is in and through these institutional structures that we can counter inequalities.*

This chapter has set the scene for understanding how and why policies in the EU on online copyright enforcement have developed. As the title of this chapter suggests, it is *not a matter of the Internet versus copyright.* The story is more complex than that. We notice that there are inherent tensions not just between, but also within actors' views and goals for the Internet and copyright. Early characteristics of the Internet denote an openness in its functioning and governance. However as capitalist forces increasingly dominate the Internet environment, the value of a flexible, decentralized, interoperable and cooperative space for technological and societal advancement is not necessarily considered. Equally struggles are present in copyright. A wider perspective is necessary in the debate on online copyright enforcement. Copyright as a system for fostering *knowledge creation* has both its costs and benefits. Moreover although I do not ignore the losses due to copyright infringement, they are not the only problem that the media industries face. Indeed copyright infringement can actually benefit society under certain conditions. Some of the authors discussed in this chapter point to a communitarian view on knowledge creation. They emphasize copyright's role in providing access to knowledge. These struggles are crucial to take into account when considering online copyright enforcement policies. New online copyright enforcement rules are likely to be framed as extensions of existing offline approaches. However policymakers should not ignore the opportunities that the Internet offers for creativity, collaboration and freedom of expression. Much comes down to *balancing market and non-market concerns*.

In this chapter I also sought to lay out how approaching online copyright enforcement from the perspective of the PEC enriches our analysis of current policy developments. The study of PEC points us to the *interaction between politics and economics*. It emphasizes structural power yet leaves some room for dynamics. Indeed policymaking on online copyright enforcement reveals the *dialectic between domination and resistance* in a capitalist market system. PEC argues that online copyright enforcement is a renewed manifestation of the age-old struggle between copyright and technology. Online, government and rights holders seek *control of information through use of surveillance and technological governance*. However as I note, this requires close scrutiny, because surveillance is a form of social control and technological governance creates strong compulsory power. In this context I also underline the importance of preserving the Internet's unique design. PEC scholar Robin Mansell offers inspiration on possible ways forward. Mansell (2012) stresses that we need not view capitalist and alternative market strategies as oppositional. There are *many shades of gray between information scarcity and abundance*. In right conditions economic growth and social justice can be achieved through both.

I have not shied away from indicating where I believe the PEC could be improved. In particular I have stressed that more attention needs to be paid to foundational and regulatory aspects of the Internet. It boils down to *infusing the PEC with more micro-level analysis and empirical observation*. Winseck (in Fuchs and Winseck 2011, 259) states that, "[w]e need more focus on textured interplay between macro and micro level analysis, theoretico-deductive approaches versus inductive yet still theory-grounded empirical observation. There are too many ungrounded analyses that regurgitate politico-theoretical propositions in light of each new round of communications media (Internet, web 2.0, et cetera) as if that constitutes analysis." I believe that analyzing ideas, interests, institutions and discourses provides a detailed empirical observation into how and why online copyright enforcement policies in the EU have developed.

The following final paragraphs narrate the story of copyright enforcement in the online environment in an alternative way—through use of five words starting with a C. They capture the PEC perspective of this study well. Online copyright enforcement revolves around continuity and change, conflict and convergence, and above all and through all control:

I observe both *continuity and change* in online copyright enforcement. The distinctive problems of the media industries remain. The media industries are experiencing turbulence due to technological advances, but importantly these changes have been ongoing for many years. They are risky businesses, contribute to commerce and at the same time to culture, have high production but low reproduction costs, and need to continually create scarcity to cope with the public good characteristic of information (Hesmondhalgh 2007). The Internet has raised hopes for a democratization of the production and distribution of knowledge. Importantly digitization and the Internet have significantly undercut the media industries' ability to create scarcity. This impact differs between media industries and within the value chain. What does this amount to? To old wine in new bottles: to strategies and resistance to *control* media content in a new digital guise. The Internet is not the demise of the media industries or copyright. This does not mean, however, that the conflicts in this new setting are not trivial, nor that the outcome is clear. Competition is fierce to get a slice of the Internet pie. Technology and policy are the result of power struggles, past and present.

Further in online copyright enforcement, we are confronted with *conflicting* rationales yet *converging* institutions. The early characteristics and ideas attached to the Internet and copyright are largely opposing. The Internet's distributed approach to information has fed alternative views on knowledge creation. The legitimacy of the current copyright model has been significantly eroded. In institutions though, a proprietarian approach to knowledge creation remains dominant. This is not surprising considering the 300-year-old history of this public policy. Stronger even, in a converging communications landscape, online copyright enforcement is deeply intertwined with IG. A driving concern of this study is that the current debate on governance *through* technology does not consider the consequences for governance *of* the technology or society. Many enforcement efforts directly target the architecture of the Internet, creating centralized points of *control* in the flow of information over the network.

An answer is sought in altering the early characteristics of the Internet, with consequences that reach far beyond the problem of online copyright infringement. Indeed online copyright enforcement fits within a trend of surveillance and controlling access to knowledge. There is little room for reflection on the value of widespread access to knowledge and privacy within an approach that advocates strong property rights and tampering with the architecture of the Internet. Online copyright enforcement policies are part of the dialectic between domination and resistance in our capitalist market system. They are key battlegrounds in setting the rules for commercial and alternative production, distribution and consumption of media.

This chapter starts to provide answers to this study's research questions. It expands on actors' ideas and interests for the Internet and copyright, the discourses used, and the existing institutional rules and settings in which online copyright enforcement policies develop. It also explains practically how content can be controlled on the Internet and argues on the effects of governance of and through technology for the open character of the Internet. As such, this chapter provides an initial, yet comprehensive analysis of power relations in the field of online copyright enforcement, setting the scene for the empirical research presented in the following chapters.

NOTES

1. My account of the history of the Internet is concise. On the one hand, it highlights key events in the development of the Internet. On the other hand, it tells the story of the unique features and culture of the Internet, building on the work of Abbate (1999).
2. It should be noted that there were similar experiments with packet-switched networks, most notably in the United Kingdom.
3. This relates to what has been coined as the "end-to-end" (e2e) principle in networking. It favors dealing with the specifications of applications at the edges of a network, leaving the center as flexible and open as possible. This has the additional advantage that innovation can occur at multiple layers in the network, and expertise of the whole network is not necessary to contribute to the development of the network. For more information on this latter argument, see Zittrain (2008).

4. CERN is the European laboratory for particle physics, located on the Swiss and French border.
5. Parts of this section were previously published in Meyer (2012).
6. A public good is non-excludable and non-rivalrous. Classic examples of public goods are national defense, air and light houses.
7. It should be noted that twelve of the thirteen US states had passed Copyright Acts prior to the signing of the Constitution (Davies 2002).
8. I include the United States in this brief look into the history of copyright, because international stakeholders in the EU online copyright enforcement debate are often American based. Think for instance of large media or technology companies. Their perception of copyright might differ from EU stakeholders.
9. Parts of this section were previously published in Meyer (2012).
10. See Sect. 2.2 for a discussion on the resistance offered to copyright through the open source, commons and access to knowledge (A2K) movements.
11. In Jessop (2009), technologies are defined as "diverse social practices that are mediated through specific instruments of classification, registration, calculation, and so on, that may discipline social action."
12. The media comprises the press, radio and television, but more broadly also entertainment industries such as film, music, gaming, publishing and performance and so on.
13. Communications industries include the media, the Internet, telecommunications and ICT.
14. For example, access to knowledge, freedom of expression, privacy and protection of minors.
15. For example, trademarks, copyright and competition.
16. For example, security and control over domain names.
17. This self-regulation corresponds with phase zero as discussed in the book's introduction.
18. Select sentences of this section can be found in Meyer and Van Audenhove (2012).
19. The label technological governance is an aggregate. In this section I mainly draw on studies pertaining to science, technology and society, and the more regulatory-oriented IG literature.

20. See Sect. 2.4 for a more detailed discussion on current uses of technology to fight piracy. Two examples of regulating copyright at a network level are tampering with the DNS and applying DPI technology.
21. The OpenNet Initiative is a collaborative research project between the Citizen Law (University of Toronto), the Berkman Center for Internet & Society (Harvard University) and the SecDev Group (Ottawa), aiming to expose and evaluate Internet filtering and surveillance practices to help better inform public policy and advocacy work in Internet regulation. "Access Controlled" and "Access Denied" are two monographs produced by the OpenNet Initiative. See OpenNet Initiative (2016b).
22. We are entering the third phase of IG.
23. Strong consumer objection to these TPMs has prompted certain sectors, in particular the music industry, to withdraw the restrictions.
24. These anti-circumvention provisions are present at all levels of legislation, from the WIPO (1996a) to the European Parliament & Council (2001a) and the Belgian Parliament (1994).
25. For instance, the EC hosted stakeholder dialogues on self-regulation of CCO from 2006 to 2010. No agreement for action was found. In the case of YouTube, negotiations with the media industries did result in cooperation. YouTube facilitates the identification of copyrighted content for rights holders and gives them the option to either file a notice for takedown or share the advertising revenues of the videos concerned with YouTube. See YouTube (2016).
26. The Office for Harmonization in the Internal Market (OHIM) took over its tasks in 2012. As of March 2016, it is known as the European Union Intellectual Property Office (EUIPO).

BIBLIOGRAPHY

February 16, 2012. C-360/10 Belgische Vereniging van Auteurs, Componisten en Uitgevers (SABAM) vs. Netlog. Court of Justice of the European Union.

January 29, 2008. C-275/06 Promusicae vs. Telefónica. Court of Justice of the European Union.

July 12, 2011. C-324/09 L'Oréal & Others vs. eBay International & Others. Court of Justice of the European Union.

March 27, 2014. C-314/12 UPC Telekabel Wien vs. Constantin Film Verleih and Wega Filmproduktionsgesellschaft. Court of Justice of the European Union.

November 24, 2011. C-70/10 Scarlet Extended vs. Société Belge des Auteurs, Compositeurs et Editeurs (SABAM). Court of Justice of the European Union.

September 3, 2014. C-201/13 Deckmyn & Vrijheidsfonds vs. Vandersteen, Dupont, Amoras II & WPG Uitgevers België. Court of Justice of the European Union.

Abbate, Janet. 1999. *Inventing the internet.* London/Cambridge, MA: MIT Press.

AGCOM. 2013. Delibera n. 680/13/CONS, Regolamento in materia di tutela del diritto d'autore sulle reti di comunicazione elettronica e procedure attuative ai sensi del decreto legislativo 9 aprile 2003, n. 70. Naples: Italian Communications Regulatory Authority.

Aguiar, Luis, and Bertin Martens. 2013. *Digital Music Consumption on the Internet: Evidence from Clickstream Data.* Seville: Institute for Prospective Technological Studies.

Aigrain, Philippe. 2012. *Sharing: Culture and the Economy in the Internet Age.* Amsterdam: Amsterdam University Press.

Ala-Fossi, Marko, Piet Bakker, Hanna-Kaisa Ellonen, Lucy Küng, Stephen Lax, Charo Sádaba, and Richard van der Wurff. 2008. The Impact of the Internet on Business Models in the Media Industries – A Sector-by-Sector Analysis. In *The Internet and the Mass Media*, ed. Lucy Küng, Robert Picard, and Ruth Towse, 149–169. London: Sage.

Andrejevic, Mark. 2007. *iSpy. Surveillance and Power in the Interactive Era.* Lawrence: University Press of Kansas.

Apple. 2009. Press Info. Changes Coming to the iTunes Store. https://www.apple.com/pr/library/2009/01/06Changes-Coming-to-the-iTunes-Store.html. Accessed 5 Oct 2016.

Beer, David. 2009. Power Through the Algorithm? Participatory Web Cultures and the Technological Unconscious. *New Media Society* 11(6): 985–1002.

Belgian Parliament. 1994. *Wet Betreffende het Auteursrecht en de Naburige Rechten.* Brussels: Belgisch Staatsblad.

Benkler, Yochai. 2006. *The Wealth of Networks. How Social Production Transforms Markets and Freedom.* New Haven/London: Yale University Press.

Bently, Lionel, Uma Suthersanen, and Paul Torremans, eds. 2010. *Global Copyright: Three Hundred Years Since the Statute of Anne, From 1709 to Cyberspace.* Cheltenham: Edgar Elgar Publishing.

Bettig, Ronald. 1996. *Copyrighting Culture: The Political Economy of Intellectual Property.* New York: Westview Press.

Bigo, Didier. 2006. Security, Exception, Ban and Surveillance. In *Theorizing Surveillance. The Panopticon and Beyond*, ed. David Lyon, 46–68. Cullompton: Willan Publishing.

Bing, Jon. 2009. Building Cyberspace: A Brief History of the Internet. In *Internet Governance. Infrastructure and Institutions*, ed. Bygrave Lee and Jon Bing, 8–47. Oxford: Oxford University Press.

Boyle, James. 2003. The Second Enclosure Movement and the Construction of the Public Domain. *Law and Contemporary Problems* 66(1/2): 33–74.

Breindl, Yana, and François Briatte. 2010. Digital Network Repertoires and the Contentious Politics of Digital Copyright in France and the European Union. *Internet, Politics, Policy 2010: An Impact Assessment*, Oxford.

Bridy, Annemarie. 2009. Why Pirates (Still) Won't Behave: Regulating P2P in the Decade After Napster. *Rutgers Law Journal* 40(3): 565–611.

Brown, Ian, and Christopher Marsden. 2013. *Regulating Code: Good Governance and Better Regulation in the Information Age*. Cambridge/London: MIT Press.

Brownsword, Roger. 2008. *Rights, Regulation, and the Technological Revolution*. Oxford/New York: Oxford University Press.

BSA. 2016. Seizing Opportunity Through License Compliance. BSA Global Software Survey. May 2016. Washington, DC: Business Software Alliance.

Burkitt, Daniel. 2001. Copyrighting Culture – The History and Cultural Specificity of the Western Model of Copyright. *Intellectual Property Quarterly* 2: 146–186.

Bygrave, Lee, and Terje Michaelsen. 2009. Governors of Internet. In *Internet Governance. Infrastructure and Institutions*, ed. Lee Bygrave and Jon Bing, 92–125. Oxford: Oxford University Press.

Campbell, John, and Matt Carlson. 2002. Panopticon.com: Online Surveillance and the Commodification of Privacy. *Journal of Broadcasting & Electronic Media* 42(2): 586–606.

Cano, Pedro, Eloi Batlle, Ton Kalker, and Jaap Haitsma. 2005. A Review of Audio Fingerprinting. *Journal of VLSI Signal Processing Systems* 41(3): 271–284.

Castells, Manuel. 2001. *The Internet Galaxy: Reflections on the Internet, Business, and Society*. Oxford/New York: Oxford University Press.

———. 2009. *Communication Power*. Oxford/New York: Oxford University Press.

Cooper, Alissa, and David Sohn. 2006. *Evaluating DRM: Building a Marketplace for the Convergent World*. Washington, DC: Center for Democracy and Technology.

Coudert, Fanny, and Evi Werkers. 2010. In the Aftermath of the Promusicae Case: How to Strike the Balance? *International Journal of Law and Information Technology* 18(1): 50–71.

Council of the European Communities. 1986. *Council Directive 87/54/EEC of 16 December 1986 on the Legal Protection of Topographies of Semiconductor Products*. Luxembourg: Official Journal of the European Communities.

————. 1991. *Council Directive 91/250/EEC of 14 May 1991 on the Legal Protection of Computer Programs*. Luxembourg: Official Journal of the European Communities.

————. 1992. *Council Directive 92/100/EEC of 19 November 1992 on Rental Right and Lending Right and on Certain Rights Related to Copyright in the Field of Intellectual Property*. Luxembourg: Official Journal of the European Communities.

————. 1993a. *Council Directive 93/83/EEC of 27 September 1993a on the Coordination of Certain Rules Concerning Copyright and Rights Related to Copyright Applicable to Satellite Broadcasting and Cable Retransmission*. Luxembourg: Official Journal of the European Communities.

————. 1993b. *Council Directive 93/98/EEC of 29 October 1993b Harmonizing the Term of Protection of Copyright and Certain Related Rights*. Luxembourg: Official Journal of the European Communities.

Davies, Gillian. 2002. *Copyright and the Public Interest*. 2nd ed. London: Sweet & Maxwell.

Deibert, Ronald. 2008. *Access Denied: The Practice and Policy of Global Internet Filtering, the Information Revolution and Global Politics*. Cambridge, MA: MIT Press.

DeNardis, Laura. 2009. *Protocol Politics: The Globalization of Internet Governance*. Cambridge/London: MIT Press.

————. 2010. The Emerging Field of Internet Governance. In *Yale Information Society Project Working Paper Series*. New Haven: Yale Law School.

————. 2012. Hidden Levers of Internet Control. *Information, Communication & Society* 15(5): 720–738.

Dutton, William, and Malcolm Peltu. 2007. The Emerging Internet Governance Mosaic: Connecting the Pieces. *Information Polity* 12(1–2): 63–81.

Dutton, William, Anna Dopatka, Ginette Law, and Victoria Nash. 2011. *Freedom of Connection, Freedom of Expression: The Changing Legal and Regulatory Ecology Shaping the Internet*. Paris: UNESCO.

Dyer-Witheford, Nick. 2002. E-Capital and the Many-Headed Hydra. In *Critical Perspectives on the Internet*, ed. Greg Elmer, 129–163. Lanham: Rowman & Littlefield.

El País. 2010a. Cable sobre la Polémica por la Ley contra la Piratería. http://elpais.com/elpais/2010a/12/03/actualidad/1291367865_850215.html. Accessed 6 Oct 2016.

————. 2010b. Cable sobre las Presiones para que España Combata la Piratería. http://elpais.com/elpais/2010b/12/03/actualidad/1291367862_850215.html. Accessed 6 Oct 2016.

EUIPO. 2016. *The Economic Cost of IPR Infringement in the Recorded Music Industry*. Alicante: European Union Intellectual Property Office.

European Commission. 2005. *COM(2005) 276 final. Proposal for a European Parliament and Council Directive on Criminal Measures aimed at Ensuring the Enforcement of Intellectual Property Rights, and Proposal for Council Framework Decision to Strengthen the Criminal Law Framework to Combat Intellectual Property Offences.* Brussels: European Commission.

———. 2009a. *COM(2009a) 467 final. Communication from the Commission to the Council, the European Parliament and the European Economic and Social Committee on Enhancing the Enforcement of Intellectual Property Rights in the Internal Market.* Brussels: European Commission.

———. 2009b. Creative Content in a European Digital Single Market: Challenges for the Future. A Reflection Document of DG INFSO and DG MARKT. Brussels: European Commission.

———. 2009c. *Final Report on the Content Online Platform.* Brussels: European Commission.

———. 2009d. *SEC(2009d) 1103 Final. Commission Staff Working Document. Accompanying Document to the Communication from the Commission to the European Parliament, the Council, the European Economic and Social Committee and the Committee of the Regions. Europe's Digital Competitiveness Report. Volume 1: i2010—Annual Information Society Report 2009d Benchmarking i2010: Trends and Main Achievements.* Brussels: European Commission.

———. 2015a. COM(2016) 288/2. Communication from the Commission to the European Parliament, the Council, the European Economic and Social Committee and the Committee of the Regions. Online Platforms and the Digital Single Market. Opportunities and Challenges for Europe Brussels: European Commission.

———. 2015b. IP/15/6261. Commission Takes First Steps to Broaden Access to Online Content and Outlines Its Vision to Modernise EU Copyright Rules. http://europa.eu/rapid/press-release_IP-15-6261_en.htm. Accessed 6 Oct 2016.

———. 2016a. *Promoting a Fair, Efficient and Competitive European Copyright-Based Economy in the Digital Single Market (COM(2016a)592 Final).* Brussels: European Commission.

———. 2016b. *Proposal for a Directive of the European Parliament and of the Council on Copyright in the Digital Single Market (COM(2016b)593 Final).* Brussels: European Commission.

European Parliament. 2012. ACTA Before the European Parliament. http://www.europarl.europa.eu/news/en/pressroom/content/20120217BKG38488/html/ACTA-before-the-European-Parliament. Accessed 6 Oct 2016.

European Parliament & Council. 1996. *Directive 96/9/EC of the European Parliament and of the Council of 11 March 1996 on the Legal Protection of Databases.* Luxembourg: Official Journal of the European Communities.

————. 2000. *Directive 2000/31/EC of the European Parliament and of the Council of 8 June 2000 on Certain Legal Aspects of Information Society Services, in particular Electronic Commerce, in the Internal Market.* Luxembourg: Official Journal of the European Communities.

————. 2001a. *Directive 2001a/29/EC of the European Parliament and of the Council of 22 May 2001a on the Harmonisation of Certain Aspects of Copyright and Related Rights in the Information Society.* Luxembourg: Official Journal of the European Communities.

————. 2001b. *Directive 2001b/84/EC of the European Parliament and of the Council of 27 September 2001b on the Resale Right for the Benefit of the Author of an Original Work of Art.* Luxembourg: Official Journal of the European Communities.

————. 2002. Decision n. 676/2002/EC of the European Parliament and of the Council of 7 March 2002 on a Regulatory Framework for Radio Spectrum Policy in the European Community (Radio Spectrum Decision). Luxembourg: Official Journal of the European Communities.

————. 2004. *Directive 2004/48/EC of the European Parliament and of the Council of 29 April 2004 on the Enforcement of Intellectual Property Rights.* Luxembourg: Official Journal of the European Union.

————. 2006. *Directive 2006/115/EC of the European Parliament and of the Council of 12 December 2006 on Rental Right and Lending Right and on Certain Rights Related to Copyright in the Field of Intellectual Property (Codified Version).* Luxembourg: Official Journal of the European Union.

————. 2009a. *Directive 2009a/24/EC of the European Parliament and of the Council of 23 April 2009a on the Legal Protection of Computer Programs (Codified Version).* Luxembourg: Official Journal of the European Union.

————. 2009b. *Directive 2009b/136/EC of the European Parliament and of the Council of 25 November 2009b amending Directive 2002/22/EC on Universal Service and Users' Rights relating to Electronic Communications Networks and Services, Directive 2002/58/EC concerning the Processing of Personal Data and the Protection of Privacy in the Electronic Communications Sector and Regulation (EC) No 2006/2004 on Cooperation between National Authorities Responsible for the Enforcement of Consumer Protection Laws (Citizens' Rights Directive).* Luxembourg: Official Journal of the European Union.

————. 2009c. *Directive 2009c/140/EC of the European Parliament and of the Council of 25 November 2009c amending Directives 2002/21/EC on a Common Regulatory Framework for Electronic Communications Networks and Services, 2002/19/EC on Access to, and Interconnection of, Electronic Communications Networks and Associated Facilities, and 2002/20/EC on the Authorisation of Electronic Communications Networks and Services (Better Regulation Directive).* Luxembourg: Official Journal of the European Union.

————. 2009d. *Regulation (EC) No 1211/2009d of the European Parliament and of the Council of 25 November 2009d establishing the Body of European Regulators for Electronic Communications (BEREC) and the Office.* Luxembourg: Official Journal of the European Union.

————. 2010. *Consolidated Version of the Treaty on the Functioning of the European Union (TFEU).* Luxembourg: Official Journal of the European Union.

————. 2011. *Directive 2011/77/EU of the European Parliament and of the Council of 27 September 2011 Amending Directive 2006/116/EC on the Term of Protection of Copyright and Certain Related Rights.* Luxembourg: Official Journal of the European Union.

————. 2012. *Directive 2012/28/EU of the European Parliament and of the Council of 25 October 2012 on Certain Permitted Uses of Orphan Works.* Luxembourg: Official Journal of the European Union.

————. 2014. *Directive 2014/26/EU of the European Parliament and of the Council of 26 February 2014 on Collective Management of Copyright and Related Rights and Multi-Territorial Licensing of Rights in Musical Works for Online Use in the Internal Market.* Luxembourg: Official Journal of the European Union.

European Union. 2006. Accession to the WIPO Treaties. http://europa.eu/legislation_summaries/internal_market/businesses/intellectual_property/l26054_en.htm. Accessed 6 Oct 2016.

————. 2011. Aspects of Intellectual Property Rights. http://europa.eu/legislation_summaries/internal_market/businesses/intellectual_property/r11013_en.htm. Accessed 6 Oct 2016.

————. 2015. Regulatory Framework for Electronic Communications. http://europa.eu/legislation_summaries/information_society/legislative_framework/l24216a_en.htm. Accessed 6 Oct 2016.

————. 2016. Regulations, Directives and Other Acts. https://europa.eu/european-union/law/legal-acts_en. Accessed 6 Oct 2016.

Farrand, Benjamin. 2011. 'Piracy. It's a Crime.' – The Criminalization Process of Digital Copyright Infringement. Neutralidad de la Red y otros Retos para el Futuro de Internet. Actas del VII Congreso Internacional Internet, Derecho y Política, Universitat Oberta de Catalunya, Barcelona.

Feenberg, Andrew. 1999. *Questioning Technology.* London/New York: Routledge.

Fisher, W. 2004. *Promises to Keep: Technology, Law, and the Future of Entertainment.* Stanford: Stanford University Press.

Foster, John, and Robert McChesney. 2011. The Internet's Unholy Marriage to Capitalism. *Monthly Review* 62(10).

Foucault, Michel. 1980. The Confession of the Flesh. In *Power/Knowledge: Selected Interviews and Other Writings, 1972–1977,* ed. Colin Gordon, 194–228. New York: Pantheon.

French Parliament. 2009a. *Loi n. 2009a-669 du 12 Juin 2009a favorisant la Diffusion et la Protection de la Création sur Internet.* Paris: Journal officiel de la République française.

———. 2009b. *Loi n. 2009b-1311 du 28 Octobre 2009b relative à la Protection Pénale de la Propriété Littéraire et Artistique sur Internet.* Paris: Journal officiel de la République française.

Frontier Economics. 2011. *Estimating the Global Economic and Social Impacts of Counterfeiting and Piracy.* London: Frontier Economics.

Fuchs, Christian. 2009. Information and Communication Technologies and Society: A Contribution to the Critique of the Political Economy of the Internet. *European Journal of Communication* 24(1): 69–87.

———. 2013. Societal and Ideological Impacts of Deep Packet Inspection Internet Surveillance. *Information, Communication & Society* 16: 1–32.

Fuchs, Christian, and Dwayne Winseck. 2011. Critical Media and Communication Studies Today. A Conversation. *tripleC* 9(2): 247–271.

Gibson, Johanna. 2007. Knowledge and Other Values – Intellectual Property and the Limitations for Traditional Knowledge. In *Emerging Issues in Intellectual Property: Trade, Technology and Market Freedom Essays in Honour of Herchel Smith,* ed. Guido Westkamp, 309–318. Cheltenham: Edward Elgar.

Giddens, Anthony. 1984. *Power, Property and the State. A Contemporary Critique of Historical Materialism.* Vol. 1. Berkeley/Los Angeles: University of California Press.

———. 1985. *The Nation-State and Violence. A Contemporary Critique of Historical Materialism.* Vol. 2. Oxford: Polity Press.

Gillespie, Tarleton. 2007. *Wired Shut: Copyright and the Shape of Digital Culture.* Cambridge: MIT Press.

Gomes, Leandro de C.T., Pedro Cano, Emilia Gómez, Madeleine Bonnet, and Eloi Batlle. 2003. Audio Watermarking and Fingerprinting: For Which Applications? *Journal of New Music Research* 32(1): 65–81.

Gordon, Wendy, and Robert Bone. 2000. Copyright. In *Encyclopedia of Law & Economics: Volume II,* ed. Boudewijn Boukaert and Gerrit de Geest. Cheltenham: Edward Elgar.

Gotzen, Frank, and Marie-Christine Janssens. 2009. *Wegwijs in Het Intellectueel Eigendomsrecht. Editie 2009.* Brugge: Vanden Broele.

Green, Leila. 2002. *Communication, Technology and Society.* London: Sage Publications.

Hajer, Maarten. 2006. Doing Discourse Analysis: Coalitions, Practices, Meaning. In *Words Matter in Policy and Planning. Discourse Theory and Method in the Social Sciences,* ed. Margo van den Brink and Tamara Metze, 65–74. Utrecht: Koninklijk Nederlands Aardrijkskundig Genootschap & Netherlands Graduate School of Urban and Regional Research.

Halbert, Debora. 1999. *Intellectual Property in the Information Age: The Politics of Expanding Property Rights.* Westport: Quorum Press.

Handke, Christian. 2010. *The Economics of Copyright and Digitisation: A Report on the Literature and the Need for Further Research.* London: UK Strategy Advisory Board for Intellectual Property Policy.

Harbers, Hans, ed. 2005. *Inside the Politics of Technology: Agency and Normativity in the Co-Production of Technology and Society.* Amsterdam: Amsterdam University Press.

Harcourt, Alison. 2008. Introduction. In *European Media Governance: The Brussels Dimension,* ed. Georgios Terzis, 13–23. Bristol: Intellect.

Harhoff, Dietmar. 2009. *Challenges Affecting the Use and Enforcement of Intellectual Property Rights.* London: UK Intellectual Property Office.

Henten, Anders, and Reza Tadayoni. 2008. The Impact of the Internet on Media Technology, Platforms and Innovation. In *The Internet and the Mass Media,* ed. Lucy Küng, Robert Picard, and Ruth Towse, 45–64. London: Sage.

Herrington, TyAnna. 2001. *Controlling Voices: Intellectual Property, Humanistic Studies, and the Internet.* Carbondale/Edwardsville: Southern Illinois University Press.

Hesmondhalgh, David. 2007. *Cultural Industries.* 2nd ed. London: Sage.

Hetland, Jarle. 2009. Sweden's Pirate Bay Members Found Guilty. *European Voice,* April 17. http://www.europeanvoice.com/article/2009/04/sweden-s-pirate-bay-members-found-guilty/64641.aspx. Accessed 6 Oct 2016.

Huygen, Annelies, Paul Rutten, Sanne Huveneers, Sander Limonard, Joost Poort, Jorna Leenheer, Kieja Janssen, Nico van Eijk, and Natali Helberger. 2009. *Ups and Down. Economische en Culturele Gevolgen van File Sharing voor Muziek, Film en Games.* Delft: Dutch Ministries for Education, Culture and Science, Economic Affairs, and Justice.

ICANN. 2016. Internet Corporation for Assigned Names and Numbers. Welcome to ICANN!. https://www.icann.org/resources/pages/welcome-2012-02-25-en. Accessed 8 Sept 2016.

IFPI. 2012. *Digital Music Report 2012. Expanding Choice. Going Global.* London: International Federation of the Phonographic Industry.

IPKat. 2014. Super-Breaking News: EU Commission Had Several Serious Doubts About Italian Communication Authority's Online Copyright Enforcement Regulation Compatibility with Fundamental Rights and EU Law. http://ipkitten.blogspot.co.uk/2014/01/super-breaking-news-eu-commission-had.html. Accessed 6 Oct 2016.

ITU. 2006. World Summit on the Information Society: About WSIS. http://www.itu.int/wsis/basic/about.html. Accessed 6 Oct 2016.

Jessop, Bob. 2009. Cultural Political Economy and Critical Policy Studies. *Critical Policy Studies* 3(3–4): 336–356.

Jones, Richard. 2005. Entertaining Code: File Sharing, Digital Rights Management Regimes, and Criminological Theories of Compliance. *International Review of Law Computers* 19(3): 287–303.

Küng, Lucy, Nikos Leandros, Robert Picard, Roland Schroeder, and Richard van der Wurff. 2008. The Impact of the Internet on Media Organization Strategies and Structures. In *The Internet and the Mass Media*, ed. Lucy Küng, Robert Picard, and Ruth Towse, 125–148. London: Sage.

Lash, Scott. 2007. Power After Hegemony: Cultural Studies in Mutation. *Theory, Culture & Society* 24(3): 55–78.

Lessig, Lawrence. 2003. *The Future of Ideas. The Fate of the Commons in a Connected World. Reprint Edition.* New York: Random House.

———. 2004. *Free Culture: How Big Media Uses Technology and the Law to Lock Down Culture and Control Creativity.* New York: Penguin Press.

———. 2006. *Code: And Other Laws of Cyberspace, Version 2.0.* New York: Basic Books.

Lievrouw, Leah. 2012. The Next Decade in Internet Time. *Information, Communication & Society* 15(5): 616–638.

Linebaugh, Peter, and Marcus Rediker. 2000. *The Many-Headed Hydra: The Hidden History of the Revolutionary Atlantic.* London: Verso.

Los, Maria. 2006. Looking into the Future: Surveillance, Globalization and the Totalitarian Potential. In *Theorizing Surveillance: The Panopticon and Beyond*, ed. David Lyon, 69–94. Cullompton: Willan Publishing.

Lyon, David. 2001. *Surveillance Society: Monitoring Everyday Life, Issues in Society.* Buckingham: Open University Press.

———. 2003. Surveillance as Social Sorting: Computer Codes and Mobile Bodies. In *Surveillance as Social Sorting: Privacy, Risk and Digital Discrimination*, ed. David Lyon, 13–30. London/New York: Routledge.

Mansell, Robin. 2012. *Imagining the Internet: Communication, Innovation and Governance.* Oxford: Oxford University Press.

Marsden, Christopher. 2010. *Net Neutrality. Towards a Co-regulatory Solution.* London: Bloomsbury Academic.

Mattelart, Tristan. 2009. Audio-Visual Piracy: Towards a Study of the Underground Networks of Cultural Globalization. *Global Media and Communication* 5(3): 308–326.

Mattelart, Armand. 2010. *The Globalization of Surveillance. The Origin of the Securitarian Order.* Trans. Susan Taponier and James Cohen. Cambridge/Malden: Polity Press.

May, Christopher, and Susan Sell. 2005. *Intellectual Property Rights: A Critical History.* Boulder/London: Lynne Riener Publishers.

McChesney, Robert Waterman. 2008. *The Political Economy of Media: Enduring Issues, Emerging Dilemmas.* New York: Monthly Review Press.

————. 2013. *Digital Disconnect: How Capitalism Is Turning the Internet Against Democracy.* New York: The New Press.

McIntyre, T.J., and Colin Scott. 2008. Internet Filtering: Rhetoric, Legitimacy, Accountability and Responsibility. In *Regulating Technologies: Legal Futures, Regulatory Frames and Technological Fixes,* ed. R. Brownsword and K. Yeung, 109–124. Oxford: Hart Publishing.

Menell, Peter. 2000. Intellectual Property: General Theories. In *Encyclopedia of Law & Economics: Volume II,* ed. Boudewijn Boukaert and Gerrit de Geest, 129–188. Cheltenham: Edward Elgar.

Metois, Eric. 1999. Audio Watermarking and Applications. http://www.metois. com/Docs/audiowatermark.pdf. Accessed 5 Oct 2016.

Meyer, Trisha. 2012. Graduated Response in France: The Clash of Copyright and the Internet. *Journal of Information Policy* 2: 107–127.

Meyer, Trisha, and Leo Van Audenhove. 2012. Surveillance and Regulating Code: An Analysis of Graduated Response in France. *Surveillance and Society* 9(4): 365–377.

Michalis, Maria. 2007. *Governing European Communications: From Unification to Coordination.* Plymouth: Lexington Books.

Mueller, Milton. 2010. *Networks and States. The Global Politics of Internet Governance.* Cambridge/London: MIT Press.

————. 2011. DPI Technology from the Standpoint of Internet Governance Studies: An Introduction. http://dpi.ischool.syr.edu/Technology_files/ WhatisDPI-2.pdf. Accessed 5 Oct 2016.

Mueller, Milton, and Hadi Asghari. 2012. Deep Packet Inspection and Bandwidth Management: Battles Over BitTorrent in Canada and the United States. *Telecommunications Policy* 36(6): 462–475.

Mueller, Milton, Andreas Kuehn, and Stephanie Santoso. 2012. Policing the Network: Using DPI for Copyright Enforcement. *Surveillance and Society* 9(4): 348–364.

Murdock, Graham. 2011. Political Economies as Moral Economies: Commodities, Gifts, and Public Goods. In *The Handbook of Political Economy of Communications,* ed. Janet Wasko, Graham Murdock, and Helena Sousa, 13–40. Chichester: Wiley-Blackwell.

Mylly, Tuomas. 2009. *Intellectual Property and European Economic Constitutional Law: The Trouble with Private Informational Power.* Gummurus: Helsinki.

Netanel, Neil. 2008. *Copyright's Paradox.* Oxford/New York: Oxford University Press.

NetNames. 2015. *Counting the Cost of Counterfeiting. A NetNames Report.* London: NetNames.

Oberholzer-Gee, Felix, and Koleman Strumpf. 2010. File Sharing and Copyright. In *Innovation Policy and the Economy, Volume 10,* ed. Josh Lerner and Scott Stern, 19–55. Chicago: National Bureau of Economic Research.

OECD. 2009. *Piracy of Digital Content*. Paris: OECD Directorate for Science, Technology and Industry.

OECD, and EUIPO. 2016. *The Economic Impact of Counterfeiting and Piracy*. Paris: Organization for Economic Co-Operation and Development.

OECD Secretary General. 2007. *The Economic Impact of Counterfeiting and Piracy*. Paris: Organization for Economic Co-Operation and Development.

OpenNet Initiative. 2016a. About Filtering. http://opennet.net/about-filtering. Accessed 26 Aug 2016a.

———. 2016b. About ONI. http://opennet.net/about-oni. Accessed 26 Aug 2016b.

Oudenampsen, Merijn, and Koen Haegens. 2009. De Hydra Is Terug. Het Veelkoppige Monster van de Internetpiraterij. *Groene Amsterdammer*.

Papathanassopoulos, Stylianos, and Ralph Negrine. 2010. Public Broadcasters in the Digital Age. In *Communications Policy. Theories and Issues*, ed. Stylianos Papathanassopoulos and Ralph Negrine, 133–147. Houndmills: Palgrave Macmillan.

Paré, Daniel. 2003. *Internet Governance in Transition*. In *Who Is the Master of This Domain?* Lanham: Rowman & Littlefield Publishers.

Perry Barlow, John. 1996. *A Declaration of the Independence of Cyberspace*. Davos: Electronic Frontier Foundation.

Reidenberg, Joel. 1998. Lex Informatica: The Formulation of Information Policy Rules Through Technology. *Texas Law Review* 73(3): 553–584.

Reyman, Jessica. 2009. *The Rhetoric of Intellectual Property: Copyright Law and the Regulation of Digital Culture*. New York: Routledge.

Rogers, Jim. 2013. *The Death and Life of the Music Industry in the Digital Age*. London: Bloomsbury.

Rooke, Richard. 2009. *European Media in the Digital Age. Analysis and Approaches*. Harlow: Pearson Education.

Searle, Nicola. 2011. *Changing Business Models in the Creative Industries: The Cases of Television, Computer Games and Music*. London: UK Intellectual Property Office.

Shahin, Jamal. 2006. A European History of the Internet. *Science and Public Policy* 33(9): 681–693.

Shapiro, Andrew L. 1999. *The Control Revolution: How the Internet Is Putting Individuals in Charge and Changing the World We Know*. 1st ed. New York: PublicAffairs.

Shemtov, Noam. 2007. Circumventing the Idea Expression Dichotomy: The Use of Copyright, Technology and Contract to Deny Public Access to Ideas. In *Emerging Issues in Modern Intellectual Property: Trade, Technology and Market Freedom Essays in Honour of Herchel Smith*, ed. Guido Westkamp, 88–108. Cheltenham: Edward Elgar.

Solum, Lawrence. 2009. Models of Internet Governance. In *Internet Governance. Infrastructure and Institutions*, ed. Bygrave Lee and Jon Bing, 48–91. Oxford: Oxford University Press.

Spanish Parliament. 2011. *Ley 2/2011, de 4 de marzo, de Economía Sostenible*. Madrid: Boletín Oficial del Estado.

———. 2014. *Ley 21/2014, de 4 de noviembre, por la que se modifica el texto refundido de la Ley de Propiedad Intelectual aprobado por Real Decreto Legislativo 1/1996, de 12 de abril, y la Ley 1/2000, de 7 de enero, de Enjuiciamiento Civil*. Madrid: Boletín Oficial del Estado.

Stalder, Felix. 2002. Opinion. Privacy Is Not the Antidote to Surveillance. *Surveillance & Society* 1(1): 120–124.

Strangelove, M. 2005. *The Empire of Mind. Digital Piracy and the Anti-Capitalist Movement*. Toronto: University of Toronto Press.

Sunder, Madhavi. 2006. IP³. *Stanford Law Review* 59(2): 257–332.

TERA Consultants. 2010. *Building a Digital Economy: The Importance of Saving Jobs in the EU's Creative Industries*. Paris: International Chamber of Commerce/ BASCAP.

Tian, YiJun. 2009. *Re-thinking Intellectual Property: The Political Economy of Copyright Protection in the Digital Era*. New York: Routledge.

Torremans, Paul. 2004. Copyright as a Human Right. In *Copyright and Human Rights*, ed. Paul Torremans, 1–20. The Hague: Kluwer Law International.

UK Parliament. 2010. *Digital Economy Act 2010*. London: Her Majesty's Stationery Office.

UN Working Group on Internet Governance. 2005. *Report of the Working Group on Internet Governance. 05.41622*. Geneva: United Nations.

United States of America. 1790. *Constitution of the United States*. Champaign: Project Gutenberg.

US Government Accountability Office. 2010. *GAO-10-423. Intellectual Property. Observations on Efforts to Quantify the Economic Effects of Counterfeit and Pirated Goods*. Washington, DC: US Government Accountability Office.

Vaidhyanathan, Siva. 2001. *Copyrights and Copywrongs. The Rise of Intellectual Property and How It Threatens Creativity*. New York/London: New York University Press.

Van Asbroeck, Benoit, and Maud Cock. 2012. The Scarlet Case. ISPs Cannot Be Ordered to Introduce General Filters on Their Network to Prevent Copyright Infringement. *AmCham Connect*, February.

van Peperstraten, Frans. 1999. *Samenleving Ter Discussie. Een Inleiding in de Sociale Filosofie*. Bussum: Uitgeverij Coutinho.

Waldfogel, Joel. 2012. Copyright Protection, Technological Change, and the Quality of New Products: Evidence from Recorded Music Since Napster. *Journal of Law and Economics* 55(4): 715–740.

Weiss, Aaron. 2008. Content Filters. Will ISPs Become the Enforcers of the Web? *netWorker* 12(1).

Werkers, Evi. 2011. Intermediaries in the Eye of the Copyright Storm. A Comparative Analysis of the Three Strike Approach Within the European Union. *ICRI Working Paper Series* 4.

Westkamp, Guido. 2007. Changing Mechanisms in Copyright's Ontology – Structure, Reasoning and the Fate of the Public Domain. In *Emerging Issues in Intellectual Property: Trade, Technology and Market Freedom Essays in Honour of Herchel Smith*, ed. Guido Westkamp, 78–103. Cheltenham: Edward Elgar.

Winseck, Dwayne. 2011. The Political Economies of Media and the Transformation of the Global Media Industries. In *The Political Economies of Media. The Transformation of the Global Media Industries*, ed. Dwayne Winseck and Dal Yong Jin, 3–48. London/New York: Bloomsbury Academic.

WIPO. 1996a. *Copyright Treaty, WO033EN*. Geneva: International Bureau of the World Intellectual Property Organization.

———. 1996b. *Performances and Phonograms Treaty, WO034EN*. Geneva: International Bureau of the World Intellectual Property Organization.

Wittem Group. 2010. European Copyright Code. http://www.copyrightcode.eu/. Accessed 6 Oct 2016.

WTO. 1994. *Agreement on Trade-Related Aspects of Intellectual Property Rights. Annex 1C of Agreement Establishing the World Trade Organization*. Marrakech: World Trade Organization.

X-Rates.com. 2016a. Exchange Rate Average 2008 (Euro, US Dollar). http://www.x-rates.com/average/?from=EUR&to=USD&amount=1.00&year=2008. Accessed 26 Aug 2016a.

———. 2016b. Exchange Rate Average 2014 (Euro, US Dollar). http://www.x-rates.com/average/?from=EUR&to=USD&amount=1.00&year=2014. Accessed 26 August 2016b.

YouTube. 2016. Content ID. http://www.youtube.com/t/contentid. Accessed 26 Aug 2016.

Yu, Peter. 2004. The Escalating Copyright Wars. *Hofstra Law Review* 32: 907–951.

———. 2007a. Digital Piracy and the Copyright Response. In *The Internet and Governance in Asia. A Critical Reader*, ed. Indrajit Banerjee, 340–359. Singapore: Asian Media Information and Communication Centre.

———. 2007b. International Enclosure, The Regime Complex, and Intellectual Property Schizophrenia. *Michigan State Law Review* 2007b:1–33.

———. 2011. Digital Copyright and Confuzzling Rhetoric. *Vanderbilt Journal of Entertainment and Technology Law* 13: 881–939.

————. 2016. International Property Rulemaking in the Global Capitalist Economy. In *The Intellectual Property Right Domain in Contemporary Capitalism*, ed. Birgitte Andersen. New York: Routledge.

Zittrain, Jonathan. 2008. *Future of the Internet – And How to Stop It*. London: Yale University Press.

CHAPTER 3

Creative Content Online: 2008 European Commission Consultation

Chapters 3 through 6 delve in-depth into the empirical cases. They all follow the structure laid out in the analytical framework: each case study is scrutinized according to its *ideas, discourses, interests and institutions.* First, as discussed in the Introduction, ideas are the proposed definitions of a policy problem, the subsequent proposed policy solutions, and the theories upon which these problem definitions and solutions are built. In this context, it is useful to note that the words italicized in the section on copyright and Internet rationales correspond with categorizations introduced on these topics in Chap. 2 (Sects. 2.1.1.2 and 2.1.2.2). Second, discourses are the involved actors' argumentation of their policy problem definitions, solutions, theories and goals. In this section, we also analyze possible discourse structuration (reproduction of discourse by government or Parliament officials and departments during the policymaking process) and institutionalization (embedding of discourse into legal and supporting policy documents at the end of the policymaking process). Third, interests are the policy goals of involved actors, and the social and economic reality in which the policy develops. Fourth, institutions are the policy legacy, and the political and legal reality in which the policy develops. The words italicized in the section on the political and legal reality correspond to the IG models introduced in Chap. 2 (Sect. 2.4.1.2). The reader might note that the discussion on interests and institutions in the case studies is relatively short. Indeed, the focus

© The Author(s) 2017   125
T. Meyer, *The Politics of Online Copyright Enforcement in the EU*, Information Technology and Global Governance,
DOI 10.1007/978-3-319-50974-7_3

here is on developments specific to the policy at hand. I kindly refer back to Chap. 2 for an in-depth overview and discussion of the socioeconomic and politico-legal contexts common to all cases. The sections in each case study build on each other. Analyzing the case studies according to this structure gives political economic insight, builds on Chap. 2 and allows for comparability between the cases. The aim is to better understand *how and why online copyright enforcement policies develop in the EU: who are the actors involved, what do they say and which institutional rules and settings do they choose?*

In all four of my case studies, the stakeholders analyzed are international, European and national, and fit into five categories: media, Internet & technology, civil society, public authorities and others. The media comprises of the press, radio and television, but more broadly also entertainment sectors such as film, music, gaming, publishing, performance and so on. Moreover it stretches across the value chain: from author & performer trade unions and collective rights management societies to companies and associations of producers and distributors. Further, Internet & technology companies and their associations cover consumer electronics, software, telecom & cable and Internet services. The category of civil society is quite narrow. It includes associations endeavoring for consumer, civil and digital rights. Public authorities are both European and national, comprising of EU public authorities, national ministries but also of individual M(E)Ps and policy officers. Finally, the category of others consists of law & consultancy companies, academics, and companies and associations not related to media, Internet and technology. My categorization of stakeholders differs from the EC's own classification. I found that using fairly small stakeholder categories results in nuanced and meaningful data.[1]

In this chapter we have a closer look at the 2008 EC public consultation on CCO in the Single Market.[2]

The EC's CCO initiative ran from 2006 until 2011. The lead Directorate General was DG Information Society and Media (INFSO), which was renamed DG Communications Networks, Content and Technology (CONNECT) in 2012. The initiative consists primarily of *non-legislative actions* to deal with the challenges related to copyrighted content in the online environment: a European Charter for Film Online, a Content Online Platform, four public consultations, a Communication, a Reflection Document and a Green Paper. Although the EC (2008a) indicated that it aimed to prepare a Recommendation on Creative Content Online for adoption by the Council and the EP, the result was a Reflection Document on Creative Content in a European Digital Single Market (European Commission 2009a). Further, in 2011 a Green Paper with a more narrow scope on the Online Distribution of Audiovisual Works (European Commission 2011) was published. In conjunction with the Green Paper on Copyright in the Knowledge Economy (European Commission 2008b), CCO has served as a basis for proposing directives on orphan works (European Parliament & Council 2012) and multiterritorial rights licensing (European Parliament & Council 2014) (Fig. 3.1).

For this first case study, I analyzed *stakeholder responses to the last three questions of the second public consultation on CCO in the Single Market* (European Commission 2008c). The consultation provides early insight into stakeholder views on online copyright enforcement. Moreover as we notice below, the selected questions are highly pertinent to this book. The public consultation was annexed to a European Commission Communication (2008a).[3] In the Communication, the Commission identifies three objectives for policymakers in dealing with CCO:

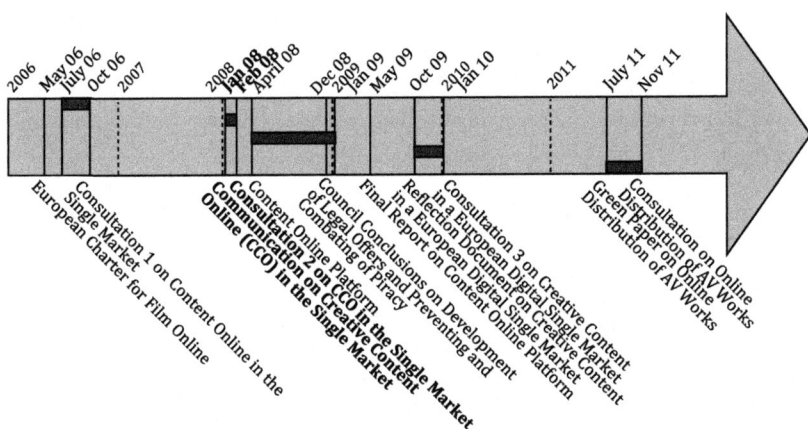

Fig. 3.1   Policy developments in Creative Content Online

Ensuring that European content achieves its full potential in contributing to European competitiveness and in fostering the availability and circulation of the great diversity of European content creation and of Europe's cultural and linguistic heritage;

Updating/clarifying possible legal provisions that unnecessarily hinder online distribution of creative content in the EU, while acknowledging the importance of copyright for creation;

Fostering users' active role in content selection, distribution and creation. (European Commission 2008a, 4)

Further "the Commission deems that there are four main, horizontal challenges which merit action at EU-level: availability of creative content; multi-territory licensing for creative content; interoperability and transparency of DRMs; and legal offers and piracy" (European Commission 2008a, 4). Dealing with copyright in the online environment requires a multifaceted approach.

The questions in the second public consultation deal specifically with the three latter challenges: multiterritorial rights licensing, DRM and legal offers and piracy.[4] The three questions analyzed in this case study concern legal offers and piracy:

How can increased, effective stakeholder cooperation improve respect of copyright in the online environment?

Do you consider the Memorandum of Understanding, recently adopted in France, as an example to [be] followed?

Do you consider that applying filtering measures would be an effective way to prevent online copyright infringements? (European Commission 2008a, 11)

I selected questions 9 through 11 as they are closely related to online copyright enforcement: cooperation, graduated response and use of filtering measures. Analysis of the responses to these questions (dating from 2008) provides *a baseline for my other cases, both in terms of substance and approach*. Stakeholders reflect on the involvement of Internet intermediaries, the need for legislative action at a European level and the suitability of the French graduated response model. Question 11 also provides unique insight into views on the use of technology to regulate.

In total 210 stakeholder contributions were analyzed (206 consultation submissions,[5] 3 Commission documents and 1 Council Conclusions). The answers to question 9 were open-ended, while the answers to questions 10 and 11 were coded as yes/no/nuanced/alternative. I opted for four (rather than binary yes/no) categories to code questions 10 and 11, as this allowed for more nuance in the analysis. The aim of the analysis was to reveal the proposed problem definitions, policy solutions and policy goals, the presence of emblematic issues and story lines, and the evidence of discourse coalitions, structuration and institutionalization.

CCO is an open invitation for policy stakeholders to determine the way forward for online copyright enforcement. It favors the development of a digital single market, but is surprisingly broad in its recommended problem definitions and policy solutions. The other three case studies start with a far more crystallized policy measure in mind. In CCO stakeholders debate without the threat of compulsory power at play. The policy outcome however, is largely non-legislative. The CCO initiative is an early example of the extent of controversy among stakeholders. The EC is at a loss concerning the appropriate way forward.

3.1 IDEAS

The lack of legal offers and of respect for copyright constitute challenges to CCO. The EC indicates in its 2008 Communication that content owners pressure it to take action. The Commission thus lists a number of complementary elements which it deems important when fighting piracy:

> Piracy and unauthorised up- and downloading of copyrighted content remains a central concern. The fight against online piracy involves a number of complementary elements: (1) developing legal offers; (2) educational initiatives; (3) enforcement of legal rights; (4) seeking improved cooperation from Internet Service Providers (ISPs) in stopping dissemination of infringing content. The idea of education and awareness-raising on the importance of copyright for the availability of content is widely supported as a tool in the fight against piracy. (European Commission 2008a, 7)

The Commission does not hesitate to identify legal offers as a means to deter copyright infringement. With the CCO initiative, the Commission aims for widespread availability of content. Approached from this angle, copyright could even be perceived as an impediment to a digital single market.

Right holders fear losing control as illegal copying in the digital environment has proven to be highly damaging. While legitimate online offer of creative content is widely regarded as one of the means of curbing illegal copying, some right holders prefer to protect existing revenue streams rather than actively licensing their rights on new platforms. (European Commission 2008a, 4)

The EC's policy goal to achieve a single market for online content comes through strongly in the follow-up Reflection Document to this Communication (European Commission 2009a). The document, jointly published by DG INFSO and DG MARKT, highlights several paradoxes. The importance of access to creative content *and* fair remuneration of creators is underlined. Illegal downloads on a large scale are acknowledged as a danger for an economically viable digital single market, *yet* new online services are seen as a response to piracy. Territoriality in copyright law is regarded as conflictual with the imperatives of a borderless single market, *but* it is also recognized as a way to maximize revenue. The tension between the protection and widespread distribution of creative content is continually emphasized. *The Commission documents on CCO* (2008a, 2009a, b) *often summarize stakeholder views and puts forward a variety of options for policy actions.* Overall however the CCO initiative tends toward a problem definition that emphasizes the importance of copyright and leans toward the increased availability and licensing of content as a policy solution. This is most pronounced in the Reflection Document (European Commission 2009a): the section on possible EU actions for the protection of rights holders does not propose measures for the enforcement of rights as one would expect, but rather deals with making available the right of authors and performers, the transparency of collective rights management societies, more collaboration with ISPs focusing on joint business models, and the provision of financial incentives through, for example, the EC Media program. Section 3.0 discusses a possible process of discourse institutionalization.

The following sub-sections set out the proposed problem definitions and policy solutions found in stakeholders' responses to the three analyzed questions. This section ends with an account of copyright and Internet rationales.

3.1.1   Problem Definitions and Policy Solutions

3.1.1.1   Increased, Effective Stakeholder Cooperation

Question 9: How Can Increased, Effective Stakeholder Cooperation Improve Respect for Copyright in the Online Environment?

Many stakeholders agree with the problem definition that breaches of copyright are a central concern and that respect for copyright in the online environment should be improved. Stakeholders either directly underline the importance of IPR and the scale of damages incurred through online piracy, or they indirectly concur by providing their views on policy solutions to improve respect for copyright.

> Digital piracy damages legitimate online commerce, and causes wider economic and societal damage. Digital piracy—unauthorized, unpaid electronic copying and distribution—competes unfairly with and undermines the business models for legitimate online content distribution. This kind of piracy, no less than physical piracy and counterfeiting, brings lost legitimate sales, lost taxes, lost jobs in upstream and downstream industries and lost innovation and competitiveness. (Microsoft 2008)

The European Consumers' Organization (BEUC), the European Telecommunications Network Operators' Association (ETNO) and British Telecommunications (BT) however, contest the Commission's use of the term "piracy". BT (2008) states that,

> [a]lthough 'piracy' can be used as an appropriate term to describe infringement of copyright works on a commercial scale, the use of the term to describe, indiscriminately, every infringement and allegation of infringement creates a barrier to constructive engagement and debate by all stakeholders. The term polarises and tends to exaggerate the level of unmeritorious behaviour by characterising any infringement as highly egregious.

The policy solutions proposed to improve respect for copyright in the online environment run along the same lines as the Commission's: development of legal offers, educational initiatives, enforcement of legal rights and ISP cooperation. Stakeholders disagree, however, on the prioritization and implementation of these solutions. Importantly although the responsibility of Internet intermediaries in the fight against piracy is stressed, it is not uncontested. Above all, it is insisted that collaboration of all stake-holders (including consumers) is required.

Thus first, most stakeholders agree that increased *stakeholder cooperation* is essential for improving respect of copyright in the online environment. The proposal of the Commission to set up a Creative Content Platform is received positively. Differences in stakeholder responses mainly pertain to the interpretation of which stakeholders to consider (and why). Some media producers think of stakeholders as only media distributors and creators. Others include *users* in the family as well, arguing that they should receive the same consideration as other stakeholders. A few author & performer organizations believe that the rights of *authors and composers* need to be safeguarded. *Verwertungsgesellschaft Bild-Kunst (VGBK)*, German collective rights management society for visual artists, refers to the imbalance in negotiation between authors and contracting companies, while the Danish Songwriters Guild argues that current EU recommendations undermine small players. Additionally, some stakeholders underline that the *European Commission (and other European institutions)* should play an active role in increasing stakeholder cooperation and improving respect of copyright in the online environment. The Association of Italian Film & Audiovisual Industries (ANICA–*Associazione Nazionale Industrie Cinematografiche Audiovisive e Multimediali*), the International Federation of Film Distributors Associations (FIADF) and the Interactive Software Federation of Europe (ISFE) argue that the EU and its member states are the principal actors in establishing a good IPR system. Alternatively, British Sky Broadcasting (BSkyB) believes legal and political initiatives should be taken on an international rather than a European level.

Second, many author & performer organizations, radio broadcasters, Internet & technology companies and a few others deem attractive, abundant and varied *legal offers* essential in the effort to improve respect for copyright. It is stressed above all that consumer demand must be met. Proposals for adapting the business models vary, however. The Digital Interoperability Forum and the European Digital Media Association (EDiMA) propose *industry-led guidelines and standards*, and British Music Rights (2008) argues for "licensing rather than policing". Other suggestions and conditions given for the development of legal offers are *alterations to the current windows release systems for audiovisual content, changes in licensing* such as increasing the transparency in the tariffs of collective rights management societies, *minimizing administrative burdens for Small- to Medium-Sized Enterprises (SMEs) and reforming the audio-*

visual remuneration system. The Association of European Radios (AER) suggests payment-per-use of audiovisual content, instead of private levies. The Internet Research and Innovation Institute Lithuania (IRII) similarly proposes *a reform of the levy system* so individuals rather than society carry the cost. The European Composer & Songwriter Alliance (ECSA) refers to a Swedish initiative of *blanket license deals* with ISPs to make downloading legal by way of a monthly license.

Third, a wide range of stakeholders stress the importance of *education* (mainly of users). Some think the Commission should take educational initiatives, like the creation of discussion groups and platforms. According to the European Bureau for Libraries, Archives and Documentation Association (EBLIDA), it must be ensured that users are aware of their rights as well as applicable restrictions. The Electronic Freedom Foundation (EFF) emphasizes that respect for copyright will only arise if interests of consumers are taken into account. Hotels, Restaurants & Cafés in Europe (HOTREC) also mentions the need for easy, speedy and affordable dispute settlement systems.

Fourth, comments are made about the current *legislation.* A variety of stakeholders criticize the *EU legal framework* for being *confusing,* thus making it difficult to comply to IPR. Accordingly BEUC and the European Information, Communications and Consumer Electronics Technology Industry Association (EICTA) share that private levies give the impression that free copying is allowed, and the Federation of European Film Directors (FERA) points to the long list of exemptions that Internet intermediaries use to justify minimal cooperation. Furthermore, while some stakeholders believe that IPR should be *adapted to the online world* and new technologies, others emphasize that a good (international and EU) framework is already in place. Along this line some stakeholders argue that it is in fact a proper *implementation of EU legislation* that is required, although the Independent Film and Television Alliance (IFTA) mentions that this has been a failure thus far. The Network of Regional Film Funds in Europe (Cine Regio), the International Music Publishers Association (IMPA), the Belgian collective managing society (SABAM) and NBC underline the importance of *case law,* such as the Belgian SABAM vs. Scarlet case to prevent illegal file sharing and the Danish Tele2 ruling to block access to two infringing sites AllofMP3.com and Pirate Bay. In opposition of the suggestions just described, the European Software Market Association (ESOMA) believes that copyright is a cultural issue and falls beyond the competency of the EC.

Finally, media stakeholders insist on the importance of *ISP cooperation* in the fight against online piracy. IMPA, Filmfolket and VMI directly challenge the role of intermediaries, calling for *stronger legal obligations* to collaborate. Some saw the reform of the Telecoms Package as an opportunity to introduce legal measures to "oblige" ISP to inform customers about what constitutes illegal practices in the online environment. SABAM and the International Association of Scientific, Technical and Medical Publishers (STM) emphasize that cooperation entails advantages for ISPs, such as freeing up bandwidth. Additionally, publishers mention the role of *search engines* in "favoring" illegal downloads and are of the opinion that they should collaborate and follow the ISPs' suit.

> ISPs and Search Engines hold a special position and are well-placed to facilitate, rather than obstruct, a culture of copyright compliance. Similar perhaps to banks and financial institutions in relation to money laundering and other improper transactions often times involving personal or private information, ISPs and Search Engines must do more to uphold the law and to explain to their customers not to confuse the Internet with a lawless environment in which copyrights can be infringed with impunity. (International Association of Scientific, Technical and Medical Publishers—STM 2008)

Alternatively, Internet & technology companies argue against improved ISP cooperation. Advestigo appeals for voluntary cooperation, but underlines that operational constraints and neutrality must be respected. Fastweb emphasizes that the sending of warning messages and disclosure of information should only happen by court order. Similarly, Microsoft does not believe that network operators should be responsible for defining illegal activity. Responses to questions 10 and 11 elaborate further on this last proposed policy solution.

3.1.1.2 Memorandum of Understanding in France

> Question 10: Do You Consider the Memorandum of Understanding, Recently Adopted in France, as an Example To [Be] Followed?

> In France, a Memorandum of Understanding between music and film producers, Internet service providers and the Government was signed on 23 November 2007. Under the agreement, France is to set up a new Internet authority with powers to suspend or cut access to the web for those who illegally file-share. (European Commission 2008a, 8)

At the time of the Commission's Communication (January 2008), many details of the French Memorandum of Understanding still needed to be worked out. The Memorandum was adopted into French law in June and October 2009. In this question 10, the EC asks whether graduated response is a policy solution to the problem of piracy. The responses were quite equally dispersed between the categories yes (34 %), no (29 %) and nuanced (33 %). Only a minority of the stakeholders expressed an alternative view (4 %).[6] While media distributors, media producers, private broadcasters, author & performer organizations, collective rights management societies and filtering software developers agree that the French Memorandum of Understanding should be considered as an example to be followed; publishers, public broadcasters, Internet & technology companies, law & consultancy companies, civil & digital rights groups and political organizations are more cautious and tend to disagree with the proposition (Fig. 3.2).

Most media stakeholders, filtering software developers and the Orange France Telecom Group *agree* with the French Memorandum. They applaud the achievement of reaching a *multistakeholder agreement* with forty-two signatories. Furthermore, the *involvement of the French authorities* and the *obligation for ISPs* to collaborate are considered crucial in the fight against

Question 10: Do You Consider the Memorandum of Understanding, Recently Adopted in France, as an Example To [Be] Followed?

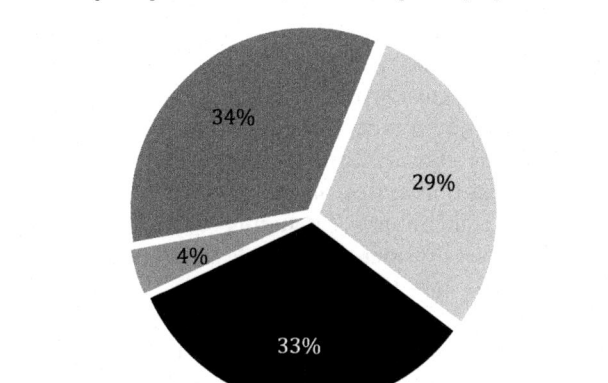

Fig. 3.2 Stakeholder views on MoU in France

online piracy. NBC mentions Recital 40 of the E-Commerce Directive to emphasize that although ISP liability is limited by the Directive, ISP cooperation is encouraged. This is interesting, as the E-Commerce Directive is most often used in opposition to the Memorandum of Understanding. Other appreciated aspects are the *setup of a special authority*, the use of *education measures* and warning messages, the focus on *legal offers* and the possibility to enforce *sanctions*. Vivendi, as a media distributor, especially welcomes the proposal for reduced VAT rates and the suspension of DRM. The French National Editors' Syndicate (SNE–*Syndicat National de l'Édition*) states that although they agree with the MoU in general, they do not believe DRM suspension would be appropriate for the publishing sector.

Internet & technology companies, civil society, public broadcasters, political organizations, law & consultancy companies, certain media stakeholders and Microsoft *disagree* with the French Memorandum. Their counterarguments mostly highlight negative aspects of the items just mentioned. Thus, they lament that *certain stakeholders were not involved* in the consultation process: consumers, collective rights management societies, performer organizations and software developers. Further, the European Competitive Telecommunication Association (ECTA), the Business Software Alliance (BSA) and Intel *oppose the imposing of requirements* and would have preferred an agreement formed on voluntary basis. eClassical. com and MacRoberts share the opinion that the MoU will further alienate the public and erode the respect for copyright. Indeed the French Organization in Defense of Digital Liberties (ODEBI–*Organisation Française de Défense des Libertés Numériques*) believes there is a conflict of interest in requesting Denis Olivennes, head of FNAC, to lead the discussions on the Memorandum, and the Green League (2008) argues that, "politicians can not be entrusted to alone hold the side of the people, as they represent all areas of life, thus also commerce."

Many opposing stakeholders (including the European Newspaper Publishers' Association) consider the *required collaboration of ISPs a possible violation of Article 15 of the E-Commerce Directive* (European Parliament & Council 2000), which stipulates that member states shall not impose a general obligation on intermediary service providers "to monitor the information which they transmit or store, nor a general obligation actively to seek facts or circumstances indicating illegal activity". According to BEUC (2008), ISPs are being transformed into "private Internet Service Police". Two open source movements (ANSOL–*Associação Nacional para o Software Livre* and Parti Pirate français) consider the MoU a reflection of the French authorities' desire to monitor and control. Furthermore, Internet companies and consumer, civil and digital rights groups strongly question the *proportionality and legality of suspending web access* for copyright infringers. It is stressed that cutting off the Internet connection of a subscriber will not only influence unauthorized copying, but also legitimate uses of the Internet. Moreover the subscriber is not necessarily the infringer. Is it proportionate and legitimate to cut off the Internet connection of a household? These stakeholders also mention the importance of the Internet in today's society to participate in public debate and communicate. The European Internet Services Providers Association (EuroISPA) argues that the MoU is contrary to the right to *freedom of expression*. BEUC is afraid of a chilling effect on free speech, as citizens and Small- to Medium-Sized Enterprise (SMEs) will play it safe rather than risk violating a law. Other fundamental rights that stakeholders deem jeopardized, are *the rights to privacy and data protection, the rights to defense and due process, and the presumption of innocence.*

Lastly, *practical issues* are mentioned. Very important is stakeholders' lack of trust in the *effectiveness of filtering*. Filtering is not considered accurate enough to distinguish between legal and illegal content and cannot provide an answer to encrypted content. Further, the GSM Europe Group and the Swedish Association for IT and Telecom Industries wonder how wireless hotspots and Internet cafés will be treated. ECTA points to the *cost* of filtering for broadband network operators. ECTA and the Hutchison Whampoa Europe–3 Group also stress the difficulty of only disconnecting the Internet when multiplay access (for instance a package-offer including broadband, television and telephone) prevails in the European market. The Hutchison Group and MacRoberts also argue that the costs of implementation will likely fall on Internet users. Finally, EFF underlines that controlling the Internet to the extent implied in the MoU constitutes a serious danger to the *open architecture of the Internet.*

At the time of the consultation, a wide cross-section of stakeholders expressed a *nuanced view*. They highlight both *positive and negative aspects* of the French Memorandum of Understanding. It should be observed that there are many correlations with the two previous discussions. Positive elements are the multistakeholder cooperation (providers, rights holders and government), the setup of a special authority, the education measures, the proposition of a reduced VAT rate and the focus on legal offers. Additionally, media stakeholders promote ISP liability. Two unique comments were made by the British Copyright Council and the Stockholm Network: the British Copyright Council finds that *the MoU lets ISPs off the hook*, and the Stockholm Network criticizes the MoU for *making IP owners concede rights*. Further, the French authorities do not believe their Memorandum of Understanding should simply be copied in other member states. It does, however, offer certain lines of thinking, such as sending of warning messages, cooperation between industry and government and a fiscal system favoring on-demand services. The UK Government (2008) also emphasizes the difficulty of applying the model in other contexts, but encourages member state dialogue, because "while the solutions might necessarily differ, the problem is common".

Negative aspects of the MoU are equally mentioned. EICTA criticizes the mandatory nature of the agreement, and Internet & technology companies find the disconnection of Internet a disproportionate measure. The VOIPEX Consortium argues that a fine would be more than sufficient. Furthermore, legal questions concerning fundamental rights (privacy, communication, data protection) and intermediary liability (E-Commerce Directive) are posed. The BBC and the European Broadcasting Union (EBU) stress the need for a means of appeal for those accused. Practical issues, such as the need to change French legislation in order to implement, the inefficiency of filtering measures and the difference between subscriber and infringer, are also discussed. Moreover, publishers wish to avoid a "one size fits all solution" and stress that *abandoning DRM* (as proposed in the Olivennes agreement) *is not desirable for the publishing sector*. ETNO and the VOIPEX Consortium are concerned that the increase of costs to high-speed broadband will negatively affect the digital divide.

Most stakeholders expressing a nuanced view deem that *the MoU is in too early a stage to evaluate* and suggest monitoring the process. Emphasis is given to the *balance* between offering legal online services and fighting copyright infringement, and between IPR and fundamental rights.

> [T]he Memorandum of Understanding in France as referred to in the consultation might be a workable solution in particular with respect to quick and cost effective dispute resolutions. However, as this model seems to be relatively new DACS favours the view that it would be preferable to monitor the activities and the effectiveness of this solution before finding European wide solutions following this example. (Design and Artists Copyright Society–DACS 2008)

Finally, four stakeholders expressed an *alternative view*. The Danish Society for Jazz, Rock and Folk Composers (DJBFA) was not aware of the Memorandum. The Federation for European Publishers (FEP) wishes to emphasize correct implementation of existing legislation, rather than to express a view on the French MoU. Further the Twentieth Century Fox Film Corporation shares that the first and preferred route should be commercial contracts and agreements, and Philips believes that the European debate should focus on meeting consumer demand.

3.1.1.3 Applying Filtering Measures

Question 11: Do You Consider that Applying Filtering Measures Would Be an Effective Way to Prevent Online Copyright Infringements?

It would indeed seem appropriate to instigate co-operation procedures ("code of conduct") between access/service providers and right holders and consumers in order to ensure a wide online offer of attractive content, consumer-friendly online services, adequate protection of copyrighted works, awareness raising/education on the importance of copyright for the availability of content and close cooperation fight piracy/unauthorised file-sharing. (European Commission 2008a, 8)

Neither the Commission Communication nor the Staff Working Document specifically mention the application of filtering measures. The Commission does, however, emphasize that instigating cooperation between access/service providers, rights holders and consumers seems appropriate and thus believes Internet intermediaries have a role to play in the fight against piracy. In this question the EC asks whether filtering measures is a policy solution to the problem of piracy. Comparable to question 10, most stakeholder contributions are distributed among the categories yes (33 %), no (34 %) and nuanced (27 %). A small number of stakeholders have been coded as alternative (6 %).[7] The stakeholders suffering most from online copyright infringements (media) are proponents of applying filtering measures. Contrarily, the organizations required to implement (Internet & technology), those defending consumer, civil & digital rights, law & consultancy companies, political organizations and research institutions are opponents. It should be noted that media distributors seem less agreed on filtering measures than they are on the French Memorandum of Understanding. The analysis also shows that within media producers, publishers are strongly opposed to filtering. Public broadcasters provide alternative views. Finally, although the France Orange Telecom Group and Rapid-Net reply positively to question 10, they oppose applying filtering measures. Throughout the contributions, it is continually emphasized that filtering is not a panacea and should be part of a package of solutions to prevent online copyright infringements (Fig. 3.3).

Many stakeholders *in favor of filtering measures* deem that they should be part of *a package of solutions.* As we will notice in the other categories, *different types of filtering* are identified. The International Federation of the Phonographic Industry (IFPI) distinguishes between content filtering based on fingerprints, protocol blocking and blocking access to infringing online locations. SABAM also mentions content filtering and P2P protocol blocking, emphasizing that they are automated filtering measures. Similarly the European Grouping of Societies of Authors and Composers (GESAC) and the French Society of Authors, Composers and Publishers of Music (SACEM–*Société des Auteurs, Compositeurs et Editeurs de Musique*) list content filtering (to be developed), P2P protocol filtering (reliable) and web 2.0 filtering (useful, but insufficient). The German Association of Video and Media Retailers *(Interessenverband des Video- und Medienfachhandels in Deutschland e.V.)* notes that although filtering

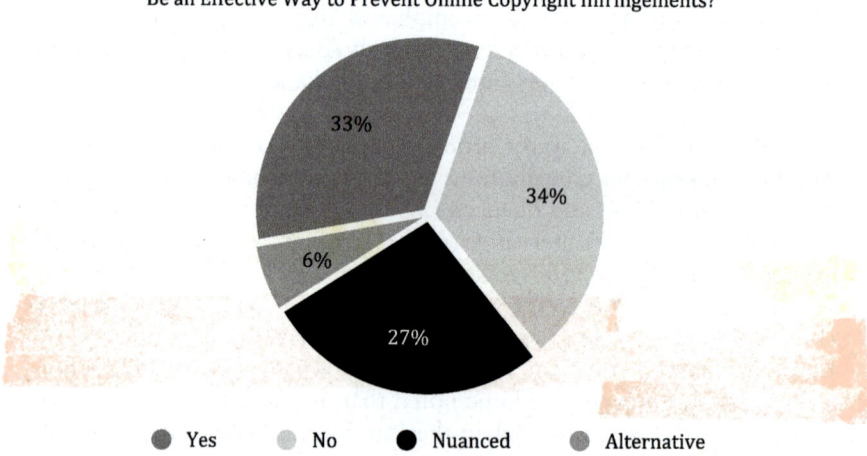

Question 11: Do You Consider that Applying Filtering Measures Would Be an Effective Way to Prevent Online Copyright Infringements?

33%

34%

6%

27%

● Yes   ● No   ● Nuanced   ● Alternative

Fig. 3.3 Stakeholder views on applying filtering measures

happens in households, it should also be implemented on websites, online services and search engines. Additionally, three software developers specializing in filtering solutions detail their approaches.

Advestigo explains that it prefers network level dynamic filtering (above static website filtering) and identification (above protocol/application traffic interdiction). Audible Magic uses a digital fingerprint technology (as opposed to watermarking). Their content recognition services are used by user generated content sites (such as MySpace and YouTube), by licensed P2P networks (such as iMesh and Kazaa) and on Internet access provider networks (mostly of university campuses). They also emphasize that private communications are not breached, as they only monitor public P2P file sharing applications. Finally ExcelMedia works on ISP backbones. They target P2P networks, and similar to Audible Magic they mention that copyrighted material is identified, not private communications. They argue that their filtering technology is legally sound, as media recognition and copyright enforcement happen in two distinct phases. Although they acknowledge that filtering can lead to the use of encryption, they believe this circumvention will slow down P2P conversations, which will promote legal versions of P2P networks.

Filtering measures are contentious and media stakeholders provide arguments to counter those opposed to applying filtering measures. Several stakeholders state that filtering is beneficial for network operators as it *helps with congestion*. NBC Universal compares content recognition technologies to sieves, very comparable to how ISPs treat spam and viruses. IFPI points out that some ISPs already monitor their networks (to throttle) and thus filtering would *not* be *too costly*. Further the association representing the recording industry believes filtering *neither violates the E-Commerce Directive, nor the rights to privacy and data protection*. Many media stakeholders argue for *increased ISP liability*. The Creative Media Business Alliance (CMBA 2008) deems that a distinction should be made between censorship and filtering of illegal content:

> Censorship and filtering of illegal content are two totally distinct matters that should remain separate. In short, filtering measures are based on content recognition technologies that are neither meant nor designed to threaten the universal right of freedom of expression.

This doesn't change the fact that false positives still occur / or do they?

Finally the Belgian SABAM vs. Scarlet court ruling clearly was the show-case argument for proponents of Internet filtering. The first instance decision required the ISP Scarlet (formerly Tiscali) to implement filtering measures to prevent P2P copyright infringement on its network. In 2011 the CJEU found that this decision was not compatible with EU law (November 24, 2011). The court case is mentioned by a total of fourteen media stakeholders.

The main arguments for *opponents of filtering measures* concern proportionality, effectiveness, encryption, cost, limited liability, right to privacy and right to freedom of expression. They are objections on societal, technical, economic and legal grounds. Concerning *different types* of filtering measures, the French Association for Internet Access & Service Providers (AFA–*Association des Fournisseurs d'Accès et de Services Internet*) shares that filtering can occur by blocking an IP address, a domain name or a URL. More important, however, is the distinction made between filtering by ISPs and Internet access providers (IAPs). Several Internet companies and publishers deem blocking by ISPs (on the level of online services) reasonable, but by IAPs (on the level of networks) disproportionate and ineffective. Further many stakeholders argue that the measures taken to combat copyright infringement are *disproportionate* compared to measures against other illegal behaviors. For instance, comparison is made between losing your driver's license and losing your Internet connection. Only in extreme circumstances is a driver's license retracted, while the French graduated response initiative proposed disconnection of Internet access after three warnings. The *Association Bordelaise des Utilisateurs de Logiciels Libres* (ABUL), a non-profit open source movement, and ESOMA contend that filtering measures are further proof of the media industries' perseverance in holding onto failed (analogue) business models.

> The EU is not well advised to step into Chinese footsteps and create precedence for online communication censorship through carriers for the sake of the financial benefit of the content industry and its inability to adapt to market environmental change. (European Software Market Association–ESOMA 2008)

The warning about the slippery slope of Internet filtering (unintended consequences) is not only brought up by ESOMA, but also by several other stakeholders, such as the European Newspaper Publishers' Association

(ENPA), the Danish IT-Political Association (Larsen), the French Pirate Party and a French association defending digital rights (ODEBI).

Internet & technology companies and civil society also oppose applying filtering measures based on *issues related to effectiveness and implementation*. In this context, the possibility to *circumvent* the technologies through encryption is deemed a very important sign of ineffectiveness. Some consider the *cost* of implementation for intermediaries, which could be passed on to Internet users, problematic. Additionally, ECTA points out that current technologies cannot distinguish well between legal and illegal content. Indeed the case is made that they tend to either *over or under block* content. AFA lists the evolution of P2P protocols, the scale of filtering required, the asymmetry of Internet traffic and the assignment of different IP addresses to users, as factors adding to the ineffectiveness of filtering measures.[8] Furthermore, some stakeholders refer to *unintended consequences* of applying filtering measures. The rise of encryption technologies was already mentioned. Several stakeholders warn that the quality of the networks and services will decrease. The Swedish Association for IT & Telecom Industries (2008) believes filtering creates a great threat for "Europe's further development as a modern, interactive and free society", while BEUC and ETNO are concerned about fragmenting consumer rights across member states.

Furthermore closely related to the arguments made about the French Memorandum of Understanding, *judicial risks* are taken into account. Stakeholders are of the opinion that filtering will not only limit illegal content/use, but *legal content/use* as well. Furthermore, requiring network operators to monitor and filter is considered contrary to *the E-Commerce Directive*. It is also shared that the decision to apply filtering measures should be taken by a public rather than a private body. BEUC and Cable Europe warn against inserting increased intermediary liability in the Telecoms Package. Other judicial risks raised concern the compatibility of Internet filtering with the *rights to privacy, data protection and freedom of expression*.

Lastly *alternative solutions* to preventing online copyright infringements are given. Several stakeholders deem that filtering should only happen at the level of the end user. EDiMA agrees with filtering at the level of services, if it has the objective of favoring the availability of content online. Others believe filtering is only warranted to combat *child abuse*. It is emphasized that the focus should be on prevention rather than on ex post remedies. *Education programs and legal offers* are preferred. Indeed

IRII considers the lack of legal offers the primary cause of online copyright infringement.

Stakeholders expressing a *nuanced view* equally mention *differences between types of filtering.* The French Association for Internet Community Sites (ASIC–*Association des Services Internet Communautaires*), Microsoft and Yahoo! consider that filtering at the level of services, when voluntary, can be beneficial, but that filtering at the level of networks presumes that surveillance is common practice. The European Publishers Council prefers TPMs over network filtering measures. Many stakeholders in this category do not deem implementation should take place before further analysis of filtering technologies are performed. Nor do they consider applying filtering measures a panacea for the prevention of online copyright infringement. For instance Yahoo! Europe (2008) believes that, "silver bullet thinking" about filtering measures should be avoided and emphasizes that there is a need for holistic approaches that work from the bottom up. Self- or co-regulatory measures are thus encouraged. Other policy solutions that need to be pursued are *educational programs, legal offers and monitoring to better remunerate artists.*

Other issues that raise uncertainty with stakeholders have already been discussed. They mainly concern *implementation:* the possibility to circumvent, the inability to distinguish well between legal and illegal content/use and the cost; *unintended consequences:* the degradation of the quality of service and the danger for an open and neutral Internet; and *judicial risks:* the restriction of legal content/use, the danger for limited ISP liability, for the right to privacy and for the right to freedom of expression. Telecom Italia underlines that an assessment of the proportionality of the measures should be made and that attention should be paid that fundamental rights are ranked higher than property rights. Telecom Italia also disapproves of the decision taken by the Belgian court in the SABAM vs. Scarlet case.

Finally various *alternative views* concerning the application of filtering measures are expressed. These stakeholders do not clearly express an opinion, but deem the problem lays elsewhere. April, a non-profit open source movement, argues that filtering should only happen at the level of the individual user. The Business Software Alliance (BSA 2008) identifies the "overboard interpretation of privacy laws" as the key issue which has prevented rights holders from "effectively investigating open and notorious piracy". Nokia argues that filtering technology should be used to generate information about traffic, and Philips is of the opinion that filtering measures should be an opt-in condition in P2P sharing software. The

Digital Media Project believes filtering measures will prove unnecessary if DRM is made interoperable.

Additionally, Liberty Global Europe provides alternative explanations to several technological issues associated with filtering, pertaining to the ineffectiveness of filtering at the level of transmission (technology is continually advancing and the Internet was built to be flexible and resilient), the availability of other protection measures (they do not believe network filtering is more effective than media-based protection) and the cost (networks were not built to be content aware).

Lastly, certain Internet & technology companies believe that ensuring the availability of legitimate attractive offers should be considered as important as applying filtering measures.

> As a matter of principle, use of technologies should not be punished rather improper use of the content. From a business point of view, we believe that fighting piracy is not only a question of implementing technology measures but of offering 'value for money'. The key to success would be to achieve the right balance between both. (Telefónica/O2 2008)

3.1.2   Copyright and Internet Rationales[9]

The copyright rationales that come through in the stakeholder contributions to the 2008 public consultation are copyright as an *economic incentive* and remuneration for the benefit of rights holders, and as access for the benefit of society *(social requirements)*. At times these objectives are considered complementary. Other times they are deemed in conflict. The Royal Institute of Technology Stockholm (KTH 2008) argues for an approach that includes new creators. Further although the third CCO objective calls for "[f]ostering users' active role in content selection, distribution and creation", this topic is reduced to orphan works and consumer access in the consequent Communication and in the Reflection Document.

Much of the stakeholder discussion regarding the Internet concerns its *commercial rationale*. The French Association for Internet Community Sites (ASIC 2008, translated from French) states that, "[i]n a context where employment and competitiveness are at the center of political debates, the new generation Internet seems to be one of those key areas of innovation from which France and Europe could benefit." The Internet is described as providing challenging new opportunities. ESOMA refers specifically to Schumpeterian competition and calls for environmental change. Some however highlight the Internet's value for citizens and the importance of its open and flexible architecture as well *(social interaction and symbolic belonging, pursuit of science)*. The Electronic Frontier Foundation (EFF 2008) argues that,

> [t]he explosion of innovation and expression that the knowledge economy has witnessed in so short a time has been built on top of networks designed to facilitate the flows of information and knowledge, not to set up checkpoints.

After this extensive look at ideas on stakeholder cooperation, graduated response and filtering, the following sections expand on the discourses, policy goals, policy legacy, socioeconomic and politico-legal context of CCO. Box 3.1 summarizes our findings on stakeholder ideas on CCO in the single market.

3.2   Discourses

Emblematic issues and story lines are woven into stakeholders detailing their problem definitions and proposing policy solutions. I identify three key discourses in the CCO 2008 public consultation. As a reminder, discourses are complex and dynamic. They are not necessarily coherent sets of arguments and can often be interpreted and adopted in various ways. This feature of discourses permits stakeholders to form coalitions without necessarily agreeing on problem definitions, policy solutions and/or goals.

3.2.1   Challenging, New Opportunities

> The availability and take-up of broadband, and the increasing possibility to access creative content and services everywhere and anytime, provide challenging new opportunities. (European Commission 2008a, 1)

Many stakeholders start their contributions with an acknowledgment that the business environment of converging media and online distribution has resulted in *challenging new opportunities*. As we have noticed, the emphasis on whether the situation is primarily challenging or rather providing new opportunities differs. The nascence of the online market spurs some stakeholders to support minimal regulatory intervention. It

Box 3.1   Ideas in creative content online

Analysis of stakeholder responses to the last three questions of the second public consultation on Creative Content Online in the Single Market (2008)

- Question 9: Stakeholder Cooperation
  - Online copyright infringement is the central policy problem
  - Stakeholder cooperation is essential, but disagreement on which stakeholders to include
  - Disagreement on the prioritization and details of policy solutions— development of legal offers, educational initiatives, enforcement of legal rights, ISP cooperation

- Question 10: French Memorandum of Understanding
  - Split views yes/no/nuanced
  - Arguments in favor: involvement of public authorities, obligation of ISP cooperation, combination of education/legal offers/sanctions vs. arguments against: disproportionality/illegality of ISP cooperation and suspension of access, ineffectiveness and cost

- Question 11: Applying Filtering Measures
  - Split views yes/no/nuanced, filtering measures are not a panacea
  - Arguments in favor: increased ISP liability, no violation of E-Commerce Directive/fundamental rights vs. arguments against: disproportionality, ineffectiveness, cost, violation of E-Commerce Directive/fundamental rights

- Copyright Rationales
  - Economic incentive, social requirements
  - Importance of cultural diversity

- Internet Rationales
  - Entrepreneurship, social interaction & symbolic belonging, pursuit of science
  - Importance of open and flexible architecture

is worth reminding that the Commission's public consultation deals not only with legal offers and piracy, but multiterritorial rights licensing and the interoperability and transparency of DRM as well. Media stakeholders call for increased ISP collaboration, even regulatory intervention, to fight online piracy. Further in the context of these challenging new opportunities, stakeholders widely adopt use of emblematic issues such as *innovation and creativity in a knowledge-based society*. Views on whether we need more or rather less copyright to achieve innovation and creativity vary. Media stakeholders emphasize the need for the EC to consider the importance of copyright in encouraging *cultural diversity*. Contrarily the Internet Research and Innovation Institute Lithuania (IRII 2008) deems that, "creative uses of copyrighted content are increasingly limited and social uses burdened. Thus, perception of copyright has changed from the instrument of creativity into the cashing instrument."

3.2.2   Gatekeepers in the Online World

Internet Service Providers are, whether they like it or not, gatekeepers in the online world. They therefore have a responsibility to help control traffic on their networks. In our case that responsibility lies with the traffic of that which is unauthorised and which infringes copyright or other intellectual property rights. (British Copyright Council 2008)

Media stakeholders across the value chain and across sectors view increased ISP cooperation and responsibility as a policy solution. They stress that ISPs benefit from the widespread distribution of copyrighted content on their networks and that these stakeholders are now part of the media value chain as well. ISPs are considered *gatekeepers, check points in the online world*. The heat is mainly directed toward network operators although there are also calls for closer involvement of search engines. Internet & technology companies, civil society and political organizations counter that increased collaboration would have the detrimental effect of ISPs serving as the *police men in the online world*. Moreover EuroISPA (2008) harshly criticizes the music industry's media campaign, stating that, "within the context of long-standing and constructive dialogue in several EU member states between ISPs and the music and film industries, media leaks and campaigns by the music industry against ISPs are very disappointing and fundamentally counterproductive. Much of what has been relayed in the press is inaccurate, misleading and does not contribute to much needed productive and proportionate self regulatory approaches."

3.2.3 Breaches to Limited Liability and Fundamental Rights

Europe has had a world-leading approach to key aspects of human rights and data protection principles. The relevant laws, directives and international legal instruments are the basis of decades of public policy development and agreement. Any agreement needs to avoid destabilising or contradicting this agreed public policy, by either breaching the letter or spirit of existing legislation or by inadvertently acting as a 'thin end of the wedge' which cause unintended consequences for European citizens. (European Internet Services Providers Association—EuroISPA 2008)

Internet & technology companies, civil society and political organizations object to increased ISP cooperation and responsibility through the proposed schemes of graduated response and filtering measures, on grounds of the limited liability provisions in the E-Commerce Directive and fundamental rights (the rights to freedom of expression, privacy and data protection, defense and due process, and presumption of innocence). They deem that the laws provide high standards and need to be upheld. Increased ISP cooperation would have a *chilling effect on citizens and companies*. Arguments against suspension of Internet access and filtering measures also relate to a lack of proportionality and effectiveness. Stakeholders across the board emphasize that there is *no panacea for online piracy*.

3.2.4 Discourse Coalitions, Structuration and Institutionalization

The discourse coalitions formed in this case study are among *media stakeholders on the one hand, and Internet & technology companies, civil society and political organizations on the other hand*. Notable exceptions are publishers (against increased ISP cooperation on grounds of freedom of expression and press), author & performer organizations and to a certain extent collective rights management societies (seeking further involvement and remuneration for authors and performers in negotiations), public broadcasters (nuanced on graduated response and filtering) and France Telecom Orange Group (involved in the French negotiations and consequently agrees with graduated response). Box 3.2 provides further insight.

It is not possible to determine whether *discourse structuration* (reproduction of discourse by government or Parliament officials and departments during the policymaking process) took place, as this case study only analyzed stakeholder contributions in January and February 2008. Exceptions to this time selection are my analysis of European Commission and Council documents: the Commission published the Final Report on the Content Online Platform in May 2009 and the Reflection Document on Creative Content in a European Digital Single Market in October 2009. The Council Conclusions on the Development of Legal Offers and Preventing and Combating of Piracy date from December 2008. Analysis of these policy documents gave insight into *discourse institutionalization* (embedding of discourse into legal and supporting policy documents at the end of the policymaking process). There was no true shift in discourse. The Commission did take up the remarks of media stakeholders concerning cultural diversity and included this theme in its Content Online Platform. Moreover, the Commission Reflection Document expands on differences between media sectors. The 2011 Green Paper looks specifically at online distribution of audiovisual works and the proposal for a Directive on multiterritorial licensing of rights limits itself to musical works. At the same time however, the Commission asserts strongly in its Reflection Document that adaptations are necessary in an online environment. Copyright is considered a possible barrier to achieving a digital single market. Further despite many stakeholders' admonitions to maintain a light touch approach to regulation, the Commission (2009a, 21) states that it "intends to continue to take a pro-active role in order to ensure a culturally diverse and rich online content market for consumers, while creating adequate possibilities for remuneration and improved conditions in the digital environment for rightholders". In summary, the Commission is open in its definition of the policy problem and solution at hand, but is clear in its goal to develop a digital single market. In comparison the Council is more vague, seeking the middle ground between various stakeholders' discourses. The Council Conclusions underline the opportunities *and* challenges of the online environment. Indeed it notes that "online piracy, which in some cultural and creative sectors is reaching a critical threshold, is likely to do lasting harm to the appropriate remuneration of copyright holders and holders of related rights; besides its consequences for the marketing of traditional media (CD, DVD, et cetera), it is a major factor holding back the

Box 3.2   Discourse coalitions, structuration and institutionalization on creative content

Analysis of stakeholder responses to the last three questions of the second public consultation on Creative Content Online in the Single Market (2008)

As the first discourse is common to all stakeholders, I only detail the discourse coalitions for the latter two discourses. I also mention stakeholders whose views do not fit the latter two discourses and/or are particularly distinctive within their category.

Challenging. New Opportunities

- Common to all stakeholders

Gatekeepers in the Online World

- Media Stakeholders
  - Companies and associations of content producers such as ICMP, IMPA, MPA, NBC, Twentieth Century Fox and VMI
  - Companies and associations of content distributors such as IFPI, Mediaset, PACT and Vivendi
  - Companies and associations of private broadcasters such as ACT, AER and BSkyB
  - Author & performer organizations and collective rights management societies such as ALADDA, DACS, FERA, GESAC and SABAM
  - Film funds such as Cine Regio and UKFC

Breaches to Limited Liability & Fundamental Rights

- Internet & Technology Industries
  - Companies and associations of fixed/mobile telecoms operators and ISPs such as AFA, BT, Cable Europe, ECTA, EuroISPA and Telefónica 02

- Civil Society
  - Civil rights organizations & associations such as BEUC, EURALVA, MUCE and UFC Que Choisir
  - Digital rights organizations such as EFF, ODEBI, Public Knowledge and ORG
  - Free and open software organizations such as ABUL, ANSOL and April

(continued)

Box 3.2   (continued)

- Media Stakeholders
  - Publisher associations such as ENPA, EPC, FEP and UK Publishers Association
  - Public broadcasters such as BBC and EBU
- Political Organizations
  - Such as Die Linke and Green League

Other
- EU Public Authorities (nuanced)
  - European Commission
  - Council of the European Union
- Media Stakeholders (positive on further artist involvement)
  - Author & performer organizations and collective rights management societies such as AEPO-ARTIS, Danish Songwriters Guild, FIM and VGBK
- Internet & Technology Industries
  - France Telecom Orange Group (positive on graduated response)
  - Filtering software providers: Advestigo, Audible Magic and ExcelMedia (positive on filtering)
  - Companies and associations of online service providers such as ASIC, Google and Yahoo! (nuanced on filtering)
  - Companies and associations of consumer electronics such as ASIMELEC, Microsoft and Panasonic (nuanced on filtering)

Discourse Structuration and Institutionalization
- Discourse Structuration
  - Not possible to determine

- Discourse Institutionalization
  - No shift in discourse—European Commission and Council of the European Union seek middle ground between various stakeholder discourses
  - European Commission—open in definition of policy problem and solution; digital single market with wide availability of content as policy goal

development of the legal provision of cultural and CCO on which, to a large extent, the dynamism of the European industry for cultural and creative content depends, and threatens cultural creativity and diversity" (Council of the European Union 2008). The Council believes that policy solutions lie in the development of legal offers *and* preventing and combating of piracy.

3.3 INTERESTS

3.3.1 Policy Goals

The policy goals of the stakeholders sometimes overlap and sometimes differ. As mentioned in the Introduction, the European Commission (2008a, 4) identifies three objectives which need to be met to make the most of the transfer of creative content to the online environment: "ensuring that European content achieves its full potential", "updating/clarifying possible legal provisions that unnecessarily hinder online distribution of creative content in the EU, while acknowledging the importance of copyright for creation", and "fostering users' active role in content selection, distribution and creation". The Commission's ultimate policy goal is to achieve a digital single market with *wide availability of creative content.* Civil society similarly seeks wide availability of content, but equally *closer involvement in policymaking processes.* Likewise authors and performers wish to put their mark on the board, asking for *more remuneration* and closer involvement in policymaking processes and private negotiations. Further in this policy initiative, publishers hope to *ward off DRM suspension* and stress the need to distinguish between media sectors. More generally media stakeholders and rights holders aim for *respect of copyright and intellectual property rights.* Their policy-specific goal is *increased ISP cooperation and liability.* They seek to communicate that piracy is a big problem. Software providers as rights holders also aim for respect of copyright. Contrarily, Internet & technology companies seek to communicate that piracy is a small problem. Their policy goal is to *ward off increased ISP cooperation and liability,* offering a wider definition of the problem at hand.

3.3.2   Social and Economic Reality

The Commission Staff Working Document accompanying the Communication (2008d) and the Reflection Document (2009a) provide insights into the social and economic reality in which the CCO initiative developed. These documents published in 2008 and 2009 address a wider range of challenges in different media sectors than can be found in the Communication and the public consultation. Piracy is identified as a problem alongside other changes in the production and distribution of media. Challenges differ between media sectors. First, the documents (European Commission 2008d, 2009a) point to the decline in the physical *music* market. They argue that the music sector was among the first to use the Internet for a distribution platform, but that its DRM tools are ill perceived by consumers. Moreover online licensing has proved difficult due to the fragmentation of rights among owners. Second, in the *film* sector DVD sales were plateauing. The lack of harmonization among the rights of performers (actors) across the EU is deemed problematic. Further statutory and contractual windowing provisions cause fragmentation in an already territorialized audiovisual market. The Commission Reflection Document (2009a) also points out that online platforms do not finance film production in the same fashion as traditional distributors do (for instance in prepurchasing rights). Nor do they play the same role in film promotion as cinema exhibitors. Actors and roles are shifting and converging in the online environment. Third, much experimenting is still present in radio and television *broadcasting*. The Commission Staff Working Document (2008d) states that advertising for online radio is small, but that television on demand has taken off. Fourth, the market for online *publishing* and ebooks remains niche and print advertising is in decline. Digitization of books and other literary and artistic works is desired, but at the time was limited by licensing difficulties for out-of-print and orphan works. Fifth, the Commission (2008d, 2009a) deems the *gaming* sector the most advanced and consistent in the online market. There seem to be less cultural and linguistic differences in the video game market.

In line with the Commission's analysis, the Council (2008) invites the Commission in its Conclusions "to contribute to improving knowledge [...] of the digital cultural economy in all its diversity, in particular of legal online offer, and of piracy: its scale, its causes and its consequences for the economy of creation and cultural diversity", thus recognizing the need for alternative problem definitions as well. Finally, a few stakeholders underline interests at play in this CCO policymaking process: big versus small players, commercial versus non-commercial interests, media versus Internet & technology industries. The Federation of European Film Directors (FERA 2008) states that,

> in light of the imbalance in the economic and lobbying power of the service providers (Information and Communication Technology/Content Distributors) versus the content creators (authors and producers) we believe in the need for a stable and harmonised legal environment which recognises the existing legal rights of European film directors to equitable remuneration.

3.4   INSTITUTIONS

3.4.1   Policy Legacy

In terms of policy legacy, the contention over ISP cooperation pertains to the implementation and acceptability of the 2000 E-Commerce Directive. Media stakeholders deem that the liability provisions are either not properly implemented or require adaptation. Internet & technology companies, civil society and political organizations draw on the EU's fundamental rights tradition to oppose graduated response and filtering measures. At the time of the CCO public consultation, the first CJEU case on online copyright enforcement had not obliged to put in place a rule for the disclosure of personal data of Internet users in the context of a civil procedure (Promusicae vs. Telefónica, January 29, 2008, Coudert and Werkers 2010). Media stakeholders accuse Internet & technology companies of hiding behind the E-Commerce Directive and data protection legislation to "get a free lunch". They think rather the Belgian SABAM vs. Scarlet case is an example to be followed. The Stockholm Network (2008) believes that,

> all relevant parties must bear their fair share of responsibility. This does not only include content creators and end users, but intermediaries including ISPs, and online content mediators and aggregators. This more balanced

approach would ensure more thorough and effective responses to piracy can be initiated, rather than the pervasive buck-passing that occurs at present.

British Telecommunications and Yahoo! urge the EC to ensure consistency across policy initiatives, avoiding unnecessary duplication between Directorate Generals. Sun Microsystems (2008) concurs stating that, "[c]ontinuing to apply patches to law that was framed prior to the existence of peer communications technologies has the unfortunate side-effect of reinforcing the commercial standing of incumbents and discriminating against innovative newcomers."

3.4.2   Political and Legal Reality

Finally, regarding political and legal reality, it is important to note that DG INFSO led the CCO initiative. Along with the Green Paper on Copyright in the Knowledge Economy (European Commission 2008b) CCO served as a basis for preparing two Directives on Certain Permitted Uses of Orphan Works (European Parliament & Council 2012) and on Collective Management of Copyright and Multi-Territorial Licensing of Rights in Musical Works for Online Uses in the Internal Market (European Parliament & Council 2014). The same line of thinking put forward in Creative Content Online Reflection Document (2009a) can also be found in the Commission flagship initiative Digital Agenda for Europe (European Commission 2010): the Commission takes on a proactive role to achieve a digital single market for citizens and companies.

Due to questions 10 and 11 on graduated response and filtering measures, many stakeholders in this case study express views on IG models and technological governance for content control. BSkyB, IMPA and NBC Universal stress the need for an international approach, as "piracy is an international phenomenon and 'solutions' should at least aspire to be internationally 'compatible'" (International Music Publishers' Association—IMPA 2008; NBC Universal 2008) *(transnational institutions and international organizations)*. Moreover stakeholders emphasize respect of copyright, making no distinction between online and offline activities. Copyright is considered valid in the physical *and* the digital world *(national governments and law)*. For media stakeholders technological governance is permissible and desirable to fight online piracy. Internet & technology companies and civil society counter that: "[t]echnological

Box 3.3   Interests and institutions in creative content

Analysis of stakeholder responses to the last three questions of the second public consultation on Creative Content Online in the Single Market (2008)

Interests

- Policy Goals
  - Diverse among stakeholders
- Social and Economic Reality
  - Stakeholders mark interests at play—big vs. small, commercial vs. non-commercial, media vs. Internet & technology
  - EC acknowledges challenges differ between media sectors

Institutions

- Policy Legacy
  - Contestation over E-Commerce Directive and fundamental rights
  - Argumentation based on Promusicae-Telefónica and SABAM-Scarlet cases
- Political and Legal Reality
  - No legislative policy outcome
  - IG—transnational institutions and international organizations, national governments and law, market and economics, code and Internet architecture

developments should be used to improve users' access not to restrict it" (Google 2008). Preservation of the Internet's current design is believed essential for innovation, freedom of expression and access to knowledge *(code and Internet architecture)*. Intel (2008) points to the non-neutrality of technology stating that,

[d]igital technologies are creating an information society with converging markets based on digital goods and services. Digital technologies are, of course, tools that obey the hands that wield them, both for good and evil.

Lastly, the *market and economics* model of IG is strongly supported in the responses to the public consultation. Many stakeholders deem legal offers an important policy solution and advocate non-intervention.

3.5   CONCLUSION: PEC CONSIDERATIONS

Voluntary collaboration and stakeholder dialogues on CCO failed. CCO illustrates the difficulty to reach an agreement on online copyright enforcement, even—or perhaps especially—in a context where there is no legislative proposal on the line. *In this public consultation there are no agreed problem definitions or policy solutions among stakeholders.* CCO provides us with extensive insights into stakeholders' polarized views on technological governance. Media stakeholders call for increased intermediary cooperation. Internet, technology and civil society actors question the proportionality, cost and effectiveness of tackling online piracy through graduated response or filtering measures. In both cases fundamental rights and limited liability are wielded as swords to advocate either for or against governance through technology. CCO focuses on commercial aspects of the Internet, although graduated response and filtering have also brought argumentations on the value of the Internet for social interaction and symbolic belonging to the fore. *Media stakeholders seek to shift the framing away from the Internet toward copyright and the role of Internet intermediaries in the media value chain.* Argumentations on cultural diversity aim to underline the value of copyright for society.

Does CCO demonstrate a standoff between Internet and media companies? Yes, but it also does more. Part of the debate revolves around access or control, legal offers or ISP cooperation. However CCO also clearly shows that there are tensions within the media sectors. Authors, performers, collective rights management societies, publishers and public broadcasters do not always tow the party line. Furthermore it seems evident that civil society organizations partner with Internet & technology companies in this case study. Civil society perceives the proposed policy solution of technological governance as requiring a choice between copyright and the Internet. Based on stakeholder contributions, the EC could not identify a middle ground.

In essence CCO is a battle of ideas. Stakeholders compete on an equal basis, advocating their views through consultation contributions. They are given almost entirely freehand to determine EC policy in this area. The side note is that the Commission remains an active policy actor in the policymaking process. It does not predetermine problems or solutions, but does aim for widespread availability of creative content in the EU. Moreover the Commission Reflection Document takes up the issue of creators' remuneration. *It could be argued that Internet & technology companies, consumers (although not necessarily citizens) and authors & performers "win" this round, as they gain productive traction with the EC. At the same time it is important to analyze CCO alongside other online copyright enforcement initiatives.* This is a non-legislative exercise, and stakeholders clearly advocate their ideas and interests in other policy venues as well. In the next chapter, we follow up on graduated response and explore the French legislative endeavor to tackle online piracy.

NOTES

1. I am aware that these categories can be contested. For instance, sometimes author & performer organizations are considered civil society. Further due to convergence companies in the Internet & technology category are also involved in media distribution. It should also be noted that Internet & technology companies are often holders of IPR (such as patents, trademarks and copyright). Finally, I consider public authorities—policymakers as stakeholders as well. In my analysis I try to consistently highlight similarities and differences between categories, sectors and stakeholders.
2. Parts of this chapter can be found in (Van Audenhove et al. 2009). I have exclusively used sections of the report for which I was responsible and which I wrote.
3. A Staff Working Document accompanied the Communication as well (European Commission 2008d).
4. Although stakeholder responses often included views on the availability of content as well.
5. All stakeholder submissions to the public consultation are available at (European Commission 2008c). I kindly refer readers interested in consulting the stakeholder opinions mentioned in the body of the text to this repository. When quoting stakeholders directly, I have included in-text references, which point back to this same online location. Throughout the chapter, stakeholders are first mentioned with their complete names, whereafter only their abbreviations are used.

6. These statistics are calculated by dividing the total amount of answers found in one category (yes: 57, no: 48, nuanced: 55, alternative: 6) by the total amount of answers submitted to question 10 (total: 172).

7. These statistics are calculated by dividing the total amount of answers found in one category (yes: 52, no: 55, nuanced: 41, alternative: 10) by the total amount of answers submitted to question 11 (total: 152).

8. The "asymmetry of traffic" refers to simultaneously filtering traffic going both up and down the network. AFA shares that most network operators are not set up to monitor both traffic flows. The "assignment of different IP addresses to users" is common practice. AFA is making the point that this hinders (but does not render impossible) the tracking of user activity.

9. In all four case studies, the words italicized in the sections on copyright and Internet rationales (ideas) and IG models (institutions) correspond with categorizations introduced on these topics in Chap. 2 (Sects. 2.1.1.2, 2.1.2.2 and 2.4.1.2).

Bibliography

January 29, 2008. C-275/06 Promusicae vs. Telefónica. Court of Justice of the European Union.

November 24, 2011. C-70/10 Scarlet Extended vs. Société Belge des Auteurs, Compositeurs et Editeurs (SABAM). Court of Justice of the European Union.

ASIC. 2008. Contribution de l'ASIC à la Consultation Publique de la Commission Européenne sur les Contenus Créatifs en Ligne. http://ec.europa.eu/archives/information_society/avpolicy/docs/other_actions/col_2008/ngo/asic_fr.pdf. Accessed 9 Oct 2016.

BEUC. 2008. Creative Content Online in the Single Market. BEUC's Position on the European Commission's Communication on Creative Content Online in the Single Market. http://ec.europa.eu/archives/information_society/avpolicy/docs/other_actions/col_2008/ngo/beuc_en.pdf. Accessed 9 Oct 2016.

British Copyright Council. 2008. Communication from the Commission to the European Parliament, The Council, The European Economic and Social Committee and the Committee of the Regions on Creative Content Online in the Single Market. Response from the British Copyright Council to the Consultation on Policy/Regulatory Issues. http://ec.europa.eu/archives/information_society/avpolicy/docs/other_actions/col_2008/ngo/bcc_en.pdf. Accessed 9 Oct 2016.

British Music Rights. 2008. Creative Content Online – Policy/Regulatory Issues for Consultation. http://ec.europa.eu/archives/information_society/avpolicy/docs/other_actions/col_2008/ngo/bmr_en.pdf. Accessed 9 Oct 2016.

BSA. 2008. Business Software Alliance Response to the Communication on Creative Content Online in the Single Market. http://ec.europa.eu/archives/information_society/avpolicy/docs/other_actions/col_2008/ngo/bsa_en.pdf. Accessed 9 Oct 2016.

BT. 2008. Content Online in the Single Market. Response by British Telecommunications PLC to the Public Consultation by DG INFSO. http://ec.europa.eu/archives/information_society/avpolicy/docs/other_actions/col_2008/comp/bt_en.pdf. Accessed 9 Oct 2016.

CMBA. 2008. Public Consultation on Creative Content Online – Policy/Regulatory Issues – Comments of the Creative Media Business Alliance (CMBA). http://ec.europa.eu/archives/information_society/avpolicy/docs/other_actions/col_2008/ngo/cmba_en.pdf. Accessed 9 Oct 2016.

Coudert, Fanny, and Evi Werkers. 2010. In the Aftermath of the Promusicae Case: How to Strike the Balance? *International Journal of Law and Information Technology* 18(1): 50–71.

Council of the European Union. 2008. *Council Conclusions on the Development of Legal Offers of Online Cultural and Creative Content and the Prevention and Combating of Piracy in the Digital Environment.* Brussels: Council of the European Union.

DACS. 2008. Stakeholder Consultation on European Commission Draft Communication on Creative Content Online in the Single Market. http://ec.europa.eu/archives/information_society/avpolicy/docs/other_actions/col_2008/ngo/dacs_en.pdf. Accessed 9 Oct 2016.

EFF. 2008. Electronic Frontier Foundation Responses to the Creative Content Online Consultation Questionnaire. http://ec.europa.eu/archives/information_society/avpolicy/docs/other_actions/col_2008/ngo/eff_en.pdf. Accessed 9 Oct 2016.

ESOMA. 2008. Creative Content Online Consultation. http://ec.europa.eu/archives/information_society/avpolicy/docs/other_actions/col_2008/ngo/esoma_en.pdf. Accessed 9 Oct 2016.

EuroISPA. 2008. EuroISPA Response to the European Commission's Content Online Consultation. http://ec.europa.eu/archives/information_society/avpolicy/docs/other_actions/col_2008/ngo/euroispa_en.pdf. Accessed 9 Oct 2016.

European Commission. 2008a. *COM(2007) 836 final. Communication from the Commission to the European Parliament, the Council, the European Economic and Social Committee and the Committee of the Regions on Creative Content Online in the Single Market.* Brussels: European Commission.

———. 2008b. *COM(2008b) 466/3. Green Paper on Copyright in the Knowledge Economy.* Brussels: European Commission.

———. 2008c. Public Consultation on Creative Content Online in the Single Market. http://ec.europa.eu/avpolicy/other_actions/content_online/consultation_2008/index_en.htm. Accessed 6 Oct 2016.

———. 2008d. *SEC(2007) 1710. Commission Staff Working Document Accompanying the Communication from the Commission to the European Parliament, the Council, the European Economic and Social Committee and the Committee of the Regions on Creative Content Online in the Single Market.* Brussels: European Commission.

———. 2009a. *COM(2009a) 467 final. Communication from the Commission to the Council, the European Parliament and the European Economic and Social Committee on Enhancing the Enforcement of Intellectual Property Rights in the Internal Market.* Brussels: European Commission.

———. 2009b. Creative Content in a European Digital Single Market: Challenges for the Future. A Reflection Document of DG INFSO and DG MARKT. Brussels: European Commission.

———. 2010. *COM(2010) 245 Final/2. Communication from the Commission to the European Parliament, the Council, the European Economic and Social Committee and the Committee of the Regions. A Digital Agenda for Europe.* Brussels: European Commission.

———. 2011. *COM(2011) 427 Final. Green Paper on the Online Distribution of Audiovisual Works in the European Union: Opportunities and Challenges Towards a Digital Single Market.* Brussels: European Commission.

European Parliament & Council. 2000. *Directive 2000/31/EC of the European Parliament and of the Council of 8 June 2000 on Certain Legal Aspects of Information Society Services, in particular Electronic Commerce, in the Internal Market.* Luxembourg: Official Journal of the European Communities.

———. 2012. *Directive 2012/28/EU of the European Parliament and of the Council of 25 October 2012 on Certain Permitted Uses of Orphan Works.* Luxembourg: Official Journal of the European Union.

———. 2014. *Directive 2014/26/EU of the European Parliament and of the Council of 26 February 2014 on Collective Management of Copyright and Related Rights and Multi-Territorial Licensing of Rights in Musical Works for Online Use in the Internal Market.* Luxembourg: Official Journal of the European Union.

FERA. 2008. European Commission Communication on Creative Content Online in the Single Market. A Contribution to the Public Consultation. http://ec.europa.eu/archives/information_society/avpolicy/docs/other_actions/col_2008/ngo/fera_en.pdf. Accessed 9 Oct 2016.

Google. 2008. Google Contribution on Creative Content Online. http://ec.europa.eu/archives/information_society/avpolicy/docs/other_actions/col_2008/comp/google_en.pdf. Accessed 9 Oct 2016.

Green League. 2008. Responses to Creative Content Online Consultation from the Information Society Working Group of the Green League (Green Party of Finland). http://ec.europa.eu/archives/information_society/avpolicy/docs/other_actions/col_2008/ngo/green_league_en.pdf. Accessed 9 Oct 2016.

IMPA. 2008. International Music Publishers Association. Public Consultation on Creative Content Online in the Single Market. http://ec.europa.eu/archives/information_society/avpolicy/docs/other_actions/col_2008/ngo/impa_en.pdf. Accessed 9 Oct 2016.

Intel. 2008. Intel Corporation Response to the 2008 Creative Content Online in the Single Market Consultation. http://ec.europa.eu/archives/information_society/avpolicy/docs/other_actions/col_2008/comp/intel_corporation_en.pdf. Accessed 9 Oct 2016.

IRII. 2008. Internet Research and Innovation Institute. In Response to the Public Consultation on Creative Content Online. http://ec.europa.eu/archives/information_society/avpolicy/docs/other_actions/col_2008/ngo/irii_en.pdf. Accessed 9 Oct 2016.

KTH. 2008. Creative Content Online – Policy/Regulatory Issues. Proposed Answers to the Commission's 11 Questions from the Music Lessons Research Group, Department for Media Technology and Graphic Arts, Royal Institute of Technology (KTH), Stockholm, Sweden. http://ec.europa.eu/archives/information_society/avpolicy/docs/other_actions/col_2008/ngo/kth_en.pdf. Accessed 9 Oct 2016.

Microsoft. 2008. Response of Microsoft to the European Commission's Communication on Creative Content Online in the Single Market. http://ec.europa.eu/archives/information_society/avpolicy/docs/other_actions/col_2008/comp/microsoft_en.pdf. Accessed 9 Oct 2016.

NBC Universal. 2008. NBC Universal Submission in Response to Commission Consultation on Creative Content on Line in the Single Market. http://ec.europa.eu/archives/information_society/avpolicy/docs/other_actions/col_2008/comp/nbc_en.pdf. Accessed 9 Oct 2016.

STM. 2008. STM Submission on the European Commission's Communication on Creative Content Online in the Single Market. http://ec.europa.eu/archives/information_society/avpolicy/docs/other_actions/col_2008/ngo/stm_en.pdf. Accessed 9 Oct 2016.

Stockholm Network. 2008. Submission to the European Commission Creative Content Online Consultation. http://ec.europa.eu/archives/information_society/avpolicy/docs/other_actions/col_2008/ngo/stockhnetw2_en.pdf. Accessed 9 Oct 2016.

Sun Microsystems. 2008. Response by Sun Microsystems to the Communication from the Commission to the European Parliament, the Council, the European Economic and Social Committee and the Committee of the Regions on

Creative Content Online in the Single Market {SEC(2007) 1710}. http://
ec.europa.eu/archives/information_society/avpolicy/docs/other_actions/
col_2008/comp/sun_ en.pdf. Accessed 9 Oct 2016.

Swedish IT and Telecom Industries. 2008. The Swedish IT and Telecom Industries
Would Like to Add the Following Comments regarding Point n. 10 and 11.
http://ec.europa.eu/archives/information_society/avpolicy/docs/other_
actions/col_2008/ngo/swed_it_tel_en.pdf. Accessed 9 Oct 2016.

Telefónica/O2. 2008. Telefónica/O2 Comments on the EC Communication on
Creative Content Online in the Internal Market. http://ec.europa.eu/
archives/information_society/avpolicy/docs/other_actions/col_2008/
comp/telefonica_o2_en.pdf. Accessed 9 Oct 2016.

UK Government. 2008. The European Commission Communication on Creative
Content Online. UK Government Response. http://ec.europa.eu/archives/
information_society/avpolicy/docs/other_actions/col_2008/ms/uk_gov-
ernment_en.pdf. Accessed 9 Oct 2016.

Van Audenhove, Leo, Luciano Morganti, John Vanhoucke, Trisha Meyer, and
Giovanni Paolo Ramirez. 2009. *Challenges for Creative Content Online: An
Assumptional Analysis on the Basis of the Communication on Creative Content
Online of the European Commission.* Brussels: IBBT-SMIT, Vrije Universiteit
Brussel and Belgacom Telindus.

Yahoo! Europe. 2008. Yahoo! Europe Response to the European Commission
Communication on Creative Content Online in the Single Market. http://
ec.europa.eu/archives/information_society/avpolicy/docs/other_actions/
col_2008/comp/yahoo_en.pdf. Accessed 9 Oct 2016.

CHAPTER 4

HADOPI: 2009 Graduated Response in France

Graduated response is a copyright enforcement mechanism, whereby Internet users are monitored and when caught infringing copyright are repeatedly warned and ultimately risk receiving a sanction. Possible sanctions include fines, technical measures and (most notably) temporary suspension of Internet access. Graduated response is not a new enforcement mechanism. Most university campuses in the United States have had a system of warnings and sanctions for copyright infringement in place for quite some time. Universities even use content recognition software to proactively scan and limit infringing transactions on their networks.[1] Furthermore, there have been examples in which ISPs who have a stake in content distribution implemented similar approaches.[2] While the issue is not new, the adoption and spread of legislation endorsing graduated response is a fairly recent phenomenon, however. Graduated response legislation has been passed in France, New Zealand, South Korea, Taiwan and the United Kingdom. Concomitantly, interest in graduated response has increased.

France was the first European country to pass legislation in 2009 introducing a graduated response mechanism to deter online copyright infringement: HADOPI 1—*Loi du 12 juin 2009 favorisant la Diffusion et la Protection de la Création sur Internet*, translated: law favoring the Dissemination and Protection of Creation on the Internet (French Parliament 2009a), and HADOPI 2—*Loi du 28 octobre 2009 relative à*

© The Author(s) 2017   165
T. Meyer, *The Politics of Online Copyright Enforcement in the EU*, Information Technology and Global Governance,
DOI 10.1007/978-3-319-50974-7_4

la Protection Pénale de la Propriété Littéraire et Artistique sur Internet, translated: law relating to the Criminal Protection of Literary and Artistic Property on the Internet (French Parliament 2009b). Contrary to the public consultations on CCO and the E-Commerce Directive and ACTA, the French problem structuring and policy recommendations lead to the adoption of new policies. For this reason I include relevant points on graduated response's history and adopted legal provisions in the introduction to this French case study. These discussions precede the sections on discourse institutionalization (4.2.4) and policy legacy (4.4.1), but are important to set the scene and aid further analysis.

Through my French interviews, it became clear that passing additional legislation to fight online piracy was in part motivated by *lenient policies in the late 1990s and early 2000s to develop broadband Internet in France.* French policymakers had turned a blind eye to copyright infringement on the network favoring faster rollout of high-speed Internet. Certain ISPs even publicly advertised that ADSL (asymmetric digital subscriber line) Internet would allow customers to download whatever they wanted whenever and wherever, despite there being few legal offers available at the time. The time had come to value copyright again and to emphasize rule of law on the Internet (Frédéric Delacroix, Marc Pic, Olivier Bomsel, Pierre Gueydier, Interviews 2013).

In 2004 a Charter of Engagements for the Development of Legal Musical Offers, the Respect of Intellectual Property and the Fight Against Digital Piracy was signed (French Ministry of Culture and Communication 2004). This Charter included the first seeds of graduated response. Rights holders would monitor P2P networks and ISPs committed to send pedagogical messages to their subscribers. However this voluntary warning mechanism was never set in place, as the French data protection authority (CNIL—*Commission Nationale de l'Informatique et des Libertés*) refused to grant rights holders permission to monitor P2P networks (Giuseppe De Martino, Marc Pic, Pierre Gueydier, Interviews 2013). CNIL (2007) deemed that the monitoring was disproportionate because it resulted in "massive data collection and could allow comprehensive and continuous surveillance of file sharing networks". In 2007 the French Council of State overruled this decision, considering that "CNIL had committed an error of assessment especially given 'the importance of the practice of music file sharing on the Internet'" (CNIL 2010, translated from French). The Council of State did uphold CNIL's analysis that ISPs were not authorized to retain subscriber data for this purpose. At this point, rights holders had already pursued a graduated response mechanism including warnings and sanctions via a legislative route.

In 2006 the French transposition of the European Union Copyright Directive (DADVSI—*Loi du 1 août 2006 sur le Droit d'Auteur et les Droits Voisins dans la Société de l'Information*, translated: Law on Author's Right and Related Rights in the Information Society) introduced provisions on DRM (French Parliament 2006). Unique to France, it also included an obligation on Internet account holders to monitor their network against copyright infringements. Further in DADVSI French policymakers sought to introduce a warning and sanction mechanism for small-scale copyright infringement. In France copyright infringement is a criminal offense, incurring sanctions of three years imprisonment and 300,000 Euros fine (*"délit de contrefaçon"*, translated: counterfeiting).[3] DADVSI introduced a small fine for small-scale copyright infringement, using counterfeiting as the basis. The Constitutional Council censured graduated response in DADVSI, because the mechanism disregarded the legal principle of equality of offenses and punishments. Different sanctions were applied to the same crime (Marc Pic, Pierre Gueydier, Valérie-Laure Benabou, Interviews 2013). On to the next step then.

In 2007 the government brokered a multistakeholder Agreement on the Development and Protection of Cultural Works and Programs on the New Networks (Olivennes 2007), affirming continued commitment to graduated response. In 2008 Nicolas Sarkozy promised throughout his presidential campaign to implement a warning and sanction mechanism. One month after the elections the French government submitted a law proposal favoring the diffusion and protection of creation on the Internet (French Ministry of Culture and Communication 2008). Graduated response was made legally enforceable with *HADOPI 1 and 2 in 2009*. Figure 4.1 provides an overview of the main graduated response policy developments in France.

When the first HADOPI law proposal was introduced, Christine Albanel, Minister of Culture and Communication described the objective of the law as "to stop the hemorrhage of cultural works on the Internet and to create the indispensable legal framework for the development of the legal offer of music, films, audiovisual works and programs, even literary works on the new communication networks" (French Ministry of Culture and Communication 2008, 3, translated from French). The first French law creates *an independent administrative authority HADOPI (Haute Autorité pour la Diffusion des Œuvres et la Protection des Droits sur Internet*, translated: High Authority for the Dissemination of Works and

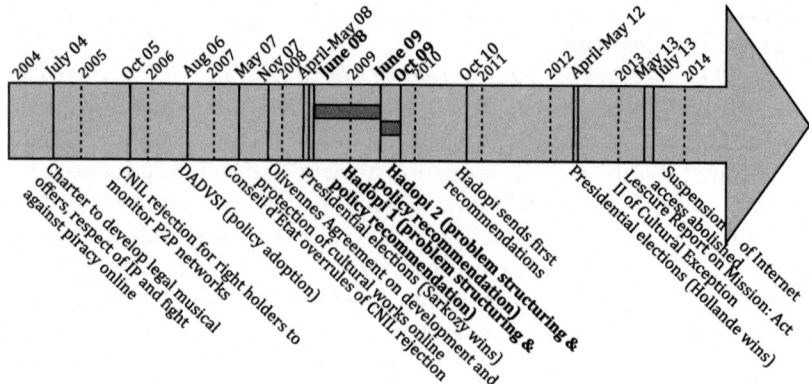

Fig. 4.1 Policy developments in HADOPI

Protection of Rights on the Internet). The French Constitutional Council censured the proposition in the first HADOPI law to authorize the administrative authority to suspend Internet access, requiring the second law to install a judicial procedure. The French government views *graduated response as a mainly educational measure*, because infringers are given repeated chances to alter their illicit behavior before being sanctioned. It is regarded as an alternative to the harsh sanctions for counterfeiting found in French IPR law. They also contend that *a strong legal framework enforcing copyright is necessary for the further development of legal offers*. Indeed the French government discourse on graduated response evokes a sense of emergency and emphasizes strong intervention. Both HADOPI laws were passed under a declaration of urgency. The policymaking process for the first HADOPI law took one year; the second HADOPI law was passed in four months. The administrative authority HADOPI has three missions: to encourage the development of legal offers and observe licit and illicit use of copyrighted works online; to regulate and monitor technical measures to protect and identify copyrighted works; and to protect copyrighted works online through graduated response. To fully understand the stakeholder ideas and discourses present in Sects. 4.1 and 4.2, I expand on each mission in the following paragraphs. The administrative authority HADOPI has been operational since 2010. It started with a generous budget of 11.4 million Euros, but this was halved to 5.5 million Euros over the period 2011 to 2014. Meanwhile HADOPI's expenses decreased from 13.8 to 8.7 million Euros. In 2015 HADOPI anticipated running a deficit for the third consecutive year (HADOPI 2015).

Concerning *legal offers* and observation, HADOPI has developed an extensive reference portal and label PUR to make it easier for Internet users to identify legal offers (Offrelegale.fr 2016). The first HADOPI law also includes provisions to shorten the release window for paid video-on-demand to four months after cinema release and to offer music catalogues free of TPMs when interoperability is an issue (French Parliament 2009a, Articles 17 & 25). For some time, the French government launched a music card for young people, doubling the amount of credits on a card purchased as an incentive to obtain music legally. Further, HADOPI conducts a wide range of studies under its *observation* function (HADOPI 2015). For instance, it tracks licit and illicit use of copyrighted works, has made recommendations on copyright infringement through streaming and direct downloading and even conducted a study on copyright exceptions. While HADOPI's budget permitted, it created Labs to fund academic discussion and research.

Concerning *TPMs*, the first HADOPI law stipulates that, at the request of rights holders, a judge can order "all measures to prevent or put an end to an infringement of an author's right or related right, against any person likely to contribute to remedy it" (French Parliament 2009a, Article 10, translated from French). The government's original law proposal included measures to block or filter content. For its part, HADOPI needs to ensure that TPMs are not used for anti-competitive purposes and does not deprive consumers of the benefit of certain legal exceptions, such as the right to a private copy. In 2013 and 2014 it provided three opinions. The authority has also been closely involved in drafting the French law proposal to adopt the WIPO Marrakech Treaty to provide copyright exceptions to persons who are bling, visually impaired or otherwise print disabled persons (HADOPI 2015). With this mission, HADOPI took over the tasks of the Authority for the Regulation of Technical Measures (ARMT—*Autorité de Régulation des Mesures Techniques*).

Concerning *copyright protection,* the HADOPI laws set in place *a graduated response mechanism,* consisting of monitoring, warnings and sanctions. Rights holders *monitor* the activities of Internet users on P2P file-sharing networks. They detect illegal uploads of copyrighted works using searches based on keyword and file size. Uploads are verified by comparing them with digital fingerprints of the copyrighted works. Rights holders gather samples of the illegal uploads and their corresponding IP addresses, which they can then communicate with the administrative authority HADOPI. Based on the IP address provided by the rights holders, HADOPI can decide to send an email to the holders of the account where illegal activity was detected, which reminds them of the obligation to secure their Internet access against copyright breaches and stresses the dangers of copyright infringement for the renewal of artistic creation and the economy of the cultural industry. The *notification* also points them to legal alternatives to obtain copyrighted works and ways to secure their Internet access. In case of renewed detection of illegal file sharing within six months of the first notification, account holders can be sent a registered letter. In case of a third detection within one year of the second notification, HADOPI can notify account holders that their file could be transferred to the judicial authorities. Taking into account the seriousness of the breach and the situation of the account holder, a judge can decide to *fine* an Internet account holder up to €1500 on the basis of gross negligence to secure their Internet access. Until July 2013 a judicial authority could also rule for the *suspension* of Internet access for a period up to one month (French Government 2013). ISPs who did not suspend access upon notification risked a fine up to €5000. During the suspension period, an account holder continued to pay the Internet subscription and was not allowed to open a new account. Contrary to DADVSI the legal basis for applying a sanction in HADOPI is gross negligence on the part of Internet account holders to secure their network against copyright infringements. At the end of 2015, HADOPI had sent 4,897,883 first notifications, 482,667 second notifications, 2712 third notifications, had deliberated over 2221 cases and referred 361 to the judicial authorities (HADOPI 2015). Judges have mainly restricted their sanctions to small fines (between €50 and €1000). One person was due to lose their Internet access. The sanction was not implemented due to the policy change in July 2013 (HADOPI 2013b, c). Figure 4.2 provides a visualization of the French graduated response procedure.

There are *several additional aspects of the first and second HADOPI laws* that do not fit directly into the three missions of HADOPI but that are relevant for the understanding of the laws and stakeholder discussions. A first important provision in HADOPI 1 concerns the publication of a list with functional specifications of *means to secure Internet access*. In this respect, HADOPI has made practical flyers on the history of the Internet, best practices on using WiFi, social media and more. An approved list of secure means has not been published (HADOPI 2016c). In the first HADOPI law ISPs are obliged to inform clients of means to secure Internet access, propose one means on HADOPI's list and

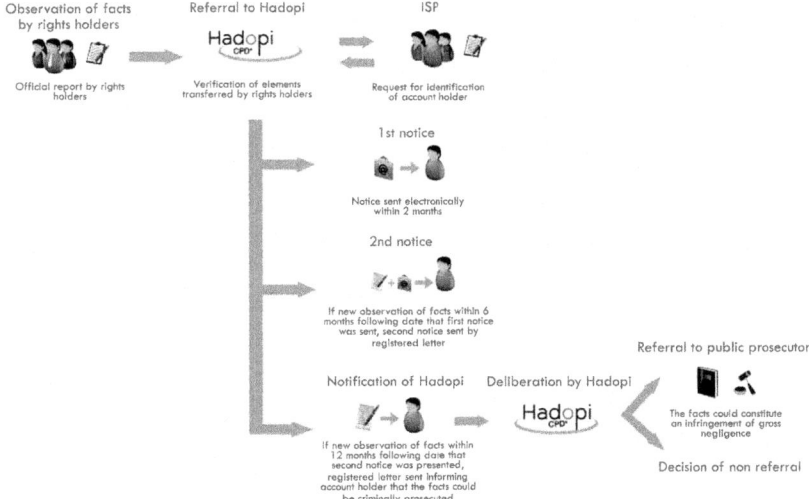

Fig. 4.2 Graduated response procedure (translated by author). Source: HADOPI. 2016c. "Réponse Graduée." accessed October 3, 2016. http://www.hadopi.fr/usages-responsables/nouvelles-libertes-nouvelles-responsabilites/reponse-graduee.

warn about the dangers and sanctions of neglecting to secure Internet access and violating copyright. HADOPI has developed a clause which can be included in charters or rental contracts and an awareness message which can be displayed when providing WiFi access (HADOPI 2016a, b). Second, the first HADOPI law also includes provisions to *educate school-going youth* on the dangers of up and downloading copyrighted works illegally, the sanctions for copyright infringement and the availability of legal offers online (French Parliament 2009a, Articles 15–16). This fits the pedagogical focus of the laws. Third, the French Parliament inserted articles in the first HADOPI law acknowledging *journalists' rights* but limiting remuneration for online publication of their works (French Parliament 2009a, Article 20), clarifying *copyright exceptions for libraries* (French Parliament 2009a, Article 21), and developing *conditions and benefits of a limited liability status for online press services* (French Parliament 2009a, Articles 27–28). One interview respondent indicated that he believed news reporting on HADOPI was particularly negative due to the provisions on journalists. It was telling that no one in the press spoke about these included provisions (Pierre Gueydier, Researcher in Sociology of Innovation, Paris, Interview 2013). Finally, the second HADOPI law introduces *distinct provisions for online copyright infringement:* a simplified criminal procedure and a complementary sanction of suspension of Internet access for a period up to one year (French Parliament 2009b, Articles 6–7). As we notice below, this special procedure for online copyright infringement and the general distinction between copyright infringement (counterfeiting) and negligence to secure the Internet access are highly contested.

For the ADA of this French case study, I have analyzed ninety-six stakeholder contributions to the policymaking processes of HADOPI 1 and 2. These include the law proposals, position papers, press releases, letters, parliamentary committee reports, Constitutional Council rulings and final laws. Contrary to ACTA (see Chap. 6), I have not studied press releases of parliamentary groups. The parliamentary committee reports are comprehensive and quite sufficient to understand the debate in the French National Assembly and Senate. Further I have analyzed relevant sections of the Lescure Report on the Act II of the Cultural Exception (2013). The report commissioned by the newly elected 2012 government, includes an evaluation of graduated response. Several newspaper articles have also been examined, as they are publications of stakeholder letters or interviews. The analysis of these stakeholder contributions provides insight into the 3Is at play when graduated response was introduced in France. It also allows for the identification of coalitions between stakeholders and their discursive struggle to become adopted and institutionalized in policy. I conducted fifteen expert interviews for this case study in May 2013. The timing of these interviews lent to an evaluative perspective of HADOPI, three years into its operation.

4.1   IDEAS

In the following sub-sections I set out the proposed problem definitions and policy solutions found in stakeholder contributions to the HADOPI 1 and 2 policymaking processes. I end with an account of copyright rationales on the one hand, and Internet rationales on the other hand. Box 4.1 provides the timelines of the Parliamentary debates. In Sect. 4.2.4 I discuss the integration of stakeholder contributions into the Parliamentary reports and final laws of HADOPI 1 and 2 (discourse structuration and institutionalization).

Box 4.1 Timeline of HADOPI parliamentary debates

HADOPI 1
Loi n° 2009-669 du 12 juin 2009 favorisant la diffusion et la protection de la création sur internet

Submission of law proposal

June 18, 2008	Submission of law proposal
October 23, 2008	Government declares urgency

Senate first reading

October 22, 2008	Report Cultural Affairs Committee
October 28, 2008	Advice Economic Affairs & Sustainable Development Committee
October 30, 2008	Adoption of law proposal, modified by Senate

National Assembly first reading

February 18, 2009	Report Legal Affairs Committee
February 18, 2009	Report Cultural Affairs Committee
March 5, 2009	Report Economic Affairs Committee
April 2, 2009	Adoption of law proposal, modified by National Assembly

Senate second reading

Joint Parliamentary Committee

April 7, 2009	Report Joint Parliamentary Committee (JRC)

Joint Parliamentary Commission reading

April 9, 2009	Adoption of law proposal by Senate, as modified by JRC
April 9, 2009	Rejection of law proposal by National Assembly, as modified by JRC

Submission of modified law proposal

April 11, 2009	Submission of law proposal, as modified by National Assembly first reading

National Assembly new reading

April 28, 2009	Report Legal Affairs Committee
May 12, 2009	Adoption of law proposal, modified by National Assembly

Senate new reading

May 12, 2009	Report Cultural Affairs Committee
May 13, 2009	Adoption of law proposal by Senate, as modified by National Assembly

Constitutional Council ruling

May 19, 2009	Request ruling Constitutional Council by 184 Deputies
June 10, 2009	Ruling Constitutional Council

(continued)

Box 4.1   (continued)

Publication of final law
June 12, 2009

Based on: French National Assembly. 2009c. "Culture: Diffusion et Protection de la Création sur Internet." Accessed October 6, 2016. http://www.assemblee-nationale. fr/13/dossiers/internet.asp

HADOPI 2
Loi n° 2009-1311 du 28 octobre 2009 relative à la protection pénale de la propriété littéraire et artistique sur internet

---

Submission of law proposal

June 24, 2009	Submission of law proposal
June 24, 2009	Government invokes accelerated procedure

Senate first reading

July 1, 2009	Report Cultural Affairs Committee
July 8, 2009	Adoption of law proposal, modified by Senate

National Assembly first reading

July 16, 2009	Report Cultural Affairs Committee
September 15, 2009	Adoption of law proposal, modified by National Assembly

Joint Parliamentary Committee

September 17, 2009	Report Joint Parliamentary Committee (JRC)

Joint Parliamentary Committee reading

September 21, 2009	Adoption of law proposal by Senate, as modified by JRC
September 22, 2009	Adoption of law proposal by National Assembly, as modified by JRC

Constitutional Council ruling

September 28, 2009	Request Constitutional Council ruling by 164 Deputies
October 22, 2009	Ruling Constitutional Council

Publication of final law

October 28, 2009

Based on: French National Assembly. 2009c. "Culture: Diffusion et Protection de la Création sur Internet." Accessed October 6, 2016. http://www.assemblee-nationale. fr/13/dossiers/internet.asp

4.1.1   Problem Definitions and Policy Solutions

HADOPI 1 and 2 were the final steps leading to legislative endorsement of graduated response in France. The policy debates were heated, particularly in the National Assembly.

Proponents of HADOPI relate the policy problem of the media industries in the online environment to piracy. *Piracy on a massive scale* causes a "hemorrhage of cultural works", threatening to "dry up the sources of creation and cultural diversity" in France. Proponents use strong words to describe copyright infringement such as a "plague", "theft" and "plundering". They point out that *policy action is urgent*, as the media industries have reached a critical threshold, experiencing a "crisis without precedence". In a joint statement, the music industry (SACEM et al. 2009, translated from French) argues that, "each passing month results in a worsening of the economic situation of the sector." In this regard HADOPI provides an indispensable policy solution that needs to be adopted as soon as possible.

The proposed judicial framework is viewed as *innovative, ambitious, just and adapted*. Proponents emphasize that graduated response provides an alternative to the harsh counterfeiting sanctions to which Internet users find themselves exposed. HADOPI is presented as a *pedagogical and preventative tool to raise awareness of copyright infringement and responsibility among citizens*. Sanctions such as the suspension of Internet access are measures of last resort necessary for users who persistently refuse to respect copyright. The French Senate's Cultural Affairs Committee (2009, 8, translated from French) states that, "everyone knows that, whatever the field, preventive action is all the more credible and effective when there is a real threat of a sanction at the end." Supporters of HADOPI contend that graduated response provides a *balance* between intellectual property and privacy and freedom of expression. The law proposal finds the middle ground between extreme repression on the one hand and extreme libertarianism on the other hand. HADOPI is particularly praised because it offers *protection from piracy but equally suitable entrepreneurial and economic models*. Some stakeholders emphasize that an attractive and rich legal offer can dissuade piracy as well. Others, including the Legal Affairs Committee of the National Assembly (2009b), argue that "damming up piracy is a precondition" to the development of legal offers.

Further, the original HADOPI 1 law proposal permitted a judge to order, at the request of rights holders, "all measures to block or filtering content infringing an author's right or related right, and all measures to restrict access to this content, against any person likely to contribute to remedy it or prevent its renewal" (French Ministry of Culture and Communication 2008, translated from French). There is consensus within the French Parliament to *remove the references to blocking and filtering*, as its efficiency, cost and large-scale deployment are doubted. Instead HADOPI will monitor experimentation in this domain. Lastly, proponents of graduated response *oppose the global license*. This is an alternative remuneration scheme based on the legalization of non-commercial file sharing and cultural contributions. Stakeholders deem the alternative remuneration scheme a "collectivist monster", "purely theoretical and inapplicable".

Opponents of graduated response take a different view. They argue that HADOPI is disproportionate and contrary to civil liberties. It is a tool for surveillance and massive control by private actors, resulting in an invasion of privacy and the launch of a Big Brother society. Opponents strongly object to the suspension of Internet access. Jacques Attali (2009a, translated from French), a French economist, writer and honorary member of the Council of State, deems HADOPI "an enclosure of free thought, freedom of information and freedom of navigation". The HADOPI law proposals reinforce the repressive arsenal against copyright infringement, creating an Internet police to criminalize end users. Opponents also object to the obligation to continue payment of the ISP subscription when Internet access is suspended. They argue that this is a double sanction. Moreover dissenting stakeholders criticize the lack of judicial involvement and the reversal of burden of proof in the first HADOPI law proposal. The simplified judicial procedure and the perceived imprecision between counterfeiting and failure to secure Internet access in the second HADOPI law proposal are also considered dangerous. These elements weaken citizens' procedural guarantees to judicial recourse and a fair trial.

Beyond considerations on proportionality and civil liberties, opponents of graduated response contend that HADOPI is inept and inefficient. La Quadrature du Net (2009b) argues that HADOPI 2 is an absurd and inefficient attempt "to reanimate a beheaded monster" that is well beyond "clinical death". Stakeholders point to the cost and collateral damages of the proposed policy. It will lock up wireless Internet and innovative Internet use. Moreover the proposed technical means of implementing graduated response—surveillance and filtering of P2P networks—are deemed weak. Opponents argue that current surveillance and filtering techniques are circumventable through encryption and result in false positives and negatives. They point to technical difficulties of suspending Internet access in certain multiplay situations, but also of securing Internet access. Indeed as mentioned in the Introduction, HADOPI has not been able to create a list with approved means to secure Internet access. Fabrice Le Fessant (Founder and Scientific Advisor at OCamlPro and INRIA Researcher) and Olivier Iteanu (Lawyer at Iteanu) contend that as a consequence HADOPI hangs over Internet users like the sword of Damocles, as these users cannot be sure that they are abiding by the law (Interviews 2013). Valérie-Laure Benabou (Professor at Université de Versailles-St-Quentin-en-Yvelines, Interview 2013) objects to the obligation to secure Internet access as well. However rather than viewing it as potential criminalization of the entire population, she argues that the obligation serves to lighten the conscience. Citizens can elude their responsibility by relying on infrastructure-based enforcement, without understanding the functionalities of the technical means, which she suggests could be discriminatory. HADOPI alienates citizens from the objective of the law which is to change copyright behavior, asking them instead to trust a technology they do not understand.

Lastly, opponents of graduated response propose alternative policy solutions. Many argue for more legal offers, including the global license, others call for a wider debate on copyright and culture in the online environment. Socialist Senator David Assouline deems that all the time spent trying to protect copyright through DADVSI, HADOPI 1 and 2 "would have been more usefully employed to build a digital cultural economy. Other solutions would have been better to protect and remunerate authors and producers than trying to 'put a dam in front of a torrent'" (French Parliament 2009c, 8, translated from French).

A number of stakeholders adopt a *nuanced view* toward graduated response. Perhaps somewhat surprising is the view of *the adult content industry*. In an interview with LeMonde.fr (2009, translated from French), Grégory Dorcel (Director General of Marcel Dorcel) remarks that HADOPI is only a *partial solution*. Rather than pursuing consumers, access needs to be blocked to file-sharing platforms. He states that, "[i]f a bag of candy is left unattended in front of children, they will not understand that we reprimand them if they take a candy. Illegal files are accessible to anyone in just three clicks. It is normal that consumers take advantage. In accusing the consumer, the file sharing platforms pass for Robin Hood, while they are making huge profits off the backs of the producers. It is unbearable!" Further *the Internet industry* carefully accepts HADOPI. Prior to the law proposals ISPs had long negotiations with rights holders to develop a graduated response mechanism. The ISP Association (AFA—*Association des Fournisseurs d'Accès et de Services Internet*) (2008) regrets that the balance found in the Olivennes Agreement is lost in the first HADOPI law proposal. In particular they criticize the lack of commitment to *develop legal offers* and the broad *references to blocking and filtering*. They also point out that the law proposal does not allow users to contest infringement allegations and that ISPs need *time to set the HADOPI procedure in place*. The Association for Community Sites (ASIC—*Association des Services Internet Communautaires*) (2008b) strongly opposes an amendment submitted by Senators of the Communist Party to tax advertising revenues of Internet actors, fearing a weakening of the nascent online sector. They stress that the neutrality and openness of the Internet must be maintained.

Multiple French and EU public authorities express nuanced views on HADOPI as well. *The French Regulatory Authority for Electronic Communications and Post* (ARCEP—*Autorité de Régulation des Communications Électroniques et des Postes*) (2008) does not object to graduated response, but points to the *technical difficulty* to suspend Internet access in certain multiplay situations and to the time that ISPs need to set the HADOPI procedure in place. Further I have included several EU documents in my analysis, in which stakeholders refer to graduated response. It is important to note that the EP, Council and Commission are aggregate bodies. First, *the EP* (2008) passed a Resolution on the Cultural Industries in Europe which underlines the value of culture for individuals and society, economic growth, social cohesion, and regional and local development. Copyright is deemed essential for the remuneration of creators and the survival of the cultural industries. The resolution stresses the importance of finding a fair balance between interests and of *avoiding the criminalization of users*. The EP (2008) specifically discourages the suspension of Internet access as a means of sanctioning copyright infringement. Second, in its Conclusions on the Development of Legal Offers of Online Cultural and Creative Content and the Prevention and Combating of Piracy in the Digital Environment, the Council (2008) contends that online piracy is reaching a *critical threshold*, threatening cultural creativity and diversity. The Council states that online piracy is holding back the development of legal offers and underlines the need for *concrete, effective, fair and proportionate solutions*. These Council Conclusions were discussed in the first case study as well. They pertain to the EC's CCO initiative and were adopted during the French Council presidency. Third, the EC (2008c) demonstrates openness toward graduated response by including a question on the Olivennes Agreement in the 2008 CCO in the Single Market consultation. At the same time, the report also admonishes rights holders for their reluctance to *make content available online*. Lastly, the European Commissioner for the Information Society and Media Viviane Reding sent a letter to a French cinematographic association ARP *(Societé Civile des Auteurs-Réalisateurs-Producteurs)* (Ecrans.fr 2008b). Reding regrets the agitated and polemic debate of the cultural sector to include graduated response in the Telecoms Package, and emphasizes that the *Commission must stay neutral* during the French policymaking debate. In this regard it is relevant to mention that the French president Nicolas Sarkozy had urged the EC President Manuel Barroso to reject Amendment 138 of the Telecoms Package. This amendment pertained to the need to involve a judge when suspending Internet access. Reding states that the *"acquis communautaire"* leaves member states with sufficient latitude to reach the right balance between the various fundamental rights affected by graduated response. The Commissioner further mentions that the Recommendation on Creative Content Online has been delayed due to the recent events. Reding will continue to endeavor to find the right balance between copyright and the fundamental rights of Internet users at a European level (Ecrans.fr 2008b).

4.1.2   Copyright and Internet Rationales

The most frequent reasoning for copyright in the analyzed texts is *economic* in nature: copyright as a *just reward for labor* and a *return on investment*. The economic reasoning is intrinsically linked with *cultural diversity and creativity*. A just reward for labor is viewed as a prerequisite, a stimulus for creativity and legal offers. Indeed, the French government and media industries assert that French cultural patrimony is endangered by lack of copyright protection.

A few stakeholders remark that culture is a public good that benefits society and for this reason needs to be preserved. More often, however, discourse pertains to the French *cultural exception*. Culture is not like any other merchandise. It requires protection from unbridled capitalism and cannot function in a competitive market. The French cultural exception makes the distinction between copyright and *"droit d'auteur"* clear. French policy actors associate copyright with commercial aspects of the media system, while *author's rights* are deemed to emphasize the intrinsic and exceptional value of art and culture. The French president Sarkozy argues that, "art constitutes the highest expression of civilization. We need to ensure that there is a civilized Internet" (Presidency of the French Republic 2009, translated from French).

In this context references are made to the *property and moral rights* of authors. In the "*droit d'auteur*" tradition, moral rights are the prime example of copyright as a *natural law;* a cultural work is the expression of its author's personality. In the HADOPI policymaking debate copyright is juxtaposed with freedom of expression and privacy. Proponents of graduated response seek to underline that copyright is a *fundamental right.* Jean-Philippe Mochon (Head of Legal and International Affairs Department at Ministry of Culture and Communication, Interview 2013, translated from French) states that it is crucial to avoid falling into the trap of opposing copyright to fundamental rights. He says that, "[t]he idea that was able to enter into the public debate is that policies protecting intellectual property are inconsistent with fundamental freedoms. This is obviously the big mistake that was committed. Our conviction is that author's rights are a fundamental freedom. Protection of author's rights is protection of a fundamental right and therefore protecting author's rights is not infringing fundamental rights but protecting fundamental rights." Valérie-Laure Benabou (Professor at Université de Versailles-St-Quentin-en-Yvelines, Interview 2013) argues that copyright has lost touch with the general public. In her view, with the increased importance of intellectual property, we have moved from an author-amateur to a producer-consumer relationship. Authors and artists have disappeared into the background, primarily companies are visible. Additionally the democratization of cultural creation has led to a desacralization of the author and his rights. Both of these changes make it more difficult to defend copyright on traditional "*droit d'auteur*" grounds. Indeed Benabou contends, France does not seem to be coping well with the changing views and expectations of the public.

Further, all stakeholders perceive the Internet as a *communication and distribution medium,* for either legal and illegal purposes *(social interaction and symbolic belonging, entrepreneurship)*. Civil society, public figures and Internet & technology associations point to characteristics of the Internet (decentralized, international, open and neutral) that they believe are endangered by HADOPI and the Telecoms Package. ASIC (2009, translated from French) emphasizes that, "the Internet is an information highway where every actor—whether a multinational or an SME, a traditional actor or not—can participate on an equal basis to offer services to end users." For these actors the Internet is deemed an *extraordinary chance* for sharing and distribution both economically and socially. The EC and Internet & technology associations stress the importance of the Internet for economic growth, employment and innovation.

Importantly, the French Constitutional Council ruled in its decision on HADOPI 1 that *considering the importance of the Internet for the exercise of human rights, only a judge could suspend Internet access*. The Constitutional Council (June 10, 2009, §12, translated from French) contends that, "free communication of thoughts and opinions is one of the most precious human rights: any citizen can thus talk, write and print freely, except in the cases of abuse of this liberty determined by law." Further it continues, "in the current state of communication means and in view of the general development of online public communication services as well as the importance of these services for the participation in democratic life and the expression of ideas and opinions, this right [free communication of thoughts and opinions] implies the freedom to access these [Internet] services." Internet access is deemed a prerequisite for freedom of expression. This has led some actors to argue that Internet access is a fundamental right.

Finally, many stakeholders perceive the information society and the Internet as *revolutionary and unstoppable*. The HADOPI 1 law proposal (French Ministry of Culture and Communication 2008) compares current developments in cultural distribution and diffusion to the invention of the printing press. Jacques Attali (2009a, b) deems the adoption of a global license scheme unavoidable. Often this revolutionary argumentation is accompanied with a strong discourse on the dangers of the Internet. The French government and media industries describe the Internet as a jungle and as an uncivilized environment where only the fittest survive. They strongly urge for regulation of the Internet; the Internet cannot be left a lawless zone. Frédéric Delacroix (Managing Director at ALPA— Association de Lutte Contre la Piraterie Audiovisuelle, Interview 2013) argues that morality and respect of rights holders have to be fostered on the Internet. With this in mind, it is interesting to note that HADOPI (2011, 9) described itself in its 2010 activity report as "the only French institute exclusively dedicated to the Internet". The EC and civil society actors interpret the reactions of the media sector (and government) to the Internet as driven by loss of control. This last paragraph serves as an appropriate transition to further discuss discourses adopted in this case study. Box 4.2 summarizes the analysis of ideas in HADOPI.

Box 4.2 Ideas in HADOPI

Analysis of stakeholder opinions on HADOPI 1 and 2 during policymaking process (2008–2009)

- Pro—graduated response is innovative, ambitious, just and adapted; there is a need for urgent action due to piracy on massive scale
- Anti—graduated response is disproportionate, contrary to civil liberties, inept and inefficient; objection to surveillance, suspension of Internet access and continued payment of ISP subscription; emphasis on need for procedural guarantees in judicial recourse and fair trial
- Nuanced—graduated response is partial solution; objection to lack of commitment to legal offers and broad references to blocking and filtering; point to technical difficulties of proposed system
- Copyright Rationales
  - Economic incentive, societal requirements, natural law
  - Cultural exception—intrinsic and exceptional value, commercial fragility of art and culture
- Internet Rationales
  - Social interaction & symbolic belonging, entrepreneurship
  - Internet is revolutionary, unstoppable *and* essential for exercise of fundamental rights

4.2   DISCOURSES

Emblematic issues and story lines are woven into stakeholders detailing their problem definitions and proposing policy solutions. I identify three key discourses in the French graduated response policymaking process.

4.2.1   *Prevention of Mass Piracy through Pedagogy*

Through this mechanism placed under the control of the High Authority for the Dissemination of Works and Protection of Rights on the Internet (HADOPI), created by the law proposal, which entrusts senior magistrates with the task of preserving the privacy of Internet users, it will be possible to build a policy that is fair because it is pedagogical, graduated, progressive and protective of the rights and freedoms of all; efficient because it associates Internet Service Providers with cinema professionals, prevention with sanction; and balanced because it disassociates the serious acts of counterfeiting, punishable with criminal sanctions, with the simple and specific file sharing acts of an end user. (Société des Auteurs et Compositeurs Dramatiques & Société Civile des Auteurs Multimedia—SACD and SCAM 2008, translated from French)

Proponents of HADOPI view the graduated response mechanism as providing a solution adapted to the *specificity of mass online piracy.* A distinction is made between counterfeiting and file sharing to argue that the criminal sanctions for counterfeiting provided in French legislation are inappropriate for the current copyright infringement situation. Indeed the French legal term for copyright infringement (counterfeiting—*"contrefaçon")* is seldom used in the policy debate. Stakeholders refer to online copyright infringement as piracy *("piratage").* Graduated response is portrayed as a *novel interpretation* of law offering a *less repressive answer to piracy.* It is primarily preventative and pedagogical. For this reason HADOPI is deemed balanced and fair.

4.2.2   Rules of the Road

Admittedly, the law proposal will not solve all the problems which the cultural industry faces. It will not end the piracy of works overnight; but it will be a milestone if it manages to 'civilize' Internet use, in the same way that policy on road safety has fostered a more responsible behavior with most motorists. (French Senate 2008b, 13, translated from French)

Proponents and some opponents of HADOPI compare graduated response to road safety policy. When motorists are caught speeding, they are given small fines. Only motorists who refuse to adapt their behavior, lose their driver's license. Although checks are periodical, the policy is considered sufficiently dissuasive. Intervention is necessary to ensure *safety and rule of law.* Similarly graduated response seeks to change online behavior through repeated awareness raising, only sanctioning gross negligence. Regulation of the Internet is deemed essential for the survival of the media industries in France.

4.2.3   Disproportionate and Unadapted Policy Solution

Since the European Parliament Resolution of 10 April [2008 on Cultural Industries in Europe] condemning the principle of graduated response, we have witnessed azimuthal attacks of the major record companies. They are trying to push through their measures which are draconian, economically unfounded and contrary to digital history. (Member of European Parliament (MEP) Guy Bono in La Quadrature du Net 2008b, translated from French)

Opponents of HADOPI argue that surveillance, filtering and suspension of Internet use and access are *disproportionate and inefficient solutions* to deal with the media industries' online problems. Graduated response jeopardizes fundamental freedoms and future developments of the Internet. Stakeholders consider *widespread distribution of content* a key Internet value. They advocate legal offers as an alternative policy solution, some go as far as asking for the legalization of file sharing. The media industries need to adjust to the economics of the online world. Access to content will foster true cultural diversity and creativity.

4.2.4   Discourse Coalitions, Structuration and Institutionalization

In the HADOPI policy debate, *the French government and media industries* form a discourse coalition in favor of graduated response (Sect. 4.2.1). *Civil society actors, some filmmakers, performing artists and public intellectuals* severely oppose the graduated response policy (Sect. 4.2.3). *The French Parliament* is split in its views. *The French Constitutional Council, Data Protection Authority, Regulatory Authority for Electronic Communications and Post, the European public authorities, the adult content sector and the Internet & technology industries* adopt a nuanced stance. They use both discourses in favor and against graduated response. Box 4.3 provides an overview of the discourse coalitions, structuration and institutionalization present in HADOPI.

Regarding *discourse structuration* (reproduction of discourse by government or Parliament officials and departments during the policymaking process), I expand on the views of the Parliamentary committees and of the Constitutional Council, as they determined the final text of the two HADOPI laws. They sought to improve the graduated response mechanism proposed by the French government. *They don't fundamen-*

tally question the policy solution but adopt arguments and discourses both for and against graduated response. The big exceptions are the requests for Constitutional Council rulings on the HADOPI laws. These Deputies strongly oppose graduated response.

In *the first HADOPI law*, the French Parliament made improvements to the functioning and independence of the administrative authority. *The Senate's Cultural Affairs Committee* (2008b) read the law proposal first. They added provisions on awareness raising by ISPs and in schools. Further the Senate's Cultural Affairs Committee removed the references to blocking and filtering. Instead HADOPI monitors and reports on experimentation by private actors. The Committee stressed that filtering's efficiency, cost and deployment on a large scale are not yet mastered. They argued that it is their task to restore the balance found in the Olivennes Agreement. For this reason the media industries' commitments to develop legal offers were also made obligatory (French Senate 2008a, b). The National Assembly added articles on journalists, libraries and online press services (French Parliament 2009c). *The Senate's Economic Affairs Committee* (French Senate 2008a) contended that the HADOPI 1 law proposal only offers a partial solution to the cultural sector's difficulties. Legal offers can also dissuade piracy. The Committee deemed that HADOPI is neither innovative nor adapted to the online environment. Indeed creating an authority for each new online policy problem will lead to a fragmentation of Internet regulation. The Committee stressed the need to respect the openness and neutrality of the Internet in order to foster growth in France. The separation between infrastructure and content must be kept in order to avoid control by state or private entities. Further *184 Deputies* (2009)[4] submitted a request for a Constitutional Council ruling on HADOPI 1. They adopted the same discourse as opponents of HADOPI: graduated response is disproportionate, circumventable, counterproductive, inapplicable, costly and dangerous for fundamental rights and liberties. *The Constitutional Council* agreed in part with the Deputies (June 10, 2009). The Deputies and the Constitutional Council underlined the importance of the Internet in democratic life. The Council ruled that only a judicial authority could suspend Internet access and that the HADOPI 1 law as adopted by the National Assembly and Senate reversed the burden of proof.

In *the second HADOPI law*, the French Parliament sought to increase the legibility, intelligibility and coherence of the text. *The Senate's Cultural Affairs Committee* (2009) debated the law proposal first. They clarified the distinction between online copyright enforcement and gross negligence, and specified that HADOPI has to delete personal data once the ISP suspends access. Moreover the Senate and National Assembly added a requirement to inform rights holders when a judicial procedure is launched (French Parliament 2009c; French Senate 2009). This would permit rights holders to become a civil party and request damages and interests. During the policy discussions on HADOPI 1 the Senate and National Assembly had also approved a provision on the continued payment of the Internet subscription during the period of suspension. *164 Deputies* (2009) submitted a request for a Constitutional Council ruling on HADOPI 2. They argued that procedural guarantees were lacking. For instance the simplified judicial procedure for online copyright infringement was criticized and rights holders should not be permitted to request damages and interests. Further Deputies considered that the continued payment of the Internet subscription is disproportionate and amounts to a double sanction. They also pointed out that it is not technically possible to suspend Internet access in some French regions. *The Constitutional Council* (October 22, 2009) rejected most objections to HADOPI 2. The Council deemed that there were sufficient procedural guarantees and that the judicial authorities would take circumstances into account. Additionally there was no manifest disproportion between the crime and sanction in requiring the continued payment of the Internet subscription. The Council did however censure the provision on damages and interests. It reasoned that although it is permissible to include such a measure in the law, rights and conditions should have been detailed. By leaving these details to a later decree the legislator violated its competence.

Regarding *discourse institutionalization* (embedding of discourse into legal and supporting policy documents at the end of the policymaking process) then, *the final text of HADOPI 1* includes the Parliament's improvements on the functioning and independence of the administrative authority, filtering is toned down, awareness raising and legal offers are boosted. Provisions on journalists, libraries and online press services are also present. Following the censure of the Constitutional Council the law does not contain provisions to sanction Internet users. *The final text of HADOPI 2* retains the Parliament's clarifications on copyright infringement and gross negligence, personal data is deleted once ISPs suspend Internet access, and Internet subscribers continue to pay during their suspension. Following the ruling of the Constitutional Council the law does not allow rights holders to claim damages and interests. *Thus after multiple failed attempts,[5] graduated response, its arguments and discourse were legally endorsed in France in 2009. A big victory for proponents.* Opponents succeeded in introducing a judicial procedure. HADOPI also contains commitments to legal offers, research and awareness raising. Filtering and blocking were largely pushed off the table.

The following sections reflect on the stakeholders' views of the socio-economic and politico-legal context in which HADOPI developed. Which interests and institutional rules are at play?

Box 4.3 Discourse coalitions, structuration and institutionalization on HADOPI

Analysis of stakeholder opinions on HADOPI 1 and 2 during policymaking process (2008–2009)
Pro—Prevention of Mass Piracy through Pedagogy

- French Public Authorities
  - ✓ Ministry of Culture and Communication, including Minister Christine Albanel
  - ✓ Ministry of Justice, including Minister Michèle Alliot-Marie
  - ✓ National Assembly and Senate
  - ✓ President Nicolas Sarkozy
- Media Industries
  - ✓ Content producer associations such as APC, SPPF and UPFI
  - ✓ Content distributor association IFPI
  - ✓ Artist & performer organizations and collective rights management societies—ARP, CSDEM, SACD, SACEM, SCAM, SCPP, SNAC, SNEP and UNAC
  - ✓ Artistes "De Gauche" and Cinéastes pour la Loi Création & Internet

Mixed—Rules of the Road

Anti—Disproportionate and Unadapted Policy Solution

- French Public Authorities
  - ✓ National Assembly and Senate
- European Public Authorities
  - ✓ MEPs Catherine Trautmann and Guy Bono (S&D)

(continued)

Box 4.3 (continued)

- Media Industries
  - ✓ Cinéastes contre la Loi Création & Internet and performer organization SAMUP
- Civil Society
  - ✓ Civil rights organization—UFC Que Choisir
  - ✓ Digital rights organization—La Quadrature du Net
- Public Intellectuals
  - ✓ Guillaume Lovet, Jacques Attali and Patrick Waelbroeck

Nuanced—Use of multiple discourses

- French Public Authorities
  - ✓ Constitutional Council
  - ✓ Data Protection Authority (CNIL)
  - ✓ Regulatory Authority for Electronic Communications and Post (ARCEP)
- European Public Authorities
  - ✓ Council of the European Union
  - ✓ European Commission
  - ✓ European Commissioner for Information Society & Media Viviane Reding
  - ✓ European Parliament
- Media Industries
  - ✓ Adult content company Marcel Dorcel
- Internet Industries
  - ✓ Company and association of fixed/mobile telecoms operators & ISPs Free and AFA
  - ✓ Association of online service providers ASIC

Discourse Structuration and Institutionalization

- Discourse Structuration
  - ✓ French parliamentary committees and Constitutional Council
  - ✓ No fundamental questioning of problem definition or policy solution, adopt
  - ✓ discourses for and against graduated response
- Discourse Institutionalization
  - ✓ HADOPI 1 and 2 final text

4.3 INTERESTS

4.3.1 Policy Goals

In terms of policy goals, stakeholders participate in the HADOPI policymaking debate to *adopt, amend or reject a graduated response mechanism*. Proponents of HADOPI are motivated to *decrease piracy, defend intellectual property rights and establish rule of law on the Internet*. Maintaining a rich and diverse culture is often mentioned as a policy goal as well. Civil society representatives however, argue that culture has been used as a pretext to defend the status quo of the media industries. For instance, UFC Que Choisir (2007, translated from French) states that, it "denounces the repressive approach and the lack of clarity of the cultural minister who, under the pretext of defending culture and its diversity, is systematically the untiring advocate of an industry that is too concentrated and not innovative enough." Opponents of HADOPI seek to *defend civil liberties and encourage access to culture*. Some aim for the *legalization of file sharing*. The Minister of Culture and Communication Christine Albanel (in French Government 2008a, b, 2009) and the Senate's Cultural Affairs Committee (2008b) contend that opponents of HADOPI support a law free Internet where unbridled and brutal liberalism rules. Lastly in my expert interviews, respondents argue that the main driver for policy action (in favor of ADSL and later HADOPI) are *economic interests*. French public authorities are motivated to support their industries. Marc Pic (Director of Digital Solutions at Hologram Industries, Interview 2013, translated from French) asserts: "[o]ne must understand that it is above all an economic equation. Why does France defend rights holders well? Because it has rights holders. Because it has power in the music and audiovisual industries." The media and Internet industries lobby hard.

4.3.2 Social and Economic Reality

Regarding the social and economic reality, multiple stakeholders including the administrative authority HADOPI and the French government emphasize *the complexity of piracy online*. HADOPI's longitudinal report on French cultural consumption on the Internet (2013a) identifies different reasons for licit and illicit cultural consumption based on user profiles.

For instance the user group *"les numerivores"* (22 % of Internet users, younger than thirty-five years old, more active than average) is hindered most by the price of legal offers and tends to search for free cultural products. Although this user group has a higher rate of illicit consumption (32 %) than other user profiles, their budget for digital cultural products is the average (€20 Euros/month). However the user group *"les passionés attentifs"* (20 % of Internet users, younger than forty-one years old) indicates that legal offers do not meet their demand. They are interested in legal offers that add value to their consumption experience. Their budget for digital cultural products is the same as *"les numerivores"* (€20 Euros/month). The Lescure Report (2013) commissioned by the French government also points out that piracy is not the only reason for harm in the media industries. Indeed Patrick Waelbroeck (Professor at Télécom ParisTech, Interview 2013) argues that,

> there were two things happening at the same time: people have confused digital transformation and the life cycle of the products with digital piracy.

For instance he states that examining independent labels rather than the major record companies provides a very different picture. Artists increasingly approach independent labels to be promoted on the Internet. Waelbroeck (Interview 2013) contends that, "it is not true that overall there is less interesting creation because of the Internet." La Quadrature du Net (2008a) remarks that the negative impact of non-commercial cultural exchange has not been determined. Further the Lescure Report (2013) fears *a sharp division between views of rights holders and the public.* The report asserts that copyright needs to be adapted to digital realities and practices. Media industries mistakenly sought to delay digital development. At the same time the Lescure Report acknowledges that technological developments sometimes harass cultural mechanisms. Foreign stakeholders are criticized for trying to escape French regulation and financing. The report contends that *relations between media and Internet industries need to be redefined.* The online sector could and should be allies rather than adversaries in digital distribution. Giuseppe De Martino (Secretary General of Dailymotion and President of ASIC—*Association des Services Internet Communautaires,* Interview 2013) argues that Internet intermediaries in France are constantly questioned in their liability status and position in the media value chain.

4.4   INSTITUTIONS

4.4.1   Policy Legacy

In terms of policy legacy, it is important to point back to *the long history* of graduated response in France. Stakeholders sought to implement a graduated response mechanism since 2004. Past non-legislative and legislative endeavors help shape the particular form that graduated response takes on in France. For instance the National Assembly (2009a, b, d, e) repeatedly referred to HADOPI as a policy instrument to complete the reflection started in DADVSI. Moreover when asked why France set up an administrative authority to deal with copyright enforcement, Francesca Musiani (Researcher at ISCC-CNRS, Paris, Interview 2013) explains that there is a state-centric paradigm in French political thought. She deems it likely that "there was little doubt in the minds of French politicians that this issue should indeed be tackled with somewhat traditional political instruments."

In the policymaking process stakeholders refer to *European initiatives* as well. In Sect. 4.1.1 we discussed the ideas that the European Parliament, Council and Commission express on graduated response. The same documents in which they share their views are used by French stakeholders to advocate their policy problems, solutions and goals. First, opponents of HADOPI draw strength and arguments from *the European Parliament Resolution on the Cultural Industries of Europe*. The resolution is portrayed as a policy position against graduated response and the suspension of Internet access. Second, stakeholders praise *the European Commission Creative Content Online policy*. The French president Sarkozy states that, "[t]his initiative is particularly welcomed because the distribution of works on digital networks is an ardent obligation. The development of an attractive legal offer on the Internet and the fight against piracy of works—one cannot exist without the other—require the mobilization of the EU institutions and Member States governments" (Ecrans.fr 2008a, translated from French). Lastly, the joint timing of the HADOPI laws and *the Telecoms Package* caused flurry. Proponents of HADOPI worried but indicated that Amendment 138 would not jeopardize the French graduated response initiative. Opponents of HADOPI were concerned about the protection of citizens and openness of the Internet. They sought support at a European level, fighting hard for safe passing of the amendment. In November 2009 the European Parliament and Council compromised on a text which calls for adequate procedural safeguards when restricting Internet access. The final text stipulates that restrictions on Internet users' access or use of services and applications through electronic communications networks "may only be imposed if they are appropriate, proportionate and necessary within a democratic society" and "their implementation shall be subject to adequate procedural safeguards in conformity with the European Convention for the Protection of Human Rights and Fundamental Freedoms and with general principles of Community law, including effective judicial protection and due process" (European Parliament & Council 2009, Article 1.3a).

4.4.2   Political and Legal Reality

Finally relating to the political and legal reality of graduated response in France, *La Quadrature du Net* deserves mention. In HADOPI the digital rights organization advocated against surveillance and infrastructure-based enforcement. La Quadrature du Net is present on both French and European levels. Pierre Gueydier (Researcher in Sociology of Innovation, Paris, Interview 2013) remarks that La Quadrature du Net has professionalized considerably over the past years. They use a campaign style called "fire marketing" which emphasizes shared values. The digital rights organization targets social networks and combines traditional offline with new online advocacy techniques. For instance in 2009 La Quadrature du Net (2009a) launched a website that tracked the activity and voting behavior of French Parliamentarians on HADOPI. The website also included details to get in touch with the elected officials. Their "political memory" website remains available and has been used at a European level. It constitutes a form of *"sousveillance"*—citizen monitoring of political decision making. In their article on digital network repertoires Yana Breindl and François Briatte (2010) state that La Quadrature du Net seeks to promote *transparency and collaboration* in policymaking through open and online advocacy. The organization upholds core values of the free and open software movement.

In terms of *technological governance* France is a mixed bag. On the one hand, HADOPI is far reaching, having endorsed surveillance of Internet use by private actors and suspension of Internet access with judicial oversight. Moreover the Lescure Report (2013) calls for more technological governance, proposing closer involvement of Internet intermediaries. On the other hand stakeholders have shown reticence toward TPMs, blocking and filtering. A study by the HADOPI Labs (Labs Hadopi 2012) pointed to the weaknesses of current filtering techniques (HADOPI 2013b). Moreover CNIL has monitored the implementation of graduated response closely, requiring high data protection standards. In this regard it is interesting to quote Marc Pic (Director of Digital Solutions at Hologram Industries, Interview 2013, translated from French). He views monitoring as a subtle and preferable form of technological regulation. Indeed Pic argues that,

> there is more interest to monitor than to prohibit. In terms of governance I have directed myself towards the facilitation of measures of surveillance rather than prohibition. It may be better to put up surveillance cameras rather than to put up barbed wire.

In the HADOPI policy debate there is a strong focus on the *national governments and law* IG model. The French government has to intervene to establish rule of law on the Internet. HADOPI is a legislative measure at a national level. Proponents of HADOPI argue that opponents advocate survival of the fittest on the Internet, hoping to keep a libertarian law free zone *(cyberspace and spontaneous ordering)*. Opponents of HADOPI disagree. Their arguments place them closer to the IG model of *code and Internet architecture*. They point to unique characteristics of the Internet and potential dangers of technological governance. Lastly the Senate Economic Affairs Committee (2008a) regrets the piecemeal approach to IG. The Committee prefers a multistakeholder dialogue independent of government *(transnational institutions and international organizations)*. It deems judicial authorities "the natural regulator of the Internet" (French Senate 2008a, 15).

Fast forward a few years. How has the debate on online copyright enforcement evolved in France? *HADOPI* has had a troubled existence. The policymaking process leading to graduated response was slow and difficult. Publicly the authority continues to suffer from a negative image, viewed as *a tool for rights holders to suspend Internet access*.[6] Both proponents and opponents of HADOPI point to *the need for alternative means to deal with online copyright infringement.* Targeting end users is not ideal. However given the restraints of the E-Commerce Directive and the reluctance of judicial authorities to pursue harsh counterfeiting sanctions against individuals, French rights holders considered graduated response the only viable enforcement option at the time (Christian Oddos, Valérie-Laure Benabou, Interviews 2013). The struggle to define the French approach to online copyright infringement continues.

This is abundantly clear in *the French government's* 2013 *Lescure Report on the Act II of the Cultural Exception.* Quintessentially French, the Lescure Report (2013) emphasizes that culture cannot be likened to other products nor left to market forces alone. The report, already partially introduced above, sets out the next steps for French culture online. The big lines of the Lescure Report are public access to works and cultural offer online, remuneration of creators and financing of creation, and protection and adaptation of IPR (French Ministry of Culture and Communication 2013). Indeed, the report offers *a varied and multifaceted approach to online copyright infringement.* Evaluating HADOPI, the Lescure Report deems that graduated response's repressive character, fueled by the threat of losing Internet access, proved exaggerated. The cost of the graduated response system is not disproportionate because illegal file sharing has decreased. However its efficiency is debated, as there seems to be a displacement to other illegal services. The report (2013) recommends *keeping but lightening the graduated response mechanism:* replace the suspension of Internet access with a small fine and move HADOPI's missions to the French audiovisual regulator (CSA— *Conseil Supérieur de l'Audiovisuel*). The Lescure Report acknowledges that the sanctions in graduated response, initially proposed as a solution to the criminal sanctions of online copyright infringement, seem disproportionate. As we discussed, the law has since been amended to remove the suspension of Internet access. The amount of the fine has not changed (maximum 1500 Euro). The transfer of HADOPI to CSA is disputed, as the audiovisual regulator's missions pertain to radio and television rather than the Internet. Further the Lescure Report seeks to *reorient the debate toward commercial scale piracy.* It does not propose legislative changes, but points to limitations in international cooperation and encourages self-regulatory schemes such as follow-the-money and dereferencing of illegal content.

These last recommendations are further explored in the 2014 Imbert-Quaretta Report evaluating effective tools to tackle commercial scale piracy. The follow-the-money approach is again promoted, complemented with the curation of a black list of massively infringing websites. The report also suggests implementing a system of notice and stay down in order to combat the reappearance of illegal content (French Ministry of Culture and Communication 2014). In 2015, the French Minister of Culture and Communication Fleur Pellerin launched a government campaign again commercial scale piracy. In this context, a Charter of Good Practices in Advertising for Copyright Protection was signed (French Ministry of Culture and Communication 2015a). Further Pellerin announced that the effectiveness of blocking injunctions through judicial procedures would be monitored and also deemed a reflection on status and responsibilities of online video platforms necessary. For instance, she suggests a simplification of procedures for reporting, withdrawal and monitoring of copyrighted content on these platforms (French Ministry of Culture and Communication 2015b). Strong parallels can be drawn to the European debate, where self-regulatory agreements on commercial scale piracy are equally sought, as well as pressure on the role of intermediaries in protecting copyrighted works applied. Box 4.4 summarizes the analysis of interests and institutions in HADOPI.

Box 4.4   Interests and institutions in HADOPI

Analysis of stakeholder opinions on HADOPI 1 and 2 during policymaking process (2008–2009)

Interests

- Policy Goals
  - ✓ Adoption, amendment or rejection of graduated response
  - ✓ Defend copyright, decrease piracy, maintain rich and diverse culture, establish rule of law on the Internet
  - ✓ Defend fundamental rights, encourage access to culture, legalize file sharing
- Social and Economic Reality
  - ✓ French government seeks to defend economic interests (first telecoms, then media)
  - ✓ Stakeholders acknowledge complexity of online piracy

(continued)

Box 4.4   (continued)

Institutions

- Policy Legacy
    - ✓ Long history of graduated response—lenient telecoms policies, charter of engagements, DADVSI, Olivennes agreement, presidential campaign promises
    - ✓ Struggle over Amendment 138 of Telecoms Package
- Political and Legal Reality
    - ✓ Legislative policy outcome—graduated response endorsed
    - ✓ Surveillance, suspension of Internet access, closer involvement of intermediaries
    - ✓ IG—national governments and law, code and Internet architecture, transnational institutions and international organizations
    - ✓ Follow up
        Lescure Report on the Act II of the Cultural Exception, multifaceted approach—public access to works and cultural offer online, remuneration of creators and financing of creation, protection and adaptation of IPRs
        Graduated response maintained, suspension of Internet access dropped
        Imbert-Quaretta Report on effective tools to combat commercial scale piracy, includes follow-the-money approach, blacklisting and notice and stay down
        French government strategy against commercial scale piracy—advertising charter signed, reflection on responsibilities of intermediaries ongoing.

4.5   CONCLUSION: PEC CONSIDERATIONS

France passed graduated response policy despite a long and difficult adoption process and a lack of agreement at a European level. The analysis of HADOPI suggests at least *four reasons why graduated response is considered an appropriate policy measure* to fight online copyright infringement in France. First as Marc Pic indicates, France has *powerful audiovisual and music industries.* Media stakeholders lobby hard, the country has economic interests to defend and its president Nicolas Sarkozy had a campaign promise to make true. Second and somewhat contrarily, the French government and media stakeholders successfully frame *culture as exceptional* and in need of protection from economic competition. Fighting online piracy protects French cultural diversity. Third, *France's state-centric paradigm* defines online copyright infringement as a public problem. Strong government intervention is not questioned. *Graduated response* is also advocated *as a soft and pedagogical approach* to online copyright enforcement, compared to the harsh legal sanctions provided against counterfeiting. Finally, the *policy history of graduated response* in France also helps the adoption of HADOPI. For instance *the DADVSI law* made Internet account holders responsible for copyright infringements on their networks. Further ISPs had been involved in previous *stakeholder agreements* to fight online piracy. This weakened their resistance to graduated response in HADOPI policy-making process.

From a political economic perspective, graduated response is about much more than fighting piracy through pedagogy, dissuasion and legal offers. What can be said about *the consequences of graduated response?* In the process of finding solutions for online copyright infringement, *fundamental decisions are taken about the type of creativity and Internet we want in the future.*

The French graduated response policy supports strong copyright, perceives the Internet as a danger and advocates the suspension of Internet access as a proportionate response to the lack of control over copyrighted works. *The fact that this interference in the code of the Internet implies monitoring of citizens is not seen as a problem.* On the contrary as we have seen, it is portrayed as a necessary step to protect cultural diversity. The analysis of stakeholder views reveals that copyright has mainly been subjected to economic reasoning. *Although the EP and French civil society indicate the potential for the Internet for non-commercial content creation, proponents of HADOPI repeatedly emphasize the relationship between cultural diversity and copyright revenues.* Civil society representatives saw graduated response as a means of protecting an overly concentrated and outdated industry.

Additionally, the striking discourse of the French government and media industries on the need to civilize the Internet and to involve intermediaries in combating piracy point in the direction of *closer Internet control.* The Internet in its current form, and thus its approach to distribution of information, are deemed threats to art and culture. In "Freedom of Speech, the Internet, and the Costs of Control: The French Example", Julien Mailland (2001) argues that a precedent of seeking to centrally control a communication network can be found in the French approach to the Minitel. France long resisted the development of the Internet, as it had introduced its own alternative communication network technology called the Minitel in the 1970s. The infrastructure supporting this video-tex technology was centralized and restricted to France, and content on the Minitel network was strongly regulated by the French government. Here again, considering the national precedent set by the Minitel, it is not surprising that graduated response legislation was adopted in France.

At the same time the efforts of HADOPI opponents should be noted. *Although opponents of graduated response did not stop the adoption of the HADOPI laws, they offered a counter discourse denting the economic copyright and uncontrolled Internet master frames* (see also Breindl and Briatte 2010). In the HADOPI policymaking process legal provisions on awareness raising and legal offers were included. Moreover proposals for blocking and filtering were removed. The French Constitutional Council stressed the importance of access to the Internet for participation in democratic life and the expression of ideas and opinions. The suspension of Internet access was highly contested. Ultimately the sanction was accepted on both a national and a European level, but important procedural safeguards including judicial review were set in place. Interestingly, there was less resistance to the idea of online surveillance. Precedents had been set in previous legislation and decisions.

The French graduated response policy adopts a proprietarian view on creativity and moves toward a closed, nationally regulated Internet environment. Moreover graduated response contributes to a further normalization of surveillance of citizens. This study does not oppose technological governance, but pleads for debates on consequences. The open, flexible and decentralized character of the Internet is not a coincidence; normative choices encouraging widespread distribution of information were made. In HADOPI societal considerations of *power inequalities between media and citizens were largely ignored*. Media stakeholders win: they see their viewpoint valorized and are given power to monitor Internet users. The following chapter explores technological governance further, zooming in on the controversial role of Internet intermediaries in the process.

Notes

1. For example, the Copysense tool offered by Audible Magic.
2. For example, the ISPs Eircom in Ireland and Virgin Media in the United Kingdom have warned their Internet subscribers about

copyright infringements. Further, stakeholders in the United Kingdom have agreed upon a Voluntary Copyright Alert Programme, implementing graduated response.

3. Unless the matter at hand pertains to distinctions between copyright, *"droit d'auteur"* and related rights, I use the term "copyright" in this case study. The section on copyright rationales will highlight some of the differences. As we see below, France's focus on *"droit d'auteur"* and culture rings out in its Report on Act II of the Cultural Exception (Lescure 2013).

4. Including Aurélie Filippetti and François Hollande who respectively became the French Minister for Culture and Communication and the French President after the 2012 elections. They were also part of the request for a Constitutional Council ruling on HADOPI 2.

5. The 2004 Charter of Engagements, the 2006 DADVSI law and the 2009 HADOPI 1 law.

6. Although several interview respondents speak quite positively about HADOPI's efforts to observe uses online. They indicate that the authority has made efforts to expand its mandate (Francesca Musiani, Cécile Méadel, Valérie-Laure Benabou, Interviews 2013). Examples are the creation of the academic Labs, the publication of a study on copyright exceptions and the launch of a study on remuneration schemes for file sharing.

BIBLIOGRAPHY

June 10, 2009. Décision n. 2009–580 DC du 10 Juin 2009. Loi Favorisant la Diffusion et la Protection de la Création sur Internet. French Constitutional Council.

October 22, 2009. Décision n. 2009-590 DC du 22 Octobre 2009. Loi relative à la Protection Pénale de la Propriété Littéraire et Artistique sur Internet. French Constitutional Council.

AFA. 2008. Projet de Loi 'Création et Internet': Pour le Respect des Accords de l'Elysée. http://www.afpi-france.com/articles/projet-de-loi-creation-et-internet-pour-le-respect-des-accords-de-l-elysee. Accessed 6 Oct 2016.

ARCEP. 2008. *Avis n. 2008-0547 de l'Autorité de Régulation des Communications Électroniques et des Postes en date du 6 Mai 2008 sur le Projet de Loi Relatif à la Haute Autorité pour la Diffusion des Œuvres et de la Protection des Droits sur Internet.* Paris: French Regulatory Authority for Post and Electronic Communications.

ASIC. 2009. L'Avenir de l'Internet Se Joue Ce Lundi à Bruxelles. http://press. dailymotion.com/wp-old/wp-content/uploads/cp_asic_bxl_27032009.pdf. Accessed 6 Oct 2016.

ASIC. 2008b. Création et Internet: L'ASIC Hostile à la Proposition Communiste de Taxer les Acteurs du 2.0. http://www.lasic.fr/wpcontent/uploads/2012/ 03/cp-asic-hadopi-taxe-30102008.pdf. Accessed 6 Oct 2016.

Attali, Jacques. 2009a. Hadopi: Réponse aux Artistes. http://www.attali.com/ actualite/blog/art-et-culture/hadopi-reponse-aux-artistes. Accessed 6 Oct 2016.

———. 2009b. Jacques Attali Répond Aux Artistes. http://www.attali.com/ actualite/blog/art-et-culture/jacques-attali-repond-aux-artistes. Accessed 6 Oct 2016.

Breindl, Yana, and François Briatte. 2010. Digital Network Repertoires and the Contentious Politics of Digital Copyright in France and the European Union. *Internet, Politics, Policy 2010: An Impact Assessment*, Oxford.

CNIL. 2007. Surveillance des Réseaux 'Peer to Peer': La CNIL Prend Acte de la Décision du Conseil d'Etat. Archived with Author.

———. 2010. Lutte Contre le Téléchargement Illégal, CNIL et HADOPI: Déjà une Longue Histoire. http://www.cnil.fr/linstitution/actualite/article/article/la-cnil-et-la-hadopi-deja-une-longue-histoire/. Accessed 11 Apr.

Council of the European Union. 2008. *Council Conclusions on the Development of Legal Offers of Online Cultural and Creative Content and the Prevention and Combating of Piracy in the Digital Environment*. Brussels: Council of the European Union.

Ecrans.fr. 2008a. Lettre Barroso. http://www.ecrans.fr/IMG/pdf/Lettre_ Barroso.pdf. Accessed 6 Oct 2016.

———. 2008b. Lettre Reding. http://www.ecrans.fr/IMG/pdf/lettrereding. pdf. Accessed 6 Oct 2016.

European Commission. 2008c. Public Consultation on Creative Content Online in the Single Market. http://ec.europa.eu/avpolicy/other_actions/content_ online/consultation_2008/index_en.htm. Accessed 6 Oct 2016.

European Parliament. 2008. *INI/2007/2153. Resolution of 10 April 2008 on Cultural Industries in Europe*. Brussels: European Parliament.

European Parliament & Council. 2009. *Directive 2009/136/EC of the European Parliament and of the Council of 25 November 2009 amending Directive 2002/22/EC on Universal Service and Users' Rights relating to Electronic Communications Networks and Services, Directive 2002/58/EC concerning the Processing of Personal Data and the Protection of Privacy in the Electronic Communications Sector and Regulation (EC) No 2006/2004 on Cooperation between National Authorities Responsible for the Enforcement of Consumer Protection Laws (Citizens' Rights Directive)*. Luxembourg: Official Journal of the European Union.

French Deputies. 2009. *Saisine du Conseil Constitutionnel en Date du 28 Septembre 2009. Projet de Loi Relatif à la Protection Pénale de la Propriété Littéraire et Artistique sur Internet.* Paris: French Parliament.

———. 2009. *Saisine du Conseil Constitutionnel Loi Favorisant la Diffusion et la Protection de la Création sur Internet.* Paris: French Parliament.

French Government. 2008a. Après la Diffusion du Sondage IPSOS sur la Lutte Contre le Piratage sur Internet, Christine Albanel Se Félicite de l'Esprit de Responsabilité des Français. http://www.culture.gouv.fr/culture/actualites/ communiq/albanel/comipsos.htm. Accessed 6 Oct 2016.

———. 2008b. Les Etats Membres de l'Union Européenne Sont Tombés d'Accord pour Retirer l'Amendement n. 138 (Dit 'Amendement Bono') du Paquet Télécom. http://www.culture.gouv.fr/culture/actualites/commu- niq/albanel/com138.html. Accessed 6 Oct 2016.

———. 2009. Christine Albanel Remercie les Sénateurs et Députés de Tous Bords Politiques qui Ont Apporté Leur Soutien au Projet de Loi Création et Internet. http://www.culture.gouv.fr/culture/actualites/communiq/albanel/com_ creation_internet_130509.html. Accessed 6 Oct 2016.

———. 2013. *Décret n. 2013-596 du 8 juillet 2013 Supprimant la Peine Contraventionnelle Complémentaire de Suspension de l'Accès à un Service de Communication au Public en Ligne et Relatif aux Modalités de Transmission des Informations Prévue à l'Article L. 331-21 du Code de la Propriété Intellectuelle.* Paris: French Government.

French Ministry of Culture and Communication. 2004. Charte d'Engagements Pour le Développement de l'Offre Légale de Musique en Ligne, le Respect de la Propriété Intellectuelle et la Lutte Contre la Piraterie Numérique. http:// www.culture.gouv.fr/culture/actualites/conferen/donnedieu/charte280704. htm. Accessed 11 Apr.

———. 2008. *Projet de Loi Favorisant la Diffusion et la Protection de la Création sur Internet.* Paris: French Government.

———. 2013. Culture-Acte 2: 80 Propositions sur les Contenus Culturels Numériques.http://www.culturecommunication.gouv.fr/Actualites/ En-continu/Culture-acte-2-80-propositions-sur-les-contenus-culturels- numeriques. Accessed 6 Oct 2016.

———. 2014. Remise à Aurélie Filippetti du Rapport de Mireille Imbert-Quaretta sur les Outils Opérationnels de Prévention et de Lutte contre la Contrefaçon en Ligne. http://www.culturecommunication.gouv.fr/Presse/Communiques- de-presse/Remise-a-Aurelie-Filippetti-du-rapport-de-Mireille-Imbert- Quaretta-sur-les-outils-operationnels-de-prevention-et-de-lutte-contre-la- contrefacon-en-ligne. Accessed 21 Sept 2016.

———. 2015a. Charte des Bonnes Pratiques dans la Publicité pour le Respect du Droit d'Auteur et des Droits Voisins. http://www.culturecommunication. gouv.fr/Actualites/Dossiers/Charte-des-bonnes-pratiques-dans-la-publicite-pour-le-respect-du-droit-d-auteur-et-des-droits-voisins/Presentation-de-la-charte. Accessed 20 Sept 2016.

———. 2015b. Stratégie du Gouvernement concernant la Lutte contre le Piratage des Œuvres sur Internet. http://www.culturecommunication.gouv.fr/Presse/Communiques-de-presse/Lutte-contre-le-piratage. Accessed 21 Sept 2016.

French National Assembly. 2009a. *Avis Fait au Nom de la Commission des Affaires Économiques, de l'Environnement et du Territoire sur le Projet de Loi, Adopté Par le Sénat, Favorisant la Diffusion et la Protection de la Création sur Internet (n. 1240), Par M. Bernard Gérard, Député.* Paris: French Parliament.

———. 2009b. *Avis Présenté au Nom de la Commission des Affaires Culturelles, Familiales et Social sur le Projet de Loi, Adopté Par le Sénat, Favorisant la Diffusion et la Protection de la Création sur Internet, Par Mme Muriel Marland-Militello, Députée.* Paris: French Parliament.

———. 2009a. *Rapport Fait au Nom de la Commission des Affaires Culturelles et de l'Éducation sur le Projet de Loi (n. 1831), Adopté Par le Sénat Après Engagement de la Procédure Accélérée, Relatif à la Protection Pénale de la Propriété Littéraire et Artistique sur Internet, Par M. Franck Riester, Député.* Paris: French Parliament.

———. 2009b. *Rapport Fait au Nom de La Commission des Lois Constitutionnelles, de la Législation et de l'Administration Générale de la République sur le Projet de Loi (n. 1240), Adopté par le Sénat Après Déclaration d'Urgence, favorisant la Diffusion et la Protection de la Création sur Internet, Par M. Franck Riester, Député.* Paris: French Parliament.

French Parliament. 2006. *Loi n. 2006-961 du 1 Août 2006 relative au Droit d'Auteur et aux Droits Voisins dans la Société de l'Information.* Paris: Journal officiel de la République française.

———. 2009a. *Loi n. 2009a-669 du 12 Juin 2009a favorisant la Diffusion et la Protection de la Création sur Internet.* Paris: Journal officiel de la République française.

———. 2009b. *Loi n. 2009b-1311 du 28 Octobre 2009b relative à la Protection Pénale de la Propriété Littéraire et Artistique sur Internet.* Paris: Journal officiel de la République française.

———. 2009c. *Rapport Fait au Nom de la Commission Mixte Paritaire (1) Chargée de Proposer un Texte sur les Dispositions Restant en Discussion du Projet de Loi Relatif à la Protection Pénale de la Propriété Littéraire et Artistique sur Internet, Par M. Franck Riester, Rapporteur, Député, Par M. Michel Thiollière, Rapporteur, Sénateur.* Paris: French Parliament.

French Senate. 2008a. *Avis Présenté au Nom de la Commission des Affaires Économiques (1) sur le Projet de Loi Favorisant la Diffusion et la Protection de la Création sur Internet (Urgence Déclarée), Par M. Bruno Retailleau, Sénateur.* Paris: French Parliament.

———. 2008b. *Rapport Fait au Nom de la Commission des Affaires Culturelles sur le Projet de Loi Favorisant la Diffusion et la Protection de la Création sur Internet, Par M. Michel Thiollière, Sénateur*. Paris: French Parliament.

———. 2009. *Rapport Fait au Nom de la Commission de la Culture, de l'Éducation et de la Communication (1) sur le Projet de Loi Relatif à la Protection Pénale de la Propriété Littéraire et Artistique sur Internet (Procédure Accélérée Engagée), Par M. Michel Thiollière, Sénateur*. Paris: French Parliament.

HADOPI. 2011. *L'Essentiel du Rapport d'Activité. 2010*. Paris: HADOPI.

———. 2013a. *Hadopi, Biens Culturels et Usages d'Internet: Pratiques et Perceptions des Internautes Français. BU3 – mai 2013a*. Paris: HADOPI.

———. 2013b. *Rapport d'Activité 2012–2013b*. Paris: HADOPI.

———. 2013c. *Réponse Graduée – Les Chiffres Clés*. Paris: HADOPI.

———. 2015. *Rapport d'Activité 2014–2015*. Paris: HADOPI.

———. 2016a. Message de Sensibilisation à Destination des Professionels. https://www.hadopi.fr/hadopi-vous/message-de-sensibilisation-destination-des-professionnels. Accessed 20 Sept 2016a.

———. 2016b. Modèle de Clause à Insérer Dans une Charte Informatique, Contrat de Bail, Contrat de Location, Etc. https://www.hadopi.fr/hadopi-vous/modele-de-charte-ou-clause-pour-les-professionnels. Accessed 20 Sept 2016b.

———. 2016c. Sécurisation de son Accès Internet. https://www.hadopi.fr/usages-responsables/nouvelles-libertes-nouvelles-responsabilites/moyens-de-securisation-labellises. Accessed 20 Sept 2016c.

La Quadrature du Net. 2008a. La CNIL S'Oppose à HADOPI, Pas le PS. http://www.laquadrature.net/fr/la-cnil-soppose-a-hadopi-pas-le-ps. Accessed 6 Oct 2016.

———. 2008b. Paquet Télécom: Guy Bono contre 'les amendements liberticides'. http://www.laquadrature.net/fr/paquet-telecom-guy-bono-contre-. Accessed 6 Oct 2016.

———. 2009a. HADOPI: Qui Veut Surveiller et Punir ?. http://www.laquadrature.net/fr/hadopi-qui-veut-surveiller-et-punir. Accessed 6 Oct 2016.

———. 2009b. HADOPI: Le Nouveau Gouvernement Poursuit l'Acharnement Thérapeutique.' http://www.laquadrature.net/fr/hadopi-le-nouveau-gouvernement-poursuit-lacharnement-therapeutique. Accessed 6 Oct 2016.

Labs Hadopi. 2012. Labs Hadopi. http://labs.hadopi.fr/. Accessed 6 Oct 2016.

Le Monde.fr. 2009. Industrie du X: 'Couper les Accès aux Sites Pirates' au lieu d'Accuser l'Internaute. *Le Monde. Archived with Author.*, September 14.

Lescure, Pierre. 2013. *Culture-Acte 2. Mission 'Acte II de l'Exception Culturelle'. Contributions aux Politiques Culturelles à l'Ère Numérique*. Paris: French Government.

Mailland, Julien. 2001. Freedom of Speech, the Internet, and the Costs of Control: The French Example. *Journal of International Law and Politics* 33(4): 1179–1234.

Offrelegale.fr. 2016. Le Site des Offres Culturelles en Ligne. http://www.offrelegale.fr/. Accessed 20 Sept 2016.

Olivennes, Denis. 2007. *Accord pour le Développement et la Protection des Œuvres et Programmes Culturels sur les Nouveaux Réseaux.* Paris.

Presidency of the French Republic. 2009. Validation, par le Conseil Constitutionnel, de la Loi relative à la Protection Pénale de la Propriété Littéraire et Artistique sur Internet. Archived with Author.

SACD, and SCAM. 2008. Projet de Loi Création et Internet. Une Chance Pour la Création, des Mesures Positives Pour les Consommateurs. Positions de la SACD et de la Scam. http://www.sacd.fr/Projet-de-loi-Creation-et-internet.8 04.0.html?&MP=450-2277. Accessed 6 Oct 2016.

SACEM, CSDEM, SNEP, SCPP, UPFI, and SPPF. 2009. Communiqué de Press SACEM, CSDEM, SNEP, SCPP, UPFI, SPPF. https://societe.sacem.fr/ ressources-presse/par-publication/Communiqués/communique-de-presse-sacem-csdem-snep-scpp-upfi-sppf. Accessed 6 Oct 2016.

UFC Que Choisir. 2007. Mission Olivennes. La Surenchère Répressive. http:// www.quechoisir.org/telecom-multimedia/image-son/musique/communique-mission-olivennes-la-surenchere-repressive. Accessed 6 Oct 2016.

CHAPTER 5

E-Commerce Directive: 2010 European Commission Consultation

As discussed in Chap. 2, the EU has set in place limited liability provisions for Internet intermediaries. This third case study takes an in-depth look at these provisions, because they are continually contested to increase the involvement of intermediaries in the fight against online piracy. In the EU, intermediary liability policy forms the center point for discussions on the use of technology to regulate behavior online.

The policy goals of the Directive on Certain Legal Aspects of Information Society Services, in particular Electronic Commerce, in the Internal Market (E-Commerce Directive, European Parliament & Council 2000) are *to remove obstacles for the development of cross-border services and to provide legal certainty to citizens and businesses in the Internal Market*. With this in mind, *Section 4 of the Directive sets out the conditions for limiting the liability of intermediary service providers (Articles 12–15)*. In essence intermediary service providers (defined as mere conduit, caching and hosting) are not liable for illegal activity or content on their networks as long as they are not aware of its presence. They do not have the obligation to monitor, but need to take action upon acquiring knowledge of illegal activity or content on their networks. The liability exemptions do not affect the possibility of a court or administrative authority of requiring the termination, prevention, removal or disabling of access to infringing information. Moreover member states may establish obligations for service providers to inform competent public authorities of

© The Author(s) 2017

T. Meyer, *The Politics of Online Copyright Enforcement in the EU*, Information Technology and Global Governance, DOI 10.1007/978-3-319-50974-7_5 illegal activities and content on their networks or to disclose information for the identification of users. Articles 12 through 15 of the E-Commerce Directive provide a scale of responsibility: liability increases proportionally with the editorial role of service providers. The more service providers intervene on their networks, the more responsibility they bear to ensure that activities and content are legal. A provider who offers a service only consisting of the transmission of information (Article 12, mere conduit) has the smallest editorial role and the least responsibility. Next follows a provider who offers a service consisting of the transmission with an automatic, intermediate and temporary storage of information (Article 13, caching). Lastly a provider offering a service consisting of the storage of information (Article 14, hosting) has the largest editorial role and the most responsibility. Finally, the E-Commerce Directive encourages the establishment of voluntary agreements among stakeholders (Article 16). Recital 40 summarizes and stipulates that, "service providers have a duty to act, under certain circumstances, with a view to preventing or stopping illegal activities; this Directive should constitute the appropriate basis for the development of rapid and reliable procedures for removing and disabling access to illegal information; such mechanisms could be developed on the basis of voluntary agreements between all parties concerned and should be encouraged by Member States."

In 2010 the EC held *a public consultation on the Future of Electronic Commerce in the Internal Market and the Implementation of the Directive on Electronic Commerce* (European Commission 2010a). The Directorate General responsible is DG MARKT. The consultation fits within a periodical re-examination of the Directive. Article 21(2) of the E-Commerce Directive states that, "[i]n examining the need for an adaptation of this Directive, the report shall in particular analyse the need for proposals concerning the liability of providers of hyperlinks and location tool services, 'notice and take down' procedures and the attribution of liability following the taking down of content. The report shall also analyse the need for additional conditions for the exemption from liability, provided for in Articles 12 and 13, in the light of technical developments." The goal of the 2010 public consultation was to *study the reasons for the limited takeoff of e-commerce*. One issue examined was intermediary liability. Following the consultation the Commission adopted an E-Commerce Action Plan (European Commission 2012b) and held a second public consultation on A Clean and Open Internet: Procedures for Notifying and Acting on Illegal Content Hosted by Online Intermediaries (European Commission

2012a). Further in 2012 the Council (2012) adopted Conclusions and the Parliament (2012) published a Resolution on the Digital Single Market. In 2015, a third public consultation was held on the Regulatory Environment for Platforms, Online Intermediaries, Data and Cloud Computing and the Collaborative Economy (European Commission 2015c). This latest consultation also included questions on the liability of intermediaries. Figure 5.1 provides a timeline of E-Commerce policy developments.

For this third case study, *I have analyzed stakeholder submissions to twelve questions on intermediary liability*. This is an important exercise, because the nature and extent of intermediaries' responsibility to curb online piracy is a recurring theme in all of my case studies. Applying the analytical framework, I have conducted an ADA with a particular focus on actors' proposed policy definitions, policy solutions and goals, and their argumentations on copyright and Internet rationales. In total 103 stakeholder contributions were analyzed (96 consultation submissions,[1] 5 Commission documents, 1 Council Conclusions and 1 Parliament Resolution). Where possible, I have structured the reporting of the problem definitions and policy solutions as yes/no/nuanced/alternative. Contrary to the CCO consultation, I have not quantified the responses, as the questions at hand were often composite. In my reporting, I have also grouped the responses to similar questions together.

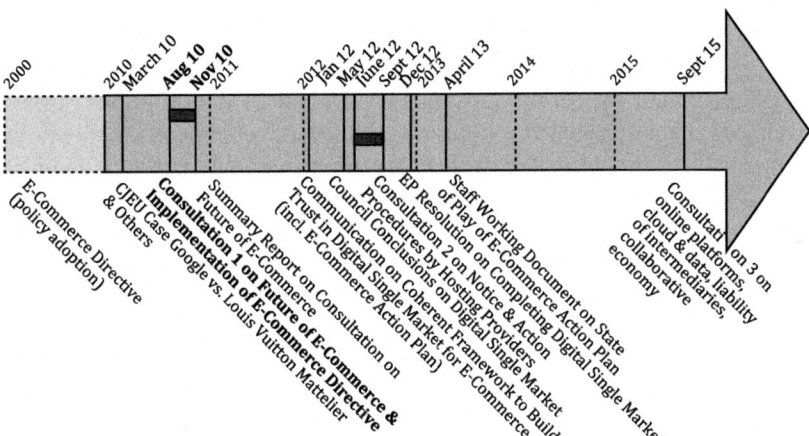

Fig. 5.1 Policy developments in the E-Commerce Directive

The Commission consultation (2010a) covers opinions on the interpretation of the provisions overall (question 52), and the terms "actual knowledge" (question 53), "expeditious" (question 54), "merely technical, automatic and passive nature" (question 66), "mere conduit", "caching" and "hosting" (question 68); awareness and opinions on notice and takedown procedures (questions 55–57) and monitoring and filtering (questions 58–60, 67); awareness of cooperation systems (question 61); experience with the liability of new intermediary service providers (hyperlinks, search engines, web 2.0 and cloud computing, questions 62–64); and opinions on law enforcement (question 69). *I have analyzed opinions on the interpretation of the provisions and terms, notice and takedown procedures, monitoring and filtering, and law enforcement.* Awareness of notice and takedown procedures, monitoring and filtering, and cooperation systems; and experience with the liability of new intermediary service providers have been excluded. The responses to questions on awareness have been omitted as they provide mainly descriptive information which can be found in other sources. The liability of new service providers is an interesting topic, but too detailed for this analysis. Stakeholders' general views on the liability of new service providers are present in their responses to the other questions on intermediary liability.

Further the Commission consultation organized stakeholders into eight categories: private individuals, consumer associations, businesses, ISPs, federations of businesses, regulated professions, professionals of information society law, and public services. *My sample of submissions consists of all EU, French and British contributions from six stakeholder categories* (private individuals and regulated professions have been excluded). I have opted to analyze all EU, French and British submissions (47, 28 and 21 contributions respectively), as there was a need to limit the amount of submissions. Limitations in research capacity were also the primary driver in excluding private individuals. It would have not been possible to obtain a representative sample while selecting among citizens. Private individuals were excluded in the CCO case study as well. There were no stakeholder submissions to issue 5 on intermediary liability among regulated professions. Thus the remaining stakeholder categories are: consumer associations, businesses, ISPs, federations of businesses, professionals of information society law, and public services. Consistent with the other case studies, I adopt a modified stakeholder categorization, comprising of media, Internet & technology, civil society, public authorities and others (see Introduction of Chap. 3 for further details). Finally analysis of the thirty-nine EU interviews is also included.

5.1 IDEAS

In the introduction to the questions on intermediary liability, the Commission (2010a) indicates that interpretation of the liability provisions has often been necessary. *Differences have been found between national courts and even within member states.* Further the consultation states that, "[t]he Internet has given counterfeiters and those involved in piracy new and powerful ways of selling their products, such as the illegal use of 'peer to peer', electronic commerce sites, on-line auction sites and e-spamming." *The Commission is open for discussion in its identification of policy problems and solutions, asking a wide range of questions on intermediary liability.* Some stakeholders provide critical (alternative) views on the questions raised, especially on filtering and voluntary cooperation, deeming that wrong solutions are being proposed for counterfeiting and piracy. Others disapprove of the consultation's focus on businesses and consumers, arguing that this disregards citizens and fundamental rights. Further the fact that *civil society was not given access to the questions on intermediary liability through the online application for consultations (Interactive Policy Making)* engendered much anger. Civil society had to submit separate documents to provide views on the issue.

Prior to their responses to the questions on liability, most stakeholders express the unsolicited (alternative) view, that they do not wish a revision, but rather *a clarification of the E-Commerce Directive.* On the one hand, civil society and Internet & technology companies emphasize the importance of the liability provisions for the development of information society services, innovation and growth, the functioning of the Internet and fundamental rights. On the other hand, this reluctance for change finds its origin in a fear shared by many stakeholders that reviewing the liability provisions will lead to heavy lobbying, yet an uncertain outcome. In the expert interviews Kostas Rossoglou (Former Senior Legal Officer at the European Consumers' Organization—BEUC, Interview 2013) phrases it the following way: "[t]o be honest, if we open the E-Commerce Directive, it is going to be Pandora's Box. We are going to lose a lot of things, it is going to be a mess and we don't know what the outcome will be. For us, the Holy Grail are the articles on ISPs' liability. For sure we are going to lose a lot of things." As we notice below, *the proposed clarifications differ greatly.*

5.1.1   Interpretation of Intermediary Liability Provisions

Overall Interpretation of the Provisions

Question 52: Overall, have you had any difficulties with the interpretation of the provisions on the liability of the intermediary service providers?

Question 65: Are you aware of specific fields in which obstacles to electronic commerce are particularly manifest? Do you think that apart from Articles 12 to 15, which clarify the position of intermediaries, the many different legal regimes governing liability make the application of complex business models uncertain?

Due to the broad formulation of the first question on the e-commerce liability provisions (question 52), stakeholder responses provide insight into their overarching problem definitions on intermediary liability. There are strong parallels with the views expressed in the CCO consultation. A wide range of stakeholders indicate that they have had difficulties with the interpretation of the provisions on the liability of intermediary service providers. Divergence in rules and case law on liability creates legal uncertainty for businesses and consumers.

Media stakeholders and rights holders consider *lack of intermediary cooperation and online piracy* as the main obstacles for the development of information society services. Their primary policy solution is *shared responsibility*. They argue that intermediary service providers have a *duty of care* in the media value chain (Recital 40, see more questions 58–60, 67 on monitoring and filtering). Georgios Mavros (Former Assistant to MEP Marielle Gallo in the EPP group, Interview 2013) states that, "all parties involved must understand that Internet is an ecosystem. For this ecosystem to thrive we need strong online content and Internet intermediaries that benefit from reasonable exceptions of liability." Moreover media stakeholders and rights holders contend that *technology has evolved significantly* since the adoption of the E-Commerce Directive and that certain service providers hide behind broad liability provisions (see more questions 53–54 on "actual knowledge" and "expeditious" removal). They argue that intermediaries who adapt or promote content for commercial purposes should not be covered by the liability regime, as their activities are not of "a mere technical, automatic and passive nature" (Recital 42, see more question 66 on CJEU case Google vs. LVMH). While most deem a clarification of the E-Commerce Directive sufficient to increase legal certainty, a few media stakeholders advocate changes to the liability provisions.

It is a fundamental principle under every legal system in Europe that any merchant has a duty of care in order to avoid that its activity or conduct generates illicit damages to third parties. The required standard of conduct is that of a reasonably careful and prudent merchant in the circumstances depending, in particular, on the nature and value of the protected interests involved, the expertise to be expected, the threat of the potential damage as well as the availability and the costs of precautionary or alternative methods. [I]f such a duty of care is found to be breached, the merchant must be held liable to compensate the victim for the damages that may have been incurred as a result of the breach. (Moët Hennessy Louis Vuitton—LVMH 2010)

Internet & technology companies see things differently. They consider *lack of uniformity in the interpretation of the liability provisions* the most pressing issue. Their primary policy solutions are clarifying that *the Directive covers both civil and criminal liability,* that *Articles 12 through 15 pertain to activities rather than actors,* and consequently that *the liability exemptions can apply to new service providers.* Moreover, Internet & technology companies and civil society deem attempts of rights holders, member states and courts to add liability on intermediaries problematic. They argue that *intermediaries are increasingly encouraged to self-regulate and to prevent infringements* (see more questions 56–57, 59–60, 67 on notice and takedown and filtering). Internet & technology companies and civil society strongly prefer *legal offers* to enforcement. Within the context of developing information society services, intermediaries welcome cooperation with rights holders.

Further and in response to question 65, some stakeholders identify additional obstacles to e-commerce.[2] Legal disparity between the E-Commerce Directive and taxation, competition and data protection laws is mentioned in particular. Media stakeholders emphasize that *data protection* legislation should not be used as a shield to hide illegal activities. Moreover Internet & technology companies and civil society are uncertain about the compatibility of the liability provisions with *injunctive relief* (see more questions 59–60, 67 on filtering). Two associations of performers' organizations GIART and AEPO-ARTIS argue that the rights of performers must not be forgotten in the development of online services, and Internet & technology companies deem cumbersome copyright licensing a problem. RSA Insurance considers the abundance of regulation an issue.

Finally, a minority of stakeholders—the International Association of Scientific, Technical and Medical Publishers (STM), British Sky Broadcasting (BSkyB), the Business Software Alliance (BSA) and some non-intermediary & non-media companies, report that they have not had any difficulties with the interpretation of the provisions on the liability of the intermediary service providers (question 52).

Interpretation of the Terms "Actual Knowledge" and "Expeditious"

Question 53: Have you had any difficulties with the interpretation of the term "actual knowledge" in Articles 13(1)(e) and 14(1)(a) with respect to the removal of problematic information? Are you aware of any situations where this criterion has proved counterproductive for providers voluntarily making efforts to detect illegal activities?

Question 54: Have you had any difficulties with the interpretation of the term "expeditious" in Articles 13(1)(e) and 14(1)(b) with respect to the removal of problematic information?

A third of the stakeholders indicate that they have had difficulties with the interpretation of "actual knowledge" and "expeditious". These terms provide guidance in Articles 13 and 14 on when and how caching and hosting providers need to take action.

Media stakeholders are particularly critical of the *narrow interpretation of "actual knowledge"* in Spain. In this member state "actual knowledge" could only be established through a court order.[3] Media stakeholders and rights holders also argue that some intermediaries are *willfully blind*, ignoring illegal activity on their networks. The IFPI 2010 states that, "[t]he safe harbour provisions, intended to provide protection from monetary liability for providers offering neutral services, have become the refuge of pirates – online services that are deliberately structured to infringe copyright." The European Publishers Council (EPC 2010) agrees, contending that, "[s]ome ISPs have deliberately exploited the fact that the exemptions in current legislation do not require any qualifying standards of corporate governance and have chosen to operate a policy of poor identification of users and slow responses to rights-holders complaints." Relating to question 54, these stakeholders deem a narrow and strict interpretation of "expeditious" preferable.

Internet & technology companies, civil society and legal professionals worry that ambiguity in the interpretation of "actual knowledge" encourages *action against legal content*. Rather than run the risk of liability or the cost of legal advice, intermediaries remove content without questioning. Article 19 (2010) puts it in the following way: "safe harbours make for overzealous harbour masters." At the same time, Internet intermediaries are concerned that they will be found liable if they voluntarily make efforts to detect illegal activities. They call for a "Good Samaritan" clause, to clarify that intermediaries do not lose their legal protection when taking voluntary action.

> These concerns are increased because it is not clear whether a provider using blocking or filtering risks losing all "mere conduit" protection from liability, or only in respect of those communications that were filtered. If an organisation that filtered some inappropriate e-mails to protect its users might thereby become liable for all copyright breaches taking place on its network, this could strongly discourage the adoption of filtering. (JANET 2010)

Following Spain's example, civil society actors deem that "actual knowledge" should only be established through a *court order*. Some stakeholders are slightly more nuanced regarding "manifestly illegal" content, arguing that action is possible if intermediaries are confident of illegality. Further a broad and flexible interpretation to "expeditious" removal of content is considered necessary, while avoiding undue delays at the same time.

Finally, some non-intermediary & non-media companies report that they have not had any difficulties with the interpretation of the terms "actual knowledge" and "expeditious". BSA provides a nuanced view. They indicate that although "actual knowledge" does not pose problems, "expeditious" does. BSA also states that intermediaries cannot turn a blind eye to infringement.

> Interpretation of the Concept of a "Mere Technical, Automatic and Passive Nature" and the Classification of "Mere Conduit", "Caching" and "Hosting"

Question 66: The Court of Justice of the European Union recently delivered an important judgement on the responsibility of intermediary service providers in the Google vs. LVMH case. Do you think that the concept of a "merely technical, automatic and passive nature" of information transmission by search engines or on-line platforms is sufficiently clear to be interpreted in a homogeneous way?

Question 68: Do you think that the classification of technical activities in the information society, such as "hosting", "mere conduit" or "caching" is comprehensible, clear and consistent between Member States? Are you aware of cases where authorities or stakeholders would categorise differently the same technical activity of an information society service?

Similar to the discussion above, questions 66 and 68 of the Commission consultation pertain to the interpretation of terms. However the emphasis here is more specifically on new services in the online environment. The CJEU Google vs. LVMH case (March 23, 2010) concerns the classification of Google's paid referencing service AdWords. Google sells sponsored links and keywords, which include registered trademarks. The Court deemed that liability exemptions need to be evaluated based on Recital 42 of the E-Commerce Directive (European Parliament & Council 2000, emphasis added):

The exemptions from liability established in this Directive cover only cases where the activity of the information society service provider is limited to the technical process of operating and giving access to a communication network over which information made available by third parties is transmitted or temporarily stored, for the sole purpose of making the transmission more efficient; this activity is of a mere technical, automatic and passive nature, which implies that the information society service provider has neither knowledge of nor control over the information which is transmitted or stored.

The facts that the referencing service is subject to payment and that keywords are linked to user search terms do not deprive Google of the liability exemptions. However the role that Google plays in the drafting of the commercial message accompanying the advertising link or in the establishment or selection of keywords is considered relevant. The CJEU (Google vs. LVMH, March 23, 2010) found that Article 14 of the E-Commerce

Directive applies to an Internet referencing service provider "in the case where that service provider has not played an active role of such a kind as to give it knowledge of, or control over, the data stored. If it has not played such a role, that service provider cannot be held liable for the data which it has stored at the request of an advertiser, unless, having obtained knowledge of the unlawful nature of those data or of that advertiser's activities, it failed to act expeditiously to remove or to disable access to the data concerned." The Court (March 23, 2010) also ruled that a trade mark owner is entitled to prohibit an advertiser from advertising on the basis of a keyword identical with that trade mark which the advertiser has selected without the consent of the proprietor "in the case where that advertisement does not enable an average internet user, or enables that user only with difficulty, to ascertain whether the goods or services referred to therein originate from the proprietor of the trade mark or an undertaking economically connected to it or, on the contrary, originate from a third party".

In response to question 66, some stakeholders think that the concept of a "merely technical, automatic and passive nature" of information transmission by search engines or online platforms is sufficiently clear to be interpreted in a homogeneous way. Others disagree. On the one hand, media stakeholders and rights holders contend that modifying or using content for commercial purposes implies that a service provider has played an *active role* and therefore should not be able to rely on liability exemptions. Some consider that AdWords is unfair competition imposed by an intermediary in a hegemonic position. On the other hand, Internet & technology companies and civil rights organizations are concerned that a narrow interpretation of a "merely technical, automatic and passive nature" could exclude new service providers from limited liability, as there is *always a certain degree of control* in their activities. Moreover, some stakeholders argue that Recital 42 of the E-Commerce Directive was wrongly applied, contending that it refers to *mere conduit and caching providers* rather than the hosting providers in question. Lastly, Bouygues Telecom, the European Newspaper Publishers' Association (ENPA) and the French Union of Manufacturers provide a nuanced view, stating that it was too early to tell the outcome. Although the CJEU had provided its judgment at the time of the 2010 consultation, the final decision on Google vs. LVMH had not yet been taken in France.

> LVMH proposes that, in the event online service providers do not limit their activities to mere storage and transmission of data at the direction of a user but rather go beyond that, by actively using, presenting, organising or modifying users' materials for commercial purposes, such online service providers do not qualify as hosting providers within the meaning of the ECD.
> (Moët Hennessy Louis Vuitton—LVMH 2010)

In response to question 68, some Internet & technology companies and other non-intermediary & non-media stakeholders think the classification of intermediary activities such as "hosting", "mere conduit" or "caching" is comprehensible, clear and consistent between member states. Others however deem that the classification of intermediary activities poses problems. With new online services in mind some stakeholders stress that the classification in the E-Commerce Directive is based on *activities rather than actors*. Depending on its activities one intermediary can be subject to multiple liability rules. Five stakeholders specify that the classification of "hosting" has proved more difficult than "mere conduit" and "caching".

5.1.2   Notice and Takedown Procedures

> Question 56: What practical experience do you have regarding the procedures for notice and take-down? Have they worked correctly? If not, why not, in your view?

> Question 57: Do practices other than notice and take down appear to be more effective? ("notice and stay down", "notice and notice" etc.)

Besides questioning the interpretation of liability provisions, the EC also seeks policy actors' views on notice and takedown procedures. Eight member states (Finland, Hungary, Lithuania, France, the United Kingdom, Portugal, Spain and Sweden) have passed legislation on notice and takedown procedures, which differ in scope of infringements covered (copyright, IPR, child abuse, terrorism or horizontal) and in level of details on requirements and obligations provided. For instance France has laws covering illegal gambling, child abuse and cybercrime, while the United Kingdom restricts itself to terrorism. The graduated response laws in these two countries can broadly be considered notice and takedown procedures as well.[4]

In the consultation stakeholders identify three main <u>problems</u> with notice and takedown procedures in the EU. First, the *lack of harmonized rules* on notice and takedown procedures is criticized. Second, media stakeholders and rights holders deem the process *costly and ineffective*. The high volume of notifications required is cumbersome and much infringing material pops again after takedown. Moreover notice and takedown procedures only work with legal online services. Third, civil society and Internet & technology companies worry that notice and takedown procedures lead to self-regulation. They emphasize that intermediaries should not act as *private police* of the Internet. Notice and takedown procedures can stifle the development of new services and the right to freedom of expression.

Stakeholders also propose <u>solutions</u> to resolve these problems. First, they argue for a *harmonized EU framework* on notice and takedown procedures. Second, media stakeholders and rights holders emphasize that public authorities do not need to be involved in notice and takedown procedures. *Cooperation between stakeholders* is preferred. With the exception of BSkyB,[5] they strongly advocate *notice and stay down procedures* to combat recurring infringements. The Interactive Software Federation of Europe (ISFE 2010) states that,

> [n]otice and takedown procedures are an important tool in addressing on-line infringements but they need to be part of an integrated approach which includes Internet Service Providers' terms of service that clearly prohibit customers engaging in illegal activities (including copyright infringement) and that contain a clear repeat infringer policy. It is helpful if these include 'notice and stay down' procedures which can be effective if strictly enforced by the ISP.

Third, civil society and some Internet & technology companies disagree and contend that *involvement of public authorities* is a prerequisite of notice and takedown procedures. *Notice and stay down procedures* are *off limits*, because they require monitoring and thus are considered contrary to Article 15 of the E-Commerce Directive. *Notice and notice procedures* are regarded with slightly *more favor*, although here too privacy concerns remain.

Lastly, a set of Internet & technology companies express a nuanced view on notice and takedown procedures. Indeed Dailymotion, eBay and Google have *voluntary procedures* in place. These companies emphasize that the schemes must not become barriers for startups. *Notice and notice procedures* are considered *worthy of closer examination*, although limitations for manifestly illegal content are recognized.

The EC has been considering stakeholders' requests for EU guidance on notice and takedown for quite some time. In 2012 the Commission (2012a) held a public consultation and stakeholder meetings on notice and action procedures. Then in 2015 a third public consultation was held on online platforms (European Commission 2015c). This included questions on notice and takedown, as well as notice and stay down, procedures. Follow up is deemed necessary. During the expert interviews a respondent in the EC (2013) reported that the preferred option for the Commission is a combination of a legislative instrument and non-binding guidance. However the respondent also stressed that a final decision has not yet been made. Indeed, this cautious approach has become typifying of EU online copyright enforcement. Change might be at hand within the context of broader copyright reforms, but as time goes on, legislation seems less likely.

5.1.3   Effective Specific Filtering Methods

Question 59: From a technical and technological point of view, are you aware of effective specific filtering methods? Do you think that it is possible to establish specific filtering?

Question 60: Do you think that the introduction of technical standards for filtering would make a useful contribution to combating counterfeiting and piracy, or could it, on the contrary make matters worse?

Question 67: Do you think that the prohibition to impose a general obligation to monitor is challenged by the obligations placed by administrative or legal authorities to service providers, with the aim of preventing law infringements? If yes, why?

Monitoring and filtering were no less controversial in 2010 than when the Commission posed the question during the CCO consultation in 2008. Consultation submissions to this section show a strong polarization of interests. In response to question 59, media stakeholders and rights holders argue that effective specific filtering methods are already in place. Internet intermediaries filter spam. Moreover fingerprinting technology permits the identification of content online, although the

Federation of European Publishers (FEP) and STM point out that it is not yet possible to detect copyrighted material in scanned PDFs. Some stakeholders deem that fundamental rights arguments do not stand, as the issue at hand is specific rather than general monitoring. Civil society, legal professionals, Internet & technology companies, non-Internet & non-media companies, BSA and ENPA state strongly that there are no effective specific filtering methods. The European Internet Service Providers' Association (EuroISPA), the French Association for Internet Community Sites (ASIC—*Association des Services Internet Communautaires*), Dailymotion, Google and Skype criticize the Commission for limiting question 59 to a technical perspective, calling for a broader impact assessment. Stakeholders reject this use of technological governance on technical, economic, legal and societal grounds.

> The question of the obligation of filtering exceeds its technical dimension by far: it concerns nothing less than the future of freedom of expression on the Internet, whereas more and more voices, in a social context marked with the fear of violence, terrorism and insecurity, rise to impose general surveillance on the Internet. (Association des Services Internet Communautaires—ASIC 2010, translated from French; Dailymotion 2010)

From a *technical* point of view, stakeholders argue that filtering methods over and under block, decrease the speed and security of the network and can be easily circumvented through encryption. From an *economic* point of view, it is feared that filtering will increase the cost of broadband, creating barriers for new entrants and consumers. From a *legal* point of view, stakeholders deem that filtering and monitoring are contrary to Article 15 of the E-Commerce Directive. They also consider that legal uses will be prevented, thus infringing the fundamental right to freedom of expression. Moreover privacy is in jeopardy and filtering methods are non-transparent. From a *societal* point of view, stakeholders consider that filtering and monitoring have chilling effects on the Internet's potential for free political and cultural discourse. Access to knowledge and innovation will be limited. Some argue that filtering discourages effective action against illegal content (such as tackling illegality at its source). Others express concern that filtering will experience a "mission creep" and be used for censorship.

Interview respondents echo these criticisms. Konstantinos Komaitis (Senior Policy Advisor at the Internet Society, Interview 2013) stresses that a crucial point with this type of enforcement relates to the costs that service providers have to incur, and more importantly whether these are ultimately borne by Internet users. He stresses that the Internet should be accessible and cheap, and that measures seeking to address issues of IG, including those of intellectual property, should respect the open architecture of the Internet and encourage *"innovation without permission"*. Innocenzo Genna (Public Affairs Advisor at EuroISPA, Interview 2013) agrees and stresses service providers' freedom to conduct business and the necessity to distinguish between access and hosting providers. He clarifies that spam is a hosting activity and that filtering at the level of access providers is neither technically feasible nor desirable. Stakeholders must be aware that *any technical measures imposed will at the same time affect economics and democracy*.

In response to question 60, the UK Local Government Regulation is the only actor who believes the introduction of technical standards for filtering could make a useful contribution to combating counterfeiting and piracy. A wide range of stakeholders express that the introduction of technical standards would make circumvention easier, as the specifications of the standards would be known. An *"arms race"* would ensue to develop more sophisticated technology. Some stakeholders emphasize that a government mandate for technical standards would stifle competition and innovation. Civil society, and Internet & technology companies take the opportunity to emphasize that meeting user demand by developing *legal offers* for CCO is preferable. Monitoring and filtering are considered wrong solutions to the right question of piracy and counterfeiting. Awareness rising among Internet users is also suggested. Cable Europe and La Quadrature du Net argue more radically for a revision of copyright exceptions and its territorial model. Further a fair number of media stakeholders and Internet & technology companies express a nuanced view on the contribution of filtering to combating counterfeiting and piracy (broader than technical standards). They deem that only filtering for *specific purposes* (such as child protection, public health or terrorism) is acceptable. Others consider that filtering should be restricted to a precise judicial system with lawful warrants and oversight.

Finally pertaining to question 67, Article 11 of the IPR Enforcement Directive and Article 8.3 of the Copyright in the Information Society Directive offer rights holders the possibility to apply for an injunction against intermediaries whose services are used by a third party to infringe a copyright or related right. This injunction is aimed at prohibiting the continuation of an infringement. Civil society, Internet & technology companies and legal professionals express concern that obligations placed by administrative or legal authorities on service providers with the aim of preventing law infringements challenge the prohibition to impose a general obligation to monitor (Article 15 E-Commerce Directive). They contend that injunctive relief fits within a trend to change intermediaries' role in copyright enforcement from passive and reactive to active and preventative. Google is particularly worried about developments in Germany, where courts encouraged monitoring and filtering, relying on disturbance liability *"Störerhaftung"* and injunctive relief *"Unterlassungsansprüche"*. Stakeholders also mention the SABAM vs. Scarlet and SABAM vs. Netlog cases (February 16, 2012, November 24, 2011). These cases were pending before the CJEU at the time of the consultation. Joe McNamee (Executive Director at European Digital Rights, Interview 2013) argues that the danger of delegating enforcement to intermediaries lies in the lack of evidence-based analysis, procedural safeguards and transparency. Injunctions should be proportionate, reasonable, the least restrictive alternative and used as a measure of *last resort*. Cable Europe (2010) states that,

[c]larification is sought from the Commission that these injunctions should only be allowed when it is proportional to the goal sought, in line with privacy rules and all other legal actions have been exhausted so that the injunction against the mere conduit service provider is used as a last resort mechanism. The burden of costs should also be on the one requesting the injunction.

Media stakeholders and rights holders call on Recital 40 of the E-Commerce Directive to advocate increased intermediary cooperation to prevent law infringements. They consider that service providers have a *duty to reasonably act as careful and prudent business operators* by removing or disabling access to infringing content in advance. In this context, the UK Local Government Regulation (2010) states that, "[s]ervice providers must work with authorities to keep their sites clean. Where a service provider can reasonably filter illegality this must be the preferred option." Applications for injunctive relief are considered difficult.

5.1.4   Lack of Investment in Law Enforcement

Question 69: Do you think that a lack of investment in law enforcement with regard to the Internet is one reason for the counterfeiting and piracy problem? Please detail your answer.

Question 69 in the consultation is the last inquiry into intermediary liability and addresses law enforcement in counterfeiting and piracy. In practice it serves as a means for stakeholders to provide a broader summary of their proposed policy solutions for online copyright enforcement. Media stakeholders and rights holders agree that a lack of investment in law enforcement training and resources is a reason for counterfeiting and piracy. They argue that counterfeiting and piracy are low priorities for officials. Some believe that there is a lack of willingness among judges and government agencies to enforce IPR. Stakeholders also urge for better disclosure of information. They point out that Article 5.1 of the E-Commerce Directive on providing general information is not respected. In this regard Matthieu Philibert (Public Affairs Manager at Impala, Interview 2013) and Niklas Lagergren (Former Vice President European Union Affairs at the Motion Picture Association, Interview 2013) contend that anonymity should mean responsibility. If service providers want their users to be anonymous, these providers should be held more responsible.

Other stakeholders disagree that a lack of law enforcement is a reason for counterfeiting and piracy. They place the problem elsewhere—primarily in a failure to adapt business models. Rene Summer (Director of Government and Industry Affairs at Ericsson, Interview 2013) says, "we don't think enforcement should be used to compensate rights holders for failed business models or for inadequate market solutions. Enforcement should be applied to those market segments, once you have a viable commercial market, that are still refusing to use those lawful services." Legal offers and online rights licensing are considered superior solutions to fight counterfeiting and piracy. Indeed Chris Sherwood (Former Director of Public Policy at Yahoo!, Interview 2013) is hopeful that in a few more years, once money is flowing digitally and content is made available digitally to consumers, the debate on online copyright enforcement will have seemed "an immense tangent, a diversion, a storm in a teacup". Further some stakeholders argue for adopting a more coherent and forward looking copyright regime. Three civil society actors (BEUC—European Consumers' Organization, La Quadrature du Net and UFC Que Choisir) and a legal professional Stefan Marsiske express the <u>alternative</u> view that counterfeiting and piracy should be tackled separately.

Both stakeholders who agree and disagree that there is a lack of investment in law enforcement, offer additional policy solutions for counterfeiting and piracy. On the one hand the value of educational campaigns is emphasized. On the other hand stakeholders believe that cooperation across borders and sectors is necessary in order to tackle counterfeiting and piracy at the source. Marco Pancini (European Senior Policy Counsel at Google, Interview 2013) states that, "we lose track that this is not supposed to be a war between user and right owners. It is supposed to be a war against criminal organizations exploiting counterfeiting and piracy online." A popular policy solution at the moment is increased cooperation of advertising and financial service providers to target infringers' money-making activities.

5.1.5   Copyright and Internet Rationales

Intellectual Property, and copyright in particular, is the vital legal infrastructure which underpins and protects all original acts of creativity, and the creative and cultural industries which depend on them. Without a robust and flexible form of legal protection for authors and their publishers, there would be little or no protection for creativity. Equally importantly, there would be no incentive to authors to continue creating new works, and no incentive for publishers to keep investing the substantial amounts—and skills—necessary to publish them and make them available in a digital age. (Federation of Publishers—FEP 2010; International Association of Scientific, Technical and Medical Publishers—STM 2010; UK Publishers Association 2010)

The copyright rationales mentioned in the stakeholder contributions to the 2010 public consultation pertain to copyright's *economic and societal* value. Media stakeholders and rights holders emphasize the essential role of copyright in providing an incentive to invest and a reward for labor. Johannes Studinger (Head of Department at UNI Media, Entertainment & Arts Global Union, Interview 2013) explains that it is important to make citizens at large understand how important IPR is "[n]ot only as a crucial basis for the business, for a sustainable digital economy but also for the remuneration of people working in the industry. And how this remuneration is not essential for the 1% stars that everyone knows but much more important for the 99% non stars who work alongside the stars in the different entertainment sectors." He argues that the mechanism provided by copyright is the step between creation and sustainability. In the consultation stakeholders underline that protecting copyright is a legitimate goal. They point to the economic and societal contributions that IPR-based industries make. The French Society of Dramatic Authors and Composers (SACD—*Société des Auteurs et Compositeurs Dramatiques*) contends that collective rights management societies have a cultural and social mission. European's cultural history and richness must be preserved. Civil society and some Internet companies disagree. They believe that, "EU lawmakers should instead reorganize the Internet-based creative economy around the emancipatory practices enabled by new technologies, such as the sharing and re-use of creative works. These practices promise a participatory culture where people can not only access, share and comment the works of others, but also use new tools to express their own" (La Quadrature du Net 2010). Citizens as producers and new bottom-up innovation are emphasized.

> The Internet is one of the most vibrant platforms for enhancing communication the world has seen since Gutenberg's press revolutionized the science of printing. The proliferation of user-generated content has democratized media, allowing any individual to reach out to a vast audience, without the constraints of traditional media. Blogs gain in importance and readership by the content and currency of their news, not their affiliations with the media of old [...] To maximize the economic, social and democratic potential of the Internet, we need policies and legal frameworks that enhance freedom of expression and privacy online. (Electronic Frontier Foundation – EFF 2010)

In their argumentation against increased intermediary cooperation, stakeholders stress the Internet's *social* value. Its potential as a venue for political and cultural discourse and its role in providing access to knowledge are particularly recognized. Further the overarching e-commerce theme of the consultation means that the Internet's *economic* rationale is mentioned. The Internet is deemed to stimulate innovation, employment and economic growth. Besides rationales, stakeholders also refer to the nature of the Internet: anarchic, open and neutral. The Law Society of England and Wales (2010) argues that, "one of the fundamental drivers for the success of internet business is universal accessibility and freedom of delivery." In this regard the limited liability provisions are considered founding legal principles for the functioning of the Internet. Rights holders take a different stance. They point to the threat of the Internet. LVMH (2010) states that, "[w]hile the internet is not in itself the source of counterfeiting, it has nevertheless become an important vehicle for the sale of fake goods worldwide." The technology is considered mature enough to apply the same rules online and offline. Box 5.1 summarizes the analysis of ideas in stakeholder responses to the consultation on the future of e-commerce.

5.2 Discourses

Discourses are policy actors' argumentation of their ideas and interests. Despite the number and the variety of questions posed in this consultation three discourses come through clearly. Parallels can be drawn with the CCO consultation in terms of discourses, coalitions and institutionalization.

5.2.1 Need to Provide Legal Certainty

The result of the last decade's changes is that the Directive's liability provisions need to be clarified to reflect the new environment and provide legal certainty to the stakeholders, and to respect the original intent of the Directive, which was to strike a careful balance between the different interests involved in order to stimulate co-operation between different parties and so reduce the risk of illegal activity on-line. (IFPI 2010)

Many stakeholders contend that diverging national rules and case law create *legal uncertainty* for businesses and consumers. In turn this lack of confidence is a barrier to the development and adoption of new information society services. Stakeholders request a *clarification of the E-Commerce Directive*. As discussed above however, the proposed nature of the clarification differs greatly among policy actors.

5.2.2 Shared Responsibility

Intellectual property and the fight against counterfeiting should be a shared responsibility with regards to society in general, and to the consumer in particular. There is no reason why this burden should fall exclusively on the right owners. This burden should be shared between intermediaries and right owners. The first have control over their own tools and the second are experts in their rights. (Colipa 2010; Walpole 2010)

Box 5.1   Ideas in the e-commerce directive

Analysis of stakeholder responses to twelve questions on limited liability provisions in public consultation on the Future of Electronic Commerce and the Implementation of the Directive on Electronic Commerce (2010)

- Questions 52 and 65: Overall Interpretation of Provisions
  - Problem definition—lack of intermediary cooperation and online piracy vs. lack of uniformity in interpretation of provisions and push for intermediaries to self-regulate
  - Policy solution—shared responsibility and intermediary duty of care vs. clarification that provisions cover civil and criminal liability and pertain to activities rather than actors
- Questions 53–54: Interpretation of "Actual Knowledge" and "Expeditious"
  - Problem definition—narrow interpretation of "actual knowledge", willful blindness vs. ambiguity in interpretation of "actual knowledge", action against legal content
  - Policy solution—broad vs. narrow interpretation of "actual knowledge" and "expeditious"
- Questions 66 and 68: Interpretation of Concept "Mere Technical, Automatic and Passive Nature" and Classification "Mere Conduit", "Caching" and "Hosting"
  - Focus is on interpretation of provisions for new online service providers
  - Majority of stakeholders deem that concept "mere technical, automatic and passive nature" and classification "mere conduit", "caching" and "hosting" pose problems
  - Modification/use of content for commercial purposes implies active role vs. always some degree of control in activities
- Questions 56–57: Notice and Takedown Procedures
  - Problem definition—lack of harmonization; costly and ineffective vs. self-regulation
  - Policy solution—harmonized EU framework; cooperation among stakeholders vs. prerequisite of public authority involvement
- Questions 59–60 and 67: Effective Specific Filtering Methods
  - Split views yes/no/nuanced

(continued)

Box 5.1 (continued)

- Problem definition—ineffectiveness, decrease in speed and security, cost, violation of E-Commerce Directive/fundamental rights, chilling effect on political and cultural discourse/access to knowledge
- Majority of stakeholders disagree on introduction of technical standards for filtering
- Injunctive relief for rights holders—intermediary duty of care vs. challenge to prohibition to impose a general obligation to monitor
- Question 69: Lack of Investment in Law Enforcement
  - Split views yes/no/alternative
  - Policy solution—development of legal offers, educational initiatives, cooperation across borders and sectors to tackle counterfeiting and piracy at source
- Copyright Rationales
  - Economic incentive, social requirements
  - Sharing and reuse of creative works
- Internet Rationales
  - Entrepreneurship, social interaction & symbolic belonging, pursuit of science
  - Stimulator of innovation, employment and economic growth, role in providing access to knowledge, venue for political and cultural discourse

Media stakeholders and rights holders call for *shared responsibility* in the detection, prevention and removal of infringing material on their networks. They deem that intermediaries are part of the *media value chain* and have a corporate and social responsibility to take *reasonable and proportionate measures* to fight counterfeiting and piracy. They are highly critical of perceived attempts to hide behind the differing interpretations of the Directive. This behavior is considered unfair—even parasitic. Media stakeholders and rights holders urge for closer cooperation in notice and takedown procedures, filtering and providing injunctive relief. A more proactive role is considered necessary.

5.2.3   Private Judge

ENPA believes that it is not the role of an Internet Access Provider to monitor the content that is published on the network and to check whether this content is lawful or not. Only a judge is able to take such decision, as the judicial authority is the only one which can put into balances the different rights and freedoms concerned, including freedom of expression. Control of content by internet access providers, in particular press content, would be considered as censorship and therefore pose a threat to the digital press freedom. (European Newspaper Publishers' Association—ENPA 2010)

Internet & technology companies, civil society, publishers and others worry about the calls for closer cooperation. They argue that there is an increased tendency to burden intermediaries with the task of private judge. Judicial safeguards are missing, endangering fundamental rights, liability exemptions and safe functioning of the Internet infrastructure. The degree to which and conditions under which privatized enforcement can take place vary among stakeholders. Many stakeholders fear a mission creep in governing through technology and argue that it should only be used as a measure of last resort.

5.2.4   Discourse Coalitions, Structuration and Institutionalization

On the one hand, *media stakeholders, other intellectual property rights holders and two UK public authorities form a discourse coalition in favor of a shared responsibility for Internet intermediaries.* Involved media stakeholders are primarily content producers & distributors in the audiovisual, music and publishing sectors, author & performer organizations and collective rights management societies. Other rights holders include luxury & clothing brands and industry associations such as the French Association of Large Companies (AFEP) and the French Union of Manufacturers (UNIFAB). Supporting UK public authorities are the Local Government Regulation and the Trading Standards Institute. Lastly, ISFE endeavors for increased cooperation in notice and takedown procedures. On the other hand, *civil society, Internet & technology companies and some legal professionals form a discourse coalition urging against tendencies to burden intermediaries with the task of private judge.* Most Internet & technology companies are Internet access & service providers and consumer electronics companies. Finally, three publishers, two software developers and the European Games Developer Federation (EGDF) express nuanced views on filtering methods. BSkyB opposes notice and stay down procedures.

As this case study primarily analyzed submissions to the 2010 E-Commerce consultation, it is not possible to determine whether *discourse structuration* took place. With regards to *discourse institutionalization*, the need to provide legal certainty is frequently adopted. The discourses on shared responsibility and private judge are more difficult to find. The focus in EU documents is on policy goals and solutions. I studied three EC documents, one Council Conclusions and one Parliament Resolution. I elaborate on these stakeholder contributions as they give insight into the EU's approach for e-commerce. Limited liability is only followed up in terms of a notice and takedown initiative. Alternative policy solutions for piracy and counterfeiting are increasingly present:

First, the Commission issued *a summary of its 2010 e-commerce consultation*. On the issue of limited liability, the document states that, "[t]he majority of respondents argued that a revision of the ECD [E-Commerce Directive]'s liability regime would be unnecessary, but thought *the existing rules require clarification*. There was general consensus in favour of developing a harmonised EU 'notice-and-takedown' procedure, but much less agreement on the precise contours of these rules" (European Commission 2010c, 10). Further it deems that, "[r]ight holders and ISPs tended to take opposing stances, with consumer and citizen organisations often agreeing with ISPs on the basis of ethical considerations" (European Commission 2010c, 10). *The summary provided by the Commission runs parallel to this case study's analysis with the exception of the synopses on filtering.* While the Commission (2010c, 13) finds that, "[r]espondents universally had doubts about the value of filtering", I distinguish between media stakeholder and rights holders' views on effective specific filtering methods (question 59, positive) and technical standards for filtering (question 60, negative). Further the Commission provides more details than presented in this case study on proposed solutions for notice and takedown procedures (questions 56–57) but less on alternative solutions for counterfeiting and piracy (questions 60 and 69). The summary limits itself to stakeholders' opinions.

The Commission's further views on limited liability were not presented until the publication of a second document: *the Communication on a Coherent Framework for Building Trust in the Digital Single Market Including the E-Commerce Action Plan* (European Commission 2012b). This document fits within the Digital Agenda framework. The policy goal is to achieve renewed, sustainable, smart and inclusive growth by 2020—and more specifically to double online sales (3.4% of retail sales in 2010) and the share of the Internet economy in EU GDP (less than 3% in 2010) by 2015. In the Communication, the Commission (2012b, 1) argues that, "[t]he Internet has revolutionised the everyday lives of Europeans in a way comparable to the industrial revolutions of the previous centuries." It points to blurring dividing lines due to convergence, but also to the patchwork of laws governing "Internet Europe". The Commission presents five priorities to *enhance legal certainty and remove barriers in the Digital Single Market*. Relevant to this case study, two of these priorities are *the development of the legal and cross-border offer of online products and services, and combating abuse and resolving disputes more effectively*. Importantly, legal offers are mentioned before enforcement. Moreover, the document states clearly that combating abuse (which is broader than IPR) must be pursued "within a framework which guarantees legal certainty, the proportionality of the rules governing businesses and respect for fundamental rights" (European Commission 2012b, 13). The document refers to the European Strategy for Intellectual Property Rights (European Commission 2011). Commission action points on developing legal offers pertain to collective rights management, private copying, a review of the Copyright in the Information Society Directive and online distribution of audiovisual works. Action points on combating abuse include the adoption of a horizontal initiative on notice and action procedures. A review of the IPR Enforcement Directive is also planned "in order to combat illegal content more effectively and in a manner which upholds the internal market and fundamental rights by improving the framework for civil law proceedings" (European Commission 2012b, 14). Lastly, cooperation between stakeholders including payment services is mentioned.

Third, *the Commission Staff Working Document accompanying the Communication on a Coherent Framework for Building Trust in the Digital Single Market* (2012d) provides further background to the identified *barriers in the development of information society services*. Divergences in national rules and case law are discussed extensively, including the distinction made by the CJEU on injunctive relief in the L'Oréal vs. eBay (July 12, 2011) and SABAM vs. Scarlet & Netlog (February 16, 2012, November 24, 2011) cases. Interestingly, *IPR* are discussed in the section Need for integration with other Digital Single Market policies > Access. Territoriality and licensing in copyright are recognized as a strategy of rights holders to maximize economic returns, but also are considered obstacles to trade. In this regard the Commission (2012d, 72) promotes legal offers, arguing that, "[p]iracy deprives creators from a fair reward whereas counterfeiting distorts the Single Market because of the unfair competition between businesses. One of the crucial means of combating piracy is the development of legal offers by providers. In parallel, the development of cross-border trade should also help increase the income of authors by attracting potential customers from all Member States."

Fourth, *the Commission Staff Working Document on the State of Play of the E-Commerce Action Plan* (2013) confirms the objectives, barriers, priorities and action points identified in the 2012 Communication. It states that the E-Commerce Action Plan was well received by stakeholders, including the Council and the Parliament. The Staff Working Document provides *an update on the action points.* It is worth noting that it mentions the Commission Communication on Content Online in the Digital Single Market (2012c). This includes the Licenses for Europe stakeholder dialogue and studies to assess the need for review of the EU copyright framework. Further the Staff Working Document (European Commission 2013) notes that extensive consultations were held on the notice and action initiative and civil IPR enforcement.

Fifth, *the Council Conclusions on the Digital Single Market and Governance of the Single Market* (2012) underline the importance of completing the digital single market and implementing the European IPR Strategy rapidly. The Council (2012, §22) is *balanced in its approach to intellectual property rights,* calling for "the modernization of Europe's copyright regime and promotion of best practices and models, while fighting piracy more effectively and taking into account cultural diversity in order to deploy the full potential of the digital economy".

Finally, *the European Parliament Resolution on Completing the Digital Single Market* (2012) *affirms the Commission's approach* to the digital single market as well. The Parliament (2012) endorses notice and action initiatives and emphasizes that "information society service providers have a duty to act under certain circumstances with a view to preventing or stopping illegal activities online" (Recital 40 E-Commerce Directive). It advocates a global approach "when addressing challenges such as data protection and piracy" and in this regard encourages "close cooperation between the EU and the Internet Governance Forum" (European Parliament 2012). Further the Commission is urged to modernize the EU's IPR framework "with a view to adaptation to the online reality of the 21st century" (European Parliament 2012). In this context the Parliament welcomes a combination of policy solutions, such as simplification of collective rights management, IPR enforcement, legal offers and harmonization of copyright exceptions and limitations. The Parliament deems that increasing the availability of legal offers will succeed in reducing piracy in the long term. Box 5.2 summarizes the analysis of discourses in stakeholder responses to the consultation on the future of e-commerce.

5.3   INTERESTS

5.3.1   Policy Goals

The 2010 E-Commerce consultation evaluates the implementation of the Directive. Respondents aim for the *further removal of barriers and provision of legal certainty*. They jointly advocate a *clarification* of the liability provisions and the establishment of the *harmonized EU framework for notice and takedown procedures*. Further media stakeholders and rights holders seek *closer cooperation of intermediaries* in the fight against counterfeiting and piracy. Civil society actors look beyond commercial interests and seek *copyright reform*. Both camps accuse each other of self-interest: rights holders protect failed business models and intermediaries hide behind liability exemptions. Large commercial interests are certainly at play in the discussion of these liability provisions. The E-Commerce Directive aims to protect works covered by IPR *and* encourage their distribution. Media stakeholders argue that the original balance in the Directive has been lost. Intermediaries have become major economic players and ignore their duty of care. UK Music (2010) states that,

> [t]he position in 2010 is very different: several intermediaries are now in an overwhelmingly strong economic position, particularly in comparison to individual composers/ performers and music publishers/ record companies who face significant challenges in protecting and enforcing their rights in the online environment.

Box 5.2   Discourse coalitions, structuration and institutionalization on the e-commerce directive

Analysis of stakeholder responses to twelve questions on limited liability provisions in public consultation on the Future of Electronic Commerce and the Implementation of the Directive on Electronic Commerce (2010)

As the first discourse is common to all stakeholders. I only detail the discourse coalitions for the latter two discourses. I also mention stakeholders whose views do not fit the latter two discourses and/or are particularly distinctive within their category.

Need to Provide Legal Certainty

- Common to all stakeholders

Shared Responsibility

- Media Stakeholders
  - Companies and associations of content producers such as FIAPF, MPA and ICMP
  - Companies and associations of content distributors such as FIAD and IFPI
  - Author & performer organizations and collective rights management societies such as Eurocopya, Eurocinema, GESAC and SACD
  - Private broadcasters such as Canal+ and TF1
  - Publisher associations such as FEP, SPQN and STM
- Intellectual Property Rights Holders
  - Companies and associations of luxury and clothing brands such as Comité Colbert, LVMH and Walpole
  - Industry associations such as AFEP, APRAM and UNIFAB
- UK Public Authorities
- Local Government Regulation and Trading Standards Institute

Private Judge

- Internet & Technology Industries
  - Companies and associations of fixed/mobile telecoms operators and ISPs such as Bouygues Telecom, Cable Europe, ETNO and EuroISPA
  - Companies and associations of online service providers such as ASIC, eBay, EDiMA, and Yahoo!

(continued)

Box 5.2 (continued)

- Companies and associations of consumer electronics such as GSMA Europe, Intel and Symantec
- Civil Society
  - Civil rights organizations & associations such as Article 19, BEUC and UFC Que Choisir
  - Digital rights organizations such as EDRi, EFF and La Quadrature du Net
- Legal Professionals such as Karmen Turk and Stefan Marsiske

Other
- EU Public Authorities (nuanced)
  - European Commission
  - European Parliament
  - Council of the European Union
- Media Stakeholders
  - British Sky Broadcasting (negative on notice & stay down procedures)
  - European Games Developer Federation (nuanced on filtering)
  - Publisher associations ENPA, EPC and FAEP (nuanced on filtering)
- Internet & Technology Companies
  - Interactive Software Federation of Europe (positive on notice/takedown procedures, nuanced on filtering)
  - Business Software Alliance (nuanced on filtering)

Discourse Structuration and Institutionalization
- Discourse Structuration
  - Not possible to determine
- Discourse Institutionalization
  - European Commission, Parliament and Council—need to provide legal certainty

5.3.2 Social and Economic Reality

Although the liability provisions in the E-Commerce Directive take a horizontal approach to illegal information (so for instance child abuse, defamation and racist content are also included), the controversy surrounding the liability provisions mainly concerns IPR infringements. A policy expert within the EC (Interview 2013) indicates that rights holders send many notices, because they are well organized and have strong financial interests. Furthermore the respondent deems that *the enforcement of intellectual property rights is contentious because the system of intellectual property rights itself is criticized.* The following comment by the European Digital Media Association (EDiMA 2010) illustrates: "[t]he starting point for this cooperation must always be that trademark rights, as with all IPR, are private rights and the primary responsibility for policing and enforcing them lies with the rights owner. The Directive must not disrupt this balance by shifting the responsibility onto the intermediaries."

Relating further to the social and economic reality of the E-Commerce consultation, stakeholders are not afraid to share their views on the effects of piracy and the functioning of copyright in their responses. Media stakeholders and rights holders deem that counterfeiting and piracy are *dangers to European creation.* TF1 (2010, translated from French) argues that, "unfortunately the making available and illegal consumption of this content supported by these sites, are sometimes judged with much leniency, even excused, as if it were normal to have access to all this content, everything and for free. However these behaviors are destroying values and strike a fatal blow against the creative sector at a national level, as well as the level of the Union." This view is restated by the European institutions, although more attention is paid overall to the making available than the protection of content in this policy initiative. Civil society actors take a macroeconomic view and consider that media revenues are being transferred to other sectors. Moreover they argue that file sharing has a neutral or even a positive impact on cultural creation. *Failures to adapt business models* have led to a legitimacy crisis in copyright. Author & performer organizations deem that the negative public perception of copyright is due to the *lack of balance between rights and interests of actors within the media value chain.* In the consultation the European Publishers Council is one of few media stakeholders who expands on other facets of copyright's difficult online experience. They identify the availability of unlicensed content as a policy problem and advocate intermediary cooperation, but argue that evolutions in the advertising market, lack of a level-playing field with aggregators and unfair competition of public service broadcasters challenge publishers as well. Lastly in terms of copyright's functioning within the internal market, stakeholders question copyright's territorial model. Media stakeholders defend this derogation of the digital single market, asserting that a territorial approach is necessary to monetize content and distinguish themselves in the market. The Commission (2012d, 71) states that, "[t]he fact that copyright protection is based on territoriality should not be seen as leading automatically to territorial licensing."

5.4   INSTITUTIONS

5.4.1   Policy Legacy

The policy legacy of the 2010 consultation are divergences in the interpretation of limited liability. Moreover the online environment evolved quickly in ten years and there is lack of clarity on the application of the liability provisions to new online service providers. In the consultation some stakeholders refer to the DMCA in the United States. Its safe harbor scheme runs parallel to the EU's limited liability provisions, but the DMCA is restricted to copyright infringements. Further at the time of the consultation the French and British *graduated response laws* had recently been adopted. Opponents criticize graduated response for violating the rights to privacy and freedom of expression. Proponents argue that graduated response does not constitute monitoring and emphasize its value in providing education on copyright protection. BSA and the UK ISP, JANET, express nuanced views on graduated response.

5.4.2   Political and Legal Reality

The outcome of the consultation in terms of the political and legal reality is that the E-Commerce liability exemptions have not been revised. Filtering for enforcement purposes does not seem to be on the table either. Instead, six years later, the EC is still considering more limited guidelines on notice and takedown procedures. In an institutional context seeking to complete the digital single market, it seems that it is views aiming to increase the availability of legal offers and simplify rights licensing that have found easier adoption.

Further, technological governance has been heavily debated in this case study. Media stakeholders, rights holders and UK public authorities call for the application of the same rules online and offline and do not hesitate to advocate technological solutions to enforce rights. This corresponds with the IG model *"national governments and law"*. Some policy actors and the EP urge for cross-border cooperation *(transnational institutions and international organizations)*. Civil society, Internet & technology companies, legal professionals and others push back strongly against tendencies to involve *code and Internet architecture* in the fight against piracy. BSA (2010) argues that, "it is important not to demonize a technology that has overwhelmingly beneficial uses." These stakeholders fear privatized enforcement and argue for safeguards. Filtering methods are opposed on technical, economic, legal and societal grounds. Moreover they deem that injunctions should be measures of last resort.

> Internet policy and lawmaking should not be using technology as a means to achieve its goals. Technology should inform policy decisions, but technology should not become the means for enforcing those decisions. (Konstantinos Komaitis, Senior Policy Advisor at the Internet Society, Interview 2013)

Box 5.3 summarizes the analysis of interests and institutions in stakeholder responses to the consultation on the future of e-commerce.

5.5   Conclusion: PEC Considerations

Although stakeholders did not use those terms, surveillance and technological governance are focal points of this consultation. *This E-Commerce case study is about the role and consequences of Internet intermediaries intervening in the network.* Stakeholders share a common ambition to clarify rather than revise the limited liability provisions in the E-Commerce Directive. Kostas Rossoglou compares revising the directive to opening Pandora's Box. *The uncertain outcome pushes many*

Box 5.3   Interests and institutions in the e-commerce directive

Analysis of stakeholder responses to twelve questions on limited liability provisions in public consultation on the Future of Electronic Commerce and the Implementation of the Directive on Electronic Commerce (2010)

Interests

- Policy Goals
  - Clarification of limited liability provisions, harmonized EU framework for notice and takedown procedures; closer intermediary cooperation vs. copyright reform
- Social and Economic Reality
  - Stakeholders argue legitimacy crisis of copyright due to failure to adapt business models vs. lack of balance between rights and interests within media value chain

Institutions

- Policy Legacy
  - Divergences in interpretation of limited liability provisions
- Political and Legal Reality
  - Limited policy outcome—*anno* 2016, notice and takedown procedures still under consideration; positive developments in legal offers and licensing
  - IG—national governments and law, transnational institutions and international organizations, code and Internet architecture

stakeholders to prefer modest policy goals. However there is much disagreement over the problem definitions and policy solutions at hand. Similar to the 2008 CCO consultation, filtering is controversial. Opponents of technological governance raise concerns about the impact on liberty and innovation. They underline the potential of the Internet for societal and economic growth. The discourse coalition of civil society, Internet & technology companies, legal professionals and others has the upper hand in the sense that the EU public authorities do not mention filtering in subsequent communications. Those requesting judicial oversight for notice and takedown procedures will be less pleased. Voluntary measures continue to be encouraged.

This consultation on e-commerce also provides insight into the problem definitions of the European Com mission, Parliament and Council on online copyright infringement. *Alongside notice and takedown procedures, the EU public authorities promote the development of legal offers as a viable solution to online copyright infringement.* Protection and distribution of copyrighted works are desired. Tensions between the E-Commerce, IPR Enforcement and Copyright in the Information Society Directives are painfully clear. As we noticed in CCO, IPR are regarded as both a policy problem and a solution in the EU's pursuit for competitiveness, jobs and growth in the digital single market. The Council Conclusions and Parliament Resolution call for the modernization of Europe's copyright regime.

Finally the commercial interests of Internet intermediaries and rights holders can converge. British Sky Broadcasting and software and game developers are good examples. In this consultation however they are largely conflictual. The stakeholder discussions center on the Internet as a commercial venue. Referring to Google, Anne Bergman-Tahon (Director at Federation of European Publishers, Interview 2013) states that, "[i]n terms of communications, I was always fascinated how a company that has a turnover of 23 billion and has been abusing certainly copyright but also personal data, appeals for 'do no evil', almost like they were a non profit organization providing good to humanity. Face it they are a capitalist company, they are trying to make profit for shareholders." The policy outcome of the public consultation on the implementation and future of the E-Commerce Directive is limited. *The role of Internet intermediaries in intervening in the network is at the crux of the online copyright enforcement debate. Its high polarization leads yet again to a political stalemate.* The liability provisions are not revised and there is no real follow-up either. Although this consultation is not IPR-centric, rights holders are loudly present. The E-Commerce consultation is another manifestation of the political economic struggle to create economic value on the Internet. Our last case study has a closer look at the continuation of this battle in the legislative attempt to pass a multilateral ACTA.

NOTES

1. All stakeholder submissions to the public consultation are available at (European Commission 2010b). I kindly refer readers interested in consulting the stakeholder opinions mentioned in the body of the text to this repository. When quoting stakeholders directly, I have included in-text references, which point back to this same online location. Throughout the chapter, stakeholders are first mentioned with their complete names, whereafter only their abbreviations are used.
2. Although the formulation of question 65 is broad (obstacles to e-commerce), most stakeholders restrict their responses to the liability provisions. Similarly I have restricted my reporting to additional obstacles related to intermediary liability.
3. In 2011 Spain adopted the "Sinde Law", which creates an expedited procedure for the blocking of websites containing copyright infringing material, when reported by rights holders to a government commission and judge.
4. For more details on formalized notice and takedown procedures, see (European Commission 2012d).
5. British Sky Broadcasting (BSkyB) considers notice and stay down procedures contrary to Article 15 of the E-Commerce Directive.

BIBLIOGRAPHY

February 16, 2012. C-360/10 Belgische Vereniging van Auteurs, Componisten en Uitgevers (SABAM) vs. Netlog. Court of Justice of the European Union.

July 12, 2011. C-324/09 L'Oréal & Others vs. eBay International & Others. Court of Justice of the European Union.

March 23, 2010. C-236/08 to C-238/08 Google vs. Louis Vuitton Mattelier & Others. Court of Justice of the European Union.

November 24, 2011. C-70/10 Scarlet Extended vs. Société Belge des Auteurs, Compositeurs et Editeurs (SABAM). Court of Justice of the European Union.

Article 19. 2010. Response to EU Consultation on E-Commerce Directive. https://circabc.europa.eu/webdav/CircaBC/FISMA/markt_consultations/ Library/Online services/The future of electronic commerce/Consumers/US PK CONSO (th 5) 782818.pdf. Accessed 9 Oct 2016.

ASIC. 2010. Contribution de l'Association des Services Internet Communautaires (ASIC) à la Consultation Publique sur l'Avenir du Commerce Électronique dans le Marché Intérieur et la Mise en Œuvre de la Directive Commerce Électronique (2000/31/CE). https://circabc.europa.eu/sd/a/141c5a35-dd4f-410d-adee-a07b5d4d6dc5/FR ASIC FED ENTR (th 1-2%265-5bis) 807533.pdf. Accessed 9 Oct 2016.

BSA. 2010. Response of the Business Software Alliance to the Commission Consultation on the Future of Electronic Commerce in the Internal Market and the Implementation of the Directive on Electronic Commerce (2000/31/EC). https://circabc.europa.eu/sd/a/5bd2b56c-2d16-4fb3-8b96-e92043e14a9c/ EU BSA FED ENTR (th 1-2%265) 808978.pdf. Accessed 9 Oct 2016.

Cable Europe. 2010. Cable Europe Answer to the Commission's Public Consultation on the Future of Electronic Commerce in the Internal Market and the Implementation of the Directive on Electronic Commerce (2000/31/EC). https://circabc.europa.eu/sd/a/98336ac9-b64c-4bce-bad6-df25c16cd75f/ EU CABLE EUROPE FED ENTR (th 1%265) 804604.pdf. Accessed 9 Oct 2016.

Colipa. 2010. Online Commerce Consultation. Colipa Contribution. https://circabc.europa.eu/sd/a/89931860-ebbc-49e7-ad4e-26b9cc513671/EU Colipa FED ENTR 779176.pdf. Accessed 9 Oct 2016.

Council of the European Union. 2012. *Council Conclusions on the Digital Single Market and Governance of the Single Market.* Brussels: Council of the European Union.

Dailymotion. 2010. Contribution de Dailymotion à la Consultation Publique sur l'Avenir du Commerce Électronique dans le Marché Intérieur et la Mise en Œuvre de la Directive Commerce Électronique (2000/31/CE). https://circabc.europa.eu/sd/a/956bbdb3-4fa1-4705-84ea-09a3bef4020c/FR DAILYMOTION ENTR (th 1-2%265) 776967.pdf. Accessed 9 Oct 2016.

EDiMA. 2010. EDiMA Response to the Public Consultation on the Future of Electronic Commerce in the Internal Market and the Implementation of the Directive on Electronic Commerce (2000/31/EC). https://circabc.europa.eu/sd/a/168a2c74-fd01-4b94-b89f-687440437d52/EU EDIMA FED ENTR (th 1-3%265%267) 800212.pdf. Accessed 9 Oct 2016.

EFF. 2010. Submission of the Electronic Frontier Foundation on the Consultation on the EU E-Commerce Directive (2000/31/EC). https://circabc.europa.eu/sd/a/7ad5a1c3-d07f-4abe-9afb-4f5698666b0b/EU EFF CONSO (th 5) 821617.pdf. Accessed 9 Oct 2016.

ENPA. 2010. ENPA Response to the Public Consultation on the Future of Electronic Commerce in the Internal Market and the Implementation of the Directive on Electronic Commerce (2000/31/EC). https://circabc.europa. eu/sd/a/2cffc3cd-ac34-4ebc-864f-cfe32b89e58f/EU ENPA FED ENTR (th 1-2%264-5) 834493 a ne pas publier.pdf. Accessed 9 Oct 2016.

EPC. 2010. Contribution from the European Publishers Council to the Review of the E-Commerce Directive. https://circabc.europa.eu/sd/a/23e27474-f646-4dab-8c52-3e10cb2c0f35/EU EPC FED ENTR 834604.pdf. Accessed 9 Oct 2016.

European Commission. 2010a. *COM(2010a) 245 Final/2. Communication from the Commission to the European Parliament, the Council, the European Economic and Social Committee and the Committee of the Regions. A Digital Agenda for Europe.* Brussels: European Commission.

―――. 2010b. *COM(2010b) 779 final. Communication of the Commission to the European Parliament, the Council, the European Economic and Social Committee and the Committee of the Regions on the Application of Directive 2004/48/EC of the European Parliament and the Council of 29 April 2004 on the Enforcement of Intellectual Property Rights.* Brussels: European Commission.

―――. 2010c. *Public Consultation on the Future of Electronic Commerce in the Internal Market and the Implementation of the Directive on Electronic Commerce (2000/31/EC).* Brussels: European Commission.

―――. 2011. *COM(2011) 287 Final. Communication from the Commission to the European Parliament, the Council, the European Economic and Social Committee and the Committee of the Regions on a Single Market for Intellectual Property Rights. Boosting Creativity and Innovation to Provide Economic Growth, High Quality Jobs and First Class Products and Services in Europe.* Brussels: European Commission.

―――. 2012a. A Clean and Open Internet: Public Consultation on Procedures for Notifying and Acting on Illegal Content Hosted by Online Intermediaries. http://ec.europa.eu/internal_market/consultations/2012a/clean-and-open-internet_en.htm. Accessed 6 Oct 2016.

―――. 2012b. *COM(2011) 942 Final. Communication to the European Parliament, the Council, the European Economic and Social Committee and the Commitee of the Regions on a Coherent Framework for Building Trust in the Digital Single Market for E-Commerce and Online Services.* Brussels: European Commission.

―――. 2012c. *COM(2012c) 789 Final. Communication from the Commission on Content in the Digital Single Market.* Brussels: European Commission.

―――. 2012d. *SEC(2011) 1641 Final. Commission Staff Working Document on Online Services, Including E-Commerce, in the Single Market*

Accompanying the Document Communication to the European Parliament, the Council, the European Economic and Social Committee and the Commitee of the Regions on a Coherent Framework for Building Trust in the Digital Single Market for E-Commerce and Online Services. Brussels: European Commission.

———. 2013. *SWD(2013) 153 Final. Commission Staff Working Document on E-Commerce Action Plan 2012-2015: State of Play 2013.* Brussels: European Commission.

European Commission. 2015c. Public Consultation on the Regulatory Environment for Platforms, Online Intermediaries, Data and Cloud Computing and the Collaborative Economy. https://ec.europa.eu/digital-single-market/en/news/public-consultation-regulatory-environment-platforms-onlineintermediaries-data-and-cloud. Accessed 6 Oct 2016.

European Parliament. 2012. *2012/2030(INI). European Parliament Resolution of 11 December 2012 on Completing the Digital Single Market.* Strasbourg: European Parliament.

European Parliament & Council. 2000. *Directive 2000/31/EC of the European Parliament and of the Council of 8 June 2000 on Certain Legal Aspects of Information Society Services, in particular Electronic Commerce, in the Internal Market.* Luxembourg: Official Journal of the European Communities.

FEP. 2010. FEP Answer to the Public Consultation on the Future of Electronic Commerce in the Internal Market and the Implementation of the Directive on Electronic Commerce (2000/31/EC). https://circabc.europa.eu/sd/a/672f3ef5-f698-42f6-b097-16eb20c06795/EU FEP-FEE FED ENTR.pdf. Accessed 9 Oct 2016.

IFPI. 2010. IFPI Response to the Commission Consultation on the Future of Electronic Commerce in the Internal Market and the Implementation of the Directive on Electronic Commerce (2000/31/EC). https://circabc.europa.eu/sd/a/7277df5c-596f-41b3-8a0c-1450534335ee/EU IFPI FED ENTR (th 1-2%265) 836295.pdf. Accessed 9 Oct 2016.

ISFE. 2010. Public Consultation on the Future of Electronic Commerce in the Internal Market and the Implementation of the Directive on Electronic Commerce (2000/31/EC). Responses by the Interactive Software Federation of Europe. https://circabc.europa.eu/sd/a/f7fa6f50-0221-44b5-a209-a37f-c4eb7452/EU ISFE FED ENTR (th 1-2%265) 835636.pdf. Accessed 9 Oct 2016.

JANET. 2010. JANET(UK)'s Response to the European Commission's Consultation 'on the Future of Electronic Commerce in the Internal Market and the Implementation of the Directive on Electronic Commerce (2000/31/EC)'.https://circabc.europa.eu/sd/a/66717321-9476-4705-840f-

3b3f814235ef/UK JANET ENTR. reply Ares 696931.pdf. Accessed 9 Oct 2016.

La Quadrature du Net. 2010. Legal Liability of Internet Service Providers and the Protection of Freedom of Expression Online. Response to the European Commission's Consultation on the E-Commerce Directive. https://circabc.europa.eu/sd/a/6c181e3b-9c4f-4252-9473-e1f1b7c4aec4/FR LQDN CONSO (th 5) 821480.pdf. Accessed 9 Oct 2016.

Law Society of England and Wales. 2010. Public Consultation on the Future of Electronic Commerce in the Internal Market and the Implementation of the Directive on Electronic Commerce (2000/31/EC). https://circabc.europa.eu/sd/a/e7ba2c62-6928-4678-9e15-00eb3aaf09e9/UK   THE   LAW SOCIETY.doc. Accessed 9 Oct 2016.

LVMH. 2010. LVMH Submission. Directorate General Internal Market & Services. EC Public Consultation on the Future of Electronic Commerce in the Internal Market and the Implementation of the directive on Electronic Commerce (2000/31/EC). https://circabc.europa.eu/sd/a/a30a7591-ab2f-4b7f-80db-3654f010f6cc/FR LVMH ENTR 804634.pdf. Accessed 9 Oct 2016.

STM. 2010. International Association of Scientific, Technical and Medical Publishers ('STM'). Response to the Public Consultation on the Future of Electronic Commerce in the Internal Market and the Implementation of the Directive on Electronic Commerce (2000/31/EC). https://circabc.europa.eu/sd/a/f755ddf4-60d2-4e22-bfde-3aa1b164462e/EU STM-ASSOC FED ENTR 719662.pdf. Accessed 9 Oct 2016.

TF1. 2010. Contribution de TF1 à la Consultation Publique sur l'Avenir du Commerce Électronique dans le Marché Intérieur et la Mise en Œuvre de la Directive Commerce Électronique. https://circabc.europa.eu/sd/a/490bfd46-4ea1-4db9-aea8-6a626c7270b9/FR TF1 ENTR (th 5) 807802.pdf. Accessed 9 Oct 2016.

UK Local Government Regulation. 2010. Local Government Regulation Response to the European Commission's Consultation on the Future of Electronic Commerce in the Internal Market and the Implementation of the Directive on Electronic Commerce (2000/31/EC). https://circabc.europa.eu/sd/a/063dabae-9c73-46fe-9ebc-e51a1e983bd6/UK Government Regulation.doc. Accessed 9 Oct 2016.

UK Music. 2010. UK Music Response to: Consultation on the Future of Electronic Commerce in the Internal Market and the Implementation of the Directive on Electronic Commerce. https://circabc.europa.eu/sd/a/8cf07d48-4b1b-4fdf-a3b4-94931f9a4ff5/uk mus.pdf. Accessed 9 Oct 2016

UK Publishers Association. 2010. Response to Public Consultation on the Future of Electronic Commerce in the Internal Market and the Implementation of the Directive on Electronic Commerce (2000/31/EC). https://circabc.

europa.eu/sd/a/5dadeb9e-4656-4385-998f-972b9ab72a14/UK PUBLISHERS ASSOCIATION FED ENTR (th 2%265) 785391.pdf. Accessed 9 Oct 2016.

Walpole. 2010. Walpole Submission to the European Commission Public Consultation on the Future of Electronic Commerce in the Internal Market and the Implementation of the Directive on Electronic Commerce (2000/31/EC).https://circabc.europa.eu/sd/a/b774ab55-25fd-4337-9caf-b2ebda98ba43/UK WALPOLE FED ENTR (th 1%264-5) 786752.pdf. Accessed 9 Oct 2016.

CHAPTER 6

Anti-Counterfeiting Trade Agreement: 2010–2012 European Parliament Discussions

Formal negotiations on the Anti-Counterfeiting Trade Agreement (ACTA, 2011 Accession Ongoing) started in June 2008 and ended in November 2010. The final text on ACTA was published in May 2011. Throughout the negotiations, the EU was represented by DG Trade and its member states. The EU's member states negotiated Section 4 of ACTA on criminal enforcement. Other negotiating parties were Australia, Canada, Japan, Republic of Korea, Mexico, Morocco, New Zealand, Singapore, Switzerland and the United States. The EP published three resolutions on ACTA, requesting public access to documents and raising concerns on transparency and state of play. In December 2011 the Council of the European Union adopted the convention unanimously. Quickly thereafter, the European Commission and twenty-two member states[1] signed ACTA in January 2012. However on the same day MEP Kader Arif (Progressive Alliance of Socialists and Democrats (S&D)) resigned as ACTA rapporteur "to denounce in the strongest manner the process that led to the signing of this agreement: no association of civil society [and] lack of transparency from the beginning" (Arthur 2012). In the weeks before and after the signature of ACTA, citizens in Europe took to the streets to protest against the trade agreement. As a consequence, European Commissioner for Trade Karel De Gucht announced his intention in February 2012 to request an opinion from the CJEU on ACTA's compatibility with the European Treaties, in particular with

© The Author(s) 2017　　　　　　　　　　　　　　　　　247
T. Meyer, *The Politics of Online Copyright Enforcement in the EU*, Information Technology and Global Governance,
DOI 10.1007/978-3-319-50974-7_6

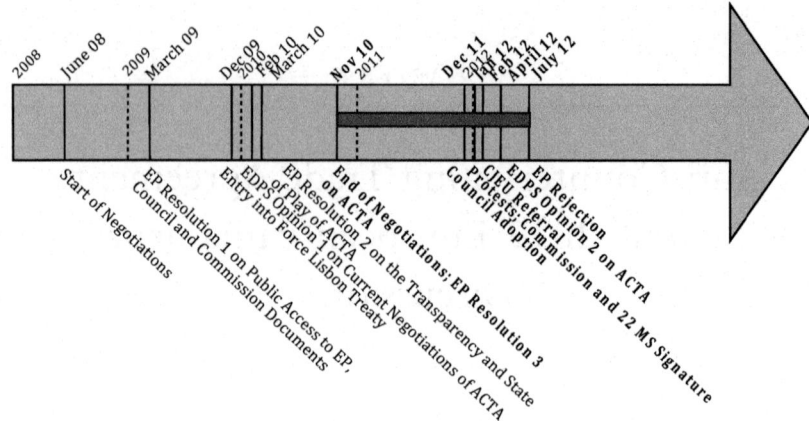

Fig. 6.1   Policy developments in the Anti-Counterfeiting Trade Agreement

the Charter of Fundamental Rights of the EU. Nonetheless citizen and civil society mobilization continued, notably through use of social media and email campaigns. In July 2012 *the EP rejected ACTA,* denying its consent and prohibiting its ratification by the EU. Trade agreements do not follow the ordinary legislative procedure in the EU. Although its role remains limited, the Lisbon Treaty's entry into force in 2009 (midway through the formal negotiations on ACTA) did provide the Parliament with some more say. The Parliament saw its consultative powers increased and importantly now votes to consent or deny the ratification of the final text of trade agreements. Thus it could not amend ACTA, but its consent was necessary for ratification of the treaty by the EU and its member states (European Parliament & Council 2010, Article 289(2), European Parliament 2016)(Fig. 6.1).[2]

For this last case study, *I have analyzed stakeholder opinions on ACTA, at an EU level, from the end of the negotiations in November 2010 until the EP's rejection in July 2012.* In practice most contributions revolve around the EP discussions in the period leading up to its vote. As stipulated in the analytical framework, I have conducted an ADA to identify emblematic issues, story lines and discourses. I focus in particular on policy actors' proposed problem definitions, policy solutions and goals, and their argumentations on copyright and Internet rationales.

Similar to the other case studies I have structured the reporting of the problem definitions and policy solutions using the categories yes/no/ nuanced. Stakeholders largely advocate either in favor or against the ratification of the trade agreement. However, contrary to the public consultations, it is not possible to identify alternative responses because documents needed to deal with ACTA in order to be included in the selection. In total ninety-nine stakeholder contributions were analyzed. These include ACTA, position papers, press releases, letters and Parliamentary committee reports. The number of stakeholders is higher than the number of stakeholder contributions, as the selection contains multiple joint contributions. Often these were statements or letters to which stakeholders could sign up. Further the longer timeframe of this case study meant that it was possible to select several contributions from one single policy actor. This is useful to identify discourse structuration and institutionalization.[3] Finally the thirty-nine EU interviews included questions on ACTA. Consequently analysis of these interviews is also included.

6.1 IDEAS

6.1.1 Problem Definitions and Policy Solutions

ACTA is a trade agreement aimed at enhanced international cooperation and more effective international enforcement for intellectual property rights. The preambles to the convention point to the necessity of IPR enforcement for economic growth, to the barriers to trade and financial harm inflicted by IPR infringement, and to the links of IPR infringement with organized crime and risks to our health and society (see Box 6.1, ACTA 2011 Accession Ongoing). Stakeholders in favor of ACTA *agree* with the trade agreement's policy solution of IPR enforcement and cooperation at an international level, arguing similar policy goals, namely that ACTA will protect industries and jobs dependent on IPR and that its adoption will *increase economic growth* and the EU's competitiveness abroad. Further stakeholders deem that ratifying ACTA will help create a level playing field abroad and send a *strong signal that IPR enforcement is a priority for the EU.* On the contrary rejecting ACTA will decrease trust and credibility in the EU as a responsible trading partner and cause the EU to fall behind in the protection of a key asset. In this regard the proposed problem definition is also repeated: IPR infringement causes

Box 6.1 Preambles to the anti-counterfeiting trade agreement

"The Parties to this Agreement,

Noting that effective enforcement of intellectual property rights is critical to sustaining economic growth across all industries and globally;

Noting further that the proliferation of counterfeit and pirated goods, as well as of services that distribute infringing material, undermines legitimate trade and sustainable development of the world economy, causes significant financial losses for right holders and for legitimate businesses, and, in some cases, provides a source of revenue for organized crime and otherwise poses risks to the public;

Desiring to combat such proliferation through enhanced international cooperation and more effective international enforcement;

Intending to provide effective and appropriate means, complementing the TRIPS Agreement, for the enforcement of intellectual property rights, taking into account differences in their respective legal systems and practices;

Desiring to ensure that measures and procedures to enforce intellectual property rights do not themselves become barriers to legitimate trade;

Desiring to address the problem of infringement of intellectual property rights, including infringement taking place in the digital environment, in particular with respect to copyright or related rights, in a manner that balances the rights and interests of the relevant right holders, service providers, and users;

Desiring to promote cooperation between service providers and right holders to address relevant infringements in the digital environment;

Desiring that this Agreement operates in a manner mutually supportive of international enforcement work and cooperation conducted within relevant international organizations;

Recognizing the principles set forth in the Doha Declaration on the TRIPS Agreement and Public Health, adopted on 14 November 2001, at the Fourth WTO Ministerial Conference"

Source: Australia, Canada, the European Union and its member states, Japan, the Kingdom of Morocco, New Zealand, the Republic of Korea, the Republic of Singapore, the Swiss Confederation, the United Mexican States, and the United States. 2011 Accession Ongoing. Anti-Counterfeiting Trade Agreement.

financial *harm*, barriers to trade, is linked to organized crime and threatens health and safety.

> Intellectual property theft on an unprecedented, global scale is depriving creators and copyright owners of the return they deserve on their massive investments of creativity, expertise, and hard work, undermining the creative sector in every country. (Motion Picture Association of America—MPAA 2011)

Besides praising the value of ACTA, proponents are also keen to address widespread criticisms of ACTA. They emphasize that ACTA will *not serve as a backdoor change to EU laws*. In the draft opinion of the EP's Legal Affairs committee on ACTA, MEP in the EPP group Marielle Gallo (2012, 3) states that, "ACTA does not create new intellectual property rights for the Contracting Parties. In other words, that which is currently protected by European legislation remains protected; that which was not protected is still not protected." Stakeholders contend that although ACTA is not as precise as corresponding international and EU laws, the *intention is not to change today's "acquis communautaire"*. Rather by building on the minimum standards of the TRIPS agreement, ACTA ensures high protection of rights outside of the EU. Business Action to Stop Counterfeiting and Piracy (BASCAP) and the International Trademark Association (INTA 2012) deem the linguistic differences in wording between ACTA and EU law inevitable and the EC (2011c) comments that the looser wording permits parties to establish an appropriate balance of rights and interests at a national level. Stakeholders try to reassure that there is no danger in the sections and wording on criminal sanctions, commercial scale, disclosure of information, injunctions, damages, due process or border measures. Nor will ACTA result in censorship, monitoring, inspection of hand luggage, criminalization of end users, graduated response or limit trade in generic medicines. Proponents argue that the EU is bound by the Charter of Fundamental Rights of the EU (European Parliament, Council, and Commission 2000) and the recent jurisprudence of the CJEU on SABAM vs. Scarlet and SABAM vs. Netlog (February 16, 2012, November 24, 2011). As a consequence, ACTA should *not be perceived as a threat to the freedom of the Internet or civil liberties*.

In *reaction to criticisms on the lack of transparency* throughout the ACTA negotiations, DG Trade emphasizes that member states were present and had first-hand information on ACTA. Moreover at the request of the EP, the Commission had pushed for the release of the draft texts on ACTA. It had also held debriefing meetings with the EP and stakeholders during the negotiations and had responded to MEP's numerous oral and written questions (European Commission 2012c). MEP in the EPP group Christofer Fjellner was also party to the requests for access to information. He states that, "we now have access to the most comprehensive documentation of any trade negotiation I've ever been involve[d] in. Despite this, the agreement has faced continuous criticism and has also been the subject of many demonstrations both in member states and on the internet" (European Parliament 2012a). Further in its correspondence with stakeholders, the Commission argues that it tried and would have *preferred to negotiate ACTA within the World Trade Organization and the World Intellectual Property Organization* (European Commission 2012a) and that an *impact assessment of the trade agreement was not necessary* as it did not exceed the EU *"acquis"* (European Commission & Parliament 2012). In this regard some proponents of ACTA evaluate the *referral to the CJEU* positively to build confidence in the treaty, while others think the consequent delay in adoption will weaken the EU's position. Lastly several stakeholders lament that many citizens' opinions had been limited to the eight-letter slogan "Stop ACTA", calling for a *reasoned debate* based on facts not rumors. In a joint letter to national governments, rights holders (2012) argue that,

> [o]ver the past two weeks, we have seen coordinated attacks on democratic institutions such as the European Parliament and national governments over ACTA. The signatories to this letter and their members stand against such attempts to silence the democratic process. Instead, we call for a calm and reasoned assessment of the facts rather than the misinformation circulating. A considered reaction is more important than ever at a time when many outside of Europe doubt the ability of the European Union institutions and its Member State governments to act together.

Opponents object to ACTA's *double, yet exclusive focus on counterfeiting and piracy.* On the one hand, they argue that it was premature to negotiate a trade agreement on a topic so heavily disputed within the EU. On the other hand, they fear that other trading partners might not have an IPR framework as developed and balanced as found in the EU. Moreover, the EP ALDE group (2012c) indicates that it has "doubts about the overall effectiveness of a 'catch-all' agreement that does *not include the countries that are the main source of counterfeit goods*". The EP Committee on Civil Liberties, Justice and Home Affairs (LIBE, European Parliament 2012a) and two digital rights organizations (European Digital Rights—EDRi 2012b; La Quadrature du Net 2012) agree that ACTA misses its target and adds little value due to the exclusion of Brazil, India and China. Some stakeholders also question the weight of ACTA as reports showed that *the United States did not consider it a binding treaty.*

Despite the reassurances that ACTA complies with the international and EU laws, many stakeholders criticize the *imprecise wording and lack of specific safeguards.*

> There is an English expression where we say the devil is in the detail. The problem with ACTA is that the devil is in the lack of details. We don't have enough information on many of the areas where in the end we will have to make a judgment on. (ACTA Rapporteur David Martin, European Parliament 2012a)

They fear that the trade agreement will be *used to change EU law* (for instance in reviewing the IPR Enforcement Directive), *endanger Internet freedom and fundamental rights* (rights to freedom of expression and information, respect for privacy and data protection, fair trial and due process, and freedom to conduct business), *increase "privatized enforcement" by intermediary service providers* (filtering, surveillance and graduated response), *stifle innovation and creativity, lead to a criminalization of Internet users, and hinder trade in generic medicines and seeds.* Indeed the EC had not issued an impact assessment of ACTA, and every external opinion and study on ACTA discouraged unconditional consent to the trade agreement. The European Data Protection Supervisor (EDPS) (2012, 16) states that, "the Agreement does not contain sufficient limitations and safeguards in respect of the implementation of measures that entail the monitoring of electronic communications networks on a large-scale. In particular, it does not lay out safeguards such as the respect of the rights to privacy and data protection, effective judicial protection, due process, and the respect of the principle of the presumption of innocence." To illustrate, opponents have difficulties with

a. the inclusion of *criminal enforcement* in the trade agreement, which stakeholders deem disrespects the position that the EP took on the Proposal for a Directive on Criminal Measures aimed at Ensuring the Enforcement of Intellectual Property Rights, and Proposal for Council Framework Decision to Strengthen the Criminal Law Framework to Combat Intellectual Property Offences (European Commission 2005);
b. the broad definition for illegal acts carried out on a *"commercial scale"* in Article 23.1 ACTA which covers "commercial activities for direct or indirect economic or commercial advantage", and the inclusion of *"aiding and abetting"* in Article 23.4 ACTA, fearing that these would lead to a criminalization of Internet users and increased intermediary liability due to the unclarity of their application in ACTA's section on enforcement in the digital environment;
c. the inclusion of all TRIPS IPR infringements (except patents and test data) under *border measures* which could cause the detention of generic medicines if suspected of ordinary trademark infringements;
d. the consequences for "privatized enforcement" in promoting *"cooperative efforts within the business community* to effectively address trademark and copyright or related rights infringement" and allowing parties to provide "competent authorities with the authority to order an online service provider to *disclose expeditiously to a right holder information sufficient to identify a subscriber* whose account was allegedly used for infringement" in Article 27.3 and 27.4 ACTA;
e. *"fair process"* in Article 27 ACTA being referred to as a fundamental principle rather than a right and legally confusing the concepts of "fair trial" and "due process"; and more.[4]

Furthermore, stakeholders opposing ACTA resent that the EC and member states skirted around the EP and traditional international forums to deal with IPR enforcement, namely the WTO and the WIPO. The ACTA negotiations are perceived as being *highly secretive, aimed at pushing higher enforcement standards on other trading partners, limit democratic participation and favor commercial interests.* Stakeholders also protest the establishment of *an ACTA committee* (ACTA, Article

36) tasked with reviewing the implementation and considering amendments to the Agreement, viewing it as another opaque regulatory body. Innocenzo Genna, ICT Consultant and Board Member of the European Internet Service Providers Association (EuroISPA, Interview 2013), aptly coins the lack of transparency and democratic process "the original sin" of ACTA.

> Of course when you hide stuff from people, people start wondering why. (Matthieu Philibert, Public Affairs Manager at IMPALA, Interview 2013)

Stakeholders also reject ACTA's referral to the CJEU, arguing that *the EP has the political responsibility* to represent the views of European citizens and to protect and promote fundamental rights "in their letter as well as in their spirit" (European Parliament 2012b). Instead *alternative policy solutions* are proposed. Much criticism pertains to the chapter on enforcement in the digital environment. This leads some to contend that a sectoral approach is desirable, treating counterfeiting and piracy separately. Further stakeholders emphasize that future copyright policymaking needs to be open and participatory, evidence based, and focused on reassessing balance and eliminating barriers in the digital single market. Socialist MEP Dimitrios Droutsas states that,

> [w]e fully respect the need for artists to be rewarded for their talents and acknowledge the challenges posed by new technologies on this issue. However, we must not accept the erosion of basic fundamental rights in Europe, and around the world, for expediency's sake. What we need is a real public debate, involving experts, organisations and individuals, in order to achieve a modern social pact, a modern regime of protecting intellectual property rights. ACTA is not and was not conceived to be this. (S&D 2012a)

Finally four stakeholders have been coded as *nuanced*, as they express reservations, but do not take a clear stance for or against ACTA. The *EP Legal Service* (2011a, b) is the most positive in its analyses, indicating that although ACTA can change EU secondary law, *no changes seem necessary "prima facie"*. Moreover it deems that ACTA is stricter than TRIPS, but that they cannot be regarded as contradictory as Article 2 ACTA gives precedence to TRIPS. According to the Legal Service ACTA does not appear to be incompatible with fundamental rights either. Indeed specific provisions guarantee the respect of fundamental rights. The EP Legal Service states that a fair balance will need to be struck in the treaty's implementation. *European academics* (D'Erme et al. 2011) come to a different conclusion. In a joint opinion they express concern about the imprecise wording and lack of safeguards. Commercial scale, border measures, disclosure of subscribers' data, injunctions and damages are examples of worrisome provisions. They call on policymakers to *withhold consent "as long as significant deviations from the EU acquis or serious concerns on fundamental rights, data protection, and a fair balance of interests are not properly addressed"* (D'Erme et al. 2011). Further then, *the authors of an external study for the EP Committee on International Trade* (Institute for Globalisation and International Regulation et al. 2011) assess that the trade agreement is compatible with the EU *"acquis"* and TRIPS. *Rejection of ACTA* is thus deemed *inappropriate* as it does not deviate significantly from the EU *"acquis"*. Moreover rejection would likely affect the EU's bargaining power. At the same time the authors consider *unconditional consent inappropriate* as there are no guarantees that ACTA's implementation will be compatible with EU law. They argue that ACTA could influence future debates on criminal measures, privacy and third party and intermediary liability. Lastly, the authors of the EP INTA study have difficulty pointing to any significant advantages for EU citizens due to the modest result of the treaty. The fourth nuanced stakeholder, *the Media Freedom Representative of the Organization for Security and Co-Operation in Europe* (OSCE 2012b), calls for a *thorough assessment of ACTA's effects on fundamental rights*. She deems that the treaty could be detrimental to freedom of expression and privacy. OSCE's Media Freedom Representative (2012a) stresses that Stop Online Piracy Act (SOPA) and Preventing Real Online Threats to Economic Creativity and Theft of Intellectual Property Act (PIPA) in the United States and ACTA show that IPR need to be reassessed to "reflect the spirit and pace of the digital age we are living in". She argues for "a *new balance* between the legitimate rights of the copyright holders and the creative exercise of everyone's right to freedom of expression in the public domain" (OSCE 2012a).

6.1.2   *Copyright and Internet Rationales*

Relating to theories and rationales of copyright, the EP Committee on Civil Liberties, Justice and Home Affairs (LIBE) highlights that IPR are protected by the EU Charter of Fundamental Rights *(natural law)*. Similarly Article 5(k) ACTA defines pirated copyright goods as "any goods which are copies made without the consent of the right holder or person duly authorized by the right holder [...]" pointing to the need for permission to use the right. In their opinion for Green/EFA, Douwe Korff and Ian Brown (2011) however, argue that consideration is due for not only the rights holder, but also the user and consumer in discussing the right to property. A range of stakeholders emphasize IPR's value in providing *market-based incentives* for innovation and creativity and its importance for economic growth in the EU. ACTA Rapporteur David Martin calls it the "raw material of the EU economy" (European Parliament 2012a).

> IP – as the 'intellectual currency' for valuing and trading inventions, brands and works created by clever and talented people – provides the market-based incentives and rewards for a virtuous circle of innovation and creativity that underpins a constantly improving stream of innovations and creative products. The companies and industries that develop and thrive on the basis of IP represent a substantial part of the jobs, tax revenues, GDP growth and competitiveness of the EU. (BASCAP and INTA 2012, 6)

The authors to the INTA study (Institute for Globalisation and International Regulation et al. 2011, 33) point out that economists have yet to agree on the best balance in IPR between "more available knowledge in the future and less accessible knowledge in the present". They urge that, "ACTA should by no means be seen as a silver bullet, as it must be supplemented by other strategic initiatives aimed at boosting the innovative capacity of the EU" (Institute for Globalisation and International Regulation et al. 2011, 46). Other stakeholders stress the balance that needs to be found in copyright for the benefit of *society*, underlining the interests of authors and consumers. The civil rights organization Article 19 (2011) remarks that there is no reference to reward for labor or sharing of benefits in the preambles or substantive provisions of ACTA. In a joint press release civil society (2012) takes it one step further, calling for changes in the EU framework to foster access and sharing of knowledge and culture:

> Access to and sharing of knowledge and culture are essential for building open and democratic societies. We call on European lawmakers to look beyond the rejection of ACTA and to work towards a new framework that nurtures our practices rather than destroying them, a framework fit for the digital age.

Lastly the Foundation for a Free Information Infrastructure (FFII 2013) takes issue with ACTA's strong enforcement focus, deeming that, "[h]igh prices for media goods, low incomes, and cheap digital technologies are the main ingredients of global media piracy."

Relating to Internet theories and rationales, opponents of ACTA stress Internet freedom and openness *(social interaction and symbolic belonging)*. Internet freedom is advocated in conjunction with fundamental rights, however, without expanding on what this means. The Internet is considered a promoter of fundamental rights and an enabler of cultural change.

> The Internet and other information and communications technology bring about a fundamental change in the political economy of communications and, through the development of new modes of production and distribution of cultural works, represent an opportunity for a more inclusive and democratic cultural sphere. (La Quadrature du Net 2010a)

Two proponents of ACTA, BASCAP and INTA (2012, 11), believe that "the Internet is a powerful tool that has expanded legitimate commerce well beyond national borders, but it also has contributed to the globalisation of illicit trade" *(entrepreneurship)*.

6.2   DISCOURSES

I identify seven discourses in the EU debate on ACTA: one common to all stakeholders, three discourses in favor of the agreement and three discourses against the agreement. The discourses sometimes overlap, sometimes contradict and importantly are contested. ACTA is strongly criticized. The pro-ACTA discourses did not convince and were not adopted by the majority of stakeholders.

6.2.1   Overarching ACTA

Discourse 1: Need to Balance Rights and Interests for Innovation, Creativity and Economic Growth

> Desiring to address the problem of infringement of intellectual property rights, including infringement taking place in the digital environment, in particular with respect to copyright or related rights, in a manner that balances the rights and interests of the relevant right holders, service providers, and users. (Preamble to ACTA 2011 Accession Ongoing)

Box 6.2 Ideas in the anti-counterfeiting trade agreement

Analysis of stakeholder opinions on ACTA at an EU level from the end of the negotiations until the European Parliament's rejection (2010–2012)

- Pro—ACTA to increase economic growth and EU competitiveness abroad, as a signal that IPR enforcement is priority, ACTA is not a backdoor change to EU law nor a threat to fundamental rights and Internet freedom
- Anti—object to ACTA's double, yet exclusive focus on counterfeiting and piracy, imprecise wording and lack of safeguards, lack of transparency and inclusiveness
- Nuanced—conflicting assessments of compatibility with EU and international law
- Copyright Rationales
  - Natural law, economic incentive
  - No reference to reward for labor or sharing of benefits in ACTA
- Internet Rationales
  - Social interaction & symbolic belonging
  - Internet as promoter of fundamental rights and enabler of cultural change

A wide range of stakeholders call for *balancing rights and interests*. There is no agreement on whether ACTA finds this balance. On the one hand, proponents deem enhanced international cooperation and more effective international enforcement for IPR necessary to promote *innovation, creativity and permit economic growth*. High protection of Europe's *"intellectual currency"* is considered essential to remain *competitive* in the global and online market place. On the other hand, opponents find that the treaty's exclusive focus on enforcement aggravates the already *shaky balance* between protection and exploitation, and between copyright and other fundamental rights. Internet companies argue that ACTA will harm their capacity to innovate and contribute to economic growth. Further many stakeholders contend that ACTA favors the *commercial interests* of rights holders. MEP in the Green/EFA group Christian Engström protests at the idea of balancing copyright and fundamental rights. He states, "[t]hese are fundamental rights. I do not want my fundamental rights balanced against an industry interest. I want my fundamental rights respected. Period" (Interview 2013).

6.2.2   Pro-ACTA

Discourse 2: ACTA Counters the Increasing Harm of IPR Infringements

The problems which ACTA seeks to address are real and growing. IPR infringements have increased substantially and continue to do so, which has negative consequences ranging from economic and job losses to health and safety dangers. (European Communities Trade Mark Association 2012)

Proponents advocate ACTA as a solution to the *growing problem of IPR infringement*. Their starting point is the *harm inflicted on the economy, health and safety*. Stakeholders argue that ACTA targets large-scale crime rather than individual Internet users. Indeed one interview respondent in the European Commission (2013) emphasizes that counterfeiting is a major source of revenue for *organized crime*. He says, "[p]eople think about handbags, but it is airbags. I had an example yesterday in the States. Something about 80,000 airbags going into cars. They were counterfeit. Not only do they not work, when they explode they catch fire. That is big, big business for criminal organizations."

Discourse 3: ACTA Requires No Change

ACTA will not change the body of EU law as it is already considerably more advanced than the current international standards. ACTA will only address the way companies and individuals can enforce their rights in court, at the borders or via the internet. It will not create new IP rights, nor will it define their acquisition, duration, scope of protection, registration, etc. ACTA countries will enforce the rights as they are defined domestically. (European Commission 2012d)

Much pro-ACTA discourse is defensive. Stakeholders seek to counter the criticism raised on both the process and substance of ACTA, arguing that the treaty will *not change international or EU law*. Remarkably the EC could not find support even among proponents of ACTA when defending its transparency in the policymaking process. In February 2012 the Commission referred ACTA to the CJEU to rebuild confidence in the Treaty.

Discourse 4: Need for Calm and Reasoned Debate

Deeming the Parliament discussions emotional, proponents of ACTA urge politicians to enter into a *calm and reasoned debate* on the substance of ACTA. This call is frequently repeated in my expert interviews. Policy developments on online copyright enforcement are viewed as intensely confrontational and polarized. Many interview respondents consider a technical debate desirable.

> For me it is time to come back to a technical debate. There is no need to talk about copyright in general. It is useless and there is nothing to gain. [ACTA] is an additional argument to come back to a technical debate and to discuss concrete proposals and solutions at the EU level. The collective management directive is a good example. It looks like it is considered a technical debate. (Cécile Despringre, Executive Director at the Society for Audiovisual Authors—SAA, Interview 2013)

Civil society organizations, however, do not support this proposed solution. They object to the narrow framing and often informal and private setting conditions imposed on such debates. Moreover Edouard Barreiro (Former Director of Public Affairs and Studies at UFC Que. Choisir, Interview 2013) states, "[t]he things are what they are. You have to choose to be on the side of those who are heard. Those who are heard are the ones with extremist positions."

6.2.3   Anti-ACTA

Discourse 5: ACTA Threatens Freedom of Citizens and the Internet

> Rather than contributing to the upholding of freedom of expression and due process rights by the dominant, private-sector players on the Internet, ACTA erodes the development of the Rule of Law in that realm. It encourages the regulation of human rights-sensitive matters by private entities, outside the formal frameworks, and without ensuring compliance with "off-line" human rights standards. (Korff and Brown 2011, 60)

The lack of clarity in ACTA provisions is a stumbling block for anti-ACTA stakeholders. They argue that ACTA *threatens freedom of citizens and the Internet*. Alternative emblematic issues in this discourse are *fundamental rights, civil liberties and the free & open Internet*.

Often stakeholders mention freedom on the Internet without further explanation. In the expert interviews, media representatives take particular issue with the proposed opposition between copyright and fundamental rights. Stakeholders believe this discourse is used in a rather abstract manner. Anne Bergman-Tahon (Director at the Federation of European Publishers—FEP, Interview 2013) finds it insulting that civil society argues that copyright prevents freedom of expression. She contends that publishers are the ones fighting for freedom of expression. "Every day and sometimes in our blood", she adds. Further Johannes Studinger (Head of Department at UNI Media, Entertainment & Arts Global Union, Interview 2013) calls for a debate on the responsibility of freedom:

> What is unfortunate is that many civil society groups have taken the stance that the solution to a free Internet is lowering of copyright levels. They do not want to see that every time you lower a right that is actually a human right it is not for better but you lower the level of civilization [...] you have to have the dialogue with civil society about the costs of freedom, about the responsibility of freedom.

Discourse 6: ACTA Lacks Democratic Credibility

> If negotiations are held in secret, if preparatory documents are kept secret, if negotiating drafts are kept secret, if legal analyses are kept secret, it is very difficult to credibly argue that ACTA was a model of transparency. The only thing that is transparent is the dishonesty. (European Digital Rights, EDRi 2012a)

Opponents of ACTA consider the process of ACTA problematic as well. The agreement *lacks democratic credibility* due to the exclusive and secretive nature of the negotiations. In this context the EP ALDE and S&D groups call the EPP group out for intending to request a secret ballot. MEP in the ALDE group, Niccolò Rinaldi states that, "[a]rguably ACTA has generated more public interest and feeling than any other international legal text that has come before this House. It is scandalous and unethical for MEPs to hide their voting behaviour on such a prominent issue from public view. They are elected to represent the citizens, not avoid them" (ALDE 2012b).

Discourse 7: Need for New Approach

Today marks a victory for European democracy and for digital freedoms. As we close the ACTA chapter we must now focus on reforming copyright management and completing the European digital single market. In any future enforcement of trade treaties we need sector specific approaches to counterfeiting and must differentiate between tangible goods and digital content. In this reform process different stakeholders should be part of an inclusive, transparent and democratic decision making process. (MEP Marietje Schaake, ALDE 2012a)

Finally stakeholders advocate *a new approach to IPR policymaking*, in process and in substance. "A modern social pact, a modern regime of protecting intellectual property rights" (S&D 2012a). There is variation in the proposed solutions, in particular to which extent copyright reform is necessary. Among opponents to ACTA, agreement can be found to involve citizens in future debates and to adopt a sectoral approach to counterfeiting and piracy.

6.2.4 Discourse Coalitions, Structuration and Institutionalization

The Council of the European Union, the European Commission, the EPP group and rights holders agree with ACTA. Except for the Council[5] these stakeholders form a first discourse coalition, emphasizing pro-ACTA discourses: the harm of IPR infringements, ACTA's compatibility with international and EU law and the need for a calm and reasoned debate. Further *the S&D, ALDE, Green/EFA & GUE/NGL political groups, the EDPS, the European Economic and Social Committee, Internet companies, civil society and a few others disagree with ACTA.* Except for Internet companies, they form a second discourse coalition, advocating anti-ACTA discourses: ACTA's threat to freedom, lack of democratic credibility and the need for a new approach to IPR policymaking. Internet companies restricted their discourse to balancing interests for innovation and economic growth. The high-volume lobbying campaign of civil society stands in contrast with the minimal involvement of Internet companies. Jérémie Zimmermann (Co-founder and Former Spokesperson for La Quadrature du Net, Interview 2013) sees the strength of the anti-ACTA coalition in the multitude and diversity of actors involved. In his words, they succeeded in networking "farmers to HIV and gay rights to vintage video games to archivists". Finally *the EP Legal Service, European Academics, the authors of the EP INTA study and the OSCE Media*

Freedom Representative express nuanced views on ACTA. Discursively the EP Legal Service fits within the pro-ACTA coalition, as it emphasizes that ACTA requires no change in international and EU law. The Legal Service also mentions the need for balancing in the implementation of the treaty. European Academics and the OSCE Media Freedom Representative join the anti-ACTA coalition, expressing concern about threats to fundamental rights. European Academics further stress the need to properly address the fair balance between rights and interests, and the OSCE Media Freedom Representative advocates a new approach to IPR policymaking. Lastly the authors of the EP INTA study are not part of a discourse coalition, as they consider that ACTA does not change international and EU law, but could influence future debates. Box 6.3 provides a list of stakeholders active on ACTA.

Regarding discourse structuration, *the majority of stakeholders adopt the overarching and anti-ACTA discourses.* I expand on *the views of the Parliamentary groups,* as MEPs' votes determined ACTA's rejection in the EU. First *the S&D group* highlights the need for balance and the value of freedom of citizens and the Internet (press releases, Feb–July 2012). While in February 2012 they communicate that they will wait before drawing conclusions on ACTA, by April 2012 this position shifts to rejection and new solutions: "[t]he sooner we reject ACTA, the sooner we can start working on concrete measures to protect copyright, trademarks and citizens rights" (MEP Hannes Swoboda, S&D 2012b). In later press releases they continue to stress ACTA's threats for fundamental rights and the need for a new approach. They also raise the issue of ACTA's democratic credibility and underline the Parliament's responsibility in defending citizens. The communication of *the ALDE group* is similar to the S&D group. Their press releases range from February to July 2012 and emphasize the threat for civil liberties and the need for a new approach. In February 2012 they welcome the verification of ACTA's conformity with fundamental rights. However by April 2012 the ALDE group shifts its position on the CJEU referral, advocating a sectoral approach which treats counterfeiting and piracy separately and involves citizens. This discourse of new solutions is repeated in following press releases. The communication of *the Green/EFA group* starts earlier (Nov 2011–July 2012) and is voluminous. The Green/EFA group commissioned two studies on ACTA's compatibility with fundamental rights, and on ACTA and access to medicines. In the resulting press releases they argue strongly that ACTA threatens fundamental rights and access to generic medicines. Further the Green/EFA group views the CJEU referral with skepticism. In February 2012 MEP Jan Philipp Albrecht states that, "[r]egardless of the outcome of an ECJ evaluation, the Greens believe ACTA is politically wrongheaded. Recent demonstrations have also shown the extent of public opposition. Against this background, the Greens will push to ensure the EP refuses to give its consent." He continues, "ACTA would block the much-needed reform of EU copyright law and instead lead to a heavy-handed and repressive enforcement of copyright with no regard to the basic rights of citizens" (Green/EFA 2012). Later press releases of the Green/EFA group continue to stress ACTA's danger for fundamental rights and access to generic medicines, and the need for copyright reform. ACTA's lack of democratic credibility is also raised. This comes through particularly strongly in a sample of French Green/EFA statements. Here the group emphasizes that the EP represents citizens rather than big industry lobbies. *The GUE/NGL group* in the EP adopts the discourses of balancing interests, threats to freedom and lack of democratic credibility. They deem that ACTA is used to extend rich countries' domination and commercial rights holders interests. Finally *the EPP group* is alone in its support of ACTA. The EPP group stresses the harm caused by IPR infringements and the need for a calm and reasoned debate. They argue that rejection will not solve the underlying problems that ACTA seeks to address and urge to wait for the CJEU's opinion.

Regarding discourse institutionalization, it is useful to analyze the views expressed in the adopted *EP recommendation on ACTA and the committee opinions*. As ACTA was rejected, these form the institutionalized discourses on the trade agreement. Five committees voted on ACTA before it was brought to the plenary: International Trade (INTA), Development (DEVE), Industry, Research and Energy (ITRE), Legal Affairs (JURI) and Civil Liberties, Justice and Home Affairs (LIBE). *Every committee proposes that the EP declines to give its consent on ACTA.* INTA drafted the EP recommendation. It recognizes the harm inflicted by IPR infringements, but deems that the "intended benefits of this international agreement are far outweighed by the potential threats to civil liberties" (European Parliament 2012b, 6). There is a need to find new approaches to balance rights and interests. Further DEVE does not provide a justification for its vote. ITRE emphasizes the need to balance and the threat for fundamental rights. It also fears that, "ACTA may contradict the ambition of the EP in the Digital Agenda to make Europe the scene for cutting edge innovation, as well as the strong ambition to promote net neutrality and access to the online digital market for all users" (European Parliament 2012b, 10). A proposal in favor of ACTA was rejected in JURI. The committee did not provide an alternative text. Finally, LIBE adopts many discourses. It acknowledges the damage of counterfeit goods to jobs, safety and health, but believes ACTA lacks democratic credibility due to the low levels of transparency. Striking "the appropriate balance" is considered crucial and "fundamental rights laundering" must not be allowed. Lastly the committee calls for "a modern social pact, a modern regime of protecting intellectual property rights" (European Parliament 2012b, 16, 17, 22).

The following sections reflect on the socioeconomic and politico legal context in which ACTA unfolds. What are policy actors' goals and which institutional rules are at play?

6.3   INTERESTS

6.3.1   Policy Goals

The contrast between policy goals of ACTA proponents and opponents is stark. While proponents desire *ratification* of the agreement, opponents advocate its *rejection*. Indeed the EU rules for trade agreements (consent) did not permit a middle ground. Building on the discussion of ideas and discourses, it is of course clear that stakeholders have policy goals beyond ratification and rejection as well. Many policy actors seek *innovation, creativity and economic growth*, even though their proposed policy solutions differ. Moreover proponents wish to underline *respect for IPR* through ACTA's ratification. Opponents see its rejection as an opportunity to *reform IPR in a more inclusive manner*. Anti-ACTA stakeholders also argue that the Commission and member states negotiated a multilateral agreement, because it provided an opportunity to *impose higher enforcement standards and avoid more balanced discussions at the international and EU level*. Further sometimes stakeholders who advocate similar problem definitions or policy solutions have differing policy goals. One interview respondent (2013) states that according to his personal interpretation Germany did not sign ACTA, because the minister in charge hoped this would boost the Liberal Party's popularity. Some proponents of ACTA similarly regard the EP's vote as an act of *political populism*. They also argue that the Parliament wished to *flex its institutional muscles*.

Box 6.3 Discourse coalitions, structuration and institutionalization on the anti-counterfeiting trade agreement

Analysis of stakeholder opinions on ACTA at an EU level from the end of the negotiations until the EP's rejection (2010–2012)

As the first discourse is common to all stakeholders. I only detail the discourse coalitions for the latter two sets of discourses. It should be noted that many representatives of the media and Internet industries did not take a formal position on ACTA, preferring no or minimal involvement.

Overarching—Need to Balance Rights and Interests for Innovation, Creativity and Economic Growth

- Common to all stakeholders

Pro—ACTA Counters the Increasing Harm of IPR Infringements, ACTA Requires No Change, Need for Calm and Reasoned Debate

- EU Public Authorities
  - Council of the European Union*
  - European Commission
  - European Parliament, European People's Party (EPP)

- Intellectual Property Rights Holders (joint 130+, May 2012)
  - Industry associations in apparel & textile, audiovisual, automobile, commercial broadcasting, cosmetics, music, publishing, software, sporting goods, toys such as IFPI and MPA
  - Industry coalitions for brands and trademarks such as INTA and European Communities Trade Mark Association (ECTA)
  - Industry coalitions against counterfeiting and piracy
  - International Chambers of Commerce such as ICC-BASCAP

Anti—ACTA Threatens Freedom of Citizens and the Internet, ACTA Lacks Democratic Credibility, Need for New Approach

- EU Public Authorities
  - European Parliament, S&D
  - European Parliament, Alliance of Liberals and Democrats for Europe (ALDE)

(continued)

Box 6.3 (continued)

- European Parliament, Greens/European Free Alliance (Green/EFA)
- \European Parliament, European United Left/Nordic Green Left (GUE/NGL)
- European Data Protection Supervisor
- European Economic and Social Committee

- Internet & Technology Industries (joint 4, April 2012)*
  - Industry associations of fixed/mobile telecoms operators, ISPs and cable companies—European Competitive Telecommunication Association (ECTA), ETNO, EuroISPA and GSMA Europe

- Civil Society (joint 50+, July 2012)
  - Civil rights organizations & associations such as Article 19, BEUC and Oxfam International
  - Digital rights organizations & associations such as EDRi, Internet Society, La Quadrature du Net and Open Rights Group
  - Free and open source software organizations & associations such as FFII

- Others
  - International Association of IT Lawyers (IAITL), Association for Arts and Media (Constant) and Reporters Without Borders
  - Opinion commissioned by EP Greens/European Free Alliance on compatibility of ACTA with fundamental rights, Douwe Korff & Ian Brown
  - Study commissioned by EP Greens/European Free Alliance on ACTA and access to medicines, Sean Flynn & Bijan Madhani *(not analyzed)*

Nuanced
- EU Public Authorities
  - European Parliament, Legal Service**
  - Others
  - Opinion drafted by European Academics (coalition 175+, February 2011),*** Robert D'Erme, Christophe Geiger, Henning Große Ruse-Khan, Christian Heinze, Thomas Jaeger, Rita Matulionyte & Axel Metzger
  - Study commissioned by EP Committee on International Trade assessing ACTA, Ansel Kamperman Sanders, Dalindyebo Bafana Shabalala, Anke Moerland, Meir Pugatch & Paolo Vergano*

(continued)

Box 6.3 (continued)

- Organization for Security and Cooperation in Europe, Media Freedom Representative***

Discourse Structuration and Institutionalization
- Discourse Structuration
  - EP groups—mainly overarching and anti-ACTA discourses
  - Shift in discourse during policymaking—recommend to reject ACTA, emphasize need for new approach
- Discourse Institutionalization
  - EP committees—recommend to reject ACTA, emphasize need for new approach to balance rights and interests

---

* These stakeholders are not part of a discourse coalition.
** This stakeholder is part of the pro-ACTA discourse coalition.
*** These stakeholders are part of the anti-ACTA discourse coalition.

[ACTA] was a pure outcome of a well orchestrated lobbying campaign with the grassroots movements very focused on key Members of Parliament who were willing to take it up as a populistic issue. (Johannes Studinger, Head of Department at UNI Media, Entertainment & Arts Global Union, Interview 2013)

Finally stakeholders contend that there are large *commercial interests* present. Malte Behrmann (Former Secretary General at the European Games Developer Federation, Interview 2013) describes the ACTA debate as a fight between Los Angeles and San Francisco. Alain Strowel (Professor at Université Saint-Louis and UCLouvain, Interview 2013) deems that the polarization in the enforcement debate is driven by greed on all sides. "Greed from the right holders, especially from commercial entities. They want to get as much money as they can get out of works of the authors, be that employees or what ever. On the other side greed by users, and by intermediaries as well. The users don't want to pay anything, sometimes it is out of greed, sometimes they don't have enough resources or access to an online payment system."

6.3.2   Social and Economic Reality

Regarding the social and economic reality, some opponents to ACTA take *issue with the proposed policy problem of harm inflicted by IPR infringement*. On the one hand, they contend that the causes of piracy are complex. On the other hand, the provisions in ACTA on damages are contested, as there is disagreement on methods for calculating damages. Further, stakeholders oppose the proposed solution to deal with counterfeiting and piracy in one policy instrument. Many argue that *infringement of tangible and intangible goods requires separate approaches*.

Expanding on the discussion of *intellectual property rights and economic growth*, the European Patent Office and the Office for Harmonization in the Internal Market jointly published a study on the contribution of IPR-intensive industries in the EU.[6] They find that, *"IPR-intensive industries contribute 26% of employment and 39% of GDP in the EU"* (EPO and OHIM 2013, 6). Moreover 90 % of EU exports are accounted for by IPR-intensive industries (EPO and OHIM 2013, 9). Further the EC (2010e)'s European Competitiveness report highlights that the creative industries account for 3.3 % of the total EU GDP and 3 % of the EU's employment.[7] The creative industries did well in the period 2000–2007, with an average employment growth of 3.5 % a year. At the time of discussing ACTA, the IFPI was optimistic that the recorded music industry had turned the corner after a shaky start in the digital environment. For instance, in their 2013 Digital Music Report (IFPI, 6) they share that, "[r]ecord companies' digital revenues for 2012 are estimated at US$5.6 billion, up an estimated 9 per cent on 2011 and accounting for more than a third of total industry revenues (34%)." By 2015, digital sales comprised the majority of global industry revenues (US$6.7 billion, 45 %) rising above physical sales for the first time (IFPI 2016). At the same time the European Competitiveness report states that growth is not uniform across the creative industries. While gaming is a particularly booming industry, employment in the publishing sector has hardly changed. Similarly although the film industry seems to be flourishing in some markets, its window release system is strained and the industry is certainly not in the clear yet (European Commission 2010e).

6.4 Institutions

6.4.1 Policy Legacy

In terms of legal arguments and policy legacy, both proponents and opponents of ACTA refer to *the CJEU cases SABAM vs. Scarlet and SABAM vs. Netlog* (February 16, 2012, November 24, 2011) to argue that the trade agreement either does or should respect EU jurisprudence on Internet monitoring. La Quadrature du Net highlights the *Telecoms Package* as additional grounds against increased intermediary cooperation. Moreover stakeholders mention Article 32 of the *Vienna Convention on the Law of Treaties* (United Nations 1969) which states that, "supplementary means of interpretation, including the preparatory work of the treaty and the circumstances of its conclusion" may be used when its interpretation "(a) leaves the meaning ambiguous or obscure; or (b) leads to a result which is manifestly absurd or unreasonable". Leaks of preparatory work on ACTA revealed that early proposals suggested graduated response as a policy solution. Stakeholders fear recourse could be had to this material as ACTA includes imprecise wording. They call for disclosure of the preparatory work.

Further, leading up to the EP discussions on ACTA, a sequence of events occurred, which Jérémie Zimmermann (Co-founder and Former Spokesperson for La Quadrature du Net, Interview 2013) described as "a blessing from the sky". First, two bills introduced in the United States, *SOPA and PIPA,* were withdrawn due to a large-scale online campaign of Internet intermediaries. This campaign included service blackouts to raise awareness of the law proposals by intermediaries such as Google and Wikipedia. Second, the United States Department of Justice seized the domain names and shut down the websites associated with the file-sharing service Megaupload. The owner of Megaupload Kim Dotcom was arrested in New Zealand. The *takedown of Megaupload* prior to a court ruling and through domain name seizure was strongly criticized. Third, shortly thereafter *the EC and twenty-two member states signed ACTA*. Again protests ensued on the streets in Europe and online. Zimmermann (Interview 2013) states, "[w]e spent a lot of energy to connect this series of events [...] This is the war against sharing, this shows how absurd it can be, this is what the world with ACTA could be. Because [with ACTA] you wouldn't even need to send the FBI, you could pressure intermediaries on the way to Megaupload to have it shut down."

Box 6.4 Interests and institutions in the anti-counterfeiting trade agreement

Analysis of stakeholder opinions on ACTA at an EU level from the end of the negotiations until the EP's rejection (2010–2012)

Interests
- Policy Goals
    - Ratification vs. rejection
    - Skirt around traditional institutions at international/EU level vs. political populism
- Social and Economic Reality
    - Stakeholders mark interests at play—big and commercial
    - IPR-intensive industries in EU provide 26 % of employment, 39 % GDP, 90 % exports

Institutions
- Policy Legacy
    - Contestation over fundamental rights
    - Argumentation based on SABAM vs. Scarlet / SABAM vs. Netlog cases, Telecoms Package
- Political and Legal Reality
    - No legislative policy outcome, successful citizen mobilization and online advocacy
    - IG—code and Internet architecture, national governments and law

6.4.2   Political and Legal Reality

Interview respondents indicate that ACTA was decided when people started protesting. Civil society perceived ACTA as a threat to freedom, in favor of commercial interests and avoiding traditional EU and international policy venues. Many stakeholders consider *ACTA as a sign of the coming of age of a new lobbying power.*

> This is a major victory for democracy and civil society and activism: against Governments['] secrecy, against the huge economic power of the large entertainment industries, against the bypassing of international decision-making. This is, in fact, a victory for global democracy. Let us never doubt the power of civil society engagement and campaigning... (Article 19 2012)

Policy actors are *not necessarily sure how to respond to these new levels of citizen participation*. Political parties and Internet companies deem that citizens should be applauded for their engagement. Chris Sherwood (Former Director of Public Policy at Yahoo!, Interview 2013) argues, "the reality is that civil society has woken up and is very excited, and rightly so, about its power to influence legislation. Part of living in a democracy is allowing that kind of thing to happen. That is part of what happened in the Arab Spring. This is all part of the same movement of moving of power to the connected people on the Internet." Proponents of ACTA argue that current discussions are too simplistic. ACTA was about sound bites, about "people voting with their tweet". They are keen to encourage citizens to contribute constructively to online copyright dialogues. For instance, one interview respondent in the Commission (2013) points out that user generated content rightly symbolizes freedom of speech on the Internet and that its value for society should be underlined. At the same time, he says, detailed discussions are needed on how to deal with infringements of moral rights, such as the use of a song in a neo-Nazi videoclip.

ACTA is illustrative of the *strong polarization* in the copyright enforcement debate, within and between stakeholder groups. So although EU *member states* were involved in the negotiations of ACTA, not all countries signed the agreement. Further *within the Parliament* the EPP group was alone in its defense of ACTA. In this policy initiative *the Commission and Parliament* took opposite views on enforcement. The ACTA debate boiled down to whether stakeholders believed this multilateral treaty on IPR enforcement was *a threat to freedom or a defense of livelihoods*. The following two paragraphs expand on this thought. ACTA was portrayed as protecting either the Internet—or IPR. Positions were juxtaposed, only alternative policy solutions tread the middle ground.

Regarding threats to freedom and relating to IG models, civil society actors view ACTA as another legislative effort to increase intermediary cooperation *(code and Internet architecture)*. In the expert interviews however, media stakeholders emphasize that the Internet is an extension of the physical world and consequently that the same rules apply online as offline *(national governments and law)*. Johannes Studinger (Head of Department at UNI Media, Entertainment & Arts Global Union, Interview 2013) deems that, "freedom is used as a Trojan horse for no regulation. No regulation does not mean freedom. Like in the physical world, no regulation on the streets would not mean freedom on the streets. So you can regulate traffic on the Internet as you can regulate traffic in the physical world. To enhance freedom." Niklas Lagergren (Former Vice President European Union Affairs at the Motion Picture Association, Interview 2013) adds that a clear distinction needs to be made between the notion of "openness" in a technical sense and the principle of "openness" in a democratic society. He contends that ensuring respect for the rule of law online will not threaten the openness of the Internet but, on the contrary, strengthen it *(against cyberspace and spontaneous ordering)*.

Regarding the defense of livelihoods, the EC admits that they failed to communicate in ACTA how IPR is important for employment and how harmful counterfeiting and piracy can be on jobs (Interview 2013). They argue that ways need to be found to explain the economics of counterfeiting and piracy. Stakeholders also find that the heavy levels of investment required for media (the economics of copyright) are misunderstood. David Touve (Director at the iLab of the University of Virginia, Interview 2013) states that rights holders essentially operate in a social trap:

> [c]opyrighted works are ultimately impossible to protect. We cannot prevent people from copy-pasting a music or movie file, performing a song in public, remixing a new recording from old recordings, etc. As a result, copyright owners are often stuck in this trap wherein the only way for them to try to earn some of the value of their copyrights arrives via the courts. Yet, suing people is not exactly perceived as friendly behaviour. As a result, on many occasions copyright owners can only pursue the value of their work if they are willing to be seen as an asshole.

As such, we can move beyond polarization only after we believe that the most interesting story to be told (or heard or read) is the one that involves the nuances that lead to collaboration and compromise. Many people make money by way of polarization, however, since nuanced debates take time and effort to understand. Polarized debates make great headlines and are easy to skim.

6.5   CONCLUSION: PEC CONSIDERATIONS

ACTA is a multilateral trade agreement aimed at enhanced international cooperation on IPR enforcement. It was negotiated outside of traditional policy venues and goes beyond international standards. ACTA's lack of transparency is strongly criticized. In the EU, the EP's consent rules for trade agreements polarized stakeholders' views. Choices were limited to either ratify or reject ACTA. Modification was not possible. In many ways, *ACTA is a battle of institutions.* The protests against ACTA send a strong signal that *citizens want to be involved in policymaking on online copyright enforcement.* Moreover similar to the other case studies, the discussions on ACTA demonstrate that *problem definitions and policy solutions proposed to deal with online piracy are contested.* Stakeholders question why the EC would enter into negotiations on online copyright enforcement policymaking at an international level, when there is no consensus on ways forward at an EU level.

In this case study, calls are made, based on copyright's social requirements, to provide *access to medicine and culture.* Civil society actors link the subject matter of ACTA with its policymaking procedure. They deem that access to and sharing of knowledge and culture help build open and democratic societies. Internet freedom is often mentioned in conjunction with civil liberties. Unfortunately what is missing is an explanation on why the design and governance of the Internet matter for fundamental rights and democracy. *In the end, ACTA's opponents—the EP, the EDPS, the European Economic and Social Committee, Internet companies, civil society and a few others—win. The Treaty is rejected.* The studies and opinions on ACTA analyzed in this case study provide mainly negative, although somewhat conflicting evaluations of its compatibility with EU secondary law and fundamental rights. It is clear that the ratification of ACTA would have been another step along a contested enforcement track and another legal recommendation for cooperative measures with Internet intermediaries. The rejection of ACTA is *an example of citizens stepping up, questioning policymaking and valuing the Internet as a public sphere.* This is positive. What is next?

After the failure to ratify ACTA, dealing with online copyright enforcement in the EU was *politically toxic.* The EC tread very carefully. They set up a stakeholder dialogue to find non-legislative solutions on copyright licensing, held public consultations, and completed reviews of the Copyright in the Information Society and IPR Enforcement Directives to decide whether to table proposals for legislative reform (European Commission 2012b). The only legislative action attempted before the new college of commissioners that took office in 2014 was the adoption of a directive on collective rights management and multiterritorial licensing for musical works online (European Parliament & Council 2014). Of late, the EC has been bolder. Adapting copyright to the digital single market is being tackled through legislative action in the field of copyright, but also audiovisual policy more broadly. At the same time, considerations are being made about how to create an effective and balanced enforcement environment. Current initiatives aim to facilitate cross-border portability and licensing of online content services, facilitate digitization and distribution of out-of-commerce works, create mandatory exceptions for research, education, cultural heritage and people with print disabilities, create an ancillary right for press publishers online, and oblige online platforms to promote European works and take appropriate and proportionate measures to protect copyright (European Commission 2016a). The latter two items fit in a discourse on sharing value generated online between market players. Initial stakeholder reactions to the legislative proposals seem to indicate that everyone have been left frustrated and disappointed; the initiatives are either too far-reaching or not nearly profound enough. *It remains to be seen whether these policy measures will find a middle ground and integrate concerns on fundamental rights and Internet freedom. Moreover it is an open question whether calls for transparent and inclusive policymaking voiced in ACTA have been heard.* The concluding chapter reflects on these thoughts further.

NOTES

1. Cyprus, Estonia, Germany, the Netherlands and Slovakia did not sign ACTA. Croatia was not a yet member of the EU when ACTA was signed (having joined the EU on July 1, 2013).
2. Select sentences of this introduction and an amended Fig. 6.1 can be found in (Meyer and Vetulani-Cęgiel 2016).
3. As defined in Chap. 1, discourse structuration and institutionalization are the reproduction of discourse by government or Parliament officials and departments during the policymaking process, and the embedding of discourse into legal and supporting policy documents at the end of the policymaking process.
4. Other objections pertain for instance to Article 8 ACTA on injunctions and Article 9 ACTA on damages.
5. The Council is involved as it adopted ACTA. However I did not find Council contributions to the EU debate on ACTA within the case study's selected timeframe.
6. The European Patent Office and the Office for Harmonization in the Internal Market (2013, p. 6) define IPR-intensive industries as "those having an above-average use of IPR per employee".

According to this study, about half of the EU industries are IPR-intensive. The period analyzed in the study is 2008–2010.
7. The EC's definition of creative industries is broad, including not only traditional media industries such as the press, radio, television, film, music, gaming, publishing, performance and more, but also professional services such as advertising, architecture and design.

BIBLIOGRAPHY

February 16, 2012. C-360/10 Belgische Vereniging van Auteurs, Componisten en Uitgevers (SABAM) vs. Netlog. Court of Justice of the European Union.

November 24, 2011. C-70/10 Scarlet Extended vs. Société Belge des Auteurs, Compositeurs et Editeurs (SABAM). Court of Justice of the European Union.

ALDE. 2012a. ACTA: An Ineffective Agreement That Puts Civil Liberties at Risk. http://www.alde.eu/press/press-and-release-news/press-release/article/acta-an-ineffective-agreement-that-puts-civil-liberties-at-risk-39459/. Accessed 6 Oct 2016.

———. 2012b. ALDE Condemns EPP Plans to Hold Secret Vote on ACTA. http://www.alde./nc/press/press-and-release-news/press-release/article/alde-condemns-epp-plans-to-hold-secret-vote-on-acta-39168/. Accessed 6 Oct 2016.

Arthur, Charles. 2012. Acta Goes Too Far, Says MEP. *Theguardian.com*, February 1.http://www.theguardian.com/technology/2012/feb/01/acta-goes-too-far-kader-arif

Article 19. 2011. Statement. European Parliament: Reject Anti-Counterfeiting Trade Agreement (ACTA). http://www.article19.org/resources.php/resource/2901/en/european-parliament:-reject-anti-counterfeiting-trade-agreement-(acta). Accessed 6 October 2016.

———. 2012. TODAY, By a Huge Majority, the European Parliament Voted to Reject ACTA. http://www.article19.org/join-the-debate.php/62/view/. Accessed 6 Oct 2016.

Australia, Canada, the European Union and its member states, Japan, the Kingdom of Morocco, New Zealand, the Republic of Korea, the Republic of Singapore, the Swiss Confederation, the United Mexican States, and the United States of America. 2011 Accession Ongoing. Anti-Counterfeiting Trade Agreement.

BASCAP, and INTA. 2012. *ACTA in the EU – A Practical Analysis*. Paris/New York: Business Action to Stop Counterfeiting and Piracy and International Trademark Association.

D'Erme, Roberto, Christophe Geiger, Henning Große Ruse-Khan, Christian Heinze, Thomas Jaeger, Rita Matulionuyte, and Axel Metzger. 2011. Opinion of European Academics on Anti-Counterfeiting Trade Agreement. *Journal of Intellectual Property, Information Technology and E-Commerce Law* 2(1): 65–72.

EDRi. 2012a. 10 European Commission Myths About ACTA. http://www.edri.org/commission_myths. Accessed 6 Oct 2016.

———. 2012b. ACTA Fact Sheet. http://www.edri.org/ACTAfactsheet. Accessed 6 Oct 2016.

EPO, and OHIM. 2013. *Intellectual Property Rights Intensive Industries: Contribution to Economic Performance and Employment in the European Union. Industry-Level Analysis Report, September 2013.* Munich/Germany: European Patent Office & Ofice for Harmonization in the Internal Market.

European Commission. 2005. *COM(2005) 276 final. Proposal for a European Parliament and Council Directive on Criminal Measures aimed at Ensuring the Enforcement of Intellectual Property Rights, and Proposal for Council Framework Decision to Strengthen the Criminal Law Framework to Combat Intellectual Property Offences.* Brussels: European Commission.

———. 2012a. *10 Myths About ACTA (Anti-Counterfeiting Trade Agreement).* Brussels: European Commission.

———. 2012b. A Clean and Open Internet: Public Consultation on Procedures for Notifying and Acting on Illegal Content Hosted by Online Intermediaries. http://ec.europa.eu/internal_market/consultations/2012b/clean-and-open-internet_en.htm. Accessed 6 Oct 2016.

———. 2012c. *COM(2011) 942 Final. Communication to the European Parliament, the Council, the European Economic and Social Committee and the Commitee of the Regions on a Coherent Framework for Building Trust in the Digital Single Market for E-Commerce and Online Services.* Brussels: European Commission.

———. 2012d. *COM(2012d) 789 Final. Communication from the Commission on Content in the Digital Single Market.* Brussels: European Commission.

———. 2013. *SWD(2013) 153 Final. Commission Staff Working Document on E-Commerce Action Plan 2012–2015: State of Play 2013.* Brussels: European Commission.

European Commission & Parliament. 2012. *Anti-Counterfeiting Trade Agreement (ACTA). List of Answers by the European Commission to Written Questions by the European Parliament (Filed Between 1 January 2010 and 31 January 2012).* Brussels: European Commission and Parliament.

European Communities Trade Mark Association. 2012. ACTA Support Letter for Members of EU Parliament. http://www.ecta.org/IMG/pdf/acta_support_letter_for_members_of_eu_parliament_2_.pdf. Accessed 6 Oct 2016.

European Data Protection Supervisor. 2012. *Opinion of the European Data Protection Supervisor on the Proposal for a Council Decision on the Conclusion of the Anti-Counterfeiting Trade Agreement Between the European Union and Its Member States, Australia, Canada, Japan, the Republic of Korea, the United Mexican States, the Kingdom of Morocco, the Republic of Singapore, the Swiss Confederation and the United States of America.* Brussels: European Data Protection Supervisor.

European Parliament. 2012a. *2012a/2030(INI)*. *European Parliament Resolution of 11 December 2012a on Completing the Digital Single Market*. Strasbourg: European Parliament.

———. 2012b. ACTA Before the European Parliament. http://www.europarl. europa.eu/news/en/pressroom/content/2012b0217BKG38488/html/ ACTA-before-the-European-Parliament. Accessed 6 Oct 2016.

———. 2012c. Everything You Need to Know About ACTA. ACTA Debate: MEPs Disagree About the Best Way Forward. http://www.europarl.europa. eu/news/en/news-room/content/2012c0220FCS38611/2/html/ACTA- debate-MEPs-disagree-about-the-best-way-forward. Accessed 6 Oct 2016.

———. 2016. Legislative Powers. Consent. http://www.europarl.europa.eu/ aboutparliament/en/0087a559c8/Consent.html. Accessed 6 Oct 2016.

European Parliament & Council. 2010. *Consolidated Version of the Treaty on the Functioning of the European Union (TFEU)*. Luxembourg: Official Journal of the European Union.

———. 2012. *Directive 2012/28/EU of the European Parliament and of the Council of 25 October 2012 on Certain Permitted Uses of Orphan Works*. Luxembourg: Official Journal of the European Union.

———. 2014. *Directive 2014/26/EU of the European Parliament and of the Council of 26 February 2014 on Collective Management of Copyright and Related Rights and Multi-Territorial Licensing of Rights in Musical Works for Online Use in the Internal Market*. Luxembourg: Official Journal of the European Union.

European Commission. 2010e. SEC(2010) 1276. European Competitiveness Report 2010. In *Enterprise & Industry Magazine*. Brussels: European Commission.

———. 2011c. *Commission Services Working Paper. Comments on the 'Opinion of European Academics on Anti-Counterfeiting Trade Agreement'*. Brussels: European Commission.

———. 2016a. *Promoting a Fair, Efficient and Competitive European Copyright- Based Economy in the Digital Single Market (COM(2016)592 final)*. Brussels: European Commission.

European Parliament, Council, and Commission. 2000. *Charter of Fundamental Rights of the European Union (2000/C 364/01)*. Nice: Official Journal of the European Communities.

European Parliament Legal Service. 2011a. *Legal Opinion Re: Anti-Counterfeiting Trade Agreement (ACTA) – Conformity with European Union Law*. Brussels: European Parliament.

———. 2011b. *Legal Opinion Re: Anti-Counterfeiting Trade Agreement (ACTA)*. *SJ-0501/11*. Brussels: European Parliament.

FFII. 2013. ACTA Analysis: The World Faces Major Challenges.http://action. ffii.org/acta/Analysis. Accessed 6 Oct 2016.

Gallo, Marielle. 2012. 2011/0167(NLE). Draft Opinion of the Committee on Legal Affairs for the Committee on International Trade on the Draft Council

Decision on the Conclusion of the Anti-Counterfeiting Trade Agreement Between the European Union and Its Member States, Australia, Canada, the Republic of Korea, the United States of America, Japan, the Kingdom of Morocco, the United Mexican States, New Zealand, the Republic of Singapore and the Swiss Confederation. Brussels: European Parliament.

Green/EFA. 2012. Referral to ECJ Hopefully a Nail in the ACTA Coffin. http://www.greens-efa.eu/acta-5394.html. Accessed 6 Oct 2016.

IFPI. 2016. *Global Music Report 2016. Music Consumption Exploding Worldwide*. London: International Federation of the Phonographic Industry.

Institute for Globalisation and International Regulation, Anselm Kamperman Sanders, Dalindyebo Bafana Shabalala, Anke Moerland, Meir Pugatch, and Paolo Vergano. 2011. *The Anti-Counterfeiting Trade Agreement (ACTA): An Assessment. EP/EXPO/B/INTA/FWC/2009-01/Lot7/12*. Brussels: European Parliament.

Korff, Douwe, and Ian Brown. 2011. *Opinion on the Compatibility of the Anti-Counterfeiting Trade Agreement (ACTA) with the European Convention on Human Rights & the EU Charter of Fundamental Rights*. Brussels: European Parliament.

La Quadrature du Net. 2012. Facts on ACTA. https://www.laquadrature.net/files/LQDN-20120207-Facts_on_ACTA.pdf. Accessed 6 Oct 2016.

La Quadrature du Net. 2010a. Future of Copyright: La Quadrature calls on the Commission to Reassert the Public's Rights. http://www.laquadrature.net/fr/node/2812. Accessed 6 Oct 2016.

Meyer, Trisha, and Agnieszka Vetulani-Cęgiel. 2016. From ACTA to TTIP: Lessons Learned on Democratic Process and Balancing of Rights. In *Transatlantic Data Privacy Relationships as a Challenge for Democracy*, ed. Dariusz Kloza and Dan Svantesson. Antwerp: Intersentia.

MPAA. 2011. Statement by MPAA CEO and Chairman Chris Dodd on the Upcoming Signing Ceremony for the Anti-Counterfeiting Trade Agreement. Archived with Author.

OSCE. 2012a. Intellectual Property Rights in the Digital Age – New Approaches Needed to Guarantee Freedom of Expression, Says OSCE Media Freedom Representative. http://www.osce.org/fom/87167. Accessed 6 Oct 2016.

———. 2012b. OSCE Media Representative Urges European Parliament to Reassess ACTA to Safeguard Freedom of Expression. http://www.osce.org/fom/88154. Accessed 6 Oct 2016.

S&D. 2012a. S&D Call to Reject ACTA Backed by Parliament's Civil Liberties Committee. http://www.socialistsanddemocrats.eu/newsroom/sd-call-reject-acta-backed-parliaments-civil-liberties-committee-1. Accessed 6 Oct 2016.

———. 2012b. Swoboda Condemns EPP Delaying Tactics with ACTA. http://www.socialistsanddemocrats.eu/newsroom/swoboda-condemns-epp-delaying-tactics-acta. Accessed 6 Oct 2016.

United Nations. 1969. Vienna Convention on the Law of Treaties.

CHAPTER 7

Lessons Learned: Online Copyright Enforcement in the European Union

This chapter brings together the various threads woven through this study. Answers have been sought and given to the research questions posed. However this chapter addresses them directly, highlighting the key story lines to understand how and why online copyright enforcement policies have developed in the EU. In this chapter, I turn to explaining the intense conflict and resulting stalemate on online copyright enforcement in the EU, bringing together the theoretical, analytical and empirical findings of this research to better understand the interplay of ideas, discourses, interests and institutions. In order to provide detailed insight into this study's main research question *how and why selected policies in the EU dealing with the online enforcement of copyright have developed*, I first answer the five operationalized sub-research questions (Sect. 7.1). Then I summarize the essential study insights (Sect. 7.2), the policy implications (Sect. 7.3) and the analytical dimensions (Sect. 7.4) of the research presented in this book. Importantly, in order to find a way forward in online copyright enforcement policies and IG, we need to come to the point where nuance and detail provide the most interesting story to tell. The chapter also provides some ideas for further avenues of research that would be fruitful pursuits given the findings presented in this book (Sect. 7.5). In this regard, the usefulness of, as well as possible improvements to, the analytical framework are explored.

© The Author(s) 2017
T. Meyer, *The Politics of Online Copyright Enforcement in the EU*, Information Technology and Global Governance,
DOI 10.1007/978-3-319-50974-7_7

7.1   RESEARCH QUESTIONS ANSWERED

At the very beginning of the study, I explained that as use of the Internet increases, interest in its regulation has grown as well. The Internet is currently governed through a myriad of policies and practices, one of which is online copyright enforcement. The Internet and technological innovation challenge the principles and practices underlying copyright. I have contended that online copyright enforcement policies are battlegrounds for debating the role of intermediaries in regulating the Internet and the nature of knowledge and cultural creation. Stakeholder opinions on IG and online copyright enforcement are polarized and conflictual. The public consultation on CCO analyzed in this study illustrates this wide variety of viewpoints well. The EC could not find a way forward. Further important attempts to formulate policy solutions for online copyright infringement were made, but failed, in ACTA. Lastly, the public consultation on the E-Commerce Directive has thus far been without result. In the vacuum of policy agreement at the EU level, certain member states have taken unilateral action to enforce copyright online. In this study I investigated the graduated response policy initiative in France. The policy outcome is fragmentation within the EU, both in terms of online copyright enforcement specifically and IG generally.

7.1.1   *Actors, Ideas and Interests*

Which actors are involved with which ideas and interests?

Copyright grants rights holders exclusive rights to reproduce, distribute and make creative content available. This means of cultural production and distribution by creating (artificial) scarcity provides a reward for labor and an incentive to invest in uncertain circumstances. At the same time copyright has always been contested. It has needed to evolve with the advent of each new technology. In the online environment, tensions between the economic and social values of creative content are particularly exposed. Information continues to be capitalized and commoditized, yet the design of the Internet encourages a "social ecology of information"—the production and distribution of creative content that draws on the work of many, is not driven by market incentives and seeks to provide benefits for society (Winseck 2011). In this study I have argued that *the struggle between proprietarian and communitarian cultural production and distribution is central to current policy debates on online copyright enforcement. It is about the domination of and resistance to copyright as a traditional means of cultural production and distribution.* Stakeholders compete for the adoption of their ideas and interests in public policy. Broadly rights holders advocate the high protection of IPR and the rule of law on the Internet, while Internet activists and industry call for the high protection of fundamental rights and the reform of IPR. It is important to state that not all stakeholders within the media industries share common problem definitions, policy solutions and goals. Some even support alternative ways of cultural production and distribution based on sharing. They tend to behave differently depending on their position in the economy and media value chain. Moreover Internet and technology companies are economic actors. They too operate on a capitalist modus operandi to increase profitability. Finally, economic interests alone do not determine public policy. Civil society successfully mobilizes Internet users with few resources. They vote with their feet—and their tweet.

In terms of actors, the empirical evidence brought to light in this study shows that rights holders in general, and content producers, content distributors, private broadcasters, author & performer organizations, collective rights management societies and film funds in particular, share common ideas and interests in favor of strong online copyright enforcement. Exceptions are some publishers, game developers, author & performer organizations and collective rights management societies who express negative, nuanced or alternative views. Publishers for instance indicate that they fear the repercussions of blocking and filtering measures on their right to freedom of the press. Further, civil society, fixed/mobile telecoms and cable operators, ISPs, online service providers, consumers' electronics companies and other stakeholders such as select political organizations, legal professionals, public intellectuals, hospitality associations, museums, libraries and universities share common ideas and interests against strong online copyright enforcement. Internet activists and industry form a de facto coalition to limit the involvement of Internet intermediaries in the fight against online piracy. Exceptions identified in the case studies are software providers who have their feet firmly grounded in both the technology and media worlds and are split in their views. Moreover French fixed/mobile telecoms and cable operators and ISPs, who previously consented to combatting online piracy, express views that are favorable to graduated response. Lastly, the case studies demonstrate divided opinions among EU, French and UK public authorities. *There is no agreement among policymakers on how to define problems, policy solutions and goals related to online copyright infringement.* At the EU level, this was painfully clear in ACTA. Except in their explicit defense of ACTA, the European Commission and Council tend to seek the middle ground between polarized views on online copyright enforcement. Within the EP, the ALDE, Green/EFA, GUE/NGL and S&D political groups oppose the international treaty. The EDPS and the European Economic and Social Committee emphasize the value of the Internet for society. At the member state level, the French government supports graduated response and its Parliaments adopts the enforcement measures. However this does not denote consensus. In France, the Constitutional Council, the Data Protection Authority (CNIL), the Regulatory Authority for Electronic Communications and Post (ARCEP) and some Parliamentarians are critical in their opinions. In the case studies, nuanced views often pertain to the proposed means and strength (rather than the principle) of online copyright enforcement. The policy outcome of the lack of agreement on online copyright enforcement is not a status quo, but a stalemate at the EU level and strong enforcement in the selected member state.

In terms of ideas and interests, the case studies and interviews expose how polarized views on online copyright enforcement are in the EU. Across coalitions, stakeholders agree on three mere points. First, they commonly argue that a multipronged approach is necessary to deal with copyright in the online environment. Stakeholders disagree however on the prioritization and details of these policy solutions. In line with the CCO public consultation, recommendations include the development of legal offers, educational initiatives, streamlined enforcement of legal rights and increased Internet intermediary cooperation. Second, policy stakeholders stress that filtering measures are not a panacea. Filtering is still considered a bridge too far in the current policy environment. This statement is encouraging from the viewpoint of technological governance, but also somewhat inconsistent with media stakeholders' call for closer intermediary involvement. Third, stakeholders agree that public policy should lead to innovation, creativity and economic growth, that the liability provisions in the E-Commerce Directive should be clarified, and that a rich and diverse culture should be maintained in France. Of course how to achieve these objectives is a different matter.

Proponents of strong online copyright enforcement advocate that massive online piracy is the main policy problem at hand. They call for urgent intervention, deeming future investments in creative content in danger. This fits the proprietarian view of knowledge creation. These stakeholders consider that the appropriate and necessary policy solution is to increase the responsibility of Internet intermediaries to tackle online piracy. They stress that intermediaries play a role in the digital media value chain and have a duty of care to limit infringements on their networks. In France, graduated response is deemed pedagogical and preventative, balancing the rights and interests of copyright holders and Internet users. Proponents of strong online copyright enforcement aim for the respect and defense of IPR and the establishment of rule of law on the Internet.

Opponents underline the problems of proposed policy solutions. Privatized online enforcement endangers limited intermediary liability and fundamental rights, stifling innovation and creativity. Further these stakeholders object to filtering measures on technical, economic, legal and societal grounds. ACTA and graduated response are considered disproportionate and lacking in democratic and judicial safeguards. Opponents of strong online copyright enforcement aim for the defense of fundamental rights and the reform of IPR. The open design of the Internet is deemed important for providing access to knowledge and culture and encouraging accountable and proportionate rule of law.

7.1.2 Discourses

Which discourses are used in these policies to argue different ideas and interests?

It is relevant to look beyond ideas and interests to discourses as well, because language frames and sets the tone for the whole policy process. Indeed it determines the scope of available problem definitions, policy solutions and goals. In this study I have argued that discourses are central to the creation and representation of meaning—the role of copyright, technology and the Internet are being (re)defined in online copyright enforcement policies.

The policy debates in the selected case studies center around existing legal rules and are economically framed. First, copyright is juxtaposed to limited liability and fundamental rights. Proponents of strong online copyright enforcement describe ISPs as gatekeepers in the online world. They point to the increasing harm of IPR infringements and advocate a shared responsibility for Internet intermediaries. However opponents of strong online copyright enforcement deem that ISPs are being pushed to become private judges in the favor of particular industrial actors. They argue that the proposed online copyright enforcement measures threaten the freedom of the Internet and citizens. Unfortunately my analysis confirms Jessica Reyman's (2009, 24) statement that stakeholders do not make "a clear distinction between a free pass to consume entertainment products and the freedom to access, build on, and contribute to an information commons". Second, discourses on online copyright enforcement stress the economics of CCO. Public authorities in particular emphasize the importance of the digital economy and the need to restore balance between rights and interests for innovation, creativity and economic growth. I believe this limits the scope for discussions on social requirements of copyright. It is worth highlighting that the French discourse is distinct in this regard. French stakeholders advocate the cultural exception—the protection of culture from unbridled capitalism.

The empirical evidence of this study shows that *views on knowledge and cultural creation are not used to win arguments in policy debates on online copyright enforcement in the EU,* adding nuance to the literature reviewed on copyright discourses in Chap. 2. Interestingly *stakeholders' emblematic issues and story lines rather relate to the intervening role of Internet intermediaries and thus to the functioning of the Internet.* This can in part be explained by one of the selection criteria for the case studies, namely the fact that policy initiatives had to include technical means of enforcement to be considered for the study. Nonetheless it would seem that Internet activists and industry find it easier to agree on common positions related to IG than to knowledge creation. As I discuss further in Sect. 7.1.4, stakeholders' views on knowledge creation remain important, because, although not present in discourse, they underlie stakeholders' views on online copyright enforcement.

Further in order to understand who gains productive power in online copyright enforcement, this study has analyzed the reproduction of discourses. In Sect. 7.1.1, I described the discourse coalitions identified across the selected case studies: rights holders vs. Internet activists and industry. Actors gather around language to advocate common ideas and interests. It is important to specify that discourse coalitions are loose in nature. Stakeholders within a particular coalition are not necessarily in full agreement. For instance I have noted nuances within the media industries, and between the Internet and technology industries and civil society. In this study I have also researched the structuration and institutionalization of discourse. These pertain to the reproduction of discourse by government or Parliament officials and departments, and to the embedding of discourse into legal and supporting policy documents respectively. The empirical results indicate little change. With the exception of ACTA, there is no shift in discourse among policymakers or in policy. The EP's rejection of ACTA is this study's anomaly. MEPs adopt anti-ACTA discourses, shifting the language and the outcome of the policy. In the other case studies only fairly minor changes to proposed ideas could be identified. The European Commission and Council tread carefully, aiming for a multipronged approach to deal with online copyright infringement. Throughout all EU case studies, the Commission consistently emphasizes wide availability of creative content as a policy goal. The public consultations on CCO and the E-Commerce Directive did not result in change. Further there is opposition to graduated response in the French parliament, but in the end it endorses the policy measure. The proposed and adopted policy discourses and goals remain the same. Stakeholders are however successful in providing policy nuance. For instance in France, the final laws include a judicial procedure and commitments to legal offers, research and awareness raising. Moreover references to filtering and blocking are largely removed.

Thus in terms of reproduction of discourses, there is no clear discursive winner in EU online copyright enforcement policies. Proponents of strong online copyright enforcement see their views adopted in graduated response; opponents win on ACTA; neither gain traction in the public consultations on CCO and the Future of the E-Commerce Directive. This investigation into online copyright enforcement discourse also teaches us that there is room for resistance and change—incremental, or as we experienced in ACTA, even radical. At the same time we need to recognize that this lack of a discursive dominance has not meant a status quo in policy. Despite the divergence of views manifest in stakeholder responses to the CCO consultation, the European Commission and Council seek strong online copyright enforcement action in ACTA.

Although ACTA may not have fundamentally altered the EU *"acquis communautaire"*, it would have served as a symbolic case for strong online copyright enforcement. Most importantly graduated response is adopted in France. *A stalemate occurs at the EU level, but strong online copyright enforcement measures are passed at the national level. The policy field in the EU is fragmented and in flux.*

7.1.3   Institutions

Which institutional rules and settings are chosen to develop these policies?

In terms of institutions, the PEC analyzes "how structures are produced and reproduced by human agents who act through the medium of these structures" (Mosco 2009, 220). In this book I have interpreted institutions as the policy legacy and the political and legal reality in which online copyright enforcement policies develop.

Policy stakeholders endeavor to influence the institutional rules and settings surrounding the use of creative content on the Internet. They present their views at an international, EU and member state level. All three levels are included in the selected case studies. Proponents of strong online copyright enforcement push for policies on enhanced cooperation, increased involvement of Internet intermediaries and the monitoring of Internet users. So ACTA is international and aimed at IPR enforcement cooperation. The CCO initiative and the E-Commerce Directive are European and relate to intermediary liability and use of technological solutions to protect copyrighted works. The graduated response initiatives are national and target Internet user behavior. At the same time we notice that the media industries are looking beyond public intervention, seeking private arrangements on online copyright enforcement. The EU and French discussions to implement a voluntary follow-the-money scheme are one such example.

New policy initiatives need to operate within the framework of existing institutional rules and settings. Along with discourse, this limits the scope of possible regulatory action. At the same time *stakeholders have the ability to select rules and settings* in advocating their ideas and interests on online copyright enforcement. Importantly, as I have noted in previous sections, much argumentation in the online copyright enforcement debate is a juxtaposition of legal provisions on copyright, limited liability and/or fundamental rights. Further, ACTA is an interesting example of how the politico-legal setting of an initiative matters. ACTA was negotiated as a multilateral trade agreement outside the established structures of the WTO and WIPO. Opponents criticize this choice. Equally however, the entry into force of the Lisbon Treaty meant that new consent rules applied in trade negotiations. This enabled the Parliament, a democratically elected public authority, to effectively veto the ratification of ACTA in the EU. Moreover, ACTA caused a massive public outcry. Interview respondents describe this civil society action as the coming of age of a new lobbying power. In ACTA concerns over democratic accountability and transparency of the policymaking process take central stage. Institutional rules play an important role in the French case study as well, as the graduated response laws were subject to accelerated policymaking processes. Stakeholders play creatively with the timing of action. Past French policies on broadband and copyright paved the way for the adoption of HADOPI. Indeed HADOPI is seen as the French government's reaction to years of lenient broadband policies and the final result of past failures to adopt graduated response. Moreover the evaluation of HADOPI after the election of French president Hollande is not surprising either. These various examples illustrate that public policy is never neutral. *Within the structure of existing institutional rules and settings on online copyright enforcement, stakeholders advocate their recommendations for new institutional rules and settings, hoping to gain compulsory and institutional power in the process.*

7.1.4   Control of Creative Content

Do these policies affect the control of creative content on the Internet?

As noted in the introduction to this study, my empirical investigation cannot fully answer to the last two sub-research questions. The case study analysis does not look at changes in the control of creative content or the architecture of the Internet directly. Rather it deals with stakeholder views on these matters. The questions are included because they provide clues as to why online copyright enforcement policies develop. The answers to these questions are mainly theoretical.

From the perspective of the PEC, online copyright enforcement policies are about protecting existing business models. The media industries seek to commercialize creative content on the Internet. For this purpose they protect their content with copyright through the imposition of scarcity. Notice and takedown procedures, filtering and blocking injunctions are technical means of controlling creative content. Online copyright enforcement policies are about the defense and protection of copyright as a means of generating revenue on the Internet. They quite narrowly portray copyright as an opportunity and the Internet as a threat for profit making in the media industries. Studying the development of online copyright enforcement policies is important because ways of thinking about cultural production and distribution on the Internet are solidified through the policymaking process. The empirical results of this study show that the adoption of new policies has proven difficult in the EU. This is due to renewed critique of the principles and practices of copyright spurred on by opportunities provided by the digital and online environment. The proprietarian basis of copyright is resisted both in discourse and in practice.

TyAnna Herrington (2001) explains that there are three views on knowledge creation: objective, subjective and transactional. Contenders of objective knowledge creation are positivist, preferring evidence obtained in a scientific manner. Supporters of subjective knowledge creation are expressivist and Romantic, viewing truth as being produced by "the lone author". Advocates of transactional knowledge creation stress the interaction between subject, object and community. In online copyright enforcement policies proprietarian and communitarian views of authorship and control of creative content are juxtaposed. A small but very vocal group of civil society actors has succeeded to enter the policy debate, arguing for a radical rethink of how knowledge is best produced and distributed. In simple terms it comes down to the rationales that stakeholders give for the existence and use of copyright and the Internet. As explained in Chap. 2, the bases for copyright are natural law, economic incentive and social requirements. The reasons for the Internet are pursuit of science, technological sharing, social interaction & symbolic belonging and entrepreneurship.

In the selected case studies, economic and social rationales for copyright and the Internet are dominant. The empirical results reveal that *when proposed and adopted, online copyright enforcement policies emphasize copyright as an economic incentive and the Internet as a vehicle for entrepreneurship. However it is also clear that resistance is strong. Civil society and other stakeholders continually question these views, stressing copyright and the Internet's role in society.* Indeed on the one hand copyright is described as the intellectual currency for the EU economy, as an incentive to create and a reward for labor. On the other hand the need to provide access to and sharing of knowledge and culture is underlined. Interestingly in ACTA, stakeholders link open access to knowledge to open and democratic societies. Some few policy actors highlight copyright as a fundamental right. In France, the intrinsic and exceptional value of art and culture is at the forefront of the policymaking debate. In general however, I have been surprised how little stakeholders use the rationale of copyright as a natural and moral right to property in the case studies. Further on the one hand the Internet is seen as stimulating innovation, employment and economic growth. On the other hand the Internet's potential as a venue for political and cultural discourse and as a provider for access to knowledge is valued. In the policy debates analyzed, it is also used for these purposes to campaign against strong online copyright enforcement. In CCO, some also defend the open and flexible architecture of the Internet, arguing for its role in the pursuit of science. Lastly in France, stakeholders describe the Internet as revolutionary and unstoppable, denoting a certain fear of technology. These stakeholders argue for applying the same rules online as offline. Thus although not present in discourse, online copyright enforcement policymaking has become an arena for battling out views on the role of copyright and the Internet in society. When adopted, online copyright enforcement policies endorse control of creative content on the Internet.

7.1.5 *"Open Character" of the Internet*

Do these policies form a possible threat to the "open character" of the Internet?

The design of the Internet encourages openness. Indeed in the early stages of the Internet's development, interoperability, cooperation, flexibility and decentralization were deemed important to build a distributed, responsive and resilient network (Castells 2001; Lessig 2006; Zittrain 2008). Throughout the study, I have contended that the openness of the Internet is worth preserving. It challenges control of creative content, but also brings about exciting opportunities for science and society. Moreover I have argued that technology is not neutral. Laura DeNardis (2010, 1) states that, the architecture of the Internet "is not external to politics and culture but, rather, deeply embeds the values and policy decisions that ultimately structure how we access information, how innovation will proceed, and how we exercise individual freedom online". For this reason we need to be cautious how we regulate through technology. Regulating through technology to monitor and shape Internet behavior for copyright purposes has wide repercussions. Importantly *in online copyright enforcement policies there are many calls for tighter control by Internet intermediaries*—this can change the open character of the Internet. Regulation through technology means regulation of technology. Currently the Internet is governed through a disparate ensemble of Internet centric, Internet-user centric, and non-Internet centric policies and practices (Dutton and Peltu 2007). In this study I have sought to show how Internet technology is governed in the field of online copyright enforcement.

The push in online copyright enforcement is to involve technological actors more closely in regulating a problem enabled by the technology. To my surprise, surveillance is not questioned in the examined cases, despite the power it grants to those monitoring. Further notice and takedown procedures and suspension of Internet access are permitted as long as procedural safeguards are in place. Filtering measures are regarded with more skepticism. Lastly proponents of strong online copyright enforcement advocate further use of blocking injunctions and cooperation of new online intermediaries. Deploying the architecture of the Internet for the enforcement of copyright entails a privatization of governance. I am not opposed to regulation through technology, but deem them measures of last rather than first resort. It is crucial that stakeholders involved in discussions on online copyright enforcement are attentive to the broader political economic picture, both regarding *the causes of change in the creative industries and the effects that existing and proposed policies have on fundamental rights and IG*. First, copyright infringement is not the only factor affecting the creative industries. There are multiple problems and multiple solutions. In my view the enforcement and reform of copyright go hand in hand. Second, I believe initiatives should always include strong fundamental rights safeguards. Although I am not in favor of graduated response on grounds of its blasé approach to the surveillance of Internet users, the built-in procedural and judicial safeguards in France significantly tone down the policy measure. Third, being attentive to the broader picture implies a critical reflection on the interlinkages with other forms of IG, such as cybersecurity, child protection and net neutrality—because IG reflects our ideas and interests on access to information, innovation and individual freedom online.

A final way in which I have sought to better understand the interaction between online copyright enforcement and technological governance is by mapping stakeholder views onto proposed models of IG. Lawrence Solum (2009) identifies five governance models advocated for the Internet: cyberspace and spontaneous ordering, transnational institutions and international organizations, code and Internet architecture, national governments and law, and market and economics. There is divergence between the models in terms of the level of governance, the stakeholders involved, and the means of governing the Internet. Considering our discussion so far, it is not surprising that proponents of strong online copyright enforcement defend the national governments and law governance model. These stakeholders do not make a distinction between online and offline activities. They consider that principles underlying the legislation should be transposed onto the Internet and the nation state is the main regulatory actor (Solum 2009; Paré 2003). On the contrary opponents of strong online copyright enforcement support the code and Internet architecture governance model. They point to the technical, economic, legal and societal difficulties of regulating through technology. Lastly some few stakeholders argue that online copyright enforcement and IG are matters for transnational institutions and international organizations. There is no agreement among policy actors on the appropriate model to govern the Internet. My case studies confirm that there is continuous pressure, but equally resistance, to shift away from the Internet's original cooperative, interoperable, flexible and decentralized design. Much remains at stake in the upcoming years. From a PEC perspective, it is crucial to lay bare the underlying reasons for governing the Internet—in order to counter abuses of power when we see them.

7.2　Essential Study Insights

Online Copyright Enforcement Policies in the European Union

> How and why have selected policies in the European Union dealing with the online enforcement of copyright developed?

As the answers to the five sub-research questions reveal, it is a combination of ideas, interests, institutions and discourses that determine how and why online copyright enforcement policies have developed in the

European Union. My aim has not been to determine causality or even which factor matters most. In fact a framework comprising of ideas, interests, institutions and discourses would have been too broad for that. Rather I have provided a thick description to prove that *the 3Is do not work in exclusion. They are deeply intertwined.* Nuance is necessary in understanding and developing online copyright enforcement policies. For instance, while the public consultation on CCO is a good example of the polarization in terms of the problem definitions, policy solutions and goals (ideas and interests) on online copyright infringement, the very nature of the non-legislative initiative encourages this wide range of contributions (institutions). Further, at first glance ACTA seems a battle of institutional rules and settings (institutions). Equally however, the EC confesses that they communicated and framed the treaty poorly in the European policymaking debate (discourses). Nonetheless I do not want to leave the reader with an incoherent, fragmented view of the online copyright enforcement tapestry. Taking a few more steps back, what are *this study's essential insights* from the perspectives of ideas, interests, institutions, discourses and PEC?

In terms of ideas, interests, institutions and discourses—first, it is clear that ideas and discourses play a central role in this contentious policy area. There is no agreement on the problem definitions and policy solutions for copyright in the online environment. Stakeholders compete to see their views and framing adopted in policy. Their *approach to knowledge creation and stance on the role of copyright and the Internet in society* determine their view on the level and type of regulatory action required on online copyright enforcement. At the same time stakeholders have to adjust their discourses to *proposed and adopted online copyright enforcement laws* which *tend to be economic rather than social in outlook.*

Second, the empirical evidence shows that the media industries and the Internet & technology industries have little in common on online copyright enforcement. *Large economic interests are opposed,* engraining the stalemate at the EU level. The question is what happens when interests align and private arrangements are found. Who will tread the middle ground? The media industries succeed at the member state level. Graduated response is adopted, albeit in a watered-down version. Equally however, ACTA teaches us that civil society can be surprisingly successful in mobilizing citizens to demand a U-turn on planned policy. In this instance combined online and offline campaigning proved effective. Moreover the

EC endeavors to remove barriers in the EU digital single market. *The positions of the Internet and technology industries and policymakers seem pivotal.*

Lastly, the policy legacy and the political and legal reality of an online copyright enforcement initiative limit the scope of possible regulatory action. The case studies indicate that *stakeholders select institutional rules and settings that support their views best.* Proponents of strong online copyright enforcement advocate use of technology to regulate because it grants direct and compulsory power. Precisely because of the Internet's embeddedness in our lives, opponents have been wary of its regulatory use. In online copyright enforcement—and in other areas of IG (just think of Edward Snowden's cybersecurity leaks)—*there is a desire to monitor and shape Internet user behavior through private actors.*

In terms of the PEC—there are also three points to highlight. First, online copyright infringement is only one reason for loss in the media industries, and the scarcity imposed by the media industries on creative content is contested on the Internet. The analyzed policy initiatives need to be seen in *the context of wider change for the media industries in the online environment.* As discussed in Chap. 2, David Hesmondhalgh (2007) indicates that there are difficulties inherent to the media industries: they are risky businesses, continually struggle to balance creative and commercial functions, experience high production costs yet low reproduction costs, and produce semi-public goods. Ways in which the media industries seek to counter these threats are by building a repertoire, forming tight alliances within and between industries, imposing artificial scarcity on products, developing easy-to-replicate formats of stars, genres and serials, and loosely controlling creators while tightly controlling distribution and marketing. The resistance to the media industries' model of content production and distribution is not unique to the online environment. Balancing between commerce and creativity is an art. *The Internet provides a new outlet for stakeholders seeking alternatives. In the online environment there is renewed hope for a society that emphasizes autonomy and equality in and through culture* (Tian 2009; Sunder 2006). Indeed copyright and the Internet give rise to different views on knowledge creation and culture. While copyright aims to protect, the Internet promotes access to content. The PEC encourages policymakers not only to seek the best way forward for innovation and economic growth, but also to take into account the opportunities that the Internet's open character provides for creativity, collaboration and freedom of expression. The Internet has been shown to act as an agent for economic, social and cultural change.

However and this is the second point, the Internet can also be a recipient of change. Lawrence Lessig (2003, 2004, 2006) contends that capitalist values increasingly dominate the online environment, encroaching on the rationales of other Internet user groups and bearing negative consequences for innovation and democracy. *Online copyright enforcement policies are about commercializing creative content on the Internet.* Proponents of strong online copyright enforcement stress copyright and the Internet's economic rationales. These stakeholders also advocate greater control of creative content through technological governance. From a PEC perspective, this should not be considered a trifle. On the one hand, digital surveillance and technology codify the views and values of those regulating. Digital surveillance and technology do not just help us in our daily activities, they also actively construct them. Will the Internet in ten years primarily be seen and used as a commercial tool? On the other hand, online copyright enforcement policies contribute to the young and moldable governance of the Internet. Jim Rogers (2013, 198) states that, *"the law is as significant in shaping the outcome of a new media as is the technology itself."* Technology is neither neutral nor fixed. In this regard, it is remarkable that in every stakeholder debate on closer intermediary involvement analyzed in this study, filtering measures, although proposed, were considered a bridge too far—disproportionate in the fight against online copyright infringement.

Lastly, this study observes a polarization of stakeholder opinions and a fragmentation of policy initiatives on online copyright enforcement. In the vacuum of agreement at the EU level, certain member states have taken their own policy action. PEC scholar Robin Mansell (2012) argues that we need a new social imaginary of the Internet. There will always be a dialectic of co-optation and resistance to the media industries' model of cultural production and distribution. At the same time it is important to realize that multiple structures and knowledges are possible. The Internet and copyright, abundance and scarcity can co-exist. Interview respondent David Touve (Director at the iLab of the University of Virginia, 2013) deems that, *"we can move beyond polarization only after we believe that the interesting story to be told (or heard or read) is the one that involves the nuances that lead to collaboration and compromise. Many people make money by way of polarization, however."* This study supports these views and has been an endeavor to provide a detailed, non-polarized analysis on the online copyright enforcement debate in the EU.

7.3   POLICY IMPLICATIONS

Strong online copyright enforcement is heavily contested in the EU. Of the four policy initiatives analyzed, one passes into law (2009 French graduated response laws), two result in stalemates (2008 EU CCO and 2010 E-Commerce Directive consultations) and one is rejected (2011 ACTA). In the vacuum of EU level policy agreement, member states have taken unilateral action. This has led to fragmentation in the policy field: a two-speed approach. Online copyright enforcement in the EU is part of an ongoing dialectic between domination and resistance. *Old and new, big and small policy actors compete for control. Control over cultural production and distribution, control over the policymaking process, control over the Internet infrastructure.*

There is no agreement on the problem definitions nor the policy solutions for copyright in the online environment. To illustrate, the EU "acquis" provides high protection of IPR. Equally however there is much pressure to complete the digital single market. Here copyright is regarded as both a problem and a solution. Intellectual property is the "intellectual currency" of Europe's knowledge-based society and thus needs protection, yet copyright's cumbersome licensing regime and territorial partitioning of markets are deemed unacceptable. Legal offers are promoted as means to stimulate economic growth, but importantly also to combat copyright infringement. The results in this book indicate that stakeholders' broader views on creativity and innovation and their stances on the roles of copyright and the Internet in society determine their ideas and interests on the specific policy issue of online copyright enforcement. Property and community-based opinions are often juxtaposed. *The Internet provides a new outlet for stakeholders seeking alternatives to the dominant economic rationale of knowledge production through the creation of artificial scarcity.* There are tensions inherent in the approaches that copyright and the Internet take to content. While the Internet encourages widespread distribution of content, copyright seeks to monetize through control.

Unsurprisingly, the analysis of the cases reveals that the meager outcome of the online copyright enforcement initiatives in the European

Union is due to the lack of common interests between the media and Internet & technology industries. *Currently the majority of Internet & technology industries have little incentive to proactively enforce copyright online.* Large economic interests are opposed. From a political economic perspective, this structural power should not be underestimated. At the same time, the cases highlight the success of civil society actors in giving pushback on online copyright enforcement policies. All stakeholders cunningly choose institutional rules and settings that favor their views. They base their arguments on existing legislation, opposing copyright to limited liability and fundamental rights. *There is no lack of pitching policy objectives, legal provisions, directives or case law against each other in the hope to gain legal and political clout. We must question whether citizens are accepted as active media producers and policy actors in online copyright discussions, and how compatible the EU's single market objective is with the preservation and flourishing of a digital commons.*

Some accuse civil society and Internet & technology companies of using arguments on freedom as a Trojan horse for no Internet regulation. Concrete solutions are indeed absent at times. Anne Bergman-Tahon (Director at the Federation of European Publishers, Interview 2013) dismisses civil society's anti-capitalist arguments. She says, "either you abolish the capitalist society and copyright should be abolished as well. You can't say because it is intangible, because it seems in the way of some big interest, we should get rid of it. Because there are so many people who depend off that sector to make a living. We live in a society where if you don't have a salary or some fees at the end of the day, you cannot live." Yvon Thiec (Director General at Eurocinema, Interview 2013) perceives the protest differently. He confesses that capitalism is now omnipresent. He indicates that, "[y]ou have no more respect. Not so long ago you did not have publicity invading all the public space. There was much more respiration in the public space. *Maybe this is making the new generation very upset, they want to be much more than capitalist consumers.*"

These points shed light on online copyright enforcement as a renewed manifestation of the struggle between domination and resistance in a capitalist market system. At the same time, I have argued that there is a need to analyze online copyright enforcement within the wider discussion on IG. *Online copyright enforcement policy initiatives consistently encourage closer involvement of Internet intermediaries through the monitoring, blocking and take down of content.* Technology reflects the values and choices of its designers, regulators and users. The Internet built with open, unfettered communication in mind, provides exciting opportunities for creativity, collaboration and freedom of expression. The role of Internet intermediaries in intervening in their networks is at the crux of the debate today. Tighter control over Internet infrastructure affects how we access information and exercise fundamental rights online. Neither technology nor policy is neutral.

What does all this mean for current policymaking? Interview respondents (2013) disagree on the desirability, feasibility and means to bridge the polarization in the current debate. Ideas on the role of copyright and the Internet in society, interests in the online media environment and institutional rules and settings are not likely to change overnight. True, through media convergence, some synergies are visible between rights holders and Internet intermediaries, resulting in, on the one hand, more legal offers, but on the other hand, also increased private enforcement. Further, the current *"EU acquis"* will continue to be incrementally clarified through rulings of the CJEU. Are stakeholders perhaps right then, as expressed in the context of the evaluation of the E-Commerce Directive, that it is best at this point not to open up the directives, as the outcome would be so uncertain? Most fundamental—and in my opinion new—to the debate are the role that civil society play and the societal views they represent on knowledge creation. Current rules do not correspond with expectations of flexible and alternative use and consequently are not respected. If only for the legitimacy of legal rules, reform is necessary. From a PEC view, there are more reasons: *governance needs to be accountable, and monopolies, wherever we find them (in the old or new media sectors), should be countered* (Mansell 2012).

If we are willing to move beyond fragmentation and polarization, this book has taught us that *the approach needs to be comprehensive.* Tensions within and between copyright and the Internet are evident. The economic- and social-oriented rationales for each medium conflict. Viewing problem definitions holistically, taking into account the various causes of copyright discontentment and media change, will lead to policy solutions that are nuanced and multifaceted. Related, it has become clear that *arguments that acknowledge the viewpoints of other stakeholders are preferable.* One-sided arguments, biased statistics and hyperbolic language may give a lead in the short term, but do not contribute to a balanced and sustainable copyright system. We also need to *stand up for weaker parties*. Copyright has sparked the interest of everyday users, who are frustrated with the strength, length and width of current copyright laws. Respect for copyright is necessary, but so is room for new and alternative uses. Further, individual authors and performers have featured less in this study, but have a clear interest in not only proper protection, but also remuneration of their works. Finally, *we should not accept that technology plays the role of adjudicator*. Technology and surveillance are to be used with caution, as they provide compulsory power to those determining and implementing the rules. If Internet intermediaries are required to play a proactive role in controlling the distribution of copyrighted content, practices will soon ripple into other policy domains and basic Internet principles start to be reversed. This is not to say that governance through technology needs to be excluded prima facie, but that safeguards need to be foreseen to preserve the openness of the Internet and the protection of fundamental rights.

Importantly the EU and France are moving forward on online copyright enforcement. Based on the theoretical and empirical insights of this study, it is straightforward where the emphasis in policy should lie. First, it is absolutely right to *tackle commercial scale piracy*. For-profit infringement is not interested in copyright exceptions and limitations. The aim is to earn cash off the back of others. Negotiations and agreements on commercial scale piracy should include civil society representation. Second, *streamlining judicial procedures* in order to increase the efficiency and effectiveness of court rulings makes sense. Rights holders suffer from the lack of a harmonized approach. Within national boundaries, but where possible also across borders, decisions on blocking and removing copyright infringing content and websites need to be reached easily and implemented widely. Facilitating judicial procedures is preferable over resorting to private arrangements. Third, a comprehensive approach requires going beyond enforcement and *looking into current contracting and licensing practices*. We need to ensure that content is available legally while rights holders are remunerated fairly. On the one hand, this implies that revenue is shared; on the other hand, it is necessary to have an open mind about the sustainability of current media business models. Fourth, *harmonization of EU limitations and exceptions* would boost the legitimacy of copyright and increase legal certainty. Similarly, although carving into protection previously granted is a difficult and painful exercise, critical assessment is advised to ensure that limitations and exceptions match societal expectations. Finally, *the limited liability provisions are the line in the sand.* We need to keep our hands off these rules, as they are key to preserving basic Internet principles. Clarification of how current definitions (such as mere conduit, caching and hosting) apply fifteen years later and a harmonized approach to notice and takedown procedures are welcome. However the current reactive approach for Internet intermediaries should remain non-negotiable. For each of these elements, transparent and accountable procedures with civil society representation and strong safeguards for recourse are necessary. In the following section, we reflect on the theoretical and analytical contributions of this study.

7.4 Theoretical/Analytical Dimensions

The PEC offers insight into the online copyright enforcement debate, because it points to the struggle between actors to gain power, especially structural power, in the online environment. It acknowledges that actors influence the development and outcome of policy. The theory of PEC lays bare abuses of power and argues that there is a constant need for checks and balances. This study builds on the theoretical foundations of PEC to provide a concrete analytical framework for studying policy. The next paragraphs expand on the contribution that I make to the PEC. I have argued that *in PEC there is need for more detailed policy analysis, in particular taking into account the role of ideas and technological governance.* PEC grapples with the "open character" of the Internet and lacks attention for the possibilities that the Internet's design permits for strong online copyright enforcement.

The PEC views politics and policy as reflections of market forces at play. The empirical evidence of this study confirms that big media and Internet interests are highly influential in the online copyright enforcement debate, yet power is more than market share alone. I have pointed to the role of ideas and discourses in the highly polarized policy field of online copyright enforcement. The lack of agreement on problem definitions, policy solutions and goals is in part driven by differences in stakeholder rationales for copyright and the Internet. *Analyzing ideas and discourses offers additional insight into the results and stalemates we observe in online copyright enforcement policies.* Stakeholders compete to structure and frame the policy problem at hand. Further, the PEC tends to be quite dismal in its prospects for change in the online environment. It observes a continued commodification of the Internet space—online activities are evaluated based on their market rather than social value. Indeed the selected case studies indicate that economics rather than social value are emphasized in proposed and adopted legislation. However I have also found that *PEC does not sufficiently consider the impact of architectural features of the Internet on power relations.* On the one hand, it underestimates the agency and hope that the Internet engenders for an alternative non-market-based culture and democracy. On the other hand, through its design the Internet opens up new avenues for monitoring and censoring information. In the PEC there is inadequate exploration into the direct and compulsory power that this governance through technology offers to regulators.

Investigating online copyright enforcement policies from a PEC perspective, especially with this micro-level focus on the role of ideas and technological governance, requires an operationalized analytical framework. For this purpose *I combined a typology of the 3Is with ADA* (Bhagwati 1989; Hajer 1995, 2002, 2006). I believe the analysis of the 3Is provides a holistic and in-depth view of the policy developments at hand. Within the case studies, ideational, socioeconomic, political and legal aspects have been elucidated. Moreover as the framework has been applied across the case studies, commonalities, trends and anomalies in online copyright enforcement policies could be observed. Further, ADA is a concrete and helpful means of researching stakeholders' ideas and discourses. More information means more detailed analysis of the struggle between domination and resistance in the development of online copyright enforcement policies. ADA also pays close attention to discourse coalitions, structuration and institutionalization in policy. This additional analysis aided my understanding of stakeholders' success rate in advocating their preferred views on online copyright enforcement. Overall, I have found that the analytical framework combining the 3Is with ADA in policy proved valuable for operationalizing the PEC's insights. Importantly *the framework is attentive to the formative role that ideas and discourses play in policymaking, while recognizing that the material reality contains resourceful market players and institutions with long legacy.*

7.5   Future Research

Finally it is appropriate to end with recommendations for future research. In this study I faced a tradeoff between the number of case studies and the level of detail in analysis. Researching four distinct case studies helped me detect trends in EU online copyright enforcement policies. Moreover the number of case studies in this study lent well to the focus of the research on the EU in general. However *a higher level of detailed analysis within the case studies would have provided increased evidence on discourse structuration and institutionalization.* In future studies I recommend including more versions of proposed legislative texts to detect subtle changes and opportunities for advocacy. Further, the emphasis on ideas and discourses in policy made the study an initial odd fit for the theory of PEC. I have extensively argued why it is important to analyze definitions, rationales and arguments to explain the polarization in online copyright enforcement. In addition the focus on policy is relevant because public policy forms the institutional frame and borders within which private practices and arrangements on online copyright enforcement operate. Nonetheless *future research could usefully consider litigation and private action on online copyright enforcement. This would permit closer investigation of the continued legal debacles and influential non-legislative agreements among stakeholders.* I also recommend *more extensive analysis of stakeholder relations.* Investigating ties between industries, civil society and public authorities (for instance through membership on boards, in councils and working groups) would provide valuable additional information on the interests at play in online copyright enforcement. Last but not least, I believe *the theoretical and analytical framework could clearly be applied to more recent policy developments in online copyright enforcement, but also in studies relating to privacy policy, cybersecurity policy or intermediary liability litigation,* adding interesting and new detail on the emerging mosaic of IG. The field will continue to evolve quickly over the coming years. It is an academic duty to contribute to an open yet non-polarized online environment. The challenge continues.

BIBLIOGRAPHY

Bhagwati, Jagdish. 1989. *Protectionism*. Cambridge: MIT Press.

Castells, Manuel. 2001. *The Internet Galaxy: Reflections on the Internet, Business, and Society*. Oxford/New York: Oxford University Press.

DeNardis, Laura. 2010. The Emerging Field of Internet Governance. In *Yale Information Society Project Working Paper Series*. New Haven: Yale Law School.

Dutton, William, and Malcolm Peltu. 2007. The Emerging Internet Governance Mosaic: Connecting the Pieces. *Information Polity* 12(1–2): 63–81.

Hajer, Maarten. 1995. *The Politics of Environmental Discourse: Ecological Modernization and the Policy Process*. Oxford: Oxford University Press.

———. 2002. Discourse Analysis and the Study of Policy Making. *European Political Science* 2(1): 61–65.

———. 2006. Doing Discourse Analysis: Coalitions, Practices, Meaning. In *Words Matter in Policy and Planning. Discourse Theory and Method in the Social Sciences*, ed. Margo van den Brink and Tamara Metze, 65–74. Utrecht: Koninklijk Nederlands Aardrijkskundig Genootschap & Netherlands Graduate School of Urban and Regional Research.

Herrington, TyAnna. 2001. *Controlling Voices: Intellectual Property, Humanistic Studies, and the Internet*. Carbondale/Edwardsville: Southern Illinois University Press.

Hesmondhalgh, David. 2007. *Cultural Industries*. 2nd ed. London: Sage.

Lessig, Lawrence. 2003. *The Future of Ideas. The Fate of the Commons in a Connected World. Reprint Edition*. New York: Random House.

———. 2004. *Free Culture: How Big Media Uses Technology and the Law to Lock Down Culture and Control Creativity*. New York: Penguin Press.

———. 2006. *Code: And Other Laws of Cyberspace, Version 2.0*. New York: Basic Books.

Mansell, Robin. 2012. *Imagining the Internet: Communication, Innovation and Governance*. Oxford: Oxford University Press.

Mosco, Vincent. 2009. *The Political Economy of Communication*. 2nd ed. London/Thousand Oaks: Sage.

Paré, Daniel. 2003. *Internet Governance in Transition*. In *Who Is the Master of This Domain?* Lanham: Rowman & Littlefield Publishers.

Reyman, Jessica. 2009. *The Rhetoric of Intellectual Property: Copyright Law and the Regulation of Digital Culture*. New York: Routledge.

Rogers, Jim. 2013. *The Death and Life of the Music Industry in the Digital Age*. London: Bloomsbury.

Solum, Lawrence. 2009. Models of Internet Governance. In *Internet Governance. Infrastructure and Institutions*, ed. Bygrave Lee and Jon Bing, 48–91. Oxford: Oxford University Press.

Sunder, Madhavi. 2006. IP³. *Stanford Law Review* 59(2): 257–332.

Tian, YiJun. 2009. *Re-thinking Intellectual Property: The Political Economy of Copyright Protection in the Digital Era*. New York: Routledge.

Winseck, Dwayne. 2011. The Political Economies of Media and the Transformation of the Global Media Industries. In *The Political Economies of Media. The Transformation of the Global Media Industries*, ed. Dwayne Winseck and Dal Yong Jin, 3–48. London/New York: Bloomsbury Academic.

Zittrain, Jonathan. 2008. *Future of the Internet – And How to Stop It*. London: Yale University Press.

BIBLIOGRAPHY

February 16, 2012. C-360/10 Belgische Vereniging van Auteurs, Componisten en Uitgevers (SABAM) vs. Netlog. Court of Justice of the European Union.

January 29, 2008. C-275/06 Promusicae vs. Telefónica. Court of Justice of the European Union.

July 12, 2011. C-324/09 L'Oréal & Others vs. eBay International & Others. Court of Justice of the European Union.

June 10, 2009. Décision n. 2009–580 DC du 10 Juin 2009. Loi Favorisant la Diffusion et la Protection de la Création sur Internet. French Constitutional Council.

March 23, 2010. C-236/08 to C-238/08 Google vs. Louis Vuitton Mattelier & Others. Court of Justice of the European Union.

March 27, 2014. C-314/12 UPC Telekabel Wien vs. Constantin Film Verleih and Wega Filmproduktionsgesellschaft. Court of Justice of the European Union.

November 24, 2011. C-70/10 Scarlet Extended vs. Société Belge des Auteurs, Compositeurs et Editeurs (SABAM). Court of Justice of the European Union.

October 22, 2009. Décision n. 2009-590 DC du 22 Octobre 2009. Loi relative à la Protection Pénale de la Propriété Littéraire et Artistique sur Internet. French Constitutional Council.

September 3, 2014. C-201/13 Deckmyn & Vrijheidsfonds vs. Vandersteen, Dupont, Amoras II & WPG Uitgevers België. Court of Justice of the European Union.

September 11, 2012. N. 11-2858 Capitol Records, Inc vs. Thomas-Rasset. United States Court of Appeals for the Eight Circuit.

Abbate, Janet. 1999. *Inventing the internet*. London/Cambridge, MA: MIT Press.

© The Author(s) 2017
T. Meyer, *The Politics of Online Copyright Enforcement in the EU*, Information Technology and Global Governance,
DOI 10.1007/978-3-319-50974-7

AFA. 2008. Projet de Loi 'Création et Internet': Pour le Respect des Accords de l'Elysée. http://www.afpi-france.com/articles/projet-de-loi-creation-et-internet-pour-le-respect-des-accords-de-l-elysee. Accessed 6 Oct 2016.

AGCOM. 2013. Delibera n. 680/13/CONS, Regolamento in materia di tutela del diritto d'autore sulle reti di comunicazione elettronica e procedure attuative ai sensi del decreto legislativo 9 aprile 2003, n. 70. Naples: Italian Communications Regulatory Authority.

Aguiar, Luis, and Bertin Martens. 2013. *Digital Music Consumption on the Internet: Evidence from Clickstream Data*. Seville: Institute for Prospective Technological Studies.

Aigrain, Philippe. 2012. *Sharing: Culture and the Economy in the Internet Age*. Amsterdam: Amsterdam University Press.

Ala-Fossi, Marko, Piet Bakker, Hanna-Kaisa Ellonen, Lucy Küng, Stephen Lax, Charo Sádaba, and Richard van der Wurff. 2008. The Impact of the Internet on Business Models in the Media Industries – A Sector-by-Sector Analysis. In *The Internet and the Mass Media*, ed. Lucy Küng, Robert Picard, and Ruth Towse, 149–169. London: Sage.

ALDE. 2012a. ACTA: An Ineffective Agreement That Puts Civil Liberties at Risk. http://www.alde.eu/press/press-and-release-news/press-release/article/acta-an-ineffective-agreement-that-puts-civil-liberties-at-risk-39459/. Accessed 6 Oct 2016.

———. 2012b. ALDE Condemns EPP Plans to Hold Secret Vote on ACTA. http://www.alde./nc/press/press-and-release-news/press-release/article/alde-condemns-epp-plans-to-hold-secret-vote-on-acta-39168/. Accessed 6 Oct 2016.

———. 2012c. Parliament Must Listen Carefully to Citizens Concerns Over ACTA. http://www.alde.eu/press/press-and-release-news/press-release/article/parliament-must-carefully-listen-to-citizens-concerns-over-acta-37926/. Accessed 6 Oct 2016.

Andrejevic, Mark. 2007. *iSpy. Surveillance and Power in the Interactive Era*. Lawrence: University Press of Kansas.

Apple. 2009. Press Info. Changes Coming to the iTunes Store. https://www.apple.com/pr/library/2009/01/06Changes-Coming-to-the-iTunes-Store.html. Accessed 5 Oct 2016.

ARCEP. 2008. *Avis n. 2008-0547 de l'Autorité de Régulation des Communications Électroniques et des Postes en date du 6 Mai 2008 sur le Projet de Loi Relatif à la Haute Autorité pour la Diffusion des Œuvres et de la Protection des Droits sur Internet*. Paris: French Regulatory Authority for Post and Electronic Communications.

Arthur, Charles. 2012. Acta Goes Too Far, Says MEP. *Theguardian.com*, February 1. http://www.theguardian.com/technology/2012/feb/01/acta-goes-too-far-kader-arif

Article 19. 2010. Response to EU Consultation on E-Commerce Directive. https://circabc.europa.eu/webdav/CircaBC/FISMA/markt_consultations/ Library/Online services/The future of electronic commerce/Consumers/US PK CONSO (th 5) 782818.pdf. Accessed 9 Oct 2016.

———. 2011. Statement. European Parliament: Reject Anti-Counterfeiting Trade Agreement (ACTA). http://www.article19.org/resources.php/ resource/2901/en/european-parliament:-reject-anti-counterfeiting-trade-agreement-(acta). Accessed 6 October 2016.

———. 2012. TODAY, By a Huge Majority, the European Parliament Voted to Reject ACTA. http://www.article19.org/join-the-debate.php/62/view/. Accessed 6 Oct 2016.

ASIC. 2008a. Contribution de l'ASIC à la Consultation Publique de la Commission Européenne sur les Contenus Créatifs en Ligne. http://ec.europa.eu/ archives/information_society/avpolicy/docs/other_actions/col_2008/ngo/ asic_fr.pdf. Accessed 9 Oct 2016.

———. 2008b. Création et Internet: L'ASIC Hostile à la Proposition Communiste de Taxer les Acteurs du 2.0. http://www.lasic.fr/wp-content/ uploads/2012/03/cp-asic-hadopi-taxe-30102008.pdf. Accessed 6 Oct 2016.

———. 2009. L'Avenir de l'Internet Se Joue Ce Lundi à Bruxelles. http://press. dailymotion.com/wp-old/wp-content/uploads/cp_asic_bxl_27032009.pdf. Accessed 6 Oct 2016.

———. 2010. Contribution de l'Association des Services Internet Communautaires (ASIC) à la Consultation Publique sur l'Avenir du Commerce Électronique dans le Marché Intérieur et la Mise en Œuvre de la Directive Commerce Électronique (2000/31/CE). https://circabc.europa.eu/ sd/a/141c5a35-dd4f-410d-adee-a07b5d4d6dc5/FR ASIC FED ENTR (th 1-2%265-5bis) 807533.pdf. Accessed 9 Oct 2016.

Attali, Jacques. 2009a. Hadopi: Réponse aux Artistes. http://www.attali.com/ actualite/blog/art-et-culture/hadopi-reponse-aux-artistes. Accessed 6 Oct 2016.

———. 2009b. Jacques Attali Répond Aux Artistes. http://www.attali.com/ actualite/blog/art-et-culture/jacques-attali-repond-aux-artistes. Accessed 6 Oct 2016.

Australia, Canada, the European Union and its member states, Japan, the Kingdom of Morocco, New Zealand, the Republic of Korea, the Republic of Singapore, the Swiss Confederation, the United Mexican States, and the United States of America. 2011 Accession Ongoing. Anti-Counterfeiting Trade Agreement.

BAE Systems Detica. 2012. *The Six Business Models for Copyright Infringement. A Data-Driven Study of Websites Considered to Be Infringing Copyright.* Guildford: Google and PRS for Music.

Barlow, John Perry. 1996. *A Declaration of the Independence of Cyberspace.* Davos: Electronic Frontier Foundation.

Barnett, Michael, and Raymond Duvall. 2005. Power in International Politics. *International Organization* 59(1): 39–75.

BASCAP, and INTA. 2012. *ACTA in the EU – A Practical Analysis*. Paris/New York: Business Action to Stop Counterfeiting and Piracy and International Trademark Association.

Beer, David. 2009. Power Through the Algorithm? Participatory Web Cultures and the Technological Unconscious. *New Media Society* 11(6): 985–1002.

Belgian Parliament. 1994. *Wet Betreffende het Auteursrecht en de Naburige Rechten*. Brussels: Belgisch Staatsblad.

Benkler, Yochai. 2006. *The Wealth of Networks. How Social Production Transforms Markets and Freedom*. New Haven/London: Yale University Press.

Bently, Lionel, Uma Suthersanen, and Paul Torremans, eds. 2010. *Global Copyright: Three Hundred Years Since the Statute of Anne, From 1709 to Cyberspace*. Cheltenham: Edgar Elgar Publishing.

Bettig, Ronald. 1996. *Copyrighting Culture: The Political Economy of Intellectual Property*. New York: Westview Press.

Betz, David, and Tim Stevens. 2011. In *Cyberspace and the State. Toward a Strategy for Cyber-Power*, ed. International Institute for Strategic Studies, *Adelphi*. Oxon: Routledge.

BEUC. 2008. Creative Content Online in the Single Market. BEUC's Position on the European Commission's Communication on Creative Content Online in the Single Market. http://ec.europa.eu/archives/information_society/avpolicy/docs/other_actions/col_2008/ngo/beuc_en.pdf. Accessed 9 Oct 2016.

Bhagwati, Jagdish. 1989. *Protectionism*. Cambridge: MIT Press.

Bigo, Didier. 2006. Security, Exception, Ban and Surveillance. In *Theorizing Surveillance. The Panopticon and Beyond*, ed. David Lyon, 46–68. Cullompton: Willan Publishing.

Bing, Jon. 2009. Building Cyberspace: A Brief History of the Internet. In *Internet Governance. Infrastructure and Institutions*, ed. Bygrave Lee and Jon Bing, 8–47. Oxford: Oxford University Press.

Bogner, Alexander, Beate Littig, and Wolfgang Menz. 2009. Expert Interviews – An Introduction to a New Methodological Debate. In *Interviewing Experts*, ed. Alexander Bogner, Beate Littig, and Wolfgang Menz, 1–13. Houndmills: Palgrave Macmillan.

BOP Consulting with DotEcon. 2015. *International Comparison of Approaches to Online Copyright Infringement*. London: UK Intellectual Property Office.

Boyle, James. 2003. The Second Enclosure Movement and the Construction of the Public Domain. *Law and Contemporary Problems* 66(1/2): 33–74.

Bradford, Neil. 1999. The Policy Influence of Economic Ideas: Interests, Institutions and Innovation in Canada. *Studies in Political Economy* 59(Summer): 17–60.

Breindl, Yana, and François Briatte. 2010. Digital Network Repertoires and the Contentious Politics of Digital Copyright in France and the European Union. *Internet, Politics, Policy 2010: An Impact Assessment*, Oxford.

Bridy, Annemarie. 2009. Why Pirates (Still) Won't Behave: Regulating P2P in the Decade After Napster. *Rutgers Law Journal* 40(3): 565–611.

———. 2010. Graduated Response and the Turn to Private Ordering in Online Copyright Enforcement. *Oregon Law Review* 89: 81–132.

British Copyright Council. 2008. Communication from the Commission to the European Parliament, The Council, The European Economic and Social Committee and the Committee of the Regions on Creative Content Online in the Single Market. Response from the British Copyright Council to the Consultation on Policy/Regulatory Issues. http://ec.europa.eu/archives/information_society/avpolicy/docs/other_actions/col_2008/ngo/bcc_en.pdf. Accessed 9 Oct 2016.

British Music Rights. 2008. Creative Content Online – Policy/Regulatory Issues for Consultation. http://ec.europa.eu/archives/information_society/avpolicy/docs/other_actions/col_2008/ngo/bmr_en.pdf. Accessed 9 Oct 2016.

Brown, Ian, and Christopher Marsden. 2013. *Regulating Code: Good Governance and Better Regulation in the Information Age*. Cambridge/London: MIT Press.

Brownsword, Roger. 2008. *Rights, Regulation, and the Technological Revolution*. Oxford/New York: Oxford University Press.

BSA. 2008. Business Software Alliance Response to the Communication on Creative Content Online in the Single Market. http://ec.europa.eu/archives/information_society/avpolicy/docs/other_actions/col_2008/ngo/bsa_en.pdf. Accessed 9 Oct 2016.

———. 2010. Response of the Business Software Alliance to the Commission Consultation on the Future of Electronic Commerce in the Internal Market and the Implementation of the Directive on Electronic Commerce (2000/31/EC). https://circabc.europa.eu/sd/a/5bd2b56c-2d16-4fb3-8b96-e92043e14a9c/EU BSA FED ENTR (th 1-2%265) 808978.pdf. Accessed 9 Oct 2016.

———. 2016. Seizing Opportunity Through License Compliance. BSA Global Software Survey. May 2016. Washington, DC: Business Software Alliance.

BT. 2008. Content Online in the Single Market. Response by British Telecommunications PLC to the Public Consultation by DG INFSO. http://ec.europa.eu/archives/information_society/avpolicy/docs/other_actions/col_2008/comp/bt_en.pdf. Accessed 9 Oct 2016.

Burkitt, Daniel. 2001. Copyrighting Culture – The History and Cultural Specificity of the Western Model of Copyright. *Intellectual Property Quarterly* 2: 146–186.

Bygrave, Lee, and Terje Michaelsen. 2009. Governors of Internet. In *Internet Governance. Infrastructure and Institutions*, ed. Lee Bygrave and Jon Bing, 92–125. Oxford: Oxford University Press.

Cable Europe. 2010. Cable Europe Answer to the Commission's Public Consultation on the Future of Electronic Commerce in the Internal Market and the Implementation of the Directive on Electronic Commerce (2000/31/EC). https://circabc.europa.eu/sd/a/98336ac9-b64c-4bce-bad6-df25c16cd75f/EU CABLE EUROPE FED ENTR (th 1%265) 804604.pdf. Accessed 9 Oct 2016.

Campbell, John, and Matt Carlson. 2002. Panopticon.com: Online Surveillance and the Commodification of Privacy. *Journal of Broadcasting & Electronic Media* 42(2): 586–606.

Cano, Pedro, Eloi Batlle, Ton Kalker, and Jaap Haitsma. 2005. A Review of Audio Fingerprinting. *Journal of VLSI Signal Processing Systems* 41(3): 271–284.

Castells, Manuel. 2001. *The Internet Galaxy: Reflections on the Internet, Business, and Society*. Oxford/New York: Oxford University Press.

———. 2009. *Communication Power*. Oxford/New York: Oxford University Press.

Center for Copyright Information. 2016. The Copyright Alert System. http://www.copyrightinformation.org/the-copyright-alert-system/. Accessed 6 Oct 2016.

CMBA. 2008. Public Consultation on Creative Content Online – Policy/Regulatory Issues – Comments of the Creative Media Business Alliance (CMBA). http://ec.europa.eu/archives/information_society/avpolicy/docs/other_actions/col_2008/ngo/cmba_en.pdf. Accessed 9 Oct 2016.

CNIL. 2007. Surveillance des Réseaux 'Peer to Peer': La CNIL Prend Acte de la Décision du Conseil d'Etat. Archived with Author.

———. 2010. Lutte Contre le Téléchargement Illégal, CNIL et HADOPI: Déjà une Longue Histoire. http://www.cnil.fr/linstitution/actualite/article/article/la-cnil-et-la-hadopi-deja-une-longue-histoire/. Accessed 11 Apr.

Colipa. 2010. Online Commerce Consultation. Colipa Contribution. https://circabc.europa.eu/sd/a/89931860-ebbc-49e7-ad4e-26b9cc513671/EU Colipa FED ENTR 779176.pdf. Accessed 9 Oct 2016.

Cooper, Alissa, and David Sohn. 2006. *Evaluating DRM: Building a Marketplace for the Convergent World*. Washington, DC: Center for Democracy and Technology.

Coudert, Fanny, and Evi Werkers. 2010. In the Aftermath of the Promusicae Case: How to Strike the Balance? *International Journal of Law and Information Technology* 18(1): 50–71.

Council of the European Communities. 1986. *Council Directive 87/54/EEC of 16 December 1986 on the Legal Protection of Topographies of Semiconductor Products*. Luxembourg: Official Journal of the European Communities.

―――. 1991. *Council Directive 91/250/EEC of 14 May 1991 on the Legal Protection of Computer Programs.* Luxembourg: Official Journal of the European Communities.

―――. 1992. *Council Directive 92/100/EEC of 19 November 1992 on Rental Right and Lending Right and on Certain Rights Related to Copyright in the Field of Intellectual Property.* Luxembourg: Official Journal of the European Communities.

―――. 1993a. *Council Directive 93/83/EEC of 27 September 1993 on the Coordination of Certain Rules Concerning Copyright and Rights Related to Copyright Applicable to Satellite Broadcasting and Cable Retransmission.* Luxembourg: Official Journal of the European Communities.

―――. 1993b. *Council Directive 93/98/EEC of 29 October 1993 Harmonizing the Term of Protection of Copyright and Certain Related Rights.* Luxembourg: Official Journal of the European Communities.

Council of the European Union. 2008. *Council Conclusions on the Development of Legal Offers of Online Cultural and Creative Content and the Prevention and Combating of Piracy in the Digital Environment.* Brussels: Council of the European Union.

―――. 2012. *Council Conclusions on the Digital Single Market and Governance of the Single Market.* Brussels: Council of the European Union.

―――. 2014. *Draft Council Conclusions on IPR Enforcement.* Brussels: Council of the European Union.

D'Erme, Roberto, Christophe Geiger, Henning Große Ruse-Khan, Christian Heinze, Thomas Jaeger, Rita Matulionuyte, and Axel Metzger. 2011. Opinion of European Academics on Anti-Counterfeiting Trade Agreement. *Journal of Intellectual Property, Information Technology and E-Commerce Law* 2(1): 65–72.

DACS. 2008. Stakeholder Consultation on European Commission Draft Communication on Creative Content Online in the Single Market. http://ec.europa.eu/archives/information_society/avpolicy/docs/other_actions/col_2008/ngo/dacs_en.pdf. Accessed 9 Oct 2016.

Dailymotion. 2010. Contribution de Dailymotion à la Consultation Publique sur l'Avenir du Commerce Électronique dans le Marché Intérieur et la Mise en Œuvre de la Directive Commerce Électronique (2000/31/CE). https://circabc.europa.eu/sd/a/956bbdb3-4fa1-4705-84ea-09a3bef4020c/FR DAILYMOTION ENTR (th 1-2%265) 776967.pdf. Accessed 9 Oct 2016.

Davies, Gillian. 2002. *Copyright and the Public Interest.* 2nd ed. London: Sweet & Maxwell.

DeBeer, Jeremy, and Christopher Clemmer. 2009. Global Trends in Online Copyright Enforcement: A Non-Neutral Role for Network Intermediaries? *Jurimetrics* 49(4): 375.

Deibert, Ronald. 2008. *Access Denied: The Practice and Policy of Global Internet Filtering, the Information Revolution and Global Politics.* Cambridge, MA: MIT Press.

della Porta, Donatella, and Michael Keating. 2008. How Many Approaches in the Social Sciences? An Epistemological Introduction. In *Approaches and Methodologies in the Social Sciences. A Pluralist Perspective,* ed. Donatella della Porta and Michael Keating, 19–39. Cambridge: Cambridge University Press.

DeNardis, Laura. 2009. *Protocol Politics: The Globalization of Internet Governance.* Cambridge/London: MIT Press.

———. 2010. The Emerging Field of Internet Governance. In *Yale Information Society Project Working Paper Series.* New Haven: Yale Law School.

———. 2012. Hidden Levers of Internet Control. *Information, Communication & Society* 15(5): 720–738.

Dutton, William, and Malcolm Peltu. 2007. The Emerging Internet Governance Mosaic: Connecting the Pieces. *Information Polity* 12(1–2): 63–81.

Dutton, William, Anna Dopatka, Ginette Law, and Victoria Nash. 2011. *Freedom of Connection, Freedom of Expression: The Changing Legal and Regulatory Ecology Shaping the Internet.* Paris: UNESCO.

Dyer-Witheford, Nick. 2002. E-Capital and the Many-Headed Hydra. In *Critical Perspectives on the Internet,* ed. Greg Elmer, 129–163. Lanham: Rowman & Littlefield.

Ecrans.fr. 2008a. Lettre Barroso. http://www.ecrans.fr/IMG/pdf/Lettre_Barroso.pdf. Accessed 6 Oct 2016.

———. 2008b. Lettre Reding. http://www.ecrans.fr/IMG/pdf/lettrereding.pdf. Accessed 6 Oct 2016.

EDiMA. 2010. EDiMA Response to the Public Consultation on the Future of Electronic Commerce in the Internal Market and the Implementation of the Directive on Electronic Commerce (2000/31/EC). https://circabc.europa.eu/sd/a/168a2c74-fd01-4b94-b89f-687440437d52/EU EDIMA FED ENTR (th 1-3%265%267) 800212.pdf. Accessed 9 Oct 2016.

EDRi. 2012a. 10 European Commission Myths About ACTA. http://www.edri.org/commission_myths. Accessed 6 Oct 2016.

———. 2012b. ACTA Fact Sheet. http://www.edri.org/ACTAfactsheet. Accessed 6 Oct 2016.

EFF. 2008. Electronic Frontier Foundation Responses to the Creative Content Online Consultation Questionnaire. http://ec.europa.eu/archives/information_society/avpolicy/docs/other_actions/col_2008/ngo/eff_en.pdf. Accessed 9 Oct 2016.

———. 2010. Submission of the Electronic Frontier Foundation on the Consultation on the EU E-Commerce Directive (2000/31/EC). https://circabc.europa.eu/sd/a/7ad5a1c3-d07f-4abe-9afb-4f5698666b0b/EU EFF CONSO (th 5) 821617.pdf. Accessed 9 Oct 2016.

El País. 2010a. Cable sobre la Polémica por la Ley contra la Piratería. http://
elpais.com/elpais/2010/12/03/actualidad/1291367865_850215.html.
Accessed 6 Oct 2016.
———. 2010b. Cable sobre las Presiones para que España Combata la Piratería.
http://elpais.com/elpais/2010/12/03/actualidad/1291367862_850215.
html. Accessed 6 Oct 2016.
ENPA. 2010. ENPA Response to the Public Consultation on the Future of
Electronic Commerce in the Internal Market and the Implementation of the
Directive on Electronic Commerce (2000/31/EC). https://circabc.europa.
eu/sd/a/2cffc3cd-ac34-4ebc-864f-cfe32b89e58f/EU ENPA FED ENTR (th
1-2%264-5) 834493 a ne pas publier.pdf. Accessed 9 Oct 2016.
EPC. 2010. Contribution from the European Publishers Council to the
Review of the E-Commerce Directive. https://circabc.europa.eu/sd/a/
23e27474-f646-4dab-8c52-3e10cb2c0f35/EU EPC FED ENTR 834604.
pdf. Accessed 9 Oct 2016.
EPO, and OHIM. 2013. *Intellectual Property Rights Intensive Industries:
Contribution to Economic Performance and Employment in the European Union.
Industry-Level Analysis Report, September 2013.* Munich/Germany: European
Patent Office & Ofice for Harmonization in the Internal Market.
ESOMA. 2008. Creative Content Online Consultation. http://ec.europa.eu/
archives/information_society/avpolicy/docs/other_actions/col_2008/ngo/
esoma_en.pdf. Accessed 9 Oct 2016.
EUIPO. 2016. *The Economic Cost of IPR Infringement in the Recorded Music
Industry.* Alicante: European Union Intellectual Property Office.
EuroISPA. 2008. EuroISPA Response to the European Commission's Content
Online Consultation. http://ec.europa.eu/archives/information_society/
avpolicy/docs/other_actions/col_2008/ngo/euroispa_en.pdf. Accessed 9
Oct 2016.
European Commission. 2005. *COM(2005) 276 final. Proposal for a European
Parliament and Council Directive on Criminal Measures aimed at Ensuring the
Enforcement of Intellectual Property Rights, and Proposal for Council Framework
Decision to Strengthen the Criminal Law Framework to Combat Intellectual
Property Offences.* Brussels: European Commission.
———. 2008a. *COM(2007) 836 final. Communication from the Commission to the
European Parliament, the Council, the European Economic and Social Committee
and the Committee of the Regions on Creative Content Online in the Single
Market.* Brussels: European Commission.
———. 2008b. *COM(2008) 466/3. Green Paper on Copyright in the Knowledge
Economy.* Brussels: European Commission.
———. 2008c. Public Consultation on Creative Content Online in the Single
Market. http://ec.europa.eu/avpolicy/other_actions/content_online/con-
sultation_2008/index_en.htm. Accessed 6 Oct 2016.

———. 2008d. *SEC(2007) 1710. Commission Staff Working Document Accompanying the Communication from the Commission to the European Parliament, the Council, the European Economic and Social Committee and the Committee of the Regions on Creative Content Online in the Single Market.* Brussels: European Commission.

———. 2009a. *COM(2009) 467 final. Communication from the Commission to the Council, the European Parliament and the European Economic and Social Committee on Enhancing the Enforcement of Intellectual Property Rights in the Internal Market.* Brussels: European Commission.

———. 2009b. Creative Content in a European Digital Single Market: Challenges for the Future. A Reflection Document of DG INFSO and DG MARKT. Brussels: European Commission.

———. 2009c. *Final Report on the Content Online Platform.* Brussels: European Commission.

———. 2009d. *SEC(2009) 1103 Final. Commission Staff Working Document. Accompanying Document to the Communication from the Commission to the European Parliament, the Council, the European Economic and Social Committee and the Committee of the Regions. Europe's Digital Competitiveness Report. Volume 1: i2010—Annual Information Society Report 2009 Benchmarking i2010: Trends and Main Achievements.* Brussels: European Commission.

———. 2010a. *COM(2010) 245 Final/2. Communication from the Commission to the European Parliament, the Council, the European Economic and Social Committee and the Committee of the Regions. A Digital Agenda for Europe.* Brussels: European Commission.

———. 2010b. *COM(2010) 779 final. Communication of the Commission to the European Parliament, the Council, the European Economic and Social Committee and the Committee of the Regions on the Application of Directive 2004/48/EC of the European Parliament and the Council of 29 April 2004 on the Enforcement of Intellectual Property Rights.* Brussels: European Commission.

———. 2010c. Public Consultation on the Future of Electronic Commerce in the Internal Market and the Implementation of the Directive on Electronic Commerce (2000/31/EC). http://ec.europa.eu/internal_market/consultations/2010/e-commerce_en.htm. Accessed 6 Oct 2016.

———. 2010d. *Public Consultation on the Future of Electronic Commerce in the Internal Market and the Implementation of the Directive on Electronic Commerce (2000/31/EC).* Brussels: European Commission.

———. 2010e. SEC(2010) 1276. European Competitiveness Report 2010. In *Enterprise & Industry Magazine.* Brussels: European Commission.

———. 2010f. *Summary of the Results of the Public Consultation on the Future of Electronic Commerce in the Internal Market and the Implementation of the Directive on Electronic Commerce (2000/31/EC).* Brussels: European Commission.

————. 2011a. *COM(2011) 287 Final. Communication from the Commission to the European Parliament, the Council, the European Economic and Social Committee and the Committee of the Regions on a Single Market for Intellectual Property Rights. Boosting Creativity and Innovation to Provide Economic Growth, High Quality Jobs and First Class Products and Services in Europe.* Brussels: European Commission.

————. 2011b. *COM(2011) 427 Final. Green Paper on the Online Distribution of Audiovisual Works in the European Union: Opportunities and Challenges Towards a Digital Single Market.* Brussels: European Commission.

————. 2011c. *Commission Services Working Paper. Comments on the 'Opinion of European Academics on Anti-Counterfeiting Trade Agreement'.* Brussels: European Commission.

————. 2012a. *10 Myths About ACTA (Anti-Counterfeiting Trade Agreement).* Brussels: European Commission.

————. 2012b. A Clean and Open Internet: Public Consultation on Procedures for Notifying and Acting on Illegal Content Hosted by Online Intermediaries. http://ec.europa.eu/internal_market/consultations/2012/clean-and-open-internet_en.htm. Accessed 6 Oct 2016.

————. 2012c. *COM(2011) 942 Final. Communication to the European Parliament, the Council, the European Economic and Social Committee and the Committee of the Regions on a Coherent Framework for Building Trust in the Digital Single Market for E-Commerce and Online Services.* Brussels: European Commission.

————. 2012d. *COM(2012) 789 Final. Communication from the Commission on Content in the Digital Single Market.* Brussels: European Commission.

————. 2012e. IP/12/1394. Copyright: Commission Urges Industry to Deliver Innovative Solutions for Greater Access to Online Content. http://europa.eu/rapid/press-release_IP-12-1394_en.htm. Accessed 6 Oct 2016.

————. 2012f. *SEC(2011) 1641 Final. Commission Staff Working Document on Online Services, Including E-Commerce, in the Single Market Accompanying the Document Communication to the European Parliament, the Council, the European Economic and Social Committee and the Committee of the Regions on a Coherent Framework for Building Trust in the Digital Single Market for E-Commerce and Online Services.* Brussels: European Commission.

————. 2012g. *Transparency of ACTA Negotiations.* Brussels: European Commission.

————. 2012h. *What ACTA is About.* Brussels: European Commission.

————. 2013. *SWD(2013) 153 Final. Commission Staff Working Document on E-Commerce Action Plan 2012–2015: State of Play 2013.* Brussels: European Commission.

————. 2014. *Communication from the Commission to the European Parliament, the Council and the European Economic and Social Committee. Towards a*

Renewed Consensus on the Enforcement of Intellectual Property Rights: An EU Action Plan. Brussels: European Commission.

———. 2015a. COM(2016) 288/2. Communication from the Commission to the European Parliament, the Council, the European Economic and Social Committee and the Committee of the Regions. Online Platforms and the Digital Single Market. Opportunities and Challenges for Europe Brussels: European Commission.

———. 2015b. IP/15/6261. Commission Takes First Steps to Broaden Access to Online Content and Outlines Its Vision to Modernise EU Copyright Rules. http://europa.eu/rapid/press-release_IP-15-6261_en.htm. Accessed 6 Oct 2016.

———. 2015c. Public Consultation on the Regulatory Environment for Platforms, Online Intermediaries, Data and Cloud Computing and the Collaborative Economy. https://ec.europa.eu/digital-single-market/en/news/public-consultation-regulatory-environment-platforms-online-intermediaries-data-and-cloud. Accessed 6 Oct 2016.

———. 2016a. *Promoting a Fair, Efficient and Competitive European Copyright-Based Economy in the Digital Single Market (COM(2016)592 Final).* Brussels: European Commission.

———. 2016b. *Proposal for a Directive of the European Parliament and of the Council on Copyright in the Digital Single Market (COM(2016)593 Final).* Brussels: European Commission.

European Commission & Parliament. 2012. *Anti-Counterfeiting Trade Agreement (ACTA). List of Answers by the European Commission to Written Questions by the European Parliament (Filed Between 1 January 2010 and 31 January 2012).* Brussels: European Commission and Parliament.

European Communities Trade Mark Association. 2012. ACTA Support Letter for Members of EU Parliament. http://www.ecta.org/IMG/pdf/acta_support_letter_for_members_of_eu_parliament_2_.pdf. Accessed 6 Oct 2016.

European Data Protection Supervisor. 2012. *Opinion of the European Data Protection Supervisor on the Proposal for a Council Decision on the Conclusion of the Anti-Counterfeiting Trade Agreement Between the European Union and Its Member States, Australia, Canada, Japan, the Republic of Korea, the United Mexican States, the Kingdom of Morocco, the Republic of Singapore, the Swiss Confederation and the United States of America.* Brussels: European Data Protection Supervisor.

European Parliament. 2008. *INI/2007/2153. Resolution of 10 April 2008 on Cultural Industries in Europe.* Brussels: European Parliament.

———. 2012a. *2012/2030(INI). European Parliament Resolution of 11 December 2012 on Completing the Digital Single Market.* Strasbourg: European Parliament.

———. 2012b. ACTA Before the European Parliament. http://www.europarl.europa.eu/news/en/pressroom/content/20120217BKG38488/html/ACTA-before-the-European-Parliament. Accessed 6 Oct 2016.

————. 2012c. Everything You Need to Know About ACTA. ACTA Debate: MEPs Disagree About the Best Way Forward. http://www.europarl.europa.eu/news/en/news-room/content/20120220FCS38611/2/html/ACTA-debate-MEPs-disagree-about-the-best-way-forward. Accessed 6 Oct 2016.

————. 2012d. *Recommendation on the Draft Council Decision on the Conclusion of the Anti-Counterfeiting Trade Agreement Between the European Union and Its Member States, Australia, Canada, Japan, the Republic of Korea, the United Mexican States, the Kingdom of Morocco, New Zealand, the Republic of Singapore, the Swiss Confederation and the United States of America. A7-0204/2012.* Brussels: European Parliament.

————. 2016. Legislative Powers. Consent. http://www.europarl.europa.eu/aboutparliament/en/0087a559c8/Consent.html. Accessed 6 Oct 2016.

European Parliament & Council. 1996. *Directive 96/9/EC of the European Parliament and of the Council of 11 March 1996 on the Legal Protection of Databases.* Luxembourg: Official Journal of the European Communities.

————. 2000. *Directive 2000/31/EC of the European Parliament and of the Council of 8 June 2000 on Certain Legal Aspects of Information Society Services, in particular Electronic Commerce, in the Internal Market.* Luxembourg: Official Journal of the European Communities.

————. 2001a. *Directive 2001/29/EC of the European Parliament and of the Council of 22 May 2001 on the Harmonisation of Certain Aspects of Copyright and Related Rights in the Information Society.* Luxembourg: Official Journal of the European Communities.

————. 2001b. *Directive 2001/84/EC of the European Parliament and of the Council of 27 September 2001 on the Resale Right for the Benefit of the Author of an Original Work of Art.* Luxembourg: Official Journal of the European Communities.

————. 2002. Decision n. 676/2002/EC of the European Parliament and of the Council of 7 March 2002 on a Regulatory Framework for Radio Spectrum Policy in the European Community (Radio Spectrum Decision). Luxembourg: Official Journal of the European Communities.

————. 2004. *Directive 2004/48/EC of the European Parliament and of the Council of 29 April 2004 on the Enforcement of Intellectual Property Rights.* Luxembourg: Official Journal of the European Union.

————. 2006. *Directive 2006/115/EC of the European Parliament and of the Council of 12 December 2006 on Rental Right and Lending Right and on Certain Rights Related to Copyright in the Field of Intellectual Property (Codified Version).* Luxembourg: Official Journal of the European Union.

————. 2009a. *Directive 2009/24/EC of the European Parliament and of the Council of 23 April 2009 on the Legal Protection of Computer Programs (Codified Version).* Luxembourg: Official Journal of the European Union.

————. 2009b. *Directive 2009/136/EC of the European Parliament and of the Council of 25 November 2009 amending Directive 2002/22/EC on Universal*

Service and Users' Rights relating to Electronic Communications Networks and Services, Directive 2002/58/EC concerning the Processing of Personal Data and the Protection of Privacy in the Electronic Communications Sector and Regulation (EC) No 2006/2004 on Cooperation between National Authorities Responsible for the Enforcement of Consumer Protection Laws (Citizens' Rights Directive). Luxembourg: Official Journal of the European Union.

———. 2009c. *Directive 2009/140/EC of the European Parliament and of the Council of 25 November 2009 amending Directives 2002/21/EC on a Common Regulatory Framework for Electronic Communications Networks and Services, 2002/19/EC on Access to, and Interconnection of, Electronic Communications Networks and Associated Facilities, and 2002/20/EC on the Authorisation of Electronic Communications Networks and Services (Better Regulation Directive).* Luxembourg: Official Journal of the European Union.

———. 2009d. *Regulation (EC) No 1211/2009 of the European Parliament and of the Council of 25 November 2009 establishing the Body of European Regulators for Electronic Communications (BEREC) and the Office.* Luxembourg: Official Journal of the European Union.

———. 2010. *Consolidated Version of the Treaty on the Functioning of the European Union (TFEU).* Luxembourg: Official Journal of the European Union.

———. 2011. *Directive 2011/77/EU of the European Parliament and of the Council of 27 September 2011 Amending Directive 2006/116/EC on the Term of Protection of Copyright and Certain Related Rights.* Luxembourg: Official Journal of the European Union.

———. 2012. *Directive 2012/28/EU of the European Parliament and of the Council of 25 October 2012 on Certain Permitted Uses of Orphan Works.* Luxembourg: Official Journal of the European Union.

———. 2014. *Directive 2014/26/EU of the European Parliament and of the Council of 26 February 2014 on Collective Management of Copyright and Related Rights and Multi-Territorial Licensing of Rights in Musical Works for Online Use in the Internal Market.* Luxembourg: Official Journal of the European Union.

European Parliament Committee on Legal Affairs. 2014. *Draft Report on 'Towards a Renewed Consensus on the Enforcement of Intellectual Property Rights: An EU Action Plan'.* Brussels: European Parliament.

European Parliament, Council, and Commission. 2000. *Charter of Fundamental Rights of the European Union (2000/C 364/01).* Nice: Official Journal of the European Communities.

European Parliament Legal Service. 2011a. *Legal Opinion Re: Anti-Counterfeiting Trade Agreement (ACTA) – Conformity with European Union Law.* Brussels: European Parliament.

———. 2011b. *Legal Opinion Re: Anti-Counterfeiting Trade Agreement (ACTA). SJ-0501/11.* Brussels: European Parliament.

European Union. 2006. Accession to the WIPO Treaties. http://europa.eu/leg-islation_summaries/internal_market/businesses/intellectual_property/l26054_en.htm. Accessed 6 Oct 2016.

———. 2011. Aspects of Intellectual Property Rights. http://europa.eu/legisla-tion_summaries/internal_market/businesses/intellectual_property/r11013_en.htm. Accessed 6 Oct 2016.

———. 2015. Regulatory Framework for Electronic Communications. http://europa.eu/legislation_summaries/information_society/legislative_frame-work/l24216a_en.htm. Accessed 6 Oct 2016.

———. 2016. Regulations, Directives and Other Acts. https://europa.eu/european-union/law/legal-acts_en. Accessed 6 Oct 2016.

Farrand, Benjamin. 2011. 'Piracy. It's a Crime.' – The Criminalization Process of Digital Copyright Infringement. Neutralidad de la Red y otros Retos para el Futuro de Internet. Actas del VII Congreso Internacional Internet, Derecho y Política, Universitat Oberta de Catalunya, Barcelona.

Feenberg, Andrew. 1999. *Questioning Technology*. London/New York: Routledge.

FEP. 2010. FEP Answer to the Public Consultation on the Future of Electronic Commerce in the Internal Market and the Implementation of the Directive on Electronic Commerce (2000/31/EC). https://circabc.europa.eu/sd/a/672f3ef5-f698-42f6-b097-16eb20c06795/EU FEP-FEE FED ENTR.pdf. Accessed 9 Oct 2016.

FERA. 2008. European Commission Communication on Creative Content Online in the Single Market. A Contribution to the Public Consultation. http://ec.europa.eu/archives/information_society/avpolicy/docs/other_actions/col_2008/ngo/fera_en.pdf. Accessed 9 Oct 2016.

FFII. 2013. ACTA Analysis: The World Faces Major Challenges.http://action.ffii.org/acta/Analysis. Accessed 6 Oct 2016.

Fischer, Frank. 2003. *Reframing Public Policy*. Oxford: Oxford University Press.

Fisher, W. 2004. *Promises to Keep: Technology, Law, and the Future of Entertainment*. Stanford: Stanford University Press.

Foster, John, and Robert McChesney. 2011. The Internet's Unholy Marriage to Capitalism. *Monthly Review* 62(10).

Foucault, Michel. 1980. The Confession of the Flesh. In *Power/Knowledge: Selected Interviews and Other Writings, 1972–1977*, ed. Colin Gordon, 194–228. New York: Pantheon.

French Deputies. 2009a. *Saisine du Conseil Constitutionnel en Date du 28 Septembre 2009. Projet de Loi Relatif à la Protection Pénale de la Propriété Littéraire et Artistique sur Internet*. Paris: French Parliament.

———. 2009b. *Saisine du Conseil Constitutionnel Loi Favorisant la Diffusion et la Protection de la Création sur Internet*. Paris: French Parliament.

French Government. 2008a. Après la Diffusion du Sondage IPSOS sur la Lutte Contre le Piratage sur Internet, Christine Albanel Se Félicite de l'Esprit de

Responsabilité des Français. http://www.culture.gouv.fr/culture/actualites/communiq/albanel/comipsos.htm. Accessed 6 Oct 2016.

———. 2008b. Les Etats Membres de l'Union Européenne Sont Tombés d'Accord pour Retirer l'Amendement n. 138 (Dit 'Amendement Bono') du Paquet Télécom. http://www.culture.gouv.fr/culture/actualites/communiq/albanel/com138.html. Accessed 6 Oct 2016.

———. 2009. Christine Albanel Remercie les Sénateurs et Députés de Tous Bords Politiques qui Ont Apporté Leur Soutien au Projet de Loi Création et Internet. http://www.culture.gouv.fr/culture/actualites/communiq/albanel/com_creation_internet_130509.html. Accessed 6 Oct 2016.

———. 2013. *Décret n. 2013-596 du 8 juillet 2013 Supprimant la Peine Contraventionnelle Complémentaire de Suspension de l'Accès à un Service de Communication au Public en Ligne et Relatif aux Modalités de Transmission des Informations Prévue à l'Article L. 331-21 du Code de la Propriété Intellectuelle.* Paris: French Government.

French Ministry of Culture and Communication. 2004. Charte d'Engagements Pour le Développement de l'Offre Légale de Musique en Ligne, le Respect de la Propriété Intellectuelle et la Lutte Contre la Piraterie Numérique. http://www.culture.gouv.fr/culture/actualites/conferen/donnedieu/charte280704.htm. Accessed 11 Apr.

———. 2008. *Projet de Loi Favorisant la Diffusion et la Protection de la Création sur Internet.* Paris: French Government.

———. 2013. Culture-Acte 2: 80 Propositions sur les Contenus Culturels Numériques.http://www.culturecommunication.gouv.fr/Actualites/En-continu/Culture-acte-2-80-propositions-sur-les-contenus-culturels-numeriques. Accessed 6 Oct 2016.

———. 2014. Remise à Aurélie Filippetti du Rapport de Mireille Imbert-Quaretta sur les Outils Opérationnels de Prévention et de Lutte contre la Contrefaçon en Ligne. http://www.culturecommunication.gouv.fr/Presse/Communiques-de-presse/Remise-a-Aurelie-Filippetti-du-rapport-de-Mireille-Imbert-Quaretta-sur-les-outils-operationnels-de-prevention-et-de-lutte-contre-la-contrefacon-en-ligne. Accessed 21 Sept 2016.

———. 2015a. Charte des Bonnes Pratiques dans la Publicité pour le Respect du Droit d'Auteur et des Droits Voisins. http://www.culturecommunication.gouv.fr/Actualites/Dossiers/Charte-des-bonnes-pratiques-dans-la-publicite-pour-le-respect-du-droit-d-auteur-et-des-droits-voisins/Presentation-de-la-charte. Accessed 20 Sept 2016.

———. 2015b. Stratégie du Gouvernement concernant la Lutte contre le Piratage des Œuvres sur Internet. http://www.culturecommunication.gouv.fr/Presse/Communiques-de-presse/Lutte-contre-le-piratage. Accessed 21 Sept 2016.

French National Assembly. 2009a. *Avis Fait au Nom de la Commission des Affaires Économiques, de l'Environnement et du Territoire sur le Projet de Loi, Adopté Par le Sénat, Favorisant la Diffusion et la Protection de la Création sur Internet (n. 1240), Par M. Bernard Gérard, Député*. Paris: French Parliament.

———. 2009b. *Avis Présenté au Nom de la Commission des Affaires Culturelles, Familiales et Social sur le Projet de Loi, Adopté Par le Sénat, Favorisant la Diffusion et la Protection de la Création sur Internet, Par Mme Muriel Marland-Militello, Députée*. Paris: French Parliament.

———. 2009c. Culture: Diffusion et Protection de la Création sur Internet. http://www.assemblee-nationale.fr/13/dossiers/internet.asp. Accessed 6 Oct 2016.

———. 2009d. *Rapport Fait au Nom de la Commission des Affaires Culturelles et de l'Éducation sur le Projet de Loi (n. 1831), Adopté Par le Sénat Après Engagement de la Procédure Accélérée, Relatif à la Protection Pénale de la Propriété Littéraire et Artistique sur Internet, Par M. Franck Riester, Député*. Paris: French Parliament.

———. 2009e. *Rapport Fait au Nom de La Commission des Lois Constitutionnelles, de la Législation et de l'Administration Générale de la République sur le Projet de Loi (n. 1240), Adopté par le Sénat Après Déclaration d'Urgence, favorisant la Diffusion et la Protection de la Création sur Internet, Par M. Franck Riester, Député*. Paris: French Parliament.

French Parliament. 2006. *Loi n. 2006-961 du 1 Août 2006 relative au Droit d'Auteur et aux Droits Voisins dans la Société de l'Information*. Paris: Journal officiel de la République française.

———. 2009a. *Loi n. 2009-669 du 12 Juin 2009 favorisant la Diffusion et la Protection de la Création sur Internet*. Paris: Journal officiel de la République française.

———. 2009b. *Loi n. 2009-1311 du 28 Octobre 2009 relative à la Protection Pénale de la Propriété Littéraire et Artistique sur Internet*. Paris: Journal officiel de la République française.

———. 2009c. *Rapport Fait au Nom de la Commission Mixte Paritaire (1) Chargée de Proposer un Texte sur les Dispositions Restant en Discussion du Projet de Loi Relatif à la Protection Pénale de la Propriété Littéraire et Artistique sur Internet, Par M. Franck Riester, Rapporteur, Député, Par M. Michel Thiollière, Rapporteur, Sénateur*. Paris: French Parliament.

French Senate. 2008a. *Avis Présenté au Nom de la Commission des Affaires Économiques (1) sur le Projet de Loi Favorisant la Diffusion et la Protection de la Création sur Internet (Urgence Déclarée), Par M. Bruno Retailleau, Sénateur*. Paris: French Parliament.

———. 2008b. *Rapport Fait au Nom de la Commission des Affaires Culturelles sur le Projet de Loi Favorisant la Diffusion et la Protection de la Création sur Internet, Par M. Michel Thiollière, Sénateur*. Paris: French Parliament.

———. 2009. *Rapport Fait au Nom de la Commission de la Culture, de l'Éducation et de la Communication (1) sur le Projet de Loi Relatif à la Protection Pénale de la Propriété Littéraire et Artistique sur Internet (Procédure Accélérée Engagée), Par M. Michel Thiollière, Sénateur.* Paris: French Parliament.

Frontier Economics. 2011. *Estimating the Global Economic and Social Impacts of Counterfeiting and Piracy.* London: Frontier Economics.

Fuchs, Christian. 2009. Information and Communication Technologies and Society: A Contribution to the Critique of the Political Economy of the Internet. *European Journal of Communication* 24(1): 69–87.

———. 2013. Societal and Ideological Impacts of Deep Packet Inspection Internet Surveillance. *Information, Communication & Society* 16: 1–32.

Fuchs, Christian, and Dwayne Winseck. 2011. Critical Media and Communication Studies Today. A Conversation. *tripleC* 9(2): 247–271.

G8. 2011. G8 Declaration. Renewed Commitment for Freedom and Democracy. G8 Summit of Deauville – May 26–27, 2011. Deauville: French Government.

Gallo, Marielle. 2012. 2011/0167(NLE). Draft Opinion of the Committee on Legal Affairs for the Committee on International Trade on the Draft Council Decision on the Conclusion of the Anti-Counterfeiting Trade Agreement Between the European Union and Its Member States, Australia, Canada, the Republic of Korea, the United States of America, Japan, the Kingdom of Morocco, the United Mexican States, New Zealand, the Republic of Singapore and the Swiss Confederation. Brussels: European Parliament.

Garnham, Nicholas. 1990. *Capitalism and Communication: Global Culture and the Economics of Information.* Thousand Oaks: Sage.

———. 2000. *Emancipation, the Media and Modernity: Arguments About the Media and Social Theory.* Oxford: Oxford University Press.

———. 2011. The Political Economy of Communication Revisited. In *The Handbook of Political Economy of Communications,* ed. Janet Wasko, Graham Murdock, and Helena Sousa, 41–61. Chichester: Wiley-Blackwell.

Gibson, Johanna. 2007. Knowledge and Other Values – Intellectual Property and the Limitations for Traditional Knowledge. In *Emerging Issues in Intellectual Property: Trade, Technology and Market Freedom Essays in Honour of Herchel Smith,* ed. Guido Westkamp, 309–318. Cheltenham: Edward Elgar.

Giddens, Anthony. 1984. *Power, Property and the State. A Contemporary Critique of Historical Materialism.* Vol. 1. Berkeley/Los Angeles: University of California Press.

———. 1985. *The Nation-State and Violence. A Contemporary Critique of Historical Materialism.* Vol. 2. Oxford: Polity Press.

Gillespie, Tarleton. 2007. *Wired Shut: Copyright and the Shape of Digital Culture.* Cambridge: MIT Press.

Goldstein, Judith, and Robert Keohane. 1993. Ideas and Foreign Policy: An Analytical Framework. In *Ideas and Foreign Policy: Beliefs, Institutions and Political Change,* ed. Judith Goldstein and Keohane Robert, 3–30. Ithaca/London: Cornell University Press.

Gomes, Leandro de C.T., Pedro Cano, Emilia Gómez, Madeleine Bonnet, and Eloi Batlle. 2003. Audio Watermarking and Fingerprinting: For Which Applications? *Journal of New Music Research* 32(1): 65–81.

Google. 2008. Google Contribution on Creative Content Online. http:// ec.europa.eu/archives/information_society/avpolicy/docs/other_actions/ col_2008/comp/google_en.pdf. Accessed 9 Oct 2016.

Gordon, Wendy, and Robert Bone. 2000. Copyright. In *Encyclopedia of Law & Economics: Volume II*, ed. Boudewijn Boukaert and Gerrit de Geest. Cheltenham: Edward Elgar.

Gottweis, Herbert. 2006. Argumentative Policy Analysis. In *Handbook of Public Policy*, ed. Guy Peters and Jon Pierre, 461–479. London: Sage.

Gotzen, Frank, and Marie-Christine Janssens. 2009. *Wegwijs in Het Intellectueel Eigendomsrecht. Editie 2009*. Brugge: Vanden Broele.

Green, Leila. 2002. *Communication, Technology and Society*. London: Sage Publications.

Green/EFA. 2012. Referral to ECJ Hopefully a Nail in the ACTA Coffin. http:// www.greens-efa.eu/acta-5394.html. Accessed 6 Oct 2016.

Green League. 2008. Responses to Creative Content Online Consultation from the Information Society Working Group of the Green League (Green Party of Finland). http://ec.europa.eu/archives/information_society/avpolicy/docs/ other_actions/col_2008/ngo/green_league_en.pdf. Accessed 9 Oct 2016.

HADOPI. 2011. *L'Essentiel du Rapport d'Activité. 2010*. Paris: HADOPI.

———. 2013a. *Hadopi, Biens Culturels et Usages d'Internet: Pratiques et Perceptions des Internautes Français. BU3 – mai 2013*. Paris: HADOPI.

———. 2013b. *Rapport d'Activité 2012–2013*. Paris: HADOPI.

———. 2013c. *Réponse Graduée – Les Chiffres Clés*. Paris: HADOPI.

———. 2015. *Rapport d'Activité 2014–2015*. Paris: HADOPI.

———. 2016a. Message de Sensibilisation à Destination des Professionels. https://www.hadopi.fr/hadopi-vous/message-de-sensibilisation-destination-des-professionnels. Accessed 20 Sept 2016.

———. 2016b. Modèle de Clause à Insérer Dans une Charte Informatique, Contrat de Bail, Contrat de Location, Etc. https://www.hadopi.fr/hadopi-vous/modele-de-charte-ou-clause-pour-les-professionnels. Accessed 20 Sept 2016.

———. 2016c. Réponse Graduée. http://www.hadopi.fr/usages-responsables/ nouvelles-libertes-nouvelles-responsabilites/reponse-graduee. Accessed 3 Oct 2016.

———. 2016d. Sécurisation de son Accès Internet. https://www.hadopi.fr/ usages-responsables/nouvelles-libertes-nouvelles-responsabilites/moyens-de-securisation-labellises. Accessed 20 Sept 2016.

Hajer, Maarten. 1993. Discourse Coalitions and the Institutionalization of Practice: The Case of Acid Rain in Great Britain. In *The Argumentative Turn in Policy Analysis and Planning*, ed. Frank Fischer and John Forester, 43–76. Durham: Duke University Press.

———. 1995. *The Politics of Environmental Discourse: Ecological Modernization and the Policy Process*. Oxford: Oxford University Press.

———. 2002. Discourse Analysis and the Study of Policy Making. *European Political Science* 2(1): 61–65.

———. 2006. Doing Discourse Analysis: Coalitions, Practices, Meaning. In *Words Matter in Policy and Planning. Discourse Theory and Method in the Social Sciences*, ed. Margo van den Brink and Tamara Metze, 65–74. Utrecht: Koninklijk Nederlands Aardrijkskundig Genootschap & Netherlands Graduate School of Urban and Regional Research.

Hajer, Maarten, and Hendrik Wagenaar, ed. 2003. *Deliberative Policy Analysis: Understanding Governance in the Network Society*. Cambridge: Cambridge University Press.

Halbert, Debora. 1999. *Intellectual Property in the Information Age: The Politics of Expanding Property Rights*. Westport: Quorum Press.

Handke, Christian. 2010. *The Economics of Copyright and Digitisation: A Report on the Literature and the Need for Further Research*. London: UK Strategy Advisory Board for Intellectual Property Policy.

Harbers, Hans, ed. 2005. *Inside the Politics of Technology: Agency and Normativity in the Co-Production of Technology and Society*. Amsterdam: Amsterdam University Press.

Harcourt, Alison. 2008. Introduction. In *European Media Governance: The Brussels Dimension*, ed. Georgios Terzis, 13–23. Bristol: Intellect.

Harhoff, Dietmar. 2009. *Challenges Affecting the Use and Enforcement of Intellectual Property Rights*. London: UK Intellectual Property Office.

Henten, Anders, and Reza Tadayoni. 2008. The Impact of the Internet on Media Technology, Platforms and Innovation. In *The Internet and the Mass Media*, ed. Lucy Küng, Robert Picard, and Ruth Towse, 45–64. London: Sage.

Herrington, TyAnna. 2001. *Controlling Voices: Intellectual Property, Humanistic Studies, and the Internet*. Carbondale/Edwardsville: Southern Illinois University Press.

Hesmondhalgh, David. 2007. *Cultural Industries*. 2nd ed. London: Sage.

Hetland, Jarle. 2009. Sweden's Pirate Bay Members Found Guilty. *European Voice*, April 17. http://www.europeanvoice.com/article/2009/04/sweden-s-pirate-bay-members-found-guilty/64641.aspx. Accessed 6 Oct 2016.

Huygen, Annelies, Paul Rutten, Sanne Huveneers, Sander Limonard, Joost Poort, Jorna Leenheer, Kieja Janssen, Nico van Eijk, and Natali Helberger. 2009. *Ups and Down. Economische en Culturele Gevolgen van File Sharing voor Muziek, Film en Games*. Delft: Dutch Ministries for Education, Culture and Science, Economic Affairs, and Justice.

ICANN. 2016. Internet Corporation for Assigned Names and Numbers. Welcome to ICANN!. https://www.icann.org/resources/pages/welcome-2012-02-25-en. Accessed 8 Sept 2016.

IFPI. 2010. IFPI Response to the Commission Consultation on the Future of Electronic Commerce in the Internal Market and the Implementation of the Directive on Electronic Commerce (2000/31/EC). https://circabc.europa.eu/sd/a/7277df5c-596f-41b3-8a0c-1450534335ee/EU IFPI FED ENTR (th 1-2%265) 836295.pdf. Accessed 9 Oct 2016.

———. 2012. *Digital Music Report 2012. Expanding Choice. Going Global.* London: International Federation of the Phonographic Industry.

———. 2013. *Digital Music Report 2013. Engine of a Digital World.* London: International Federation of the Phonographic Industry.

———. 2015. *Digital Music Report 2015. Charting the Path to Sustainable Growth.* London: International Federation of the Phonographic Industry.

———. 2016. *Global Music Report 2016. Music Consumption Exploding Worldwide.* London: International Federation of the Phonographic Industry.

IMPA. 2008. International Music Publishers Association. Public Consultation on Creative Content Online in the Single Market. http://ec.europa.eu/archives/information_society/avpolicy/docs/other_actions/col_2008/ngo/impa_en.pdf. Accessed 9 Oct 2016.

Institute for Globalisation and International Regulation, Anselm Kamperman Sanders, Dalindyebo Bafana Shabalala, Anke Moerland, Meir Pugatch, and Paolo Vergano. 2011. *The Anti-Counterfeiting Trade Agreement (ACTA): An Assessment. EP/EXPO/B/INTA/FWC/2009-01/Lot7/12.* Brussels: European Parliament.

Intel. 2008. Intel Corporation Response to the 2008 Creative Content Online in the Single Market Consultation. http://ec.europa.eu/archives/information_society/avpolicy/docs/other_actions/col_2008/comp/intel_corporation_en.pdf. Accessed 9 Oct 2016.

IPKat. 2014. Super-Breaking News: EU Commission Had Several Serious Doubts About Italian Communication Authority's Online Copyright Enforcement Regulation Compatibility with Fundamental Rights and EU Law. http://ipkitten.blogspot.co.uk/2014/01/super-breaking-news-eu-commission-had.html. Accessed 6 Oct 2016.

IRII. 2008. Internet Research and Innovation Institute. In Response to the Public Consultation on Creative Content Online. http://ec.europa.eu/archives/information_society/avpolicy/docs/other_actions/col_2008/ngo/irii_en.pdf. Accessed 9 Oct 2016.

ISFE. 2010. Public Consultation on the Future of Electronic Commerce in the Internal Market and the Implementation of the Directive on Electronic Commerce (2000/31/EC). Responses by the Interactive Software Federation of Europe. https://circabc.europa.eu/sd/a/f7fa6f50-0221-44b5-a209-a37f-c4eb7452/EU ISFE FED ENTR (th 1-2%265) 835636.pdf. Accessed 9 Oct 2016.

ITU. 2006. World Summit on the Information Society: About WSIS. http://www.itu.int/wsis/basic/about.html. Accessed 6 Oct 2016.

JANET. 2010. JANET(UK)'s Response to the European Commission's Consultation 'on the Future of Electronic Commerce in the Internal Market and the Implementation of the Directive on Electronic Commerce (2000/31/EC)'. https://circabc.europa.eu/sd/a/66717321-9476-4705-840f-3b3f814235ef/UK JANET ENTR. reply Ares 696931.pdf. Accessed 9 Oct 2016.

Jessop, Bob. 2004. Critical Semiotic Analysis and Cultural Political Economy. *Critical Discourse Studies* 1(1): 1–16.

———. 2009. Cultural Political Economy and Critical Policy Studies. *Critical Policy Studies* 3(3–4): 336–356.

Joint Civil Society. 2012. Down with ACTA! The EU Must Protect Our Commons. http://www.article19.org/resources.php/resource/3355/en/down-with-acta!-the-eu-must-protect-our-commons. Accessed 6 Oct 2016.

Joint Rights Holders. 2012. Please Support ACTA for the Good of Europe. Letter to National Governments. http://www.inta.org/Advocacy/Documents/February152012Governments.pdf. Accessed 6 Oct 2016.

Jones, Richard. 2005. Entertaining Code: File Sharing, Digital Rights Management Regimes, and Criminological Theories of Compliance. *International Review of Law Computers* 19(3): 287–303.

Kern, Florian. 2011. Ideas, Institutions, and Interests: Explaining Policy Divergence in Fostering 'System Innovations' Towards Sustainability. *Environment and Planning C: Government and Policy* 29: 1116–1134.

Korff, Douwe, and Ian Brown. 2011. *Opinion on the Compatibility of the Anti-Counterfeiting Trade Agreement (ACTA) with the European Convention on Human Rights & the EU Charter of Fundamental Rights*. Brussels: European Parliament.

Krikorian, Gaelle, and Amy Kapczynksi, eds. 2010. *Access to Knowledge in the Age of Intellectual Property*. New York: Zone Books.

KTH. 2008. Creative Content Online – Policy/Regulatory Issues. Proposed Answers to the Commission's 11 Questions from the Music Lessons Research Group, Department for Media Technology and Graphic Arts, Royal Institute of Technology (KTH), Stockholm, Sweden. http://ec.europa.eu/archives/information_society/avpolicy/docs/other_actions/col_2008/ngo/kth_en.pdf. Accessed 9 Oct 2016.

Küng, Lucy, Nikos Leandros, Robert Picard, Roland Schroeder, and Richard van der Wurff. 2008. The Impact of the Internet on Media Organization Strategies and Structures. In *The Internet and the Mass Media*, ed. Lucy Küng, Robert Picard, and Ruth Towse, 125–148. London: Sage.

La Quadrature du Net. 2008a. La CNIL S'Oppose à HADOPI, Pas le PS. http://www.laquadrature.net/fr/la-cnil-soppose-a-hadopi-pas-le-ps. Accessed 6 Oct 2016.

———. 2008b. Paquet Télécom: Guy Bono contre 'les amendements liberticides'. http://www.laquadrature.net/fr/paquet-telecom-guy-bono-contre-. Accessed 6 Oct 2016.

———. 2009a. HADOPI: Qui Veut Surveiller et Punir ?. http://www.laquadrature.net/fr/hadopi-qui-veut-surveiller-et-punir. Accessed 6 Oct 2016.

———. 2009b. HADOPI: Le Nouveau Gouvernement Poursuit l'Acharnement Thérapeutique.' http://www.laquadrature.net/fr/hadopi-le-nouveau-gouvernement-poursuit-lacharnement-therapeutique. Accessed 6 Oct 2016.

———. 2010a. Future of Copyright: La Quadrature Calls on the Commission to Reassert the Public's Rights. http://www.laquadrature.net/fr/node/2812. Accessed 6 Oct 2016.

———. 2010b. Legal Liability of Internet Service Providers and the Protection of Freedom of Expression Online. Response to the European Commission's Consultation on the E-Commerce Directive. https://circabc.europa.eu/sd/a/6c181e3b-9c4f-4252-9473-e1f1b7c4aec4/FR LQDN CONSO (th 5) 821480.pdf. Accessed 9 Oct 2016.

———. 2012. Facts on ACTA. https://www.laquadrature.net/files/LQDN-20120207-Facts_on_ACTA.pdf. Accessed 6 Oct 2016.

Labs Hadopi. 2012. Labs Hadopi. http://labs.hadopi.fr/. Accessed 6 Oct 2016.

Laffey, Mark, and Jutta Weldes. 1997. Beyond Belief: Ideas and Symbolic Technologies in the Study of International Relations. *European Journal of International Relations* 3(1): 193–237.

Lash, Scott. 2007. Power After Hegemony: Cultural Studies in Mutation. *Theory, Culture & Society* 24(3): 55–78.

Law Society of England and Wales. 2010. Public Consultation on the Future of Electronic Commerce in the Internal Market and the Implementation of the Directive on Electronic Commerce (2000/31/EC). https://circabc.europa.eu/sd/a/e7ba2c62-6928-4678-9e15-00eb3aaf09e9/UK THE LAW SOCIETY.doc. Accessed 9 Oct 2016.

Le Monde.fr. 2009. Industrie du X: 'Couper les Accès aux Sites Pirates' au lieu d'Accuser l'Internaute. *Le Monde. Archived with Author.*, September 14.

Lescure, Pierre. 2013. *Culture-Acte 2. Mission 'Acte II de l'Exception Culturelle'. Contributions aux Politiques Culturelles à l'Ère Numérique.* Paris: French Government.

Lessig, Lawrence. 2003. *The Future of Ideas. The Fate of the Commons in a Connected World. Reprint Edition.* New York: Random House.

———. 2004. *Free Culture: How Big Media Uses Technology and the Law to Lock Down Culture and Control Creativity.* New York: Penguin Press.

———. 2006. *Code: And Other Laws of Cyberspace, Version 2.0*. New York: Basic Books.

Lievrouw, Leah. 2012. The Next Decade in Internet Time. *Information, Communication & Society* 15(5): 616–638.

Linebaugh, Peter, and Marcus Rediker. 2000. *The Many-Headed Hydra: The Hidden History of the Revolutionary Atlantic*. London: Verso.

Los, Maria. 2006. Looking into the Future: Surveillance, Globalization and the Totalitarian Potential. In *Theorizing Surveillance: The Panopticon and Beyond*, ed. David Lyon, 69–94. Cullompton: Willan Publishing.

LVMH. 2010. LVMH Submission. Directorate General Internal Market & Services. EC Public Consultation on the Future of Electronic Commerce in the Internal Market and the Implementation of the directive on Electronic Commerce (2000/31/EC). https://circabc.europa.eu/sd/a/a30a7591-ab2f-4b7f-80db-3654f010f6cc/FR LVMH ENTR 804634.pdf. Accessed 9 Oct 2016.

Lyon, David. 2001. *Surveillance Society: Monitoring Everyday Life, Issues in Society*. Buckingham: Open University Press.

———. 2003. Surveillance as Social Sorting: Computer Codes and Mobile Bodies. In *Surveillance as Social Sorting: Privacy, Risk and Digital Discrimination*, ed. David Lyon, 13–30. London/New York: Routledge.

———. 2007. *Surveillance Studies: An Overview*. Cambridge/Malden: Polity.

Mailland, Julien. 2001. Freedom of Speech, the Internet, and the Costs of Control: The French Example. *Journal of International Law and Politics* 33(4): 1179–1234.

Mansell, Robin. 2012. *Imagining the Internet: Communication, Innovation and Governance*. Oxford: Oxford University Press.

Marsden, Christopher. 2010. *Net Neutrality. Towards a Co-regulatory Solution*. London: Bloomsbury Academic.

Mathijsen, P.S.R.F. 2010. *A Guide to European Union Law as Amended by the Treaty of Lisbon*. 10th ed. London: Sweet & Maxwell.

Mattelart, Tristan. 2009. Audio-Visual Piracy: Towards a Study of the Underground Networks of Cultural Globalization. *Global Media and Communication* 5(3): 308–326.

Mattelart, Armand. 2010. *The Globalization of Surveillance. The Origin of the Securitarian Order*. Trans. Susan Taponier and James Cohen. Cambridge/Malden: Polity Press.

May, Christopher, and Susan Sell. 2005. *Intellectual Property Rights: A Critical History*. Boulder/London: Lynne Riener Publishers.

McChesney, Robert Waterman. 2008. *The Political Economy of Media: Enduring Issues, Emerging Dilemmas*. New York: Monthly Review Press.

———. 2013. *Digital Disconnect: How Capitalism Is Turning the Internet Against Democracy*. New York: The New Press.

McGillivray, Fiona, Iain McLean, Robert Pahre, and Cheryl Schonhardt-Bailey. 2001. *International Trade and Political Institutions: Instituting Trade in the Long Nineteenth Century.* Cheltenham: Edward Elgar.

McIntyre, T.J., and Colin Scott. 2008. Internet Filtering: Rhetoric, Legitimacy, Accountability and Responsibility. In *Regulating Technologies: Legal Futures, Regulatory Frames and Technological Fixes,* ed. R. Brownsword and K. Yeung, 109–124. Oxford: Hart Publishing.

Menell, Peter. 2000. Intellectual Property: General Theories. In *Encyclopedia of Law & Economics: Volume II,* ed. Boudewijn Boukaert and Gerrit de Geest, 129–188. Cheltenham: Edward Elgar.

Metois, Eric. 1999. Audio Watermarking and Applications. http://www.metois. com/Docs/audiowatermark.pdf. Accessed 5 Oct 2016.

Meyer, Trisha. 2012. Graduated Response in France: The Clash of Copyright and the Internet. *Journal of Information Policy* 2: 107–127.

Meyer, Trisha, and Leo Van Audenhove. 2010. Graduated Response and the Emergence of a European Surveillance Society. *Info* 12(6): 69–79.

———. 2012. Surveillance and Regulating Code: An Analysis of Graduated Response in France. *Surveillance and Society* 9(4): 365–377.

Meyer, Trisha, and Agnieszka Vetulani-Cęgiel. 2016. From ACTA to TTIP: Lessons Learned on Democratic Process and Balancing of Rights. In *Transatlantic Data Privacy Relationships as a Challenge for Democracy,* ed. Dariusz Kloza and Dan Svantesson. Antwerp: Intersentia.

Michalis, Maria. 2007. *Governing European Communications: From Unification to Coordination.* Plymouth: Lexington Books.

Microsoft. 2008. Response of Microsoft to the European Commission's Communication on Creative Content Online in the Single Market. http:// ec.europa.eu/archives/information_society/avpolicy/docs/other_actions/ col_2008/comp/microsoft_en.pdf. Accessed 9 Oct 2016.

Miège, Bernard. 1989. *The Capitalization of Cultural Production.* New York: International General.

Mosco, Vincent. 2009. *The Political Economy of Communication.* 2nd ed. London/ Thousand Oaks: Sage.

MPAA. 2011. Statement by MPAA CEO and Chairman Chris Dodd on the Upcoming Signing Ceremony for the Anti-Counterfeiting Trade Agreement. Archived with Author.

Mueller, Milton. 2010. *Networks and States. The Global Politics of Internet Governance.* Cambridge/London: MIT Press.

———. 2011. DPI Technology from the Standpoint of Internet Governance Studies: An Introduction. http://dpi.ischool.syr.edu/Technology_files/ WhatisDPI-2.pdf. Accessed 5 Oct 2016.

Mueller, Milton, and Hadi Asghari. 2012. Deep Packet Inspection and Bandwidth Management: Battles Over BitTorrent in Canada and the United States. *Telecommunications Policy* 36(6): 462–475.

Mueller, Milton, Andreas Kuehn, and Stephanie Santoso. 2012. Policing the Network: Using DPI for Copyright Enforcement. *Surveillance and Society* 9(4): 348–364.

Murdock, Graham. 2011. Political Economies as Moral Economies: Commodities, Gifts, and Public Goods. In *The Handbook of Political Economy of Communications*, ed. Janet Wasko, Graham Murdock, and Helena Sousa, 13–40. Chichester: Wiley-Blackwell.

Murdock, Graham, and Peter Golding. 2005. Culture, Communication and Political Economy. In *Mass Media and Society*, ed. James Curran and Michael Gurevitch, 70–92. London: Arnold.

Mylly, Tuomas. 2009. *Intellectual Property and European Economic Constitutional Law: The Trouble with Private Informational Power*. Gummurus: Helsinki.

NBC Universal. 2008. NBC Universal Submission in Response to Commission Consultation on Creative Content on Line in the Single Market. http://ec.europa.eu/archives/information_society/avpolicy/docs/other_actions/col_2008/comp/nbc_en.pdf. Accessed 9 Oct 2016.

Netanel, Neil. 2008. *Copyright's Paradox*. Oxford/New York: Oxford University Press.

NetNames. 2015. *Counting the Cost of Counterfeiting. A NetNames Report*. London: NetNames.

Oberholzer-Gee, Felix, and Koleman Strumpf. 2010. File Sharing and Copyright. In *Innovation Policy and the Economy, Volume 10*, ed. Josh Lerner and Scott Stern, 19–55. Chicago: National Bureau of Economic Research.

OECD. 2009. *Piracy of Digital Content*. Paris: OECD Directorate for Science, Technology and Industry.

OECD, and EUIPO. 2016. *The Economic Impact of Counterfeiting and Piracy*. Paris: Organization for Economic Co-Operation and Development.

OECD Secretary General. 2007. *The Economic Impact of Counterfeiting and Piracy*. Paris: Organization for Economic Co-Operation and Development.

Offrelegale.fr. 2016. Le Site des Offres Culturelles en Ligne. http://www.offrelegale.fr/. Accessed 20 Sept 2016.

Olivennes, Denis. 2007. *Accord pour le Développement et la Protection des Œuvres et Programmes Culturels sur les Nouveaux Réseaux*. Paris.

OpenNet Initiative. 2016a. About Filtering. http://opennet.net/about-filtering. Accessed 26 Aug 2016.

———. 2016b. About ONI. http://opennet.net/about-oni. Accessed 26 Aug 2016.

OSCE. 2012a. Intellectual Property Rights in the Digital Age – New Approaches Needed to Guarantee Freedom of Expression, Says OSCE Media Freedom Representative. http://www.osce.org/fom/87167. Accessed 6 Oct 2016.

———. 2012b. OSCE Media Representative Urges European Parliament to Reassess ACTA to Safeguard Freedom of Expression. http://www.osce.org/fom/88154. Accessed 6 Oct 2016.

Oudenampsen, Merijn, and Koen Haegens. 2009. De Hydra Is Terug. Het Veelkoppige Monster van de Internetpiraterij. *Groene Amsterdammer*.

Papathanassopoulos, Stylianos, and Ralph Negrine. 2010. Public Broadcasters in the Digital Age. In *Communications Policy. Theories and Issues*, ed. Stylianos Papathanassopoulos and Ralph Negrine, 133–147. Houndmills: Palgrave Macmillan.

Paré, Daniel. 2003. *Internet Governance in Transition*. In *Who Is the Master of This Domain?* Lanham: Rowman & Littlefield Publishers.

Perry Barlow, John. 1996. *A Declaration of the Independence of Cyberspace*. Davos: Electronic Frontier Foundation.

Presidency of the French Republic. 2009. Validation, par le Conseil Constitutionnel, de la Loi relative à la Protection Pénale de la Propriété Littéraire et Artistique sur Internet. Archived with Author.

Reidenberg, Joel. 1998. Lex Informatica: The Formulation of Information Policy Rules Through Technology. *Texas Law Review* 73(3): 553–584.

Rein, Martin, and Donald Schön. 1996. Frame-Critical Policy Analysis and Frame-Reflective Policy Analysis. *Knowledge and Policy: The International Journal of Knowledge Transfer and Utilization* 9(1): 85–104.

Reyman, Jessica. 2009. *The Rhetoric of Intellectual Property: Copyright Law and the Regulation of Digital Culture*. New York: Routledge.

Rogers, Jim. 2013. *The Death and Life of the Music Industry in the Digital Age*. London: Bloomsbury.

Rooke, Richard. 2009. *European Media in the Digital Age. Analysis and Approaches*. Harlow: Pearson Education.

S&D. 2012a. S&D Call to Reject ACTA Backed by Parliament's Civil Liberties Committee. http://www.socialistsanddemocrats.eu/newsroom/sd-call-reject-acta-backed-parliaments-civil-liberties-committee - 1. Accessed 6 Oct 2016.

———. 2012b. Swoboda Condemns EPP Delaying Tactics with ACTA. http://www.socialistsanddemocrats.eu/newsroom/swoboda-condemns-epp-delaying-tactics-acta. Accessed 6 Oct 2016.

SACD, and SCAM. 2008. Projet de Loi Création et Internet. Une Chance Pour la Création, des Mesures Positives Pour les Consommateurs. Positions de la SACD et de la Scam. http://www.sacd.fr/Projet-de-loi-Creation-et-internet.8 04.0.html?&MP=450-2277. Accessed 6 Oct 2016.

SACEM, CSDEM, SNEP, SCPP, UPFI, and SPPF. 2009. Communiqué de Press SACEM, CSDEM, SNEP, SCPP, UPFI, SPPF. https://societe.sacem.fr/ressources-presse/par-publication/Communiqués/communique-de-presse-sacem-csdem-snep-scpp-upfi-sppf. Accessed 6 Oct 2016.

Schiller, Herbert. 1969. *Mass Communications and American Empire*. New York: Augustus M. Keeley Publishers.

———. 1973. *The Mind Managers*. Boston: Beacon Press.

Schiller, Dan. 2000. *Digital Capitalism: Networking the Global Market System*. Cambridge, MA: MIT Press.

———. 2008. *How to Think About Information*. Urbana: University of Illinois Press.

Schmidt, Vivien. 2010. Taking Ideas and Discourse Seriously: Explaining Change Through Discursive Institutionalism as the Fourth 'New Institutionalism'. *European Political Science Review* 2(1): 1–25.

Searle, Nicola. 2011. *Changing Business Models in the Creative Industries: The Cases of Television, Computer Games and Music*. London: UK Intellectual Property Office.

Shahin, Jamal. 2006. A European History of the Internet. *Science and Public Policy* 33(9): 681–693.

Shapiro, Andrew L. 1999. *The Control Revolution: How the Internet Is Putting Individuals in Charge and Changing the World We Know*. 1st ed. New York: PublicAffairs.

Shemtov, Noam. 2007. Circumventing the Idea Expression Dichotomy: The Use of Copyright, Technology and Contract to Deny Public Access to Ideas. In *Emerging Issues in Modern Intellectual Property: Trade, Technology and Market Freedom Essays in Honour of Herchel Smith*, ed. Guido Westkamp, 88–108. Cheltenham: Edward Elgar.

Sirois, André, and Janet Wasko. 2011. The Political Economy of the Recorded Music Industry: Redefinitions and New Trajectories in the Digital Age. In *The Handbook of Political Economy of Communications*, ed. Janet Wasko, Graham Murdock, and Helena Sousa, 331–357. Chichester: Wiley-Blackwell.

Smythe, Dallas. 1977. Communications: Blindspot of Western Marxism. *Canadian Journal of Political and Social Theory* 1(3): 1–27.

———. 1981. *Dependency Road: Communications, Capitalism, Consciousness and Canada*. Norwood: Ablex Publishing.

Solum, Lawrence. 2009. Models of Internet Governance. In *Internet Governance. Infrastructure and Institutions*, ed. Bygrave Lee and Jon Bing, 48–91. Oxford: Oxford University Press.

Spanish Parliament. 2011. *Ley 2/2011, de 4 de marzo, de Economía Sostenible*. Madrid: Boletín Oficial del Estado.

———. 2014. *Ley 21/2014, de 4 de noviembre, por la que se modifica el texto refundido de la Ley de Propiedad Intelectual aprobado por Real Decreto Legislativo 1/1996, de 12 de abril, y la Ley 1/2000, de 7 de enero, de Enjuiciamiento Civil*. Madrid: Boletín Oficial del Estado.

Stalder, Felix. 2002. Opinion. Privacy Is Not the Antidote to Surveillance. *Surveillance & Society* 1(1): 120–124.

STM. 2008. STM Submission on the European Commission's Communication on Creative Content Online in the Single Market. http://ec.europa.eu/

archives/information_society/avpolicy/docs/other_actions/col_2008/ngo/stm_en.pdf. Accessed 9 Oct 2016.

―――. 2010. International Association of Scientific, Technical and Medical Publishers ('STM'). Response to the Public Consultation on the Future of Electronic Commerce in the Internal Market and the Implementation of the Directive on Electronic Commerce (2000/31/EC). https://circabc.europa.eu/sd/a/f755ddf4-60d2-4e22-bfde-3aa1b164462e/EU STM-ASSOC FED ENTR 719662.pdf. Accessed 9 Oct 2016.

Stockholm Network. 2008. Submission to the European Commission Creative Content Online Consultation. http://ec.europa.eu/archives/information_society/avpolicy/docs/other_actions/col_2008/ngo/stockhnetw2_en.pdf. Accessed 9 Oct 2016.

Strangelove, M. 2005. *The Empire of Mind. Digital Piracy and the Anti-Capitalist Movement*. Toronto: University of Toronto Press.

Sun Microsystems. 2008. Response by Sun Microsystems to the Communication from the Commission to the European Parliament, the Council, the European Economic and Social Committee and the Committee of the Regions on Creative Content Online in the Single Market {SEC(2007) 1710}. http://ec.europa.eu/archives/information_society/avpolicy/docs/other_actions/col_2008/comp/sun_ en.pdf. Accessed 9 Oct 2016.

Sunder, Madhavi. 2006. IP³. *Stanford Law Review* 59(2): 257–332.

Swedish IT and Telecom Industries. 2008. The Swedish IT and Telecom Industries Would Like to Add the Following Comments regarding Point n. 10 and 11. http://ec.europa.eu/archives/information_society/avpolicy/docs/other_actions/col_2008/ngo/swed_it_tel_en.pdf. Accessed 9 Oct 2016.

Telefónica/O2. 2008. Telefónica/O2 Comments on the EC Communication on Creative Content Online in the Internal Market. http://ec.europa.eu/archives/information_society/avpolicy/docs/other_actions/col_2008/comp/telefonica_o2_en.pdf. Accessed 9 Oct 2016.

TERA Consultants. 2010. *Building a Digital Economy: The Importance of Saving Jobs in the EU's Creative Industries*. Paris: International Chamber of Commerce/BASCAP.

TF1. 2010. Contribution de TF1 à la Consultation Publique sur l'Avenir du Commerce Électronique dans le Marché Intérieur et la Mise en Œuvre de la Directive Commerce Électronique. https://circabc.europa.eu/sd/a/490bfd46-4ea1-4db9-aea8-6a626c7270b9/FR TF1 ENTR (th 5) 807802.pdf. Accessed 9 Oct 2016.

Tian, YiJun. 2009. *Re-thinking Intellectual Property: The Political Economy of Copyright Protection in the Digital Era*. New York: Routledge.

Torremans, Paul. 2004. Copyright as a Human Right. In *Copyright and Human Rights*, ed. Paul Torremans, 1–20. The Hague: Kluwer Law International.

UFC Que Choisir. 2007. Mission Olivennes. La Surenchère Répressive. http://www.quechoisir.org/telecom-multimedia/image-son/musique/communique-mission-olivennes-la-surenchere-repressive. Accessed 6 Oct 2016.

UK Department for Business Innovation & Skills, Intellectual Property Office, Department for Culture Media & Sport, Vince The Rt Hon Dr Cable, and Sajid The Rt Hon Javid. 2014. New Education Programme Launched to Combat Online Piracy. https://www.gov.uk/government/news/new-education-programme-launched-to-combat-online-piracy. Accessed 6 Oct 2016.

UK Government. 2008. The European Commission Communication on Creative Content Online. UK Government Response. http://ec.europa.eu/archives/information_society/avpolicy/docs/other_actions/col_2008/ms/uk_government_en.pdf. Accessed 9 Oct 2016.

UK Local Government Regulation. 2010. Local Government Regulation Response to the European Commission's Consultation on the Future of Electronic Commerce in the Internal Market and the Implementation of the Directive on Electronic Commerce (2000/31/EC). https://circabc.europa.eu/sd/a/063dabae-9c73-46fe-9ebc-e51a1e983bd6/UK Government Regulation.doc. Accessed 9 Oct 2016.

UK Music. 2010. UK Music Response to: Consultation on the Future of Electronic Commerce in the Internal Market and the Implementation of the Directive on Electronic Commerce. https://circabc.europa.eu/sd/a/8cf07d48-4b1b-4fdf-a3b4-94931f9a4ff5/uk mus.pdf. Accessed 9 Oct 2016

UK Parliament. 2010. *Digital Economy Act 2010*. London: Her Majesty's Stationery Office.

UK Publishers Association. 2010. Response to Public Consultation on the Future of Electronic Commerce in the Internal Market and the Implementation of the Directive on Electronic Commerce (2000/31/EC). https://circabc.europa.eu/sd/a/5dadeb9e-4656-4385-998f-972b9ab72a14/UK PUBLISHERS ASSOCIATION FED ENTR (th 2%265) 785391.pdf. Accessed 9 Oct 2016.

UN Working Group on Internet Governance. 2005. *Report of the Working Group on Internet Governance*. 05.41622. Geneva: United Nations.

United Nations. 1969. Vienna Convention on the Law of Treaties.

United States of America. 1790. *Constitution of the United States*. Champaign: Project Gutenberg.

US Copyright Office. 1998. *The Digital Millennium Copyright Act of 1998. U.S. Copyright Office Summary*. Washington, DC: US Copyright Office.

US Government Accountability Office. 2010. *GAO-10-423. Intellectual Property. Observations on Efforts to Quantify the Economic Effects of Counterfeit and Pirated Goods*. Washington, DC: US Government Accountability Office.

Vaidhyanathan, Siva. 2001. *Copyrights and Copywrongs. The Rise of Intellectual Property and How It Threatens Creativity*. New York/London: New York University Press.

Van Asbroeck, Benoit, and Maud Cock. 2012. The Scarlet Case. ISPs Cannot Be Ordered to Introduce General Filters on Their Network to Prevent Copyright Infringement. *AmCham Connect*, February.

Van Audenhove, Leo, Luciano Morganti, John Vanhoucke, Trisha Meyer, and Giovanni Paolo Ramirez. 2009. *Challenges for Creative Content Online: An Assumptional Analysis on the Basis of the Communication on Creative Content Online of the European Commission*. Brussels: IBBT-SMIT, Vrije Universiteit Brussel and Belgacom Telindus.

van Peperstraten, Frans. 1999. *Samenleving Ter Discussie. Een Inleiding in de Sociale Filosofie*. Bussum: Uitgeverij Coutinho.

Vennesson, Pascal. 2008. Case Studies and Policy Tracing: Theories and Practices. In *Approaches and Methodologies in the Social Sciences. A Pluralist Perspective*, ed. Donatella della Porta and Michael Keating, 223–239. Cambridge: Cambridge University Press.

Waldfogel, Joel. 2012. Copyright Protection, Technological Change, and the Quality of New Products: Evidence from Recorded Music Since Napster. *Journal of Law and Economics* 55(4): 715–740.

Walpole. 2010. Walpole Submission to the European Commission Public Consultation on the Future of Electronic Commerce in the Internal Market and the Implementation of the Directive on Electronic Commerce (2000/31/EC). https://circabc.europa.eu/sd/a/b774ab55-25fd-4337-9caf-b2ebda98ba43/UK WALPOLE FED ENTR (th 1%264-5) 786752.pdf. Accessed 9 Oct 2016.

Wasko, Janet, Graham Murdock, and Helena Sousa. 2011. Introduction: The Political Economy of Communications: Core Concerns and Issues. In *The Handbook of Political Economy of Communications*, ed. Janet Wasko, Graham Murdock, and Helena Sousa, 1–10. Chichester: Wiley-Blackwell.

Watson, James. 2003. *Media Communication: An Introduction to Theory and Process*. 2nd ed. Basingstoke/New York: Palgrave Macmillan.

Weatherley, Mike. 2014a. 'Follow the Money': Financial Options to Assist in the Battle Against Online IP Piracy. A Discussion Paper by Mike Weatherley MP Intellectual Property Adviser to the Prime Minister. http://www.olswang.com/media/48204227/follow_the_money_financial_options_to_assist_in_the_battle_against_online_ip_piracy.pdf. Accessed 6 Oct 2016.

———. 2014b. Search Engines and Piracy. A Discussion Paper by Mike Weatherley MP Intellectual Property Adviser to the Prime Minister. http://www.olswang.com/media/48165108/search_engines_and_piracy_mike_weatherley_mp.pdf. Accessed 6 Oct 2016.

Weiss, Aaron. 2008. Content Filters. Will ISPs Become the Enforcers of the Web? *netWorker* 12(1).

Wendt, Alexander. 1998. On Constitution and Causation in International Relations. *Review of International Studies* 24: 101–118.

Werkers, Evi. 2011. Intermediaries in the Eye of the Copyright Storm. A Comparative Analysis of the Three Strike Approach Within the European Union. *ICRI Working Paper Series* 4.

Westkamp, Guido. 2007. Changing Mechanisms in Copyright's Ontology – Structure, Reasoning and the Fate of the Public Domain. In *Emerging Issues in Intellectual Property: Trade, Technology and Market Freedom Essays in Honour of Herchel Smith*, ed. Guido Westkamp, 78–103. Cheltenham: Edward Elgar.

Winseck, Dwayne. 2011. The Political Economies of Media and the Transformation of the Global Media Industries. In *The Political Economies of Media. The Transformation of the Global Media Industries*, ed. Dwayne Winseck and Dal Yong Jin, 3–48. London/New York: Bloomsbury Academic.

WIPO. 1996a. *Copyright Treaty, WO033EN*. Geneva: International Bureau of the World Intellectual Property Organization.

———. 1996b. *Performances and Phonograms Treaty, WO034EN*. Geneva: International Bureau of the World Intellectual Property Organization.

Wittem Group. 2010. European Copyright Code. http://www.copyrightcode.eu/. Accessed 6 Oct 2016.

WTO. 1994. *Agreement on Trade-Related Aspects of Intellectual Property Rights. Annex 1C of Agreement Establishing the World Trade Organization*. Marrakech: World Trade Organization.

Wu, Tim. 2010. *The Master Switch: The Rise and Fall of Information Empires*. London: Atlantic Books.

X-Rates.com. 2016a. Exchange Rate Average 2008 (Euro, US Dollar). http://www.x-rates.com/average/?from=EUR&to=USD&amount=1.00&year=2008. Accessed 26 Aug 2016.

———. 2016b. Exchange Rate Average 2014 (Euro, US Dollar). http://www.x-rates.com/average/?from=EUR&to=USD&amount=1.00&year=2014. Accessed 26 August 2016.

Yahoo! Europe. 2008. Yahoo! Europe Response to the European Commission Communication on Creative Content Online in the Single Market. http://ec.europa.eu/archives/information_society/avpolicy/docs/other_actions/col_2008/comp/yahoo_en.pdf. Accessed 9 Oct 2016.

YouTube. 2016a. Content ID. http://www.youtube.com/t/contentid. Accessed 26 Aug 2016.

———. 2016b. Copyright on YouTube. https://www.youtube.com/yt/copyright/. Accessed 6 Oct 2016.

Yu, Peter. 2004. The Escalating Copyright Wars. *Hofstra Law Review* 32: 907–951.

―――. 2007a. Digital Piracy and the Copyright Response. In *The Internet and Governance in Asia. A Critical Reader*, ed. Indrajit Banerjee, 340–359. Singapore: Asian Media Information and Communication Centre.

―――. 2007b. International Enclosure, The Regime Complex, and Intellectual Property Schizophrenia. *Michigan State Law Review* 2007:1–33.

―――. 2011. Digital Copyright and Confuzzling Rhetoric. *Vanderbilt Journal of Entertainment and Technology Law* 13: 881–939.

―――. 2016. International Property Rulemaking in the Global Capitalist Economy. In *The Intellectual Property Right Domain in Contemporary Capitalism*, ed. Birgitte Andersen. New York: Routledge.

Zittrain, Jonathan. 2008. *Future of the Internet – And How to Stop It*. London: Yale University Press.

Index

Note: Page numbers followed by "n" denote notes.

© The Author(s) 2017
T. Meyer, *The Politics of Online Copyright Enforcement in
the EU*, Information Technology and Global Governance,
DOI 10.1007/978-3-319-50974-7

Printed by Printforce, the Netherlands